*f*P

Michael Norton

How to make a difference—
one day at a time

FREE PRESS

New York   London   Toronto   Sydney

*f*P

FREE PRESS
A Division of Simon & Schuster, Inc.
1230 Avenue of the Americas
New York, NY 10020

Originally published in Great Britain in 2005 by Myriad Editions Ltd
Published by arrangement with Myriad Editions Ltd
First Free Press Edition January 2007

For information about special discounts for bulk purchases,
please contact Simon & Schuster Special Sales:
1-800-456-6798 or business@simonandschuster.com

Manufactured in the United States of America

10   9   8   7   6   5   4   3   2   1

Library of Congress Cataloging-in-Publication data is available.

ISBN-13: 978-0-7432-9778-3
ISBN-10:   0-7432-9778-4

Contents

WAYS TO
CHANGE THE
WORLD

Themes

 Community and neighborhood
Getting to know your city or neighborhood, ways of brightening it up, bringing fun and laughter into local life, working with socially excluded people and with prisoners.

 Culture and creativity
Connecting up with people, new ideas for getting your message across, communicating through language and stories, listening in to get inspired.

 Democracy and human rights
Fighting for freedom of information, participating in elections, lobbying your elected representatives, human rights and human wrongs around the world.

 Discrimination
Fighting for disability rights, tackling racism and sexism (and all the other -isms in society), dealing with violence and abuse.

 Employment and enterprise
Sharing skills and resources, open access software, Internet collaboration, social enterprise, microcredit.

 Environment
Global warming, pollution, pesticides and toxins, conservation of species and resources, trees and forests, sustainable living, waste and recycling, transportation.

 Globalization and consumerism
Multinationals and responsible business practice, fairer trade and ethical consumption, consuming less.

 Health
Battling HIV/AIDS, malaria, and other global diseases, water and sanitation, better health, sports and fitness, hunger and obesity, food and diet.

 International development
Achieving the Millennium Development Goals, addressing inequality and social injustice in the world with skills, money, and ideas, recycling to benefit the world's poor, paying off foreign debt, enhancing livelihoods, and using appropriate technology.

Peace
Ridding the world of weapons, waging war on war, promoting peace, preventing genocide.

Volunteering and citizenship
Getting your message across, being nice to others, gearing up for action, having the right attitudes, donating cash and raising money, giving in kind, volunteering your time.

Young people
Improving education and schools, fighting for children's rights, supporting children in need, dealing with child abuse, providing opportunities for play and exercise, being a young activist.

Introduction

What's the big idea?

The world is full of all sorts of problems, including

HIV/AIDS, which is infecting more and more of the world's population

A widening North-South divide

War and terror (and the "War on Terror")

All the "isms" (racism, sexism, ageism, etc.) that deny people opportunities

Environmental degradation and pollution

A scarcity of water for living and working

Hunger for far too many of the world's population

A lack of universal primary education

Corruption and bad governance in too much of the world

Abuse of human rights (including slavery and torture)

Global warming, which will have an impact on almost everything

...and many more.

We all have our own ideas about what's wrong with the world. We argue about which are the most important issues. But everyone agrees that things could be a lot better than they are and that something really does need to be done. But what? Do we just leave it to governments and international institutions? Or are there things we can do that will actually make a difference?

The issues that confront us may seem so huge, so complicated, so difficult to deal with that it's hard to believe that anything we can do will have a meaningful impact. But there are a lot of us in the world. A lot of people doing a lot of little things could have a huge impact. And by doing something, we are also demonstrating that lots of people really do care.

Together we can change the world. That is the idea underlying this book. Through the way we live, the adjustments we make in our lives, and the action we take on issues that really concern us, we can begin to make a difference.

This book has an idea a day for changing the world. Most are quite simple, can be done from home, and will not take up that much time. Some require a bit more time, energy, and commitment.

Get going on changing the world. You can make a start at anytime. But the best time is right now! Just open the book to today's date, read, enjoy, be inspired to action...and do something.

Visit www.365act.com: To complement the book, we have created a website that includes all the 365 ideas and many more. You will also be able to click on the weblinks to go straight to the sources of information listed in the book.

This book is just a starting point for an ideas bank for changing the world. We need your help, your ideas, the feedback from what you have tried to do in order to help us make our dream—of people everywhere doing all they can to change the world—a reality.

We look forward to hearing from you.

New Year's REVOLUTION

The best way to predict the future is to invent it.

—Alan Kay

New Year's Day is traditionally a time for looking forward, when we resolve to make a fresh start, do better, try harder, live up to expectations. But all too often these resolutions evaporate by the time we have cleared up the remains of the previous night's party and almost certainly by the time we get in to work the next day. And if nothing is changing in the world around you, and the same old problems—war, famine, injustice, torture, poverty, disease—are reported in the news day after day, you may feel as though there is little point in resolving to give up smoking, lose those extra pounds, walk to work. So here's a suggestion: instead of watching, wracked by guilt, as world events unfold on your TV screen, bring about a New Year's Revolution. Change your life by resolving to change the world.

Taking the first step is important. Once you've gotten started, everything will get a lot easier. So, today, commit yourself to taking that first crucial step. Once you have resolved to make poverty history, to stop global warming (or whatever it is you want to do), the first thing you need is a plan of action. So make a plan. Set targets for what you want to achieve. Be ambitious. But make sure that your plan is achievable.

At the end of the year, you will want to review your progress. You will want to know whether you achieved your goals. You will want to see how much impact you have had on the issue. You will want to learn from your experience. And you will then need to plan what to do next.

www.mygoals.com/about/NewYearsTips.html

Don't be frightened of failure.
Do something, and try your best to succeed.

But even if you don't, you will have shown that you care enough to want to do something, you will probably have made some difference, and you will have learned a lot from the experience—which you can put into practice next time.

...resolve to change the world

Make a New Year's Resolution.

Go to www.tomphillips.co.uk/portrait/sbec and download the portrait of Samuel Beckett ringed by these words:

No matter
Try again
Fail again
Fail better

Cut this picture out, frame it, and put it somewhere you will see it every day. Let Samuel Beckett's words become your motto for the efforts you will be making to change the world.

JANUARY 1 *New Year's Day*

4

MAKE *amends*

It is almost certain that there is someone you've done wrong to, harmed, had a huge argument with, insulted, become estranged from to a point where you are not speaking, lost contact with. ♦♦ You've thought about this person more times than you can count, but for some reason, you've never made an effort to wipe the slate clean. ♦♦ Make amends. Bury the past by apologizing for what you've done. Admit responsibility. Heal the situation. In doing this, you will have done good, and you will have one less thing to worry about.

Whole communities can make amends. In Greensboro, North Carolina, on November 3, 1979, members of the Ku Klux Klan and the American Nazi Party killed five people and wounded ten others, as activists gathered for a rally and conference for racial and social justice. ♦♦ Twenty-five years later, the City of Greensboro decided to confront the past in the style of the Truth and Reconciliation Commission that Nelson Mandela so successfully instituted for postapartheid South Africa. The past can never be erased, but people and communities can make amends—and move forward.

Greensboro Truth and Community Reconciliation Project: www.gtcrp.org

Pavel's story

Forced to work in a carpentry shop by day, locked in barracks at night, Pavel Kotlyarov will never forget the hunger and the hardship. Pavel, a Ukrainian, was one of millions forced into slave labor by the Nazis. "They fed us so badly, the only thing we were thinking about was a piece of bread."

Fifty years later, some German students in Gersthofen, the town where Kotlyarov was enslaved, tried to make amends for the past. They sent Kotlyarov and other former slave laborers from Kiev a letter of apology and money that they had collected as a gesture of compensation.

The German government has paid compensation of $1,000 each to Ukraine's 600,000 surviving former slaves, but the students, as well as many others in Germany, feel the need to do more.

Cities have been sponsoring trips to Germany and raising money to provide aid packages for former slaves, who are mostly now in their 80s or even older.

...and clear your conscience

Make amends. Today's the day to do it!

Pick up the phone, write a letter, or send an email to someone you have hurt, or someone you have lost contact with. It doesn't matter whether it is your fault or theirs that you are no longer speaking. It doesn't matter if they choose not to respond. You've taken the first step. That's what's important.

♦♦ **What you need:** a little humility

♦♦ **Time invested:** about 10 minutes

♦♦ **The pay-off:** a clean conscience

2 JANUARY

Change in the world's climate is a cause for intense concern. Heat waves, droughts, monsoons, and hurricanes are breaking all previous records. These are the most obvious signals of climate change and are already proving costly in terms of human life, but there are others that are more surreptitious and likely to be even more deadly.

Warmer average temperatures are causing ice to melt. In Antarctica, vast areas of ice sheet are disintegrating. In parts of Canada, Alaska, Siberia, the melting of the permafrost is undermining roads, airports, and buildings. Most significantly, there are signs that the huge ice sheet over Greenland is beginning to thin, releasing millions of cubic kilometers of fresh water into the North Atlantic. ♣ Mountain glaciers in temperate zones are retreating, and as they shrink, summer water flows will start to drop sharply, creating severe shortages of water for irrigation and power in areas that rely on mountain watersheds. ♣ Melting ice, and increasing temperatures that cause seawater to expand, are likely to lead to a rise in sea level of around 3 feet over the next 100 years. Some low-lying areas will simply cease to exist; others will experience catastrophic flooding.

These climate changes are being caused by the emission of greenhouse gases. The scale of the problem means that coordinated government action will be required if climate change is to be slowed down. But it is the sum of our own individual choices and actions that is causing the problem.

Change One Sweet Whirled Name: www.lickglobalwarming.org
COIN—Climate Outreach and Information Network: www.coinet.org.uk

How to cut your carbon emissions by 50%
In the UK, George Marshall did everything he could to reduce his personal carbon emissions. In just one year he achieved a reduction of 50% through energy saving and changes to his lifestyle. To encourage others and even whole communities to do the same, he set up COIN—Climate Outreach Information Network. One of their ideas is Carbon Pioneers, a group of 100 people who commit to reducing their emissions, and then encourage and support each other through the process.

...needs to be stopped

Take a carbon pledge to reduce your own carbon emissions. And get all your friends to do the same. The average European emits directly and indirectly around 13 tons of carbon a year into the atmosphere. Pledge to cut back 5–10% of your carbon emissions. For example:

♣ **Replace three standard lightbulbs** with low-energy bulbs and save 300 lbs. of carbon emissions a year.
♣ **Turn the thermostat down** by 40° and save 600 lbs. a year.
♣ **Install a modern programmable thermostat** and save 1,000 lbs. a year.
♣ **Travel 15 miles fewer each week** by car and save 900 lbs. a year.

Pledge to cut your personal carbon emissions by at least 1 ton a year at www.lickglobalwarming.org

JANUARY 3

COFFEE *at a fair price*

Fair-trade coffee provides a higher income and greater security for small producers than is offered by the vagaries of the world market. ⚽ The current fair-trade price for coffee is more than double the market price, which can fluctuate wildly. In 1994 coffee reached a high of $2 per pound, a rise caused by frost and drought in Brazil, but by 2001 prices had fallen to 50 cents—where they have pretty much remained since. ⚽ The impact of low coffee prices is felt particularly by small family producers, who depend on this cash crop for their livelihood. In countries such as Ethiopia, Uganda, and Honduras, coffee is a particularly important export commodity, and a slump in prices can depress the whole economy.

Some recent trends in coffee production: More coffee is being produced than is being consumed, much of it funded by agricultural development schemes. The price has dropped as a result. ⚽ New technology is being used to remove the bitterness from the lower-priced robusta variety, making it taste more acceptable to consumers. This means more robusta coffee is being consumed. It is grown intensively, on large estates, which are introducing increasing mechanization, considerably reducing the need for labor. What 1,000 people might achieve on a small estate in Guatemala can be achieved by 12 people on a state-of-the-art mechanized farm in Brazil. ⚽ Sales of premium coffees (single-estate coffees, speciality brands, fair-trade, organic, and shade-grown, sometimes called bird-friendly) are all growing rapidly. Fair-trade coffee represents 1% of the US market, and 2% in the UK.

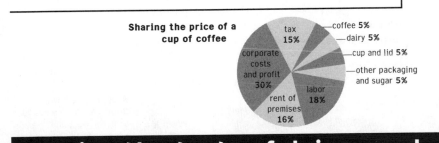

Sharing the price of a cup of coffee

tax 15%
coffee 5%
dairy 5%
cup and lid 5%
other packaging and sugar 5%
corporate costs and profit 30%
labor 18%
rent of premises 16%

...enjoy the taste of doing good

Buy and drink fair-trade coffee. The higher price will help small farmers.

Ask whether a cup of coffee made with fair-trade coffee is a fairly traded cup of coffee. Roasted ground coffee wholesales at around $4 per pound. A pound is sufficient to make 50 cups of coffee. When you buy a coffee in a coffee shop, the coffee costs about 8 cents. The consumer will be paying $1.50 and up. The grower will get only about 3 cents of this, even at fair-trade prices.

Write to the managing directors of a coffee chain and ask them to

⚽ **Sell only fair-trade coffee** through their outlets.

⚽ **Include a voluntary premium** of a few cents per cup to be added to your bill and paid to the Fairtrade Foundation to benefit small coffee producers.

4 JANUARY

start DRINKING

When you have a drink with your friends, there are a number of things you can do to support the local economy and help the environment.

Reduce your beer miles. This is the distance the beer has traveled from the brewery to get to you, the consumer. Support your local brewer—and your local whisky distiller and winemaker.

Choose bottles of wine that have natural cork stoppers. Oak corks biodegrade. The oak cork woodlands in Portugal and Spain produce over 80% of natural cork. These woodlands support a huge population of wildlife and are at risk of being felled to create even more intensively farmed fields when they no longer fulfill an economic purpose.

Recycle all your bottles and cans.

Buy organic beer and wine. Organic producers don't use pesticides that can harm wildlife and contaminate water sources. Organic beer and wine will contain fewer additives, so you won't have such a killer headache when you wake up.

Drink real ale, and keep traditional breweries in business. And why not brew your own?

Campaign for Real Ale: www.camra.org.uk

How to brew your own beer—all you need to know, from Brew Your Own: www.byo.com

The Brew Your Own website has some adventurous recipes:

Black Pear Oyster Stout has oysters as an ingredient. There's no strong oyster flavor, but the brew does have a slight salty/briny character.

Wild Rice Helles Bock, a strong, light-colored beer made with wild rice.

Original Hempen Ale, a dark ale made with roasted hemp seeds, which contain a trace of THC, which is the active ingredient in marijuana. But hemp is completely legit!

Smoked Maple Amber Ale uses maple sap (you can improvise by adding water to maple syrup). For a strong smoky flavor, use hickory smoke.

Stonehenge Stein Beer uses hot stones to heat the wort and caramelize the sugars; making it requires heat-resistant tongs and some ingenuity.

...for the environment

Try brewing your own beer. You could start with something simple, or try one of the exotic varieties listed above, which were compiled to celebrate the first ten years of *Brew Your Own* magazine.

Or, if that is too daunting, make a point of drinking local beers. If your local store or bar doesn't offer any, ask why not.

JANUARY 5

HUMAN RIGHTS *and wrongs*

Open your newspaper—any day of the week—and you will find a report from somewhere in the world of someone being imprisoned, tortured, or executed because his opinions or religion are unacceptable to his government. The newspaper reader feels a sickening sense of impotence. Yet if these feelings of disgust all over the world could be united into common action, something effective could be done.

—Peter Benenson

Amnesty International was started in 1961 by Peter Benenson, a British lawyer, after he read about the imprisonment of two Portuguese students who had drunk a toast to liberty in a Lisbon restaurant. This was during Portugal's 32-year rule by right-wing dictator Antonio Salazar. ❧ Benenson wanted to harness the enthusiasm of people all over the world concerned about human rights abuse. ❧ Local supporters were asked to adopt three "prisoners of conscience," one from the West, one from the Soviet Bloc, and one from the nonaligned world. They energetically campaigned for the release of their prisoners by writing letters, mobilizing political support, and showing the jailers (and the prisoner) that the prisoner had not been forgotten.

Human rights violations are as numerous today as when Amnesty was founded. Amnesty International, based in the UK, and Human Rights Watch, based in the USA, are the world's two leading human rights organizations. Amnesty campaigns on issues of violence against women, arms control, the death penalty, torture, refugee rights, child soldiers, and many others.

Amnesty International: www.amnesty.org
Human Rights Watch: hrw.org

Resources for human rights activists:
Human Rights Network International: www.hrni.org
International Service for Human Rights: www.ishr.ch

The Amnesty Urgent Action Network

A peasant activist "disappears" in Mexico...in Turkey, a journalist is arrested and at risk of torture...environmentalists in Kenya are imprisoned and beaten...an elderly political prisoner in Indonesia is denied insulin for his diabetes...

Every day Amnesty receives information like this. If an immediate international response is needed to deal with a specific human rights violation, the Urgent Action Network is set in motion.

Members of the network send a flood of letters to try to right the wrong. They may be trying to save someone from torture, death, or medical neglect, from an unfair trial, a judicial death penalty or political killing, or from forcible repatriation to a country where they may be at risk of further human rights abuse.

...urgent action is needed

Here are two simple things you can do:

❧ **Download a screensaver** from the Amnesty website and remind yourself every day that human rights are the foundation of freedom, justice, and peace in the world.

❧ **Join Amnesty's Urgent Action Network** and participate in campaigns on urgent issues. www.amnesty.org/pages/ua-index-eng

6 JANUARY

visit the HUNGER SITE

Every day 24,000 people die from hunger. Three-quarters of the deaths are of children under the age of five. 🌐 A website that focuses the power of the Internet on the eradication of world hunger was launched in June 1999. A visitor to the Hunger Site just clicks the Give Free Food button and a cup of food is donated to feed a hungry person. 🌐 The food donation is paid for by a sponsor, and the cost of running the site is paid for by the advertisements of up to 10 sponsors and the sale of merchandise (such as jewelry, crafts, T-shirts, and wristbands).

More than 200 million visitors gave more than 300 million cups of food in the site's first five years. In a typical month in 2005, 3.2 million people visited the site, and 3.6 million cups of food. weighing a total of 228 tons, were distributed as a result of this online clicking. 🌐 The food is distributed to those in need by Mercy Corps (through food donations and food-for-work programs in over 70 countries in Africa, Asia, Eastern Europe, the Middle East, and Latin America) and by America's Second Harvest (which collects food to help feed an estimated 26 million hungry people in the USA).

The Hunger Site: www.thehungersite.com
Mercy Corps: www.mercycorps.org
America's Second Harvest: www.secondharvest.org

Hunger in the world

Ten percent of children in developing countries die before the age of five. *(CARE)*

The majority of hunger deaths are caused by chronic malnutrition. Families are simply not getting enough to eat because of their extreme poverty. Famine and wars cause just 10% of hunger deaths. *(The Institute for Food and Development Policy)*

Chronic malnutrition also causes impaired vision, listlessness, stunted growth, and greatly increased susceptibility to disease. *(United Nations World Food Program)*

It is estimated that one in six people in the world suffers from hunger and malnutrition, about 100 times as many as those who actually die from it each year. *(Food and Agriculture Organization of the United Nations)*

It can take just a few simple resources for impoverished people to grow enough food to become self-sufficient: these include seeds, tools, access to water, and improvements in farming techniques. *(Oxfam)*

...and provide a square meal

🌐 **Visit the Hunger Site daily and trigger a donation.** It will cost you nothing, but you will be feeding a hungry person. There is a facility on the site for you to be sent a reminder each day.

🌐 **Develop a start-up routine for your computer** that automatically gets your computer (or all the computers in your office) to visit the Hunger Site each morning and trigger a donation.

🌐 **Tell all your friends.** There is a facility on the site to do this, or you can send an e-card by asking them to click on this weblink: www.thehungersite.com/seasonoflight.swf

JANUARY 7

FOREIGN DEBT *send cash*

During the 1970s and 1980s, the world's poorest countries were encouraged to borrow. The idea was that they would invest in projects that would produce an economic return sufficient to repay the loans. This did not happen. Instead they got saddled with a huge amount of debt and annual interest payments that they simply could not afford to repay. 🌐 Jubilee Year in the Bible is a time to wipe out outstanding debts. The Jubilee Debt Campaign focused on the year 2000 as a date to clear the debts of the world's poorest countries.

The Heavily Indebted Poor Countries initiative was set up in 1996 by the World Bank and International Monetary Fund. The original debt of the world's 52 poorest and most indebted countries totaled $375 billion. The initiative aimed to write off $100 billion of multilateral and bilateral debt. In return, countries would spend the debt relief on health, education, and development. 🌐 There were 42 countries eligible. Of these, Benin, Bolivia, Burkina Faso, Ethiopia, Ghana, Guyana, Madagascar, Mali, Mauritania, Mozambique, Nicaragua, Niger, Senegal, Tanzania, and Uganda completed the process; $46 billion was written off.

The Jubilee Debt Campaign continued to press for 100% cancellation of unpayable debt for every poor country. The leaders of the world's richest nations at the G8 summit in July 2005 agreed to write off all World Bank, IMF, and African Development Bank debt for the 18 poorest African nations.

Jubilee Debt Campaign: www.jubileeusa.org
African Forum and Network on Debt and Development: www.afrodad.org
Paris Club, the network of 19 developed countries dealing with third-world debt: www.clubdeparis.org/en/

Third-world debt burden

Total external debt of low-income countries: $523 billion, of which $300 billion relates to Africa.

Total debt service being paid every day by low-income countries: $100 million.

For every $1 received in grants, low-income countries pay $2.30 to service debt.

Debt cancellation works

In Benin, 54% of the money saved has been spent on health.

In Tanzania, debt relief enabled primary school fees to be abolished, which led to a 66% increase in school attendance.

In Mozambique, debt relief enabled all children to be offered free immunization.

In Uganda, debt relief enabled 2.2 million people to gain access to water.

...to help pay it off

Help mend the finances of Sierra Leone. Sierra Leone has a population of nearly 5 million. It is a country which until recently has been in the grip of civil war. It was ranked lowest on the Human Development Index. It is the poorest country in the world.

Put what you can afford in an envelope (cash or money order) and send it to the Bank of Sierra Leone, Siaka Stevens Street, Freetown, Western Area, Sierra Leone. Mark it for attention of the governor, Dr. J. D. Rogers. Indicate that it is to help repay the country's debt and that you would like a receipt.

Even if the money gets lost on the way, your gesture shows that individuals as well as governments can make a difference.

learn TURNTABLISM

Turntablism is a subgenre of hip-hop. One who engages in *turntablism* is a *turntablist:* a term created in 1994 by DJ Supreme, from New Rochelle, New York, to describe the difference between a DJ who just lets records play and one who actually manipulates the sounds of a record. This term was later popularized by DJ Babu of the Beat Junkies and Dilated Peoples, who inscribed his mixtapes as "mixed by Babu the Turntablist."—*Wikipedia*

Turntablism is a way of creating musical compositions by using vinyl records and phonographic equipment.

The Tutoritool teaches the basic skills behind turntable music creation. It is a double vinyl package containing two sides of lessons on the most popular scratch techniques, and then showing how these can be used for composition. It includes:

- Lessons and examples of the baby scratch, chirps, cuts and stabs, the transformer scratch, the flare, and the crab.
- Compositional lessons in turntable beat, bass line, verse and chorus creation. Practice with a virtual turntable band before sharing your skills with other turntablists.
- A booklet with lessons and information on all the techniques required to become a turntable musician.
- A specially designed sticker sheet for marking up your favorite sounds on the record.
- A comprehensive beat suite of hip-hop, rock, jazz, and drum 'n' bass beats for both practice and turntable accompaniment with included samples.
- Multipitch instruments that change pitch over each revolution using popular sounds and instruments (guitars, keyboards, trumpets, vocals, and many more).
- Virtual vocalist groove, to make your turntable sing.
- Jugglers beats, to hone your beat juggling skills with beats that loop on every revolution of the record.

HipHop Directory, turntabling resources on the web:
www.hiphopdirectory.com/Deejaying/Turntablism/index.php
International Turntablist Foundation: www.hip-hop.com

James Kelly, aged 19, developed a training course in turntablism, which is particularly aimed at young people who don't fit easily into traditional education, so that they can achieve a recognized national qualification and be encouraged to continue with education.

It is the first-ever such course, and is being promoted worldwide by Pedestrian, an arts organization based in the UK.

...start scratching now

- **Get the taste.** Sample beat juggling and scratching on the Pedestrian website.
- **Learn the skills.** Get the Tutoritool, or take a course.
- **Now that you're an accomplished DJ,** use your new skills to run a disco. Charge an entry fee, and use any money you make to change the world.

SEEING *is understanding*

There is much common ground among religions, but it is the differences that are highlighted. Religions seem to have grown from similar impulses—the desire to understand the place of human beings in the universe, the need to comprehend the mysteries of life and death, and the wish to experience meaning and happiness in the face of suffering. ✤ The troubles between Unionists and Nationalists (Protestants and Catholics) in Northern Ireland, the continuing conflict in Israel and Palestine (Jews and Muslims), the Kashmir problem between India and Pakistan (Hindus and Muslims), and the Tamil Tiger separatist movement in Sri Lanka (the Hindu minority in a largely Buddhist country) may all be based on very real grievances, but they all demonstrate how religious differences can create divisions within communities and societies, and how this can perpetuate intolerance and lead to violence. ✤ The world would be a better place if there were greater religious tolerance.

Virtual Religion Index, hyperlinks to a wealth of resources on the major religions: virtualreligion.net/vri/

Faith and Food, dietary practices and beliefs of nine religions: www.faithandfood.com

The world's major religions are

Buddhism	Islam	Mormonism
Christianity	Jainism	Quakerism
Confucianism	Judaism	Sikhism
Hinduism		

But there are differences within religions, such as those between Catholic, Protestant, Orthodox, and evangelical Christianity, or between Sunni and Shiite Muslims.

...promote religious tolerance

Develop a better understanding of the world's religions. Here's a simple way. Get a group of friends together. Ask each to research one religion or denomination on the Internet by reading the main religious text (Bible, Qur'an, etc.), and talking to people of that faith.

Now go to the services of as many religions and denominations as you can and observe at first hand the different practices. But a word of caution: first contact the church, temple, or mosque to confirm that outsiders are welcome at services and to find out about dress and behavior protocol.

Here are some questions to ask yourselves:
✤ What are the basic tenets of the religion?
✤ How are concepts of peace and nonviolence highlighted by the religion?
✤ Has the getting-to-know-it process confirmed or dismissed any preconceptions you held?
✤ Does the religion promote tolerance of other religious beliefs? Does it actively seek to convert nonbelievers? And does it see itself as the world's only true religion?
✤ How are women treated compared with men?
✤ What does the religion say about forgiveness?
✤ Does the religion promote charity? If it does, is there an underlying motivation for undertaking selfless acts and giving to those in need?
✤ Are interfaith services and other events held?

10 JANUARY

what's the BIG IDEA?

Are you someone who bores your friends, endlessly going on about the best way to deal with the burning issue of the day? Or maybe you are something of a lateral thinker, for whom simple everyday problems have elegant and imaginative solutions. ♟ Instead of keeping your good ideas to yourself (and your long-suffering nearest and dearest), you now have a chance to share them with the wired world.

The Idea-a-Day website was launched in August 2000, and one original idea has been published on this site every day since then. ♟ You can arrange for the idea of the day to be sent to you simply by submitting your name and e-mail address. ♟ You also can submit your own ideas, and they will be posted on the site if they are imaginative enough. ♟ All ideas posted on the site since its inception remain on the site, and it is the intention that the site will continue forever.

Some 500 of the best ideas have been published in *The Big Idea Book* by David Owen, founder of Idea-a-Day; details of this book are on the website.

www.idea-a-day.com

Some ideas from the Idea-a-Day website:

Meeting posts in city centers. There would be 12 posts set out in a big circle in a public square in the city center. The post at due north would be 12 o'clock. Going clockwise round the circle, the posts would be 1 o'clock, 2 o'clock, etc. You would then say to a friend, "Hey, let's meet for a drink after work, at six o'clock in the city center." You would have agreed when *and* where.

Being able to vote *against* a candidate in an election. You would still have just one vote, but you could use it to vote either for or *against* a particular candidate. This would make it much easier to run a campaign against a person or a party that you don't want to see in power.

Cordoning off places of natural beauty or which have some cultural significance. The police will use "Do not cross this line" tape not just at a crime scene, but for an ancient manhole cover or to mark where an IRA bomb was detonated or where David Beckham proposed to Posh Spice.

The International Language of Love: a language school which is also a dating agency. You get paired up with someone for some "intimate tête-à-tête conversation." By talking together, you each learn the other's language. You would fill in a normal dating agency form to ensure that you are an ideal match with the person you are paired with.

Audio recordings of celebrities sleeping. Buy this, and when you go to bed, you can pretend that you are sleeping with your favorite pop star or A-list celebrity.

...one for each new day

♟ **Subscribe to the Idea-a-Day website and receive an idea a day.** This should set you thinking about things you could do to change the world.

♟ **Then come up with your very own brilliant idea**—and submit it.

JANUARY 11

WEAR *a wristband*

Wristbands are a way of showing that you support a particular cause.
Since Lance Armstrong's Livestrong campaign for cancer survivors, which was run in association with Nike, they have replaced ribbons as the must-have fashion accessory. For some wristbands, the demand has been so high, because of celebrity endorsement, that they have become virtually unobtainable. ⚥ Most wristbands cost around $4. Try to buy direct from a charity rather than from a commercial supplier; then you know that all proceeds will be going to the cause:

Keep a Child Alive, AIDS drugs for children in Africa, *red*:
www.keepachildalive.org

Make Poverty History, a campaign to end global poverty, *white*:
www.makepovertyhistory.org

Livestrong with Lance Armstrong, surviving cancer, *yellow*: www.livestrong.org

Someone You Know Has Lupus, lupus awareness, *purple*: www.lupus.org

Orange Ukraine, solidarity with Ukraine's Orange Revolution, *orange*:
orangeukraine.squarespace.com

Get in the Pink, the fight against breast cancer, *pink*: www.breastcancer.org

Max Life, juvenile (Type 1) diabetes, *orange*: www.charitybands.com

Beat bullying with a wristband

Beat Bullying was an antibullying campaign run in Britain by BBC Radio 1 and the Department for Education and Skills in 2004. They produced a bright blue wristband for young people to wear in solidarity with the campaign. They got celebrities such as footballers Wayne Rooney and Rio Ferdinand and music acts such as Franz Ferdinand and Scissor Sisters to support the campaign and be seen wearing the wristband.

This created a huge demand, not all of which could be met. Eventually, 1 million were handed out before the campaign was closed. They were so popular that some were being traded for up to $60 on eBay.

PEACE

...show that you care

⚥ **Buy a wristband and support a cause.** Wear it with pride and tell other people why the cause is important.

⚥ **Selling wristbands can be a good way of fund-raising.** Try to get a celebrity to wear yours, for maximum publicity. To order a wristband for your cause, go to BAND-ITS.com at www.mpglink.com/bands or find other suppliers on Google.

become a VIRTUAL ACTIVIST

The Internet is ideal for bringing thousands of people together for a common purpose. It enables you to contact lots of people extremely quickly. It allows them to make an immediate response. And you don't have to spend a lot of money on printing and postage. ☗ The anti-World Trade Organization demonstration in Seattle in 1999 first awoke the world to the power of Internet activism. Ideas and information had spread around the world with a click of a mouse, plans had been developed and shared, and people had come to Seattle in huge numbers to fight for fairer trading arrangements for the developing world.

The starting point for Internet activism is to create an e-mail list of individuals and organizations that might be interested in hearing about what you are doing. Here are some tips for doing this:

Collect the e-mail addresses of as many friends, colleagues, helpers, and supporters as possible. Research the media, potential funders, people you want to influence, and anyone else you would like to communicate with regularly. Include a space for e-mail addresses in all your promotional material, so that anyone interested can let you know.

Produce a regular e-newsletter to let people know what you are doing in an electronic format.

Take promotional material to any conference or workshop you attend. This could include a postcard so that those who are interested can send you their contact details.

Give people the opportunity to get involved. Suggest some simple things for people to do to help your campaign. Ask for their views and ideas. Suggest that they pass on your details to anyone they know who might be interested.

A picture gallery of Seattle 1999: www.globalarcade.org/wto/photo.html
The World Trade Organization History Project: depts.washington.edu/wtohist

Tuesday, November 30, 1999—termed N30 by anti-WTO activists—dawned gray and cloudy as I made my way up Pike Street to Victor Steinbrueck Park on the Seattle waterfront. By the time I arrived at 7 a.m., over 1,000 demonstrators had gathered, ranging from environmentalists to union members to advocates for human rights for the people of Tibet. Soon the crowd began to march toward the Seattle Convention Center, site of the long-awaited meeting of the World Trade Organization, a group of government representatives who set the international

rules regarding trade and tariffs. WTO delegates were scheduled to attend an opening ceremony that morning at the historic Paramount Theater at 8th and Pine, but protesters were determined to ensure that WTO business did not proceed as usual. As delegates arrived, demonstrators—some dressed in sea turtle costumes and others carrying giant puppets—formed a human barrier to deny them entry...
—Liz Highleyman, www.black-rose.com

...through the Internet

Learn the skills of Internet activism. Read the training materials on
☗ NetAction: www.netaction.org/training
☗ Backspace.com: www.backspace.com/action/all.php

AIDS *Memorial Quilt*

In June 1987, a small group of people came together in San Francisco. Their aim was to create a memorial for those who had died of AIDS and to promote a better understanding of the disease and its impact. This meeting led to the foundation of the AIDS Memorial Quilt. ☺ Since that day, more than 44,000 individual 3 ft. x 6 ft. memorial panels have been sewn—each commemorating the life of someone who has died of AIDS and contributed by friends, lovers, or family members. The quilt is exhibited from time to time, either as a whole or just a part. All the panels contributed will eventually be put on a database and form a "virtual quilt."

The Quilt
> is a creative way of remembering a life cut short.
> provides a strong visual illustration of the scale of the AIDS pandemic.
> creates public awareness of HIV and AIDS.
> raises funds for the fight against AIDS.

You don't have to be an artist or a sewing expert to contribute a panel. You can use paint, needlework, iron-on transfers, or appliqué—whatever technique you like. You can create a panel privately, or you might follow the tradition of "quilting bees" by involving friends, family, and colleagues. ☺ Contributing a panel is absolutely free, but donations are welcomed. The organizers (the NAMES Project) suggest a voluntary contribution of $100 a year to process and care for each panel, and $200 to add a new panel to the quilt.

The NAMES Project Foundation and the AIDS Memorial Quilt: www.aidsquilt.org

How to design a panel

The finished, hemmed panel must be exactly 3 ft. x 6 ft. Leave an extra 3 in. on each side for the hem.

Use a panel to commemorate just one individual.

Include the name of the person you are commemorating, and also additional information such as date of birth and death, hometown, and special talents.

Use medium-weight, nonstretch fabric (such as a cotton or poplin).

Sew things on. Don't glue them, as glue will deteriorate.

If you want to include a photo or a letter, the best idea is to photocopy it onto an iron-on transfer, iron this onto a piece of cotton fabric, and then sew the fabric onto your panel.

...sew a panel

☺ Contribute a panel to commemorate someone you know who has died of AIDS.

☺ Contribute a panel to an unknown victim of AIDS—just like the Tomb of the Unknown Soldier, which provides a remembrance to all those who might otherwise be forgotten.

14 JANUARY

Even though you are consciously committed to egalitarianism and strive to behave without prejudice, you may still possess strong hidden negative prejudices or stereotypes. You believe that you see and treat people as equals, but hidden biases may still influence how you think and what you do. ✖ Psychologists at Harvard, the University of Virginia, and the University of Washington have created Project Implicit and launched a series of tests on the Internet—"Implicit Association Tests"—that aim to detect any hidden bias in people's attitudes.

The test on racial bias: The first task is to sort faces identifiable racially as either black or white. The second task is to sort words associated with positive qualities *(peace, pleasure, friend)* or negative qualities *(violent, failure, awful)*. Next, participants are asked to sort words into combined categories, assigning positive words and white faces to one column, and negative words and black faces into the other. As the items flash on the screen—peace, white face, awful, black face, friend—the vast majority of people continue to have little trouble doing the sorting. ✖ The signals of bias appear in the next step, when people are asked to reverse the process: to group positive words with black faces, and negative words with white faces. Theoretically, this task should have precisely the same level of difficulty as the previous step. However, most test takers take longer and make more errors when trying to group good qualities with blacks (and in other versions of the test, with other socially excluded groups). ✖ Over 3 million tests have been completed. Consistently, the test shows bias against stigmatized groups, whether they be Aboriginals in Australia or Turks in Germany. The bias appears to cross racial lines.

In other versions of the test, people show strong preferences for young versus old. And both men and women have far more difficulty grouping women's names with words having to do with science *(chemistry, biology)*, than with words relating to art *(drama, poetry)*.

Project Implicit: implicit.harvard.edu
Fight hate, promote tolerance: www.tolerance.org
A British website about race, racism, and life: www.britkid.org

The website www.tolerance.org is for people interested in countering bigotry and promoting diversity, whether at home, at school, in the workplace,

or in the community. It supports antibias activism through its online resource bank and downloadable public service announcements. It tells you ten ways to fight hate and provides 101 tools for tolerance.

...test yourself and find out

Take a Demonstration Test at Project Implicit to test your bias regarding age, gender, race, or nationality. Each test will take around 10 minutes to complete. At the end of the test, you will be given a summary of your results.

After taking the test on race, read the Tolerance.org tutorial to learn more about stereotypes and prejudice and their impact on society.

STAND UP FOR *your rights*

> *Now, I say to you today, my friends, even though we face the difficulties of today and tomorrow, I still have a dream. … I have a dream that one day this nation will rise up and live out the true meaning of its creed: "We hold these truths to be self-evident, that all men are created equal."*
>
> —Martin Luther King Jr., at the March on Washington, August 28, 1963

Is there an issue you feel really strongly about? Is there an injustice that is so outrageous that you boil with rage and feel that you have to do something about it? ♛ Take your inspiration from Rosa Parks (see below). This previously very ordinary woman did something that was both very simple and very extraordinary. Her single action changed the course of her own life and was a trigger for the Civil Rights Movement. ♛ So stand up for your beliefs by starting a campaign or undertaking some sort of nonviolent direct action.

Until her death in 2005 at the age of 92, Rosa Parks worked with youth through the Rosa and Raymond Parks Institute. Find out more about Rosa Parks: http://en.wikipedia.org/wiki/Rosa_Parks

Rosa Parks, civil rights pioneer

Rosa Parks worked as a seamstress in Montgomery, Alabama, at a time when the southern states practiced segregation by law. She was arrested on December 1, 1955, for refusing to give up her seat on a segregated bus to a white male passenger, as demanded by the bus driver. She was tried and convicted of violating a local ordinance. Her act sparked a citywide boycott of the bus system by blacks.

The Montgomery Bus Boycott started on December 5, 1955, and lasted 381 days. Rosa Parks's courage catapulted her into world history, and she is now affectionately referred to as the mother of the modern-day Civil Rights Movement.

The boycott also brought a young Baptist minister, Dr. Martin Luther King Jr., to world prominence.

...sitting down ain't easy

Do something!

♛ **What?** Is there an issue or an injustice that you feel really strongly about? Then do something that addresses that issue or injustice.

♛ **When?** Today. Now's the time to get started.

♛ **Who?** You, of course!

♛ **How?** You decide. But taking that first step is the most important thing.

Hear the voice of Dr. Martin Luther King Jr. at the King Center: www.thekingcenter.org

Street papers being sold by homeless or socially excluded people are a familiar sight in many of our cities. Vendors buy bulk copies at a 50–60% discount and then resell them, keeping the profit. They are given some training and identification, allocated a location, and asked to comply with a code of conduct. 🏠 The organizers behind these papers aim to

help homeless people help themselves by providing them with a means of earning an income and a dignified alternative to begging.

support their reintegration into society, through a philosophy of "a hand up, not a handout." Any profit made by the paper is used to support homeless people.

The *Big Issue* in London was inspired by the first street paper, *Street News* in New York. There are now more than 400 vendors in London, who all told sell 131,000 copies of each issue. There are separate *Big Issues* for the North, the South West, Scotland, and Wales. 🏠 In the last ten years, the Big Issue Foundation has worked with 5,398 people, of whom 407 have gone on to further education, 281 have been rehoused, and 75 have been helped into permanent employment.

Street papers now exist in many big cities. The International Network of Street Newspapers has 55 members in 28 countries, with a combined annual circulation of 26 million copies. The North American Street Newspaper Association has members in 40 US and Canadian cities.

Vendor Code of Conduct
No begging
No drinking
No swearing
No harassment of the public

Big Issue website: www.bigissue.com
International Network of Street Papers (INSP): www.street-papers.com

John's Story: Aged 33, having lost his job and split up with his partner, John found himself homeless, friendless, and jobless. He started selling the *Big Issue* to earn money but wanted to go back to school. The Big Issue Foundation helped him enroll in a suitable course and provided a grant toward tuition fees. "Two years ago I was living on the streets in a cardboard box. Now I'm a mature student at the University of London."
—from the Big Issue Foundation

...keep buying the *Big Issue*

🏠 **Buy a copy of your city's street paper.** Do this on a regular basis, and smile when you do it. Why not engage in small talk with the vendor? When you get to know your local vendor, why not take him or her out for a coffee at your local coffee shop?

🏠 **Download** *Street Papers, a Guide to Getting Started* from the website of the North American Street Paper Assn. or the International Network of Street Papers.

JANUARY 17

MONEY *talks*

Everyone uses money. Even if you are a serious credit-card addict, you will almost certainly have some bills in your purse or wallet. 👤 Money speaks to the masses. It promises food in your stomach, a warm home, entertainment and enjoyment, and a better tomorrow. But you can also make your money serve a purpose different from just buying you a cup of coffee and a doughnut.

You can make your money speak to the world. People pay attention to money—and to red ink. So use red ink to put messages on your money, which will be passed from person to person as the money is spent. 👤 Some suggestions for hard-hitting facts to inscribe on your paper money:

Over 1 billion people have to survive on less than a dollar a day.

Across the world, 842 million people will go to bed hungry tonight.

One in five women experience a rape or attempted rape in their lifetime.

Guns kill 34,000 Americans every year.

Wear a condom. Today 14,000 people will become infected with HIV/AIDS.

Perform a random act of kindness to someone today.

Give this money to someone who really needs it.

Make amends with someone today. Tell them you're sorry.

Make way for others. Let someone else go first.

Spread a little happiness. Smile at a stranger.

Explore the world of paper money: www.banknotes.com
Find out all about money: en.wikipedia.org/wiki/Money

...give it a voice

Use your money to spread the word.

👤 **Take all the bills in your wallet** and write a simple but hard-hitting fact on each side. Don't write all over the note, or someone might not be able to use it. Write round the edges.

👤 **Your message will be spread** to everyone who gets possession of the money. Try to write something lively and interesting. so that people will want to read it. You could even direct the reader to a website.

*think*LONG-TERM

Ten thousand years is about as long as the history of human technology. We have fragments of pots that old. But it is a blink of an eye in the history of the world.

I cannot imagine the future, but I care about it. I know I am part of a story that starts long before I can remember and continues long beyond when anyone will remember me. I sense that I am alive at a time of important change, and I feel a responsibility to make sure that the change comes out well. I have hope for the future.

—Danny Hillis

Progress is often measured by how quickly things happen and how cheap things become. It has been nearly 10,000 years since the end of the last ice age and the beginnings of civilization. The Long Now Foundation was established in the year they call 01996. It seeks to promote slower and better thinking and to foster creativity within a framework of the next 10,000 years.

The 10,000-year clock: One of the projects of the Long Now Foundation is a clock that will tick only once a year; the century hand will advance once every 100 years, and a cuckoo will come out at each millennium. The clock will last for 10,000 years. It is being built by Danny Hillis, and a prototype is exhibited at London's Science Museum.

Long Now Foundation: www.longnow.org
World Future Society: www.wfs.org

The World Future Society is a neutral clearinghouse for ideas about the future, including forecasts, recommendations, and alternative scenarios. These ideas will help people to anticipate what may happen in the next five, ten, or more years ahead. And when people can visualize a better future, then they can start to create it. The society has local branches in more than 100 cities. These are some forecasts from the society:

More emphasis will be placed on skills that cannot be automated. These "hyper-human" skills include caring, judgment, intuition, ethics, inspiration, friendliness, and imagination.

With global climate change, coral reefs will see greater changes in the next 50 years than they have faced in the last half million years.

...and predict the future

Predict the future. You can make a long-term prediction about the future on the Long Now website and give your reasons for the prediction. To do so costs $50. You can vote on predictions that other people have made. You can also challenge a predictor with a bet of at least $200 that his or her prediction will not come true: whoever wins donates their winnings to a nominated charity. Place your bet at www.longbets.org.

Some predictions to bet on:

🏮 **By 2020** bioterror or bioerror will lead to 1 million casualties in a single event.

🏮 **By 2020** solar energy will be as cheap or cheaper than that produced by fossil fuels.

🏮 **By 2060** the total population of humans will be less than it was in 2004.

JANUARY 19

COMPUTERS *working*

The most obvious way to fight HIV/AIDS is to wear a condom. But we're not all having crazy, fun sex all the time. Fortunately (or unfortunately) many of us aren't having any sex at all most of the time. ☺ Regardless of whether you are out and about trying to get laid or have joined a monastery, you can be fighting HIV/AIDS. The people working at the Scripps Research Institute have put their geeky brains together and come up with an easy way for you to help in the search for an HIV/AIDS vaccine.

It takes an unimaginable amount of computer power to conduct the data searches necessary to create a new vaccine. Your computer sits idle with its computing power not being used, while it could be helping in this search. ☺ Scripps has devised a computer program—FightAIDS@Home—that you can download onto your desktop. This program puts your computer to work when you aren't using it. ☺ When your computer has completed a computation, the results are packed up and sent back to the Scripps Research Institute, ready for its researchers to collect and analyze. ☺ When you want to use your computer for your own purposes, the FightAIDS@Home program instantly and automatically turns your computing power to the task you are doing.

Download the Scripps program: fightaidsathome.scripps.edu/help.html
The United Nations Program on AIDS: www.unaids.org
Avert, a good source of information on AIDS: www.avert.org

AIDS around the world

According to UNAIDS, more than 60 million people have been infected with HIV since the epidemic began in the 1980s.
In the 45 most affected countries, it is projected that 68 million people will die prematurely as a result of AIDS between 2000 and 2020. The projected toll is greatest in sub-Saharan Africa, where 55 million additional deaths are expected.

The average life expectancy in sub-Saharan Africa is currently 47 years. Without AIDS, it would have been 62 years. Life expectancy at birth in Botswana (which, at 38.8%, has the highest adult prevalence rate in the world) has dropped below 40 years—a level not seen in that country since before 1950.

Current HIV prevalence levels only hint at the much greater lifetime probability of becoming infected. In Lesotho, for example, it is estimated that a person who turned 15 in 2000 has a 74% chance of becoming infected with HIV by his or her 50th birthday.

...to discover an AIDS vaccine

Over 5 million people will have contracted HIV/AIDS in 2006.

Don't you think it's time to come up with a vaccine? Well, why don't you help in the search?

Download the free Scripps program and follow some simple instructions. There are well over 10,000 computers working on this project.

news REPORTING

The growth of the Internet is changing the balance of power between journalists and readers. Dan Gillmor, in his book *We the Media*, writes

Big media...treated the news as a lecture. We told you what the news was. You bought it, or you didn't....Tomorrow's news reporting and production will be more of a conversation or a seminar. The lines will blur between producers and consumers, changing the role of both in ways we're only beginning to grasp. The communication network itself will be a medium for everyone's voice, not just the few who can afford to buy multimillion-dollar printing presses, launch satellites, or win the government's permission to squat on the public airways.

Dan's book discusses some momentous changes that are taking place. Here are three examples:

OhMyNews: in Korea everyone can be a reporter. When launched in 2000, the website OhMyNews had 727 citizen reporters, called "guerrillas," who posted news based on their own informed perspectives, which were usually antiestablishment. Immediately, huge numbers of people put themselves forward, wanting to report the news, and OhMyNews changed from a weekly to a daily format. ♪ By 2004, some 32,000 people had registered as citizen reporters. OhMyNews publishes approximately 200 articles a day, around 150 of these produced by their citizen reporters. OhMyNewsInternational, English version: english.ohmynews.com

The Memory Hole: giving the news they don't want you to know. The Memory Hole preserves and disseminates material that is in danger of being lost or hard to find or not widely known. For example, it used the Freedom of Information Act to get into the public domain photos of dead US soldiers being brought back from Iraq in flag-draped caskets. www.thememoryhole.org

Indymedia: a global media network. Indymedia is a network of individuals and independent and alternative media activists and organizations offering grassroots coverage of important social and political issues. It was originally set up as an information clearinghouse for journalists during the WTO's meeting in Seattle in 1999. ♪ There is now a network of Indymedia organizations spanning the globe and providing a radical, accurate, and passionate telling of the truth. "We work out of a love and inspiration for people who continue to work for a better world." www.indymedia.org

Download Dan Gillmor's book free on the We the Media website: wethemedia.oreilly.com

...anyone can do it

♪ **Subscribe** to *Indymedia* for a different slant on the news.

♪ **Report the news.** When you have something important to contribute, call up a journalist; write a letter to the editor; call a phone-in show...

QUALITY *of life*

Quality of life is not just about national and personal wealth. There are lots of other factors to take into account. But how can you compare one country with another? ♪ The British Economist Intelligence Unit has devised a Quality of Life Index, which tries to measure how good a country is to live in. In 2005, 111 countries were surveyed. The survey scored each country's performance in nine different areas:

Material well-being *gross domestic product (GDP) per person*
Health *life expectancy at birth*
Quality of family life *divorce rate*
Community life and social cohesion *rate of church attendance or trade union membership*
Gender equality *ratio of male and female earnings*

Climate and geography *geographical latitude, to distinguish between warmer and colder climates*
Job security *unemployment rate*
Political freedom *index devised by Freedom House on political and civil liberties*

Ireland comes out on top because, according to the report, "it successfully combines the most desirable elements of the new (high GDP per head, low unemployment, political liberties) with the preservation of certain cosy elements of the old, such as stable family and community life." ♪ Zimbabwe, despite its great climate, comes in at the bottom. With widespread food shortages, one of the world's highest HIV/AIDS infection rates, 200% inflation, 70% unemployment, and a complete erosion of political freedom, life there has become very tough for its citizens.

Quality of Life Index: www.economist.com

The scores out of ten for those ranked top and bottom:

Top 6 countries	Bottom 6 countries
1 Ireland (8.333)	106 Tajikistan (4.754)
2 Switzerland (8.068)	107 Tanzania (4.753)
3 Norway (8.051)	108 Nigeria (4.505)
4 Luxembourg (8.015)	109 Botswana (4.313)
5 Sweden (7.937)	110 Haiti (4.090)
6 Australia (7.925)	111 Zimbabwe (3.892)

These are the rankings for selected other countries:
USA 13, Canada 14, UK 29, China 60, India 73, South Africa 92, and Russia 105.

...Ireland 8.3, Zimbabwe 3.9

♪ **Assess how you feel about your own quality of life.** Is there any way you can improve it?

♪ **Do something to improve the quality of life in your country.** You can't do anything about your climate (heating it up by contributing to global warming doesn't count), but there may be lots of other things you can do through campaigning or direct action.

♪ **Do something for the people of Zimbabwe or Haiti.** Go to the Human Rights Watch website to find out about some of their problems: hrw.org.

22 JANUARY

lost in TRANSLATION?

Do you want to send out a message in many different languages? Maybe you need to mount some text on a website, produce multilingual leaflets about a campaign, or publish a manifesto setting out your ideas—all in a range of languages. You might want to translate some practical advice into Spanish for the local Hispanic community. ♦ You could find an English speaker who is fluent in other languages to do the translation for you. But there is now another way. The Altavista Babel Fish Translation program will translate web pages or 150-word blocks of text at the click of your mouse. It will translate from English into

Chinese	Italian
Dutch	Japanese
French	Korean
German	Portuguese
Greek	Spanish

It's a free service—although you can purchase more advanced software from Altavista. You will need to load special fonts onto your computer for translating into Chinese, Japanese, Korean, and Greek. ♦ As an automatic translator, Babel Fish works best when the text you wish to translate uses proper grammar. Slang, misspelled words, poorly placed punctuation, and complex or lengthy sentences can all cause a page to be translated incorrectly. If you want a polished translation, the computer-generated text will need to be properly edited.

Babel Fish: world.altavista.com

...here's an easy way to do it

♦ **Go to the Babel Fish website** at world.altavista.com and translate a leaflet or a page of your website into another language.

Allez au site Web de Poissons de Babel à world.altavista.com et traduisez un prospectus ou une page de votre site Web dans une autre langue.

Vaya al Web Site de los Pescados de Babel en world.altavista.com y traduzca un prospecto o las páginas de su web site a otra lengua.

Gehen Sie zur Babel Fisch Website auf world.altavista.com und übersetzen Sie ein Faltblatt oder die Seiten ihrer Website in eine andere Sprache.

Go on. Try it!

♦ Next time you travel abroad, write down 20 or 25 useful phrases that you might need to use (such as "Which restaurant sells the best pizza in town?" or "I want to e-mail my mother. Where is the nearest Internet café?") and translate them into the languages of all the countries you will be visiting.

JANUARY 23

SWITCH OFF *the Internet*

We are basically trying to persuade people for just one day to do something, do anything, that involves the real world—meeting people, walking, cycling, or just getting out. By all means use e-mail to prearrange to meet up with people—but do turn it off on the day itself.

—The Global Ideas Bank

The Internet is wonderful in so many different ways. It has transformed the way we live. We can contact people instantly, wherever they are. We can involve large groups of people in discussions and capture their ideas. We can plan things together, without ever needing to meet. We have access to a world of information at the click of a mouse. We can download films and music...

But on the other hand, the Internet glues us to our computer monitors, isolates us from our fellow human beings. Large offices have become eerily silent. We will now e-mail someone a message, rather than call them up or walk ten yards to the next office to say hello.

We need to create a balance between the World Wide Web and the real wide world we live in. Turn your computer off for one day a week, leave your laptop at home, get out into the real world—and get a life!

Find out about the next Internet-Free Day: www.globalideasbank.org

If you type into Google "end of Internet," you get about 118 million English pages alone. This is one of the first:

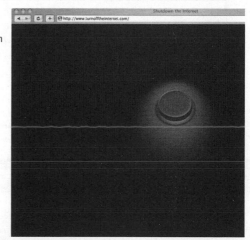

The End of the Internet

Congratulations! This is the last page.

Thank you for visiting the End of the Internet. There are no more links.

You must now turn off your computer and go do something productive.

Go read a book, for pete's sake.

—www.turnofftheinternet.com

...and get a life

- **Test your addiction to the Internet** at www.netaddiction.com/resources/internet_addiction_test.htm

- **Switch off your computer on Internet-Free Day,** which is the last Sunday in January. And keep it switched off for the whole day! To find out about the next Internet-Free Day, go to www.globalideasbank.org.

- **Organize your very own Internet-free day** in your office, at your college, or in your community.

where on EARTH

Google Earth provides aerial maps of the whole world. You can explore the world from the comfort of your desktop. Here are two interesting places to visit:

Mumbai is the commercial capital of India. It had a population of 18.3 million in 2005. It is the home of India's major financial institutions such as the Reserve Bank of India and the Stock Exchange, and is the corporate HQ in India for many Indian and multinational companies. It is also the home of India's Bollywood film industry. Mumbai attracts migrants from all over India, most coming to the city to seek a better life.

Dharavi, Mumbai, India: Near the airport is Dharavi, "Asia's largest slum," housing around 1 million people. In the midst of the wealth of Mumbai, which has some of the highest property prices in the world, it comes as a shock to see the squalid conditions in which so many Indians have to live. Yet Dharavi is a hub of energy, industry, enterprise…and hope for a better tomorrow.

Los Angeles is the second-largest city in the US, with a population of 3.95 million in the city itself and of 17.5 million in the wider metropolitan area. The city is a main point of entry for immigrants to the US attracted by its warm climate, the glamour of the Hollywood film industry, and the opportunity to live the "American dream." LA is home to some of the richest people on the planet. It also has a large and growing Mexican and Mexican American population.

18th Street, East Los Angeles: Not so far from the palatial residences of Beverly Hills, where film stars live in gated luxury, is 18th Street, the center of LA's gangland culture. *"La vida loca"* or "the crazy life" is what people call the gangland life, with its daily gun crime, drug scene, and carjackings.

Google Earth: www.earth.google.com
Catch up with the latest Bollywood news: www.planetbollywood.com
Catch up with the latest Hollywood news: www.hollywoodreporter.com
See the iconic HOLLYWOOD sign at: www.hollywoodsign.org

...do 6.5 billion people live

Visit Dharavi on Google Earth
Read *Rediscovering Dharavi: Stories from Asia's Largest Slum* by Kalpana Sharma, Penguin Books India, 2000.

Visit LA's 18th Street on Google Earth
Find out more about gangland culture on 18th Street:
www.streetgangs.com/18thstreet.html
www.aliciapatterson.org/APF1602/Rodriguez/Rodriguez.html

Visit your hometown on Google Earth; go to where you live
Find out as much as you can about the people living in these three locations. Think about the lottery of life—the inequalities that exist in the world and within communities, the different living conditions and the different opportunities that people have. Think about what you can do to reduce inequalities in your community and in the wider world.

JANUARY 25

OLD SPECS *new owners*

A pair of eyeglasses could transform someone's life. One billion people in the developing world need eyeglasses but cannot afford them (the cost can exceed three months' salary); 50% of children in institutions for the blind in Africa would be able to read normal or large print with eyeglasses. ● So people have to live their lives in a haze of half-sight.

Where they can afford to, people change their eyeglasses as their eyesight changes. Some people want the latest designer brands. Around 4 million pairs of glasses are thrown away each year in North America. ● These could help people in the developing world see, but only if a simple way of recycling them can be found.

Unite for Sight: www.uniteforsight.org

The story of Unite for Sight

In the USA, 10 million people are blind or visually impaired. Many of them do not have access to health care and are unaware of the importance of having an annual eye examination to maintain sight. Even if they have health insurance, they may be fearful of eye surgery or perceive blindness—due to cataracts or diabetes—as a natural part of aging.

Unite for Sight was started in 2002 by a Yale sophomore named Jennifer Staple to mobilize medical students to address the eye problems of the medically underserved population of New Haven, Connecticut. Volunteers screen people for eye disease, educate children and adults about eye health and blindness

prevention, and identify eye problems that require follow-up treatment.

Such was the success of the program that after three years it was expanded to other universities and then internationally. Unite for Sight has now introduced a scheme for recycling old eyeglasses.

Today over 4,000 Unite for Sight volunteers in 90 chapters, based at universities, medical schools, corporations, and high schools around the world, provide eye care to over 400,000 people.

...transform someone's outlook

- ● **Donate your eyeglasses.** Unite for Sight distributes donated reading and distance glasses and also nonprescription sunglasses to children and adults in Africa, Asia, and Latin America. Reading glasses and sunglasses are especially needed! Fill in your details at www.uniteforsight.org/donate_eyeglasses.php.

- ● **Start a collection in your community.** Ask all your friends and workmates to hand over their discarded eyeglasses. Get publicity in the local media. You might be able to collect lots of pairs of unused and unwanted spectacles. Doing this could make a significant impact on the lives of others.

All glasses should be in good condition, with two unscratched lenses. Unfortunately, bifocals and progressive lenses are of no use.

give BLOOD

It must be a wonderful feeling to save someone's life. Although medical professionals, firefighters, and lifeguards experience that satisfaction time and again, it seems beyond the reach of the rest of us. But you too can save a life simply by donating about an hour of your time—and a pint of your blood.

Few of us can predict when we might need a blood transfusion. And if we are lucky enough never to need one, then it is almost certain that our children, our parents, or a friend will need one sometime in the future. Giving blood couldn't be easier. It's quick, simple, and safe. And all that most people feel is the satisfaction that they are helping to save lives.

Most people can give blood. If you're generally in good health, between the ages of 17 and 59, and weigh at least 110 lbs., you could start giving blood today. And when you do, find out how easy it is to save someone's life. ☺ If you are pregnant or have just had a baby, are taking antibiotics, have contracted or think you may have contracted HIV, had malaria, inject drugs, or are a hepatitis carrier, then you will not be able to give blood. There are other criteria you have to pass as well, so contact the National Blood Service in advance, and they will send you a simple health check form.

When you arrive to give blood, someone will go through your health check form. If it is safe for you to be a donor, then a drop of blood will be taken from your finger and tested to make sure you're not anemic. And if you're still OK, then just under a pint of your blood will be taken—a procedure that lasts about ten minutes.

www.givelife.org

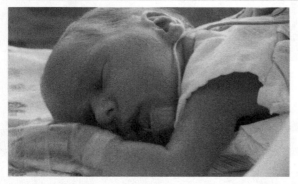

Helen's story

When Helen was born, she was premature and weighed only 4 lbs 3 oz. When she was only a few weeks old, she caught a chest infection and stopped breathing. She had to be put on a ventilator to keep her alive, and be pumped full of antibiotics to combat the infection. It seemed as though she might lose the battle.

A blood test revealed that she was anemic, and a blood transfusion was needed. Just a small amount of blood, donated on the spot by one of the hospital's support staff (who had been prescreened), changed her from a pasty white to a healthy pink and saved her life. She has never looked back.

...and save a life

If you're able to, give blood. Do it regularly.

Call up your local hospital or a national blood transfusion service for details of how to do it.

JANUARY 27

HOUSES *for sustainability*

The Tree People Center in Los Angeles is a building with lots of green features. These include:

Extensive landscaping and a "green roof" planted with native vegetation, which reduces heat absorption in summer.

Bicycle storage and changing facilities so as to encourage cycle use.

A "water harvesting" storage tank and simple filtration to collect rainwater with which to irrigate the gardens.

Low-flow plumbing and waterless fixtures to reduce water use.

Renewable energy supply for at least half of the building's energy consumption.

On-site solar panels that produce 20% of the building's electricity requirements.

Insulated floors, walls, and roofs, which reduce heat loss in winter and heat gain in summer.

Recycled building materials, produced locally or from sustainable sources, wherever possible.

Low-fume-emitting paints, coatings, adhesives, carpets, and sealants used for decoration, which improve indoor air quality.

Daylight illumination, where possible, to minimize use of artificial light.

In the UK, the Peabody Housing Trust built a Zero (fossil) Energy Development (ZED) of low-cost housing in Sutton in South London and has published a handbook, *From A to ZED*, which sets out some basic principles for green development.

Take a green buildings tour at http://tours.virtuallygreen.com.
Find out about ZED buildings at www.zedfactory.com.

You can't change the design of an existing building, but there are things you can do to make it greener. Using lessons from the Tree People Center, you might improve the way your house deals with

Water: Store your roof-water runoff, or use it to recharge the groundwater. Use more water-efficient home appliances. What about installing a composting toilet? Plant a garden on any flat roof, and collect and use rainwater to water it.

Energy: Make sure that your roof and hot water tank are properly insulated, and use seals on windows and doors to reduce heat loss. Make sure that the curtains are not obstructing daylight through the windows, and paint the walls white or a light color to maximize natural illumination.

...create a greener home

🌳 **Take a Green Buildings virtual tour** and visit a green building without leaving the comfort of your home. You can find out why the building was built, what materials it's made of, and what key design concepts were incorporated to make it a green building. You can visit the Tree People Center, the Cleveland Environmental Center, and several other green buildings. The list is growing, and there's no admission charge!

🌳 When you have completed your visit, think about what you can do to make your own home just that little bit greener.

fight the SUV MENACE

Do you live in the depths of the country and frequently have to drive off-road? If not, then you have little need to drive an SUV (Sport Utility Vehicle) or 4x4. Nevertheless, these huge cars have become very popular, despite being dangerous both for pedestrians and the environment. One in four vehicles sold in the USA is an SUV, and the proportion continues to rise. The same trend is now apparent in Europe.

The SUV is seen as a passport to freedom and the great outdoors. TV commercials depict them climbing snow-capped mountains or tearing through desert sand dunes. In reality, the only off-road action most of these vehicles are likely to see is when they are accidentally driven across a grass median!

SUVs are the most polluting form of passenger transport available. Every gallon of gasoline burned emits more than 26 lbs. of carbon dioxide, and SUVs have gargantuan appetites. Some SUVs do as little as 13 miles per gallon in town and not a great deal more on the open road. This gas puzzling makes them a major contributor to climate change. 🌳 Their enormous engines spew out twice as much carbon monoxide, hydrocarbons, and nitrogen dioxide as "greener" passenger cars. These chemicals cause ozone and other pollutants to build up around cities, leading to poor air quality, which in turn causes people to suffer from headaches, eye and throat irritation, and, in the long term, lung damage.

The US Friends of the Earth website dedicated to SUVs is www.suv.org.

Buy a cleaner car

When you choose your next car, do some research. There is a huge range of different models and they vary enormously in their environmental impact. Pay attention to fuel  emission ratings, miles per gallon in the city and on the highway. Cars powered by noncarbon fuels are gaining in popularity, thanks to rising gas prices and fears of global warming. Consider buying an electric car or a hybrid. Use a carpool whenever possible.

The site www.greenercars.com will help you choose the "greenest car" for your needs.

...get the off-roads off the road

Download fake parking tickets from www.wastemonsters.org.uk/ TrueGenericFeb06-Web.pdf. Put them under the windshield wipers of SUVs. They will give the owner a real shock. The information they contain will show everything that's wrong with an SUV.

JANUARY 29

SLOTHS *slowing down*

What does it mean to be a sloth? Is a sloth lazy and dirty? Is a sloth stupid and slow? Is a sloth really slothlike? You will be surprised to find out how sloths actually live, and why we could all benefit from emulating them. An incident in the coastal jungle of Ecuador inspired the creation of the Sloth Club. A group of ecotourists encountered a three-toed sloth tied up in a concrete cage in a kitchen, awaiting the moment when it would be killed and eaten. Anja Light, singer and activist with the Australian Rainforest Information Centre, and several members of the Japanese Action for Mangrove Reforestation saw something in the defenselessness of the sloth that moved them to do something.

They saw all the injustice and suffering in the world reflected in the act of binding a harmless animal for three days and killing it for a tiny amount of meat: the torture of prisoners of conscience, children in poor countries starving while the rich world doesn't notice, abuse of animals, senseless warfare, and degradation of the planet. The sloth is also a symbol of the forest, and the Ecuadorian forest is being destroyed at a frightening pace. It suddenly became very important for these people to find a way to release this sloth, in order to try to lessen the amount of suffering in the world, even if only for a moment. So they paid less than $5 for it and then released it downriver.

They created the Sloth Club to protect the animal's habitat and to change our way of thinking and living. The Sloth Club promotes the concept of doing less, living simply, and finding joy in our life without consuming an endless chain of meaningless things. "We want to shift from a culture of the 'more, faster and tougher' to that of 'less, slower and non-violent.' The three-toed sloth can be our greatest teacher in how to do this."

The objectives of the Sloth Club:

Establish a sloth sanctuary in Ecuador.

Create a fund to help protect and restore the forests where sloths live.

Support communities in those forests to improve the quality of their lives.

Lead a cultural movement inspired by the sloth's low-energy, cyclical, symbiotic and nonviolent lifestyle.

Promote "sloth businesses"—those that are ecologically and socially conscious.

Sloth Club: www.slothclub.org

The three-toed sloth

This harmless vegetarian lives in the rainforests of Central and South America and spends most of its life upside down about 100 feet above the ground. It has only half the muscle weight of other animals of the same size. As a result, the sloth moves only very slowly, but is light enough to climb thin branches, and therefore less likely to be attacked by predators. The sloth lives in harmony with the environment. Its fur even grows green-blue algae that support many species of insect. No wonder it has such a beatific smile.

...to protect and restore

Join the Sloth Club. But don't rush!

get a technological FIX

You scratch. Then it becomes like malaria, you get a high fever. If the fly has previously bitten a rabid animal, and it bites you, you could get rabies.

—Ndith

This is the worst kind of insect bite. Ndith lives in Kathekani in southern Kenya, where both cattle and people are affected. Her neighbor, Paul, lost all his cows to trypanosomiasis, a disease carried by the bloodsucking tsetse fly.

If the tsetse fly is allowed to spread unchecked, it will devastate the lives and livelihoods of many thousands more Kenyan farmers. Much of Kenya is dry, and crops fail three out of four years. Many families raise animals such as chickens, goats, and cows. It is the one way they can meet their basic needs. ☻ Twenty years ago, the tsetse fly wiped out 80% of the livestock in Kathekani. Across Africa, 55 million people and their livestock are under threat.

But there is a solution. Tsetse fly traps can eliminate 99% of flies. Farmers work together to build and maintain barriers of fly traps, which are erected in key locations. In Kathekani, ten traps kill 20,000 flies every day. ☻ One trap costs only $40 to build. The trap is designed to look enough like a cow to trick the tsetse fly. The fly is lured to the trap by the smell of cow's urine contained in a bottle. The flies fly toward the blue cloth on either side of the trap. The black cloth in the middle invites the flies to settle. They then fall into the trap and die.
☻ The tsetse fly trap is one of many technological solutions developed by Practical Action. Other ideas that have been turned into action include:

Building roads in Sri Lanka.
Harnessing local river power in Zimbabwe.
Water harvesting, terracing, donkey plows, and damp-proof grain storage in Sudan.
Solar driers to preserve food and earthquake-proof housing in Nepal.
Solar lanterns in Kenya.
Fish breeding in Bangladesh.

Practical Action: www.practicalaction.org

Intermediate Technology Development Group (now Practical Action) was set up following the 1973 publication of E. F. Schumacher's book *Small Is Beautiful: Economics as if People Mattered.* Small-scale water harvesting instead of big dams is a good example of his pioneering idea of small-scale solutions to problems, developed and implemented with local participation.

...find simple solutions

☻ **Do a global challenge.** Practical Action supporters have cycled the world, run the Andes, and done other extraordinary things to raise money for ITDG. Take a year or two off and do the same.

☻ **Design a machine for turning seawater into drinking water.** Of all the earth's water, 97% is saltwater found in oceans and seas; 2% is frozen. Only 1% of the earth's water is available for drinking. Your invention could transform the world.

JANUARY 31

GIVE UP *apathy*

If the sheer weight of the world's problems induces apathy, and you don't know where to direct your energies (assuming you have any), there is a website just for you. It saves you the trouble of trawling the Internet, providing one-stop shopping for anyone wanting to make a difference.

The Anti-Apathy movement starts with the idea that we should all be engaged in doing *something* for a better world, and our apathy is one of the reasons things are not changing for the better. Anti-Apathy aims to get cynical and disengaged people to connect with key issues and organizations by showing them how they can help create a more just, more democratic, and more sustainable world through their awareness and action. The website provides a list of 24 key organizations. All you have to do is express an interest in five of them, and *act* on the information they send you.

Some of the organizations included on the website:

Amnesty International *human rights*
The Big Issue Foundation *homelessness*
Center for Alternative Technology *low-energy technologies*
Fair Trade Foundation *fair trade*
Friends of the Earth *environment*
Grass Roots Collective *arts and media*
Slow Food *responsible eating and living*

Soil Association *organic agriculture*
Space Hijackers *use of public spaces*
Surfers against Sewage *marine and river pollution*
Survival International *tribal peoples around the world*
World Development Movement *tackling global poverty*

Anti-Apathy: www.antiapathy.org

WORN AGAIN

These unique sneakers, made from recycled prison blankets, towels, parachutes, and suit jackets are available from the Anti-Apathy website.

...start to make a difference

This is your own personal action plan. Get moving!

The first five steps to conquering apathy:

Admit that a life addicted to apathy is a life half lived.

Come to believe that the power to change things and restore society lies within each and every one of us.

Ponder the question, "What can I do?" And while you're at it, list some answers to this question.

Make a list of all the things you do in your everyday life that cause stress to the planet and to society.

Act on your discoveries. Find alternatives, or just stop doing the things that cause harm.

—*adapted from Anti-Apathy's 12 steps to personal recovery*

1 FEBRUARY

become a GROUNDHOG

On February 4, 1841, in Morgantown, Pennsylvania, storekeeper James Morris wrote in his diary, *"Last Tuesday, the 2nd, was Candlemas Day, the day on which, according to the Germans, the Groundhog peeps out of his winter quarters, and if he sees his shadow, he pops back for another six weeks' nap, but if the day be cloudy he remains out, as the weather is to be moderate..."* This is believed to be the origin of Groundhog Day, which falls on February 2.

Punxsutawney, Pennsylvania, is the home of weather-forecasting groundhog Punxsutawney Phil. He made his first prediction in 1887 when he saw a shadow— which meant that there were still 6 more weeks of winter. No shadow means that spring is just around the corner. Since that first prediction, Phil has seen his shadow 95 times, and not seen a shadow 16 times. In 9 years before 1900, there was no record. Perhaps Phil failed to get up. Or maybe his shadow was so big, he took to his bed without telling anybody.

Other weather-forecasting groundhogs have names such as Connecticut Chuckles, Pennichuk Chuck, Unadilla Bill, and French Creek Freddie. There's probably a weather-forecasting groundhog near where you live.

Punxsutawney Phil: www.groundhog.org
Punxsutawney community website: www.punxsutawney.com
Other weather-forecasting groundhogs:
www.groundhogsday.com/groundhogcentral.php

Long-range weather forecasts are available from

World Meteorological Organization: www.worldweather.org
Long-Range Weather: www.longrangeweather.com
Climate Prediction Center: www.cpc.ncep.noaa.gov
Old Farmer's Almanac: www.almanac.com/weather/index.php

Start your own Groundhog Club chapter

Carry on the tradition of Groundhog Day in your community. Set up a Groundhog Day chapter with your friends and neighbors. Follow these easy steps:

- Get ten or more people to agree to become members of the *Punxsutawney Groundhog Club*. Each has to complete a membership form and have a good sense of humor. Membership costs $10 per year.

- Agree to perpetuate and celebrate Groundhog Day robustly and heartily.

- Report your activities and events for the *Groundhog Club Newsletter* and website.

- Complete a chapter application form (joining fee $75 with a banner, or $30 without).

...is spring just around the corner?

Crawl out of bed today and see if you can see your shadow.

- If you can, crawl back into your hole. Then start a Groundhog Club chapter. And next year set yourself up as a climate predictor. Give yourself a sassy name. Become your community groundhog. Go out on February 2 to look for your shadow.

- If you can't, then get out of your hole. Spring is just around the corner. Resolve to do one thing today that will contribute to a better world and to get at least 10 other people to join you in doing this. Address global warming by switching your central heating down by one degree (or two degrees if you can bear it). Stay cheerful, though; it'll soon be spring.

AIR PORTS *for all*

Wi-Fi (wireless Internet) hot spots are springing up in public spaces all over the developed world, giving us Internet access wherever we go. But the people who stand to benefit most from the Wi-Fi revolution are those in the developing world—in countries and districts where roads and telephones are rudimentary, rare, or nonexistent.

Wi-Fi comes brightly painted. A bicycle rickshaw, decorated to resemble a Hindu temple carriage but carrying a computer with a Wi-Fi connection, travels round villages in Uttar Pradesh, India. ✋ The driver is a computer instructor, who gives classes to young and old, providing the villagers with the skills necessary to run their own webcam, which in turn will enable them to participate in online learning. ✋ The rickshaw can also carry medical diagnostic equipment.

Wi-Fi helps isolated communities stay in contact. Yak farmers in remote regions of Nepal are using a Wi-Fi connection to stay in touch with family and friends, get help with health problems, and trade online. ✋ The project was started by teacher Mahabir Pun, who had been given some computers for his school but could not get on line. With no telephone lines, he decided to adopt a wireless solution. ✋ Signals are sent from a server about 30 miles away, to a solar-powered relay station on a tree up the mountainside. This station sends the signal to another relay station (also solar- and wind-powered), from where it is distributed to five villages.

Find out more about
The infothela bicycle rickshaw at www.iitk.ac.in/MLAsia/infothela.htm.
The Nepal Wireless Networking Project at nepalwireless.net.

The MagicBike: Internet connectivity on two wheels

The MagicBike was developed by Yury Gitman in New York. It is a mobile Wi-Fi hotspot that gives free Internet connectivity wherever the bicycle is ridden or parked. It is ideal for art and culture events, emergency access, public demonstrations, and communities who are at the struggling end of the digital divide.
http://www.yuryg.com/yury

...bring Wi-Fi to your community

Get connected to the Internet by setting up your own Wi-Fi connection.

✋ **Join with your neighbors** to set up a wireless base station that all of you can use. Share the costs.

✋ **Use the money you save** to do something to bridge the digital divide.

✋ **Subscribe to www.bytesforall.org,** an online magazine on IT and development.

Keeping costs down and profits up is the name of the game for fashion retailers such as Gap and Diesel, and sports labels such as Adidas, Nike, and Puma. One way they keep costs low is to use sweatshop workers to produce their goods. ⚽ Sweatshops can range in size from hi-tech factories for 10,000 workers to individuals working from home. What they have in common is that the workers are required to work long hours for low wages, often in unhealthy and unsafe conditions.

Over 23.6 million people work in sweatshops, in 160 countries around the world. Many of them are young women and teenagers, producing cheap clothing for western consumers. About 80% work under conditions that systematically violate local and international laws. ⚽ Some firms have pledged to clean up their act, issuing "codes of conduct" and supporting the campaign against global poverty, but in reality the situation is getting worse as poor countries compete for low-wage jobs. With complex production systems, involving thousands of suppliers, work is often subcontracted to sweatshops, which remain "off the books," hidden from view.

Now is the time to demand that retailers eliminate the global sweatshop system. They control the industry, and they can end it. But we consumers may have to forgo the pleasure of purchasing piles of dirt-cheap clothes.

PeopleTree Fairtrade clothing is now sold by Top Shop: www.ptree.co.uk

In 2003 British soccer star David Beckham "earned" over $20 million by endorsing companies like Adidas. Indonesian sweatshop workers producing for Adidas earn the equivalent of $600 a year.

Women sewing $17.99 Disney shirts in Bangladesh were paid just 5 cents for each shirt they sewed, while former Disney boss Michael Eisner made about $63,000 per hour.

...look behind the label

Buy a No-Sweat T-shirt or sweatshirt. Next time you shop, ask the store the following:

⚽ Do you have a list of the factories that make your products, with information on the wages and working conditions in each factory? Can you provide me with a copy of it?

⚽ Does your store guarantee that the workers who made this product were paid a living wage, enough to support their families?

⚽ Does your store have a code of conduct that protects human rights and forbids child labor and unsafe conditions in all the factories that make the products you sell? How do you enforce these rules?

FEBRUARY 4

TOILETS *you've got one*

Most of us take a flushing toilet for granted. Yet more than half the people in the world have no access to any kind of toilet at all, let alone one we would consider acceptable. ● Lack of toilets is a major health issue. It is important to prevent other people, animals, and in particular insects from coming into contact with human waste, for that is how many diseases are spread. Diarrhea kills over 2 million children a year. Many of these deaths could be prevented by proper sanitation.

Lack of sanitation is also a gender issue. Boys and men find it much easier, and less embarrassing, to urinate and even defecate in public. Women dare not be caught relieving themselves. They either have to get up before dawn, or wait until nightfall, which can be bad for their health, as well as being uncomfortable.

Many schools in the developing world have no toilets at all—even large secondary schools with several thousand pupils. This is unpleasant for all concerned but especially difficult for teenage girls. Many agencies recognize that latrines in schools are key to the education of girls and that well-educated young women are, in turn, key to the social and economic development of some of the world's poorest nations. ● So the answer to many of the world's problems is more toilets in schools.

WaterAid: www.wateraid.org
IRC International Water and Sanitation Centre: www.irc.nl

The simplest pit latrine is a hole in the ground, with a cover to prevent insects from entering. Some also have ventilation pipes to take away odor and insects.

A more luxurious version is a pour-flush latrine, which has a U-bend kept continually full of water to create a seal. Each user takes water in with them to pour down the latrine.

These simple devices have to be properly managed, and resited when they become full.

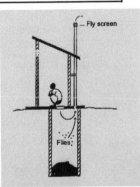

...now give one to someone else

If everybody with a toilet helped provide one for someone without, the problem would be solved. There are plenty of international development agencies working on sanitation. Find a scheme you like, and start raising money for it. According to WaterAid:

● **$16** pays for enough cement to produce four latrine slabs in Malawi.

● **$30** buys an ecological sanitation latrine in Mozambique.

● **$700** pays for a school sanitation block for 150 boys and girls in India.

Ask people at work to help. Construct two collecting boxes. Put one in the men's and one in the women's toilet at your workplace, with a poster inviting people to drop a coin in the box every time they use the toilet.

5 FEBRUARY

minimally invasive EDUCATION

Mere curiosity will lead groups of children to explore, and this will result in their learning.

Dr. Sugata Mitra of NIIT—a leading computer training and software company in India—came up with the idea of **Minimally Invasive Education (MIE).** The NIIT office was located next to a slum, where the children had no access to computers, and were not particularly familiar with the English language. A hole was made in the wall of the office, and a computer was installed there with a monitor and a mouse, accessible from the street through this hole in the wall.

Within three months, the children had achieved a certain level of computer skills without any instruction at all. They were able to browse the Internet, download songs, go to cartoon sites, and work on MS Paint. They even invented their own vocabulary to define terms on the computer; for example, *sui* (needle) for the cursor, *channels* for websites, and *damru* (Shiva's drum) for the hourglass (busy) symbol. By the fourth month, the children were able to accomplish tasks such as creating folders, cutting and pasting, creating shortcuts, moving/resizing windows, and using MS Word to create short messages, which they were able to do without using a keyboard.

Ten more kiosks have been set up in towns and cities across India, and 100 are planned. When the idea was discussed, parents and children strongly opposed removing the original kiosk. The kiosk is still there, and approximately 80 children use it daily.

Read about the Hole-in-the-Wall project at www.hole-in-the-wall.com

Children working intently at the Stok Learning Station in Ladakh in the Himalayas, another hole-in-the-wall project.

A Stok Learning Station.

...it's a hole-in-the-wall thing!

- **Find out** as much as you can about the **Hole-in-the-Wall** project. Write a simple manual about it.
- **Bring the idea to the attention** of organizations working in education and urban issues—in your own country as well as in the developing world.
- **And next time you travel**, try to find an organization working in a slum and discuss with them how they might set up a **Hole-in-the-Wall** project in their community (with your support?).

FEBRUARY 6

WAR GAMES *now's your chance*

I am a slightly liberal Republican, completely confused about the whole "Weapons of Mass Destruction" thing. I love riddles, puzzles, games, and all that jazz. More than anything, I love the concept of treasure hunts. I developed the "Find those Weapons" treasure hunt to raise the $25,000 I needed to go back to college, but also to make use of the Iraq trivia I had collected and to raise money for charity.

In December 2003, I released the game. People had to hunt for Weapons of Mass Destruction by searching through thousands of real-life documents relating to the Iraq war. The winner would receive a $5,000 solid gold trophy and a bag of cash; another bag of cash would be sent to their favorite charity plus a barrel of oil would be sent to President George W. Bush. Over 1,000 people played the game, which was solved in August 2004. —Shane Messer

Some issues are really complex, and the only way to understand what is happening is to make a careful study of the facts. But let's face it, this can be very boring. So why not make a game out of it?

Collect as much relevant information about the issue as possible. For the Iraq war, a lot of information was available on official and private websites: leaflets from the war, maps of the area, records of the costs of different aspects of the war, statements made by all the people involved, etc.

Assemble all this information, and devise a number of questions, which players will solve by carefully reading through the documents. ♣ A simple question might be something like: *B____ and B____ were the two most outspoken proponents of the war.* ♣ The answer is of course *Bush* and *Blair*. Another might be, *How many UN Resolutions referred to Weapons of Mass Destruction?* The questions are then circulated to all the players, and the first player to come up with all the right answers is declared the winner.

The more people who play, the better. ♣ So get as much publicity as you can for your game—which is not hard. You might think about charging a participation fee to help you cover your costs and pay for the prizes.

Shane Messer's game to hunt for Weapons of Mass Destruction is on www.findthoseweapons.com.

The US military issued its soldiers a deck of 55 cards of the most wanted people in Iraq. Saddam was the ace of spades. View these cards at www.defenselink.mil/news/Apr2003/pipc10042003.html.

A replica set of cards can be obtained from a number of sources, including www.greatusaflags.com.

"Try 'em" is a card game of the USA's "most wanted," with Dick Cheney as the ace of spades. It is on a spoof World Trade Organization website, www.gatt.org/regime/.

...to find those WMD

♣ **Take any issue you like**, and create a game.

♣ **Play your game with your friends**—or launch it on the Internet.

women hold up **HALF THE SKY**

Sometimes our thinking is clouded by false assumptions. Think about this:

A father and son are driving home. They are involved in a bad car accident and are rushed to hospital. Both are in critical condition. A surgeon comes to the emergency room to try to save the boy, takes one look at the patient, and says, "I can't operate on this boy, he's my son." But the boy's father is lying on a trolley next to him.

What is the surgeon talking about? The answer is actually quite simple. Of course, the surgeon is the boy's mother.

Challenging gender inequality has to start with a simple shift in thinking. Think of women as leaders, as activists, as experts, as contributors, and not as passive onlookers or victims. ✖ The reality is that women can have a huge influence within their community. This is why most poverty programs focus on women as agents of change. As Chairman Mao said, "Women hold up half the sky." ✖ It was Sudanese women who organized the Wunlit tribal summit to bring an end to hostilities between the Dinka and Nuer peoples. The resulting covenant guaranteed peace between the tribes, who agreed to share rights to water, fishing, and grazing land, which had been key points of conflict. ✖ And in spite of the ongoing violence, it is Israeli and Palestinian women who are working together through Jerusalem Link to convey a joint vision of a just peace.

For stories of some of the world's leading women activists, visit www.adventuredivas.com.

Some notable women effecting change in India:

Vandana Shiva has been a leading researcher and activist on biodiversity, conservation, and protecting people's rights from threats to their livelihoods and the environment. www.vshiva.net

Ela Bhatt started SEWA, the Self Employed Women's Association, which represents 250,000 self-employed workers. SEWA runs health and maternity programs and has set up its own bank. www.sewa.org

Kiran Bedi was the first woman officer in the Indian Police Service. Since 2003, she has been civilian police adviser in the Dept. of Peacekeeping Operations for the UN. She also set up the India Vision Foundation to work in the field of prison reform and crime prevention. www.kiranbedi.com

...challenge gender inequality

Women are underrepresented at the top level in organizations. Not enough women sit on charity boards in relation to their proportion in the population or the potential contribution they could make.

Find an organization that is doing work that you really care about. Research the composition of its board. And if you feel that women (or young people, or minority people, or older people) are underrepresented, then write to the chairperson pointing this out. Ask for a response.

ORGAN DONATION *a gift of life* ☺

Transplants save lives, but there is a desperate need for more organs, and the more people discuss their wishes regarding donation, the more lives can be saved. More than 90,000 people are waiting for an organ, and around 6,500 people die each year while waiting for a transplant.

Transplants depend entirely on the generosity of donors and their families who are willing to make this lifesaving gift. ☺ You can donate your organs, but only if you have expressed a wish in writing during your lifetime (or orally in front of two witnesses), or if the person in possession of your body at the time of your death is willing to donate your organs and has no reason to believe you would not have wished this. ☺

Organs that can be donated include	Tissue that can be donated includes
heart	corneas
lungs	skin
kidneys	bone
pancreas	heart valves
liver	tendons
small bowel	

Corneas can be transplanted to restore the sight of a person who has a severe eye disease or injury. ☺ Bone and tendons are used for reconstruction after an injury or during joint replacement surgery. ☺ A bone transplant can prevent limb amputation in patients suffering from bone cancer. ☺ Heart valves are used to help children born with heart defects and adults with diseased or damaged valves. ☺ Skin grafts are used as protective dressings to help save the lives of people with severe burns. ☺ Tendons can be used to restore mobility.

Register online as an organ donor at www.organdonor.gov.

In the US as of August 2006,

☺ More than 92,000 candidates are on the waiting list to receive an organ.

☺ More than 9,300 transports were performed as a result of the generosity of 4,800 donors.

...that costs you nothing

☺ **Make known your wish to be an organ donor.** Tell your partner, your family, and your friends. Tell your doctor.

☺ **Join the Organ Donor Register** and carry an organ donor card. This will alert those who are dealing with you in an emergency situation.

☺ **Get nine of your friends and family to register too.** This is a gift of life that costs you nothing but will help to tackle an interntional shortage of donors.

collect your SMALL CHANGE

Loose change in your pocket really does burn a hole—or at least wears away at your pocket linings. And bulky purses full of change only add to the weight most of us end up lugging around with us. ♦♦ The only thing to do is *offload it*. Empty your pockets or your purse each night and save the change in a jar, a piggy bank, under your mattress, or wherever you like.

You'll be amazed at how quickly your spare change mounts up. And you probably won't even miss it! ♦♦ At the end of the year—or whenever the container gets full—you will then have the pleasure of deciding which project to donate the money to. You might decide to give it to a project near home, or to respond to one of the many charitable appeals in the media. Even small sums of money can make a huge difference.

Here are some good online giving websites:

Global Giving, a marketplace for high impact social and economic development projects around the world: www.globalgiving.com

Give India has lots of different types of project, and many give you several options for giving. Surf the site, and you might end up by building a well, sponsoring a child's education, or helping provide eye operations: www.giveindia.org

First Giving, a website with lots of options for giving both at home and abroad: www.Firstgiving.com

...and donate a fortune

What a difference your small change can make! There are all sorts of interesting causes you can donate to. Put your money to work changing the world.

You could give

♦♦ $10 to send four carefully selected books to Africa: www.bookaid.org

♦♦ $30 for an adult cataract operation: www.sightsavers.org

Or you could be more ambitious and choose a longer-term project on the Global Giving website. Here are two examples in El Salvador:

♦♦ Enable one farming family to buy the land that they are working. Cost: $7,535

♦♦ Save the El Imposible rainforest, helping over 50 volunteers working with SalvaNATURA to ensure that the trees don't get cut down. Cost $10,000.

These are suggestions just to illustrate the good that you could be doing with your money. Make a big change with your small change!

FEBRUARY 10

TOOLS *in the right hands*

Giving them a tool enables people to make a living for themselves and their family. It is the same principle as teaching a hungry person how to fish, rather than just handing out fish. 🌍 In countries such as Tanzania and Ghana, it can be extremely difficult and far too expensive for people to buy the tools they need to make a living. This is tough for the people involved. But there's an imaginative solution.

Tools for Self-Reliance (TFSR) collects and sends over half a million pounds' worth of high-quality tools every year to six countries in Africa. The tools they send are used by skilled craftspeople to earn a living. TSFR also trains people how to use and take care of their tools.

The tools most requested are for

woodworking

blacksmithing

building and plumbing

shoemaking and leather working

car and bicycle repairing

metalworking and tinsmithing

Shipping costs are the same for good tools or bad tools, so wherever possible only the best are sent.

Tools for Self-Reliance: www.tfsr.org

My African people have great skills, initiative, and energy. They work so hard to develop their communities and their continent, against such heavy odds. But you cannot work with bare hands.

—Archbishop Desmond Tutu speaking to the BBC about Tools for Self-Reliance

...foster self-reliance

Organize a tool collection drive.

🌍 Contact Tools for Self Reliance. They will supply you with a list of needed tools.

🌍 Contact your friends, family, and local businesses. Tell them what you are doing and what you need. Ask them to donate tools.

rig an ELECTION

The Zimbabwe opposition leader Morgan Tsvangirai (Movement for Democratic Change) said that there was no point in contesting the 2005 elections for the Senate because the government would rig them—and anyway the Senate has no real power. The MDC claims that previous elections were seriously rigged and that opposition politicians and supporters have been harassed, imprisoned, and even murdered.

The spokesman for the ruling Zanu-PF party, Comrade Webster Shamu, said, *"We would like to congratulate the people of Zimbabwe for once again showing their commitment to Zanu-PF and what the party and leadership stand for. The elections and the results have once again demonstrated that the people of Zimbabwe cannot be bought or sold."*

Movement for Democratic Change: *www.mdczimbabwe.org*
Zanu-PF: www.zanupfpub.co.zw
Lynn Landes, on open voting and democracy in America:
www.ecotalk.org/VotingSecurity.htm

How to rig an election in Zimbabwe

1. *Install cronies to oversee the poll.* Robert Mugabe chose Justice Chiweshe to chair the Election Commission.
2. *Gerrymander constituency boundaries.* Justice Chiweshe redrew the parliamentary map to favor Zanu-PF.
3. *Ban likely opponents from voting.* Up to 3.4 million Zimbabweans living abroad were unable to vote.
4. *Ensure that all likely supporters vote.* Senior ranks of the army, air force, police, and prisons service were rewarded with business opportunities. Junior ranks were threatened with being fired if they voted MDC.
5. *Reduce independent election scrutiny.* Western inspectors were banned. Those from Iran, China, and Russia were admitted.
6. *Stuff the electoral rolls with the names of dead people.* There appeared to have been 1 million dead voters.
7. *Double the number of polling booths and place them in regime strongholds.* In 2005, 8,000 new polling booths made it hard for the observers to do the monitoring.
8. *If all else fails, falsify the result.* Votes were counted in polling booths, results phoned to a "constituency center," then a "national logistics center" in Harare. Mugabe loyalists ran the process.

...make democracy work for you

- Make up your own mind about what is happening in Zimbabwe, a once prosperous country now suffering famine and hyperinflation. Find out as much as you can. Look at all points of view. Write a letter of support to either Morgan Tsvangirai or President Robert Mugabe—whomever you deem to be in the right.
- Make sure you vote at the next election.
- Make an impact on the election. Form your own voter bloc. Find 10 people who agree to vote your way. Ask each of them to find 10 more people. Set up a webgroup. Quiz the politicians. On the basis of their policies and promises, decide whom to support. Get out your vote behind your chosen candidate.

PLANT *a sunflower*

The scientific name for sunflower is *Helianthus,* derived from *helios,* meaning "sun" and *anthos,* meaning flower. Its head follows the sun from sunrise until sunset in order to better gather the sun's rays. The sunflower is making a silent, simple, and spontaneous statement that it is nature and sunlight that provide for us.

On June 4, 1996, the defense ministers of the US, Russia, and Ukraine met at the Pervomaisk missile base to celebrate Ukraine's transfer of its nuclear warheads to Russia for dismantling. The ministers planted sunflowers where missiles were once buried. US Secretary of Defense William Perry stated, "Sunflowers instead of missiles in the soil would ensure peace for future generations."

The Sunflower Project is dedicated to taking the 1996 Ukrainian missile gesture and fostering a worldwide campaign to encourage people everywhere to plant sunflowers throughout their cities, towns, communities, and countryside as living symbols of peace and to celebrate our connection to nature.

The Sunflower Project: www.sunflowerproject.org

The Sunflower Petition

To all people everywhere: The Sunflower Project is a global appeal to all people on planet Earth concerned about nuclear war, pollution, violence, injustice, and threats to the balance of nature—to plant at least one sunflower seed in a sunny place where it will be noticed.

This simple act of planting a seed will demonstrate the energy, simplicity, and practicality of nature. The incredible sunflower turns its head to follow the sun and provides seeds to eat, fiber for materials, medicine to heal, a golden yellow dye, and oil. It offers shade and beauty. It is a symbol of our hope for Nature and for Peace.

We make a collective, conscious, and powerful statement by planting sunflowers where they will be noticed—in vacant lots, fields, along roadways, city streets, at schools, surrounding toxic waste sites, reservoirs, threatened open space, along stretches of railroad, parking lots, playgrounds, around places of worship, and in gardens.

We encourage all to plant a sunflower seed and watch it grow to become a majestic symbol—to summon harmony between humans and with nature, toward peace on earth.

...for peace and prosperity

Click and sign the Sunflower Petition on the Sunflower Project site.

Plant a sunflower in your garden, on wasteland, or wherever. The larger varieties grow up to a height of 11 ft. After they have flowered, snack on the seeds. They're nutritious, 24% protein and containing lots of minerals and vitamins.

learn a new language SIGN UP

Sign is the primary means of communication for many profoundly deaf people. It is in effect their first language. ⊗ Sign uses hand gestures that are interpreted visually. Each word has its own gesture. There are also signs for each letter of the alphabet. ⊗ There are two different versions of sign: British Sign Language (BSL) and American Sign language (ASL). And just as with spoken language, there are colloquialisms and slang.

Social inclusion is one of the dominant ideas of our age—finding ways of including people whatever their difficulties or disabilities, for example, enabling people with learning difficulties to attend regular schools and making public buildings accessible for wheelchairs. ⊗ If you meet a profoundly deaf person, find out how he or she prefers to communicate. Learning to sign will show your commitment to a just, tolerant, and inclusive society. It isn't hard. Many words are based on gestures that reflect the essence of the word. For example:

How are you?

Open your hands and touch your chest with them, then move them outwards, making them into fists with raised thumbs.

Hungry

With a clenched fist draw a circle on your stomach. The same actions are used to sign the country, Hungary.

Thank you

With straight fingers put your hand to your chin and gently bring it forward, once or twice.

For BSL, contact www.british-sign.co.uk or www.learnbsl.org
For ASL, contact www.masterstech-home.com/ASLDict.html www.signlanguage.org

I Love You (ASL)

...and speak to deaf people

Get started in sign. Here's a simple phrase to get you going. First, find someone you want to say this to. And then say it to him or her. With passion!

I (Point to yourself.)

LOVE (Cross either your closed or flat hands over your heart with palms facing in.)

YOU (Point to the person you are addressing.)

KNITTING *cast off*

Peace Fleece seeks to find a common ground across political and religious divides. It was started by Peter Hagerty and Marty Tracy in Maine in 1985 when they bought wool from the Soviet Union in the hope that through trade they could help diffuse the threat of nuclear war. ✹ Since then they have created links with shepherds in Russia, Kyrgyzia, Israel, and Palestine, as well as in Montana, Ohio, Texas, and Maine, seeking to develop a mutual understanding and economic interdependence.

Combining wools from around the world into one yarn symbolizes peace. In response to the Iraq war, Peace Fleece came up with "Baghdad Blue," a vibrant new Peace Fleece color as bright as the desert sky. All profits from the sale of Baghdad Blue are donated to Neve Shalom/Wahat al Salaam, an international community in Israel founded by a Dominican monk, Father Bruno Hussar.

Knitting can itself be a political act. Knitting is about self-sufficiency and designing it yourself, as an alternative to responding to the whims of the fashion industry and buying garments made in developing-world sweatshops. Boys who knit challenge gender stereotypes. So believes Cast Off, a guerrilla knitting group launched in the UK in 2000 by designer Rachael Matthews and artist Amy Plant.

Peace Fleece: www.peacefleece.com
Cast Off: www.castoff.info/shop.asp

In Neve Shalom peace village
Jews, Christians, and Muslims live in peace, each one faithful to his or her own faith and traditions, while respecting others. The village is the setting for a school for peace. The inspiration is the biblical passage: "Nation shall not lift up sword against nation, neither shall they learn war any more."

Peace is an art. It doesn't happen spontaneously; peacemaking has to be learned. You can go to Neve Shalom/Wahat al Salaam as a volunteer. For more information about the village and the peace school, go to www.nswas.com.

...knit and purl for peace

If you've never knitted, now's the time to learn.

✹ Order some Peace Fleece wool and make a sweater.

✹ Or use the yarn to try out some of the wackier ideas on the Cast Off website. They include a dishcloth, shoelaces, a first-aid kit, a blindfold, a deluxe lipstick case, an exfoliating sponge cover, and even a knitted hand grenade that doubles as a purse.

15 FEBRUARY

the One-Straw REVOLUTION

My method of "do-nothing" farming is based on four major principles:

1 No cultivation (that is, no plowing and no hoeing)
2 No fertilizer
3 No weeding
4 No pesticides

I will admit that I have had my share of failures during the forty years that I have been at it. But because I was headed basically in the right direction, I now have yields that are at least equal to or better than those of crops grown scientifically in every respect. And most importantly my method succeeds at only a tiny fraction of the labor and costs of scientific farming, and my goal is to bring this down to zero.

At no point in the process of cultivation or in my crops is there any element that generates pollution, in addition to which my soil remains eternally fertile...and I guarantee that anyone can farm this way.

—Masanobu Fukuoka, author of *The One-Straw Revolution*

Masanobu Fukuoka is a Japanese farmer who devised a revolutionary method of farming. Plowing the land, large-scale monoculture, and chemical fertilizers and pesticides were all discarded. To everybody's surprise, year by year his yields rose, eventually exceeding those obtained using modern farming techniques. ☀ Disciples all over the world continue to experiment with Fukuoka's methods of natural farming. These challenge the whole basis of the world's agricultural policies. ☀ Fukuoka believes they can also be used to transform the arid lands of Africa.

The One-Straw Revolution is available on Amazon. For details contact oibs@bom2.vsnl.net.in.

Other books that have revolutionized thinking:
Gaia by James Lovelock. The earth's biosphere is seen as a self-regulating entity with its own capacity to keep the planet healthy in the long term.

Small Is Beautiful: Economics as if People Mattered by E. F. Schumacher, the inspiration for appropriate technology.

Pedagogy of the Oppressed by Paolo Freire, which influenced a generation on the role of education in the fight for social justice.

Rules for Radicals by Saul Alinsky, which gives practical ideas for effective organizing. His techniques are used by community organizers around the world.

Limits to Medicine: Medical Nemesis, the Expropriation of Health and *De-schooling Society*, both by Ivan Illich, two books that show the need for radical new approaches for the two public services that have the most impact on our lives.

All these books were written a generation ago. But their ideas remain relevant.

...change your thinking

Make a list of your own six books to change the world. Encourage others to read them.

MEETING UP *is fun*

We believe that the world will be a better place when everyone has access to a local Meetup Group. That is our goal.

Meetup.com helps people find others who share their interest or cause. This can be a starting point for creating or joining a lasting and influential local community group. 👊 Meetups are usually informal, held monthly, open to anyone— you can bring along friends if you like—and held in public places such as cafés and parks, although some take place in offices or private houses. 👊 Some meetups are based on activities such as knitting or speaking a foreign language; others focus on a cause—such as planning a women's rights march or getting a political candidate elected; others are self-help groups at which people can swap information and stories.

There are literally thousands of local meetup groups for thousands of interests all over the world. There are meetups for

Spanish speakers	Quit-smoking optimists	Trigger-happy
Philosophy freaks	Poker-playing nuts	photographers
Elvis fans	Quilting sororities	Stiff-upper-lipped expat
Atkins dieters	Marathon trainers	Brits
Red Sox supporters	Pekinese dog walkers	Linux lovers
Alternative-energy bores	Harry Potter aficionados	Bloggers with attitude
Wine lovers	Pregnant women	Environment savers

Over 1 million people all over the world have joined local meetup groups, which have brought communities together, shaken up politics, given people a voice...and provided a lot of fun. *United we meet up!*

Meetup: www.meetup.com

The Meetup Bill of Rights for members

The right to meet: Free, local monthly Meetups should be open to all.

The right to privacy: Your e-mail address will not be shared without permission.

The right not to get annoying ads: No pop-up ads, no spam.

The right to meet about almost anything: Meetup.com is nonpartisan and nondenominational. Everyone should have access to a meetup group about almost anything (except hate and obscenity).

The right to choose where to meet: Meetups can take place anywhere. If it is a place of business, buy a drink to thank your host location!

...a chance to learn, do, change

Meet up. Join a meetup near you that brings a group together around a topic that interests you. If there isn't one, start your own group.

stop eating SHRIMP

Huge quantities of shrimp are produced in developing countries. More than 4 million tons are shipped annually for consumption by the rich world. And this is causing major environmental problems in the poor world.

Shrimp fishing is a major threat to marine life and ecosystems: 75% of shrimp are fished, mostly by boats dragging huge conical trawling nets over estuaries, bays, and continental shelves. ⏣ This method destroys the seabed and scoops up whatever lies in the path of the trawler. About 10 pounds of dead fish, turtles, and other marine species are discarded for every pound of shrimp caught. Shrimping accounts for 33% of the world's discarded catch, while producing less than 2% of our seafood.

Nor is shrimp farming the answer. Shrimp farming destroys fields and rural livelihoods in coastal areas. When fishponds are built, chemicals, fertilizer, and saltwater inevitably leach out into the soil, degrading the land and making it unusable for agriculture. The average shrimp farm provides 15 jobs on the farm and 50 for security around the farm, while displacing up to 50,000 people through loss of traditional fishing and agriculture. ⏣ It destroys natural coastal environments. Nearly 25% of the world's remaining tropical mangrove forests have been destroyed over the past 20 years, most of them to make way for shrimp farms. ⏣ Each pound of farmed shrimp requires 2 to 4 pounds of fish protein, which is mainly derived from captured wild fish.

Find out more from the WorldWatch Institute:
www.worldwatch.org/pubs/goodstuff/shrimp.

Ecuador's shrimp industry has expanded rapidly over the past 30 years. It now takes up some 500,000 acres of former mangrove forests, salt flats, and agricultural land along the coast.

Corrupt government officials and land-hungry illegal shrimp producers collude to rob coastal people of their traditional fishing and food-gathering lands, and traditional mangrove forestry activities such as charcoal making and wood production can no longer be carried out.

Coastal village people wanted to evict illegal shrimp producers and reforest the devastated mangrove areas around Muisne. Supported by Greenpeace and Fundecol, and using only shovels, pieces of wood, and their bare hands, they cut out a breach in an illegal shrimp pond, drained the water, and planted mangrove seedlings to try to restore what had been destroyed.

...and help the environment

Pledge to stop eating shrimp. For every 1,000 people who stop eating shrimp, more than 6 tons of marine life will be saved per year.

Grassroots environmental groups are working with international activists to develop more ecologically sound shrimp farming. In Sri Lanka, for example, the Small Fishers Federation (www.shrimpaction.com/SFFL.html) and the Mangrove Action Project (www.earthisland.org/map/) work with shrimp farmers to curb mangrove destruction and protect fish habitat. Visit their websites and lend your support.

FEBRUARY 18

E-MAIL *Bill Gates*

Bill Gates receives about 4 million e-mails a day. Much of this is spam—unwanted, unsolicited mail sent to him because of his wealth, or because some people believe he exercises too much control on the virtual world, or just because he is Bill Gates III.

All this unwanted e-mail should focus his mind on the fact that spam is a major Internet problem—as well as a time-consuming nuisance. Up to 80% of all e-mail traffic is spam, much of it trying to sell pornography or aids to increase your sexual performance, or some sort of scam that aims to part greedy fools from their money.

As the biggest software company in the world, Microsoft is in a position to take action—to protect all of us from receiving spam and to stop it from being sent. 🐌 Bill Gates has a department that sifts through the mountain of e-mail he gets each day. So he won't actually read what you send him. But if his mail mountain continues to rise, perhaps he will be spurred to action.

E-mail Bill: billg@microsoft.com or askbill@microsoft.com
The unofficial Bill Gates website: www.zpub.com/un/bill
Microsoft Corporation, with the official Bill Gates web pages and contact details
for the company: www.microsoft.com
The Bill and Melinda Gates Foundation: www.gatesfoundation.org

Today's problems are solvable. While the world around us fuels our sense of urgency, it also fuels our optimism. We believe that by increasing equity and opportunity, the world will become a better place for generations to come.... As the years ahead bring more advances in health and learning, we share the global responsibility to ensure that they reach the people who need them most.
—Bill Gates and Melinda French Gates

Bill and Melinda are putting their money where their mouth is.
The Bill and Melinda Gates Foundation has an endowment of $27 billion and funds initiatives in global health, libraries, and schools—and community initiatives in the Pacific Northwest, where Microsoft is located. Bill is not only the richest person on the planet but also the most philanthropic.

...to put a stop to spam

E-mail Bill Gates and tell him that you are fed up with receiving pornographic e-mails, Nigerian fund-transfer scams, and advertisements for cheap Viagra, and tell him that you expect Microsoft to find a workable solution. Ask him to do something about spam; ask him to do it now!

The Microsoft website does have tips for hiding your address from spammers, avoiding phishing and other e-mail scams, blocking junk mail, and reporting spammers to the authorities: www.microsoft.com

nonviolent DIRECT ACTION

Nonviolent direct action can be an effective way of getting things changed. It is often misunderstood and criticized as being too radical, too political, or even illegal. It is certainly radical, often political, and may even challenge the law, but it has a long tradition of success: **†† The Boston Tea Party**, when tea was dumped into the sea, was the starting point for America's independence. **†† Gandhi's Salt Marches** highlighted the injustice of British rule in India and mobilized popular support for the Quit India campaign. And Gandhi successfully built nonviolent direct action into a political philosophy. **††** Peter Hain (subsequently a British cabinet minister) led the **Antiapartheid** campaign to stop South African sportsmen from touring the UK by digging up rugby fields. **†† The Civil Rights Movement** involved sit-ins and boycotts to end segregation. **†† Friends of the Earth** in the UK started by returning nonreturnable bottles to Schweppes's head office. Such stunts are now a common campaigning technique.

The environmental movement has incorporated significant components of direct action in its campaigns to stop nuclear power, to save ancient forests, to achieve a global ban on high-seas drift-net fishing, and to end dumping on the high seas. Ditto the antiwar movement, the Campaign for Nuclear Disarmament, and the efforts to stop the growing of genetically modified crops.

Greenpeace: www.greenpeace.org
Ruckus Society: ruckus.org

The functions of direct action:

Alarm—to get attention to a burning problem or issue

Reinforcement—to get publicity to support your campaign

Planned escalation—to raise the stakes and show you mean business

Morale—to raise spirits and renew energy.

Before you take action, you need to clearly define the issue, who is responsible, and what you want to achieve. You need to design an action that will have impact. You also need to know the law and what your rights are.

...create change

Get skilled in organizing. The *Ruckus Society* is a resource center for organizers. You are asked to make a donation of $100, but nobody is refused for lack of funds. They also have a range of resources for direct action, including an *Action Planning Manual* and a practical guide to *Hanging Yourself from a Billboard* or other outdoor structure—downloadable free from their website.

If you want to campaign for the environment, join Greenpeace. They use direct action effectively. Visit the Greenpeace website, and play games on themes such as GM foods, toxic chemicals, oil discharges, nuclear waste, global warming, and wind farms. These will make you think. And you may then decide to get involved.

FEBRUARY 20

CAN YOU SAY *adios in Ainu?*

Only eight elderly people spoke Ainu on Hokkaido Island, Japan, by the late 1980s. But once it was decided to do something, the language was revived. ✊ Cornish died out in 1777. Using surviving written documents, descendants of Cornish speakers began to learn their former language and speak it to their children. Road signs began appearing in Cornish and English. Now about 2,000 people speak Cornish.

Why is this important? Without words to express them, knowledge and ideas begin to disappear. The loss of any one language means a reduction in the sum total of human thought and knowledge and an impoverishment of the human race. ✊ It is predicted that at least half the world's 6,000 or so languages still in existence will be dead or near death by the year 2050. An *Atlas of Endangered Languages* reports that 50 European languages are in danger, with France having 14 near death. In Siberia, in the Russian Federation, nearly all the 40 or so local languages are disappearing. ✊ Languages are becoming extinct at twice the rate of endangered mammals and four times the rate of endangered birds. While there are huge campaigns to preserve animal and plant species, there is far less concern about preserving the world's languages.

Foundation for Endangered Languages: www.ogmios.org
Ethnologue, an online resource on lesser-known languages: www.ethnologue.com
International Mother Language Day is UNESCO's campaign to highlight the importance of linguistic diversity: www.un.org/depts/dhl/language
Free Online Language Courses: www.word2word.com/coursead.html

First-language speakers in the world today
Source: Ethnologue

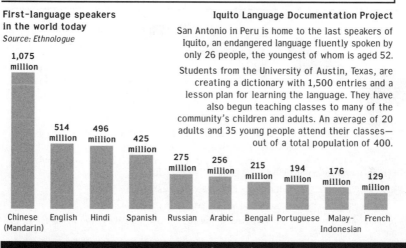

Iquito Language Documentation Project

San Antonio in Peru is home to the last speakers of Iquito, an endangered language fluently spoken by only 26 people, the youngest of whom is aged 52.

Students from the University of Austin, Texas, are creating a dictionary with 1,500 entries and a lesson plan for learning the language. They have also begun teaching classes to many of the community's children and adults. An average of 20 adults and 35 young people attend their classes—out of a total population of 400.

Chart values: Chinese (Mandarin) 1,075 million; English 514 million; Hindi 496 million; Spanish 425 million; Russian 275 million; Arabic 256 million; Bengali 215 million; Portuguese 194 million; Malay-Indonesian 176 million; French 129 million.

...save a vanishing language

Do something to revive an endangered language.

✊ Find out more. Investigate the languages that are indigenous to your own locality or region.

✊ Take a course in or buy a recording of an endangered language.

✊ Go to www.word2word.com/coursead.html for free resources for learning 100 different languages online. Get started with Cornish or Cherokee.

say *NO to* PLASTIC BAGS

Bags that you use for just a few minutes may last for between 15 and 1,000 years. Every time you go shopping at the supermarket and accept a plastic bag at the checkout, you'll be doing something that harms the environment—even if you walk or cycle to get there. Even biodegradable bags take years to degrade.

Plastic bag litter creates huge problems. The bags can trap birds or kill livestock (if eaten). One farmer in Australia found eight plastic bags in the stomach of a dead calf: the loss of this calf cost him around $500. And when a dead animal decays, the plastic bags will be reingested by other animals—a cycle that will continue for many years. ♣ That's not all. Plastic bags can block drains and foul waterways. They can accumulate along the roadside or on beaches. They can be a blot on the landscape as well as an environmental hazard.

Government action can help. In Ireland, where a law was introduced in 2002 that taxed retailers on the nonreusable bags they issued, plastic checkout bag usage was reduced by 90%. That was a saving of nearly 1 billion bags in just one year. ♣ In Australia, retailers were required to reduce their use of plastic bags by 25% during 2004 and by 50% by 2005.

Customers also need to act. Use reusable bags when you go shopping. Recycle any plastic bags you take home with you as liners for your waste paper baskets or as freezer bags.

Did you know...

There are now over 46,000 pieces of plastic waste in every square mile of the world's oceans. Plastic-bag litter kills at least 100,000 birds, whales, seals and turtles every year.

During the manufacture of plastic bags, benzene gas, a known carcinogen, enters the atmosphere.

Plastic can take centuries to decompose. When it is burned, poisonous dioxins and hydrogen cyanide enter the soil and natural water supply.

In Australia at least 80 million bags end up as litter each year.

In China plastic bags blowing around are called "white pollution."

In South Africa there are so many bags in the countryside that they have become known as the "national flower."

...save the environment

Just say No! to plastic bags. Buy cloth bags, jute bags, straw bags, bags made out of recycled bottle tops. Use these instead. Take one with you whenever you go out shopping. And use it again and again and again.

STREETS *for people*

There was a time when streets comfortably accommodated a full range of human activity. In villages, towns, and cities, they were places for trading, socializing, playing, entertaining, meeting, and demonstrating in. They were also routes for travel and the movement of goods. Until the motor age, all this was kept in balance. Today the balance has been lost. Streets have become traffic corridors, cutting swaths through local communities. Traffic management is more important than the quality of local life. Streets are dirty and dangerous. Communities everywhere suffer.

Let's give the streets back to the people. Let them be living streets.
This 10-point manifesto has been adapted from the Pedestrian Association's Living Streets campaign in the UK:

1. **Lots of people out and about.** Living streets need people living on them, walking down them, and overlooking them. There needs to be a mix of housing, shops, offices, restaurants, schools, and places of worship within reasonable walking distance.
2. **A balance between people and traffic.** Streets have become ugly and intimidating for pedestrians. Streets should be designed for people as well as for traffic.
3. **Traffic volume and speed** should not be too high. Traffic kills people. Too much traffic also kills communities.
4. **The street environment.** People are being overwhelmed by clutter on the pavements, squeezed between the buildings and the traffic.
5. **Street upkeep.** Streets need to be properly managed to get rid of litter, dog fouling, dumped cars, petty vandalism, and graffiti.
6. **Safe and well-lit streets.** If people don't feel safe, they won't use the streets.
7. **Facilities to relax.** Living streets have benches and walls where people can pause and pass the time.
8. **A nice place to be.** The street environment needs to be attractive and interesting.
9. **Accessibility.** Access in and out should be made easy.
10. **Information for pedestrians.** Maps and signs for pedestrians should be informative and helpful.

The Living Streets campaign: www.livingstreets.org.uk
Reclaim the Streets campaign: http://rts.gn.apc.org

...put pedestrians first

Do a liveability survey to see how much the street where you live or shop scores on the 10 points. Score each point out of 10, and the total out of 100. Are you satisfied with the result? If not, come up with some ideas for what to do.

23 FEBRUARY

become the EXPERT

When a new issue hits the headlines, experts are in great demand. The broadcast media are desperate to fill their airtime, and print journalists need help in filling their column inches. Policy makers often seek out experts for advice. ♦♦ The world needs information about so many different issues. There must be something on which you have more information than anyone else or in which you are interested or about which you are concerned enough to go out and collect all the information. ♦♦ With work you can become *the expert* on your subject.

Tell people about the importance of what you know. You could, for example

> **Write and publish a report.** This makes you an instant expert. Make sure the report contains accurate facts and is well designed and produced.
>
> **Contact relevant journalists** to tell them about it. Make them believe that you are *the expert*.
>
> **Get publicity for your ideas.** You'll have to work at this. Organize a stunt to get media attention.
>
> **Collect as much information as you can**, and put it on a website. Google-bomb it to make sure that your website comes up first when people are searching on a related keyword.
>
> **Get references and endorsements** from as many prominent and respected people as you can.
>
> **Send out a press release** whenever the issue is topical.

You might then turn from being *the expert* to being *a pundit*, and be asked for your views on a range of topics.

> **Read** *The Know-It-All: One Man's Humble Quest to Become the Smartest Person in the World*, by A. J. Jacobs.

Some ideas to get you thinking:

Steven Millman wrote to every chocolate manufacturer to ask if they used slave labor in any stage of the production of the chocolate they were selling. This made him the expert on the use of slave labor in chocolate.

Documenting change over time enables you to compare what things were like then and what they are like now. You will have real evidence of change. Keep a diary, take photographs, collect published information and press clippings.

...know your facts

♦♦ **Think of a topic that really interests you**—preferably one that nobody else is expert on, and something that is or is likely to become important and newsworthy. Start collecting as much information as you can. Then put up a website and write a definitive article for Wikipedia, the open-source Internet encyclopedia at en.wikipedia.org

♦♦ **Get a group of 100 young people to be "the voice of youth"** on topics as diverse as gender and democracy. If the group is representative, their views will be more authoritative. Get advice from a polling agency on how to construct such a group.

FEBRUARY 24

INFLUENCE *the media*

> *You ask me what I came into the world to do. I came to live out loud.*
> —Emile Zola

The internet has provided us all with an opportunity to make our views known. Political blogging is an effective way of keeping democracy alive using the latest technology. ♀ Use your freedom of expression as an individual to keep government transparent and accountable—locally or nationally. Even if you live under a tyrannical government, the Internet may still provide a space for you to express your views.

"Blog" is short for "web-log"—an Internet diary reflecting the ideas, experiences, and views of the blogger, often linked to other web-based information. ♀ People blog for every reason under the sun. Some just do it to keep a diary, some because they are keen to share their ideas or expertise. And some do it for a political purpose. ♀ Some people just want to share their secrets.

These are some good examples of political blogs:

www.andrewsullivan.com—a British-born gay Republican with great sources and a sharp outlook on American politics.

Baghdad Burning, an award-winning blog from where it's happening:
http://riverbendblog.blogspot.com

www.instapundit.com—a hyperactive blogger who focuses on the intersection between technology and individual liberty.

Most blogs have the following features for easy access:

Photographs and links to text, audio, and video files and to other websites.

One or more columns, with new content put prominently in the largest column. Side columns include links to other blogs, previous posts, or reader comments.

Updates published in reverse chronological order, so regular readers just need to read what's at the top.

Frequent updates, sometimes daily, sometimes several times an hour.

...become a political blogger

Become a blogger. A free basic blogging service that will help you get started is www.blogspot.com. Setting up a blog will take you less than five minutes. Then how much time and energy you put into making it really good and in finding readers is up to you.

♀ **Are there issues in your community that no one is addressing**: traffic, homelessness, gangs, police brutality? Become the voice that brings this issue to the forefront so it can no longer be ignored.

♀ **Provide the latest news**. Praise and criticize government officials. See that they live up to the promises that got them elected. Research the candidates running in the next election. Find out about their campaigning platforms and their stance on important issues.

25 FEBRUARY

give up GROUPTHINK

Do you ever find yourself listening to a group discussion, disagreeing with what is being said, or feeling that an important point is being missed, but afraid to speak up? It is quite likely that others are feeling the same way. This is groupthink.

We will all find ourselves in a groupthink situation sometime. It might be about a tiny issue or something much more important. Whatever it is, speak up; get your point of view heard; influence the discussion *and* the decision. Your view is important and needs to be heard.

Six symptoms of groupthink

1 Believing there are good reasons for what you know are poor decisions, and explaining away facts that do not support the line of thought.
2 Believing what you are doing is morally correct, even when the evidence suggests otherwise.
3 Using shared negative and positive stereotypes to inform the decision.
4 Exercising direct and indirect pressure on members of the group who would like to express contrary views.
5 Self-censorship: failure to speak up means that your views remain hidden.
6 Maintaining an illusion of unanimity, where silence is taken for assent.

And six ways to avoid groupthink

1 Understand how groupthink affects decision making.
2 Find someone neutral to chair the group.
3 Give space for everyone to express his or her views.
4 Always compare the proposed decision with a less popular alternative. Ask someone to play devil's advocate.
5 After reaching what seems to be a consensus, encourage people to express their doubts.
6 Break into several smaller groups to discuss the issue and suggest a course of action. Then try to reach a consensus.

Read *1984* by George Orwell, a frightening parable of Stalinist Russia and a couple's attempt not to conform: www.online-literature.com/orwell/1984

Watch *12 Angry Men,* an Oscar-winning film in which the Henry Fonda character is the only juror to believe that the defendant is not guilty: www.filmsite.org/twelve.html

> Here are some examples of groupthink in recent history:

The treatment of the Jews in Nazi Germany: people must have known what was happening was wrong. The McCarthy crusade against Communism in the 1950s. The Salem witch trials which Arthur Miller used as a parable of McCarthyism in his play *The Crucible.*

...speak up if you disagree

Next time you go to a meeting, don't remain silent. Speak up. Say what you think. Don't be frightened of seeming foolish. Others in the group may also not be happy with how the discussion is going, and welcome your intervention.

If you are chairing a group, encourage everyone to say what he or she thinks, and make sure everyone's point of view is respected. Sharing ideas leads to better decisions—and better decisions are needed for a better world.

FEBRUARY 26

FREECYCLE *for fun*

"Think globally, recycle locally." The Freecycling Network has been set up for those who want to recycle things rather than throw them away. 🏠 Whether it's a chair, a fax machine, a piano, or an old door, your local Freecycling group will provide you with an opportunity to advertise the things you no longer need in the hope that you can find someone who would like them. 🏠 Or if you're looking to acquire something yourself, this is a good place to start.

Freecycling helps keep good stuff out of landfills. It is a virtual response to a global problem. There is just one rule: everything that is advertised must be free. 🏠 There are now over 1,500 cities all over the world with a Freecycling group, with over 525,000 members in total. The largest group is in Portland, Oregon, with over 10,000 members. 🏠 Freecycling can be started in any city, and is open to any individual who wants to participate. Groups are run by a local volunteer, who facilitates the group. The Freecycling Network gives itself a pat on the back by saying, "This is grassroots action at its best!"

Freecycle: freecycle.org

The Freecycling Oath of Honor

Those starting a new Freecycling group take the following oath:

I pledge to be a really nice and patient person when moderating our new Freecycle web page.

I promise to use the Freecycle name only for our noncommercial *Yahoo* group.

I will remain open to the occasional democratic discussion on our web page but will know when to make the tough calls and decisions in order to spare the rest the long debates.

With great honor I shall also keep spam, ads, and money makers out of my group with the "two strikes, you're out" rule.

I'll suggest people give preference to nonprofits when giving stuff away.

And, finally, I shall come clean of my rat pack ways and clean out my own garage before asking the same of others.

...find homes for your discards

Check if there is a local Freecycling group for your city, town, or neighborhood. If there is, join it. Dispose of your old stuff and get new stuff by Freecycling. Enjoy!

If there isn't a local Freecycling group, then start one. The Freecycle website tells you what you need to do to get started. It essentially means moderating a Yahoo group while being a passionate advocate for recycling.

be a good NEIGHBOR

In these days of high-speed communications, you can feel close to someone thousands of miles away. The sense of a global village is being used by NABUUR, a Dutch foundation, to help give urban and rural communities in developing countries (which they call "villages") access to the resources they need to solve their problems: information, expertise, experience gained by projects that work elsewhere, ideas for funding.

This is how NABUUR works:

1 A community is in urgent need of help. After an assessment, the village is given a page on NABUUR.com. A representative of the local community then describes an urgent question or problem that needs to be solved.

2 People who want to help sign up as virtual neighbors of that village. They look for answers to the question, working together with other good neighbors.

3 The best solutions are then put forward to the village. A neighborhood representative discusses these with the community.

4 The community decides what to do, and the solutions are implemented. The good neighbors are able see the results through photos and stories posted on NABUUR.com.

5 A new question may then be put forward, and the process starts all over again.

The neighbors mainly help by searching for information on the Internet, contacting organizations that could be helpful, using their creativity and other skills, and providing specific expertise and advice.

NABUUR is the brainchild of Siegfried Woldhek, who was previously the chief executive of WWF Netherlands.

NABUUR Foundation: www.nabuur.com

Welcome to Chimaltenango, Guatemala: The Kaqchikel Maya who live in Chimaltenango are the direct descendants of the pre-Columbian Maya. The majority are peasant farmers, growing maize, beans, and vegetables. The population has grown rapidly in recent years. This has led to widespread deforestation. To stem the tide, the community wants to develop ecotourism. The area has much to offer: beautiful forests (despite the deforestation), volcanoes, ancient temples, and indigenous arts and crafts. The community needs information on what tourists find interesting, what sorts of activities could be developed, and how to promote Chimaltenango as an ecotourist destination.

...help in someone else's village

Become a good neighbor. Choose from approximately 60 villages in Africa, Asia, and Latin America with problems covering community development, income generation, education, environment, sanitation, agriculture, health, and much more.

Go to NABUUR.com and select a village that interests you. Become a neighbor of that village. Get to work. Post your answers and ideas on the discussion board for that village.

FEBRUARY 28

A DAY OFF *clear your head*

Today is an extra day added to the calendar to keep it aligned with the seasons. Why not mark it by taking the day off, if you can, and doing something out of the ordinary: an extreme sport, an act of generosity—something you've been meaning to do for four years? ♣ If you're usually a very busy person, you could treat it as a day to get yourself back in alignment and just chill out. Do whatever you think you need to do most. Of course this could include thinking up some really great ideas for changing the world.

Here are some suggestions, but don't feel pressured to do any of them!

Soak in a hot tub. Relax. And start thinking about how to change the world.

Ask your friends to come round and celebrate Leap Day with you. Ask them to bring a bottle and one good idea.

Take your local street newspaper seller for a cup of coffee and a chat. Ask him or her to give you one idea for doing something about homelessness.

Surf the Internet. Type in two or three words that best describe the issue you are interested in, and see what appears. Follow up any interesting links that are suggested.

Write a prominent government official (or any other famous person), and ask him or her to give you one good idea for what you and other people can do to make the world a better place.

Check out these idea websites:
Why not?: www.whynot.net
Global Ideas Bank: www.globalideasbank.org
Idea Explore www.ideaexplore.net
Idea-a-Day: www.idea-a-day.com
Creativity Pool: www.creativitypool.com
Premises Premises: www.premisespremises.com
ShouldExist: www.shouldexist.org
Half Bakery: www.halfbakery.com

And these idea blogs:
World Changing:
www.worldchanging.com
Global Ideas Bank blog:
www.globalideasblog.com
The New Café: http://newcafe.org

The Innovation Tools website catalogs the best resources for innovation, creativity, and brainstorming: www.innovationtools.com

...make room for new ideas

Organize an impromptu "ideas party" for changing the world.

♣ **Decide on an issue you really care about.** Identify some of the problems around that issue. For each problem, ask everyone to come up with one practical idea that they—either by themselves or as a small group—could do that would have some impact (however small) on the problem.

♣ **List all the ideas** and then select those that are relatively simple to do and likely to have some impact. At the end of the evening, review all the good ideas, and ask each person to do at least one thing from the list.

♣ **Eat, drink, be merry**—and get your creative juices flowing.

Leap Day **29 FEBRUARY**

keep up with THE NEWS

There's so much information on the web, and so little time to sift through the billions of web pages. Keeping up to date with the news can be extremely time-consuming.

How about getting the latest news and features delivered to your desktop? Now news updates can be sent straight to your computer using a service called RSS. No more hopping from site to site looking for new information updates; RSS sends it to you directly.

RSS stands for Really Simple Syndication. It enables you to choose websites you're interested in and get their news delivered to your computer or BlackBerry. RSS makes it easy for people to access multiple blogs and news websites simultaneously. Instead of surfing 20 web pages, you'll see new content on your favorite sites at the click of a button. To use RSS, simply install an RSS reader and log your favorite websites. Then click the update button, and your RSS reader lists all new items on your preferred websites by headline, brief description, date, and time.

RSS news reader downloads: for Windows: www.newzcrawler.com; for Mac: ranchero.com/
RSS at How Stuff Works, for interesting facts about almost everything: www.howstuffworks.com/rss-feeds.htm

Websites offering Really Simple Syndication:

A growing number of websites offer RSS, including news providers such as Reuters, the BBC, and CNN. As Really Simple Syndication becomes more widely used, more information providers will offer the service.

Here are a few websites already offering RSS:

National Public Radio: www.npr.org/rss/index.html
CNN: www.cnn.com/services/rss/
Reuters: today.reuters.com/rss/newsrss.aspx
Wired: www.wired.com/support/rss _instructions.html

...with Really Simple Syndication

Get started with RSS.

🔦 **Get a news reader.** One may be included in your browser software, or you can download one from the Internet. There are lots of programs available, although free versions have fewer features.

🔦 **Check your favorite website for an RSS link.** If it has one, click on the link and choose the categories of information you want to be updated on. Then follow the instructions on how to hook up, and get news updates from this site to your computer.

MARCH 1

WASTE *stamp it out*

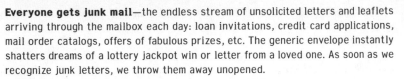

Everyone gets junk mail—the endless stream of unsolicited letters and leaflets arriving through the mailbox each day: loan invitations, credit card applications, mail order catalogs, offers of fabulous prizes, etc. The generic envelope instantly shatters dreams of a lottery jackpot win or letter from a loved one. As soon as we recognize junk letters, we throw them away unopened.

Junk mail is a complete waste of paper, extra weight for the postal worker to carry, and extra rubbish for the sanitation worker to cart away, not to mention personal aggravation for us.

Direct Marketing Association: www.the-dma.org/consumers/offmailinglist.html

Do it yourself—stop junk mail, e-mail, and phone calls—a free guide: www.obviously.com/junkmail

New American Dream: www.newdream.org
Forest Ethics: www.forestethics.org/

How to make junk mail more environmentally friendly

New American Dream and Forest Ethics are calling on five of the USA's biggest catalog companies (all of whom currently use little or no recycled paper) to start greening the 600 million catalogs they produce each year.

Help persuade mail-order companies to make their catalogs more environmentally friendly. Write a letter urging companies sending you mail to reduce the frequency of their mailings, and to start printing on at least 10% recycled content immediately. Ask them to commit to improving this to 50–60% over the next five years. Tell your friends to do the same.

...stop junk mail

If you're fed up with junk mail, you'll be glad to know you can do something about it:

🌳 **Get in touch with the Direct Marketing Association** and tell them you don't want to receive unsolicited mail. Mailing-list organizations servicing the direct marketing industry will delete your name from the addresses sold to marketers. Your name will be removed for five years and you should start to notice a reduction in junk mail after three months. It's much better to stop junk mail at the source rather than recycle, and this organization will show you how to do it.

🌳 **Check the box on any reply form** you fill out stating you do not want information about future special offers.

🌳 **Do not fill in the warranty applications for consumer goods,** as the forms are often used as a way of collecting names and addresses. Your rights are protected under law.

2 MARCH

go on a CARBON DIET

The US is responsible for 25% of the world's energy consumption—most of which is generated by burning fossil fuels. ♣ Each American is directly or indirectly responsible for the release of 22 tons of CO_2 each year. ♣ The world annual total of carbon emissions is 7.2 billion tons, which is four times the 1950 level. ♣ The earth's capacity to absorb CO_2 is fairly constant, and the excess adds to the concentration of greenhouse gases in the atmosphere.

Cut your CO_2 emissions. When it comes to CO_2, most of us in the rich world are overindulging. To prevent the climate from changing even more, we all need to go on a CO_2 diet.

Play the Carbon Game to get some commonsense ideas for saving energy and money and reducing your impact on global warming:
www.pbs.org/wgbh/warming/carbon

The Home Energy Saver will help you identify the best ways of saving energy in your home: hes3.lbl.gov/hes/hes.taf?f=top

60

Some tips for living lite

Buy locally grown fresh produce wherever possible. This cuts down on the air miles used in getting the food to you.

Don't leave the TV and other appliances on standby: 8% of electricity consumed at home is from items you aren't using.

Ensure that your home and your hot water tank are properly insulated.

Use more energy-efficient household appliances. Switch to low-energy bulbs for all or most of your lighting.

Purchase goods from suppliers who have teamed up with a carbon reduction company to offset some or all of the carbon cost of what you are purchasing.

Drive more slowly. If you do 60 mph rather than 80 mph on the highway, you will use 25% less fuel. But better still, cut out some journeys, and travel wherever possible by bicycle or on foot—or Rollerblade, if you really want some fun.

...get a taste for living lite

♣ **Make a 24-hour personal energy log** to see how much you are consuming. Use the form at fp.arizona.edu/khirschboeck/nats101gc/energy_log.htm.

♣ **Plant one tree.** This will consume more than enough CO_2 to offset the CO_2 you are breathing out. It's nice to know that a tree is working to reduce your body's carbon emissions!

♣ **Live lite.** Go on a carbon diet. Change your lifestyle to cut down on your own CO_2 emissions.

MARCH 3

TOXINS *in your TV*

Many electronic products contain toxic chemicals. Small amounts of these chemicals can cause widespread pollution once the product has reached the end of its useful life and is discarded.

What is being done? One solution is to put pressure on the manufacturers to remove toxic chemicals from their products. Samsung, Nokia, Sony, and Philips have all promised to do this as soon as they realistically can.

> **If your cellphone is made by** Motorola, Panasonic, Sharp, Siemens, Sony Ericsson...
>
> **Or if your TV is made by** Akai, Bang & Olufsen, Daewoo, Grundig, JVC, Panasonic, Sharp...
>
> **Or if your computer is an** Acer, Apple, Dell, Fujitsu-Siemens, HP/Compaq, IBM, Panasonic, Toshiba, Tulip...

...your pressure could push these companies to follow the good example of those that have already made a decision to phase out toxic chemicals.

Do the Toxic Tech Test at the Greenpeace website:
www.greenpeaceweb.org/consumingchemicals/ddtest.asp

Form letter you could send to a manufacturer

Dear Sir/Madam,

I have a product from your company *(insert name of company)*. As a customer of your company, I am asking if the computer/electronic equipment *(insert item and model)* I have bought from you contains toxic chemicals.

Toxic chemicals, if used by your company in the production of these products, would cause damage to the environment and to people. I am particularly concerned about brominated flame retardants and phthalates.

More and more companies are choosing to phase out all these toxic chemicals in all their products and production. If your products contain toxic chemicals, are you planning to phase all these chemicals out of your products or not?

If you do *not* plan to phase out all these toxic chemicals, then I will consider buying from a different company next time.

Yours sincerely,

Your Name, your e-mail

...take the Toxic Tech Test

Go to the Greenpeace website:

🌳 **Do the Toxic Tech Test.**

🌳 **Send a letter to a manufacturer** of the electronic product you have just bought. The site provides a form letter, with space for you to fill in your details.

4 MARCH

join the GREAT ESCAPE

Stuck in a job you don't like? Dissatisfied with the work you are doing? Feeling that your values are at odds with those of your employer? Want to fulfill your potential, do something more meaningful, and exploit your talents and creativity?

You are not alone. Many people settle for a job that gives them a certain status and brings in a reasonable income, but this may not be what they really want to be doing. You only have one life, so try to use it to do what you really want to do—something you feel passionate about, where you can make a positive contribution and get real satisfaction.

The Escape Club was set up for people like you, by Alok Singh and Satu Kreula. These two pioneers of change saw many of their friends unhappy at work and wanted to help them find a way of improving their situation. The Escape Club provides people making a career change with what they need: specific tools, courses, connections with people who can help, real-life stories, etc. The club also includes lots of feedback and ideas from members.

The Escape Club: www.escape-club.org

Advice from an Escapee

Never let your perceived limitations hold you back. Take a chance. Accept a risk and go for it.

Get passionate about something and turn it into your work.

Remember to do the groundwork: plan your move and fuel it with passion.

Be flexible enough to pull your ideas apart every so often, look at what works and what doesn't, and take the plan forward from there.

Be humble enough to ask for help and guidance.

—Helena Dennison, June 2004

...change your career

Make your own great escape.

Read the archive of the Escape Club's monthly newsletter, *Escape Stories*. Each issue has real-life stories of people who said, "Okay isn't good enough." and went on to pursue what inspired them in their lives.

You'll read about the changes they made, but you'll also find out what their journeys were like, what obstacles they faced, how they overcame these, and the advice they'd give to others contemplating a career change.

There is a resource section with inspirational books and other resources. And there is information on workshops, courses, and networking events that you can attend to support you on your escape journey.

MARCH 5

CONVERSE *over a coffee*

When people get together over a cup of coffee, they put the world to rights. Chatting informally with others is a great way to generate ideas, solve problems, and get to know others better. But these days it feels like nobody has the time to listen or swap thoughts.

In Rawthmell's Coffee House in London in 1774, a group of friends decided to take time to talk. They wanted to discuss all kinds of problems and to see how, together, they could do something to make the world a better place. They set up an organization now known as the Royal Society of Arts (RSA).

To celebrate its 250th anniversary, the RSA teamed up with Starbucks to organize coffeehouse gatherings so that people could exchange thoughts and come up with great ideas to see the world through its next 250 years.

www.thersa.org/250/chc.asp

The Knights of The Square Table

Right in the center of Bangalore, at Koshy's coffeehouse, a group called the Knights of the Square Table meet every morning from eleven to noon. Prem Koshy explains how it began:

A few of us used to sit at this table, discussing everything under the sun. One of us might mention someone who needed help. This might be to do with drugs, alcohol, food, or another health problem. One of the group could always find an answer. We've helped an 11-year-old boy who was paralyzed, taught hypnosis to a man suffering chronic pain, and helped someone with edinoma (a growth on the lung). Our services are completely gratis. Our policy is no demands, no expectations.

The Knights aren't trying to save the world, but they are trying to help people.

...brew up some great ideas

Set up your own coffeehouse challenge for your city, town, or neighborhood.

 Organize a regular meeting, perhaps once a month. Find a local coffeehouse that will make a great venue and talk to the manager about your plans. Select the subjects for discussion. Invite a speaker to kick off the proceedings and find a moderator to make sure everything runs smoothly.

Publicize the event in the local press, and wait to see who turns up. The rest will depend on the ideas and the energy of the group.

save the RAINFOREST

Originally there were 6 million square miles of tropical rainforest worldwide. Today, as a result of deforestation, just over 2 million square miles remain. The rainforest continues to shrink rapidly: almost two acres disappear every second. This destruction leads to soil erosion, loss of biodiversity, and an increase in carbon dioxide in the atmosphere.

But you can do something to help. You can save acres of the rainforest by visiting one of the many click-to-donate sites. Click and make a donation to the rainforest (and many other good causes) in seconds. You can buy acres of rainforest much more cheaply than you can buy land in the US. For a donation of $45 through World Land Trust you can buy an acre in the Amazon Basin in Ecuador. For a donation of just $280 you can save 1,500 rainforest trees.

To save the rainforest for free, visit www.therainforestsite.com.
Or visit www.worldlandtrust.org to buy acres of rainforest.

Click-to-donate sites

There are many opportunities to donate to good causes, sometimes for free. Look at www.donationjunction.com for joint promotions with commercial companies who donate in return for publicity. Choose the cause you like, see what the money will go toward, and click away. The more sites, the better! The more clicks, the more you give! All these sites are paid for by advertising, sales of gift items, and online donations.

More click-to-donate sites
The Hunger Site: www.thehungersite.com
The Literacy Site: www.theliteracysite.com
Race for the Rainforest: rainforest.care2.com
Race for the Ocean: oceans.care2.com
Race for the Primates: primates.care2.com
The Ecology Fund: ecologyfund.com
Die Wald Seite (for rainforests): www.diewaldseite.de
WildGlobe: www.wildglobe.com

Solve Poverty (education for young people): www.solvepoverty.com
PovertyFighters (microcredit): www.povertyfighters.com
For an up-to-date listing of click-and-donate sites, see www.thenonprofits.com.

...with a click of your mouse

Visit the Rainforest Site daily at www.therainforestsite.com and save an area of rainforest land for free. Just click on the Save Our Rainforests button. Your click triggers a donation from the sponsors of the site. Each click saves 11.4 square feet of rainforest—about as much space as you take up sitting at your computer. So far, visitors' clicks have preserved nearly 29,000 acres in the following areas:

🌳 The Atlantic Rainforest Preserve in Paraguay

🌳 The Calkumal Bio-Reserve in Mexico

🌳 The Reserva Comunal Tanshiyacu Tahuayo in Peru

🌳 Brazil's Atlantic Forest

MARCH 7

WOMEN'S *day*

The history of International Women's Day:

In 1909, after a declaration by the Socialist Party of America, the first US National Woman's Day was held on February 28.

In 1910, the Socialist International meeting in Copenhagen established an International Women's Day to honor the movement for women's rights and to assist in achieving universal suffrage for women. The first International Women's Day was held on March 19, 1911.

In 1913, as part of the peace movement on the eve of World War I, Russian women observed their first International Women's Day on the last Sunday of February 1913.

In 1917, with 2 million Russian soldiers dead in the war, Russian women again chose the last Sunday in February to strike for "bread and peace." Four days later the czar was forced to abdicate and the new provisional government granted women the right to vote. That Sunday fell on February 23 on the Julian calendar then used in Russia, which was March 8 on the Gregorian calendar used elsewhere.

International Women's Day has become a global opportunity to celebrate acts of courage and determination by ordinary women in the advancement of women's rights.

International Women's Day: www.un.org/events/women/iwd

The Nobel Peace Prize has been awarded to 12 women since it was founded in 1901:

1905 **Bertha von Suttner** (Austria), who helped set up the Nobel Peace Prize
1931 **Jane Addams** (USA), pioneering sociologist and leader of the women's peace movement
1946 **Emily Balch**, cofounder of the Women's International League for Peace and Freedom
1976 **Mairead Corrigan and Betty Williams** (Northern Ireland), peace activists
1979 **Mother Teresa** (Calcutta, India), working with the most marginalized
1982 **Alva Myrdal** (Sweden), campaigner for nuclear disarmament
1991 **Aung San Suu Kyi** (Burma), opposition leader and prisoner of conscience
1992 **Rigoberta Menchú** (Guatemala), for protecting the rights of indigenous peoples
1997 **Jody Williams** (USA), for working to ban and clear land mines
2003 **Shirin Ebadi** (Iran), for improving the status of women and children in Iran *(see right)*
2004 **Wangari Maathai** (Kenya), for tree planting

...to celebrate achievements

Find ways to promote the achievements of women in creating social change:

❌ **Spend 15 minutes researching a current woman leader** whose achievements and ideas have impressed you.

❌ **Interview a woman in your community** who is doing admirable things. This could be a person of power or a cleaning lady. What's important is what she is doing to change the world.

❌ **Tell at least five people about this amazing woman** and what she has achieved.

down with TOBACCO

Tobacco is the cause of 1 in 10 adult deaths worldwide (around 5 million people a year), and this is projected to double by 2020 if current smoking trends continue. Half of those who smoke today (around 650 million people) will be killed by tobacco.

Many smokers live in developing countries, where the international tobacco companies are now concentrating their marketing efforts. Smoking and poverty are closely linked, with poor people spending a greater proportion of their income on tobacco—which means that they have less to spend on health, education, and nutrition.

More than 160 countries so far have signed the UN Framework Convention on Tobacco Control and are committed to protecting nonsmokers and banning tobacco advertising. The states of New York, Delaware, and California were the first in the US to ban smoking. In New York, the ban covers bars, certain restaurants, betting parlors, bowling alleys, pool halls, and even company cars. In California, smoking is now banned in prisons.

Bhutan aims to become the first country in the world to become completely tobacco-free. The sale of tobacco products and smoking in public places in this tiny Himalayan kingdom have already been banned in 19 of the country's 20 districts, and the ministry of health provides support for anyone wanting to quit.

Read about the Great American Smokeout:
www.cancer.org/docroot/PED/ped_10_4.asp

Tobacco, the killer facts:

Every year 5,600 billion cigarettes are smoked. That's 875 for every person in the world.

There are 1.1 billion smokers, but only 15% live in rich countries. Despite warnings, 30% of adults still smoke in North America, Europe, and Japan.

There are 4.8 million premature deaths a year from smoking-related illnesses. WorldWatch predicts that smoking will become the world's biggest killer by 2030, causing over 10 million deaths a year.

...it kills

☺ **If you're a smoker, quit.**

☺ **Be a pain in the butt.** Tell everyone you know who smokes, and any smoker whose smoke is curling into your face, how harmful smoking is to them and how unpleasant and dangerous to those around them.

☺ **Download information on smoking and pregnancy.** Hand it out to friends and colleagues who are or intend to become pregnant. You'll be giving a baby a better chance of good health.

☺ **Talk to the manager in bars and restaurants** about providing smoke-free zones, where these aren't yet provided.

MARCH 9

BUILD YOUR OWN *website*

Do you really exist? French philosopher René Descartes declared, *"Cogito ergo sum,"* which is Latin for "I think, therefore I am." He was looking for certainties in life. One thing he was absolutely certain about was that he was thinking. And this led him to another certainty—that in order to think, he must exist.

"I don't have a website, therefore I don't exist." If someone wants to find out more about you, your ideas, your organization, and the cause you are involved with, the first thing they will do is type your name into Google. If the search comes up with nothing, then as far as the searcher is concerned, you just don't exist. In the Internet age, you need a virtual web identity.

Seven steps to setting up a website: www.havingmyownwebsite.net

Virtually Ignorant, an online web design course for beginners: www.virtuallyignorant.com

WebSpawner.com, a free and easy way to create your own webpage: www.webspawner.com

Charity Focus was founded in 1999 by 23-year-old Nipun Mehta and four of his friends from the San Francisco Bay Area. They decided that most nonprofit organizations at that time couldn't afford to create good websites, so they offered to build websites free for charities. Quite soon demand began to grow exponentially. Charity Focus now receives around 40 requests a week. It can't help everybody, so it concentrates on smaller organizations without a current web presence. The service is volunteer-run and completely free, apart from domain and web hosting charges (which have to be paid to third parties).

Charity Focus has developed a pledging system, a charity shop facility for selling things from websites, enlightening banners of inspiring quotations instead of advertisements, and a quote-for-the-day e-mail service.

—charityfocus.org

...tell the world you exist

Design a website

- For yourself, or
- For your community, or
- For the organization or ideas you are putting your energies into.

If you don't know how to do this, you can

- Find a professional website designer, or
- Visit WebSpawner.com and teach yourself, or
- Find a virtual volunteer.

BOOKS ONLINE

Recycle your old books. You can sell new, used, and collectible books, your no-longer-needed college textbook, bargains you have found at tag sales or used book shops, whatever. Here are two online bookselling services you can use.

Abebooks.com: For $25 a month, you can register as a bookseller. The site charges you 8% sales commission and a 5.5% credit card processing fee. You have your own online bookstore. All you need to do is register as a bookseller, enter and upload your inventory of books, and start selling. Already 13,500 booksellers are using this service to sell 80 million books online.

Find out more. Buy the *Insiders Guide to Selling Books on Amazon* at Infoheaven Digital E-Books:

http://infoheaven.bravepages.com/Amazon/sell%20book.htm.

This costs $16.88, but you can apply for a full refund within 90 days.

Public libraries

You don't need to buy new books. Conserve nature's resources instead:

Go to your local library and read or borrow a book.

Borrow books from your friends.

Buy secondhand.

William James Sidis, a child prodigy, mathematician, polymath, and chronicler of 100,000 years of North American history, held the public library to be an American invention, citing the first town library established in Boston in 1698. Find out about public libraries in your area: www.publiclibraries.com.

Abebooks: www.abebooks.com
World Environmental Organization: www.world.org/reuse/Books

...and buy them secondhand

What to do with your old books and magazines

Recycle all the books you no longer need. Get your books into the hands of new readers (this will save trees), and use any cash you raise to support a good cause.

Advice from the World Environmental Organization:

🌳 Donate books to a library.

🌳 Sell study books directly to other students: let *them* save a ton of money.

🌳 Set up a table at your community center where people can drop off old magazines for others to buy. Then donate the money to charity.

ABOLISH *capital punishment*

The death penalty is no more effective a deterrent than life imprisonment. It is also evident that the burden of capital punishment falls upon the poor, the ignorant and the underprivileged members of society.

—US Supreme Court Justice Thurgood Marshall

Governments all over the world are ending capital punishment. Each year since 1976, three more countries have abolished the death penalty. But judicial killing continues to be used in some parts of the world. The US, China, Iran and Saudi Arabia today account for over 80% of recorded executions. ♪ The US has executed over 800 people since 1976, and over 3,700 men and women are held on death row. Despite popular support for the death penalty, it does not stop violence. Other reasons for pressing for its abolition are that it affects poor and black people disproportionately, and that it is irreversible (and evidence can turn up when it is too late, demonstrating the innocence of an executed prisoner).

Befriending a person on death row by writing to them regularly allows an element of humanity to enter an inhumane system. Organizations exist to advise you about what is involved and tell you whether they feel you are suitable as a pen friend. If so, they put you in contact with a prisoner who is under sentence of death. Here is a quote from a death row prisoner with a Human Writes pen friend:

> *As a condemned man I have felt alone and isolated and completely cut off from everybody and the world. Human Writes gave me hope by connecting me to compassionate people....I love watching the world through your eyes.*

Human Writes: www.humanwrites.org
Cyberspace Inmates: www.green.colossus.net/cyberspace-inmates/death.htm
Receive execution alerts from the National Coalition to Abolish the Death Penalty: www.ncadp.org/execution_alerts.html

Ernest Willis was the 117th death row prisoner to be freed in the US since 1973. He had been sentenced to death 17 years previously, for allegedly setting a fire that killed two people. The district judge held that the state had administered medically inappropriate antipsychotic drugs without Willis's consent, had suppressed evidence favorable to Willis, and had provided ineffective legal representation at his trial. The district attorney hired a fire expert to examine the evidence, and his conclusion was that there was not a single item of physical evidence supporting a finding of arson. He concluded Willis "simply did not do the crime....I'm sorry this man was on death row for so long."

...champion human rights

Become a pen friend of a prisoner on death row: Here's how to do it.
Go to www.prisonpenpals.com

12 MARCH

The framework for naming plants and animals is based on the Linnean binomial system devloped 250 years ago, which gives a *genus* name to the larger group, and *species* name to the members within it.

While an ordinary person will use a common name like "tent caterpillar" to identify an insect eating tree leaves, entomologists and botanists will be much more specific. The forest tent caterpillar *(Malacosoma disstria)* eats a variety of trees including quaking aspen *(Populus tremuloides)* and red maple *(Acer rubrum)*. The eastern tent caterpillar *(Malacosoma americanum)* feeds primarily on wild black cherry *(Prunus serotina)*.

New mammal discoveries are rare but occur occasionally. Canadian gaming site GoldenPalace.com paid $650,000 at auction for the right to name a monkey— *Callicebus audeipalatii*—as a publicity stunt.

Insects and plants make up 80% of all living things. And there are possibly 10 million invertebrates and 125,000 plant forms still to be scientifically described.

The George W. Bush Slime-Mold Beetle: Entomologists Quentin Wheeler and Kelly Miller had 65 new species of slime-mold beetle to name. They started with descriptive names, then their wives' names, then names of pop characters such as Darth Vader (who resembles a beetle), and then political heroes. Wheeler is a fan of President George W. Bush, so he named beetles for Bush, Cheney, and Rumsfeld. He got a thank-you call from Bush himself. *"He seemed to understand that the honor was in having a whole new life-form named after you, not necessarily what its eating preferences are."*

The International Commission on Zoological Nomenclature publishes a code: www.iczn.org.
International Association for Plant Taxonomy:
www.botanik.univie.ac.at/iapt/index_layer.php.
Name Your Own Rose: www.name-your-own-rose.com.
The Central Bureau for Astronomical Telegrams has guidelines for naming comets:
http://cfa-www.harvard.edu/icq/cometnames.html.
Information on naming comets: www.ss.astro.umd.edu/IAU/csbn/cnames.shtmlne.

...or a rose or a comet

Name a comet: Are you an avid astronomer with a telescope trained on the skies? If so, you might discover a comet. The first comet to be credited internationally as "belonging" to an astronomer was the comet predicted by Edmund Halley in 1705 to return 1758 (being the same comet that had been seen in 1607 and 1682). Halley's comet is the most famous comet. Your discovery might allow you to go down in history as the next Halley!

Name a Rose: For £100 you can name your own rose. The price includes the naming certificate, registration on the Rose List, post and packing for sending the rose to you, and instructions for planting and care. Name Your Own Rose has a limited number of new cultivars each year for naming. Yours might become the next best-selling variety! Guidance on choosing a name for your rose is given on their website.

MARCH 13

TOXIC TOURS *organize your own*

Our society spews out unbelievable quantities of effluent and waste, all of which has to be disposed of. But mostly this process is kept hidden from us. 🌳 What we see are rows of attractively designed products on the shelf, not the factories manufacturing either the packaging or the contents, nor the solid waste they produce and the chemicals they discharge.

We don't see the mountains of garbage collected from our houses and piled up in landfills. Nor do we see human waste and how that's disposed of. This is the hidden backside of our society. If we knew the mess we were causing, we might choose to live differently and be a lot more environmentally conscious.

Play a toxic waste team-building exercise:
www.wilderdom.com/games/descriptions/ToxicWaste.html

International dumping of toxic waste

In November 1998, the cargo ship *Chang Shun* slipped into Cambodia's southern port of Sihanoukville. The cargo was unloaded and dumped 9 miles away. Soon villagers nearby started to complain of diarrhea, headaches, and vomiting.

Dumping toxic waste is a serious problem for poor countries, who may need the money but do not have the resources for proper waste treatment or public safety. The Basel Convention controlling shipments of toxic waste was adopted in 1989. The Basel Action Network (BAN) campaigns on toxic waste issues, including ship breaking, electronic waste, mercury pollution, and ratification of the Basel ban on exporting hazardous waste from rich to poor countries.

...go on a waste watch

Organize a toxic tour to raise community awareness and to stimulate action on pollutants and those who are generating them.

🌳 **Take members of the public and local decision makers** to see how waste is disposed of in and around your town or city. Visit any or all of the following: a local sewage treatment facility, a landfill site, a waste incinerator (if one is nearby), a municipal recycling center, a hospital (to look at medical waste disposal), a local manufacturer using chemicals to see how they dispose of effluents, and a factory chicken farm or a pig production unit.

🌳 **You will all be intrigued and horrified** at how much we waste and how our waste is disposed of. Discuss the problem, and develop a plan of action to do something about it.

14 MARCH

run a **BANANA REPUBLIC**

General Sani Abacha was the military dictator of Nigeria, Africa's most populous country, from 1993 until his death from a heart attack in 1995. He is estimated to have stolen between $2 and $5 billion of his country's wealth—up to 10% of the country's oil revenues.

Corruption is a fact of life in many countries. Corrupt leaders steal their country's natural resources and extort bribes from companies who wish to do business. Corruption has dire economic and social consequences:

- It traps millions of people in poverty and misery.
- It undermines democracy and the rule of law.
- It distorts national and international trade.
- It jeopardizes sound governance and ethics in the private sector.
- It breeds social, economic, and political crises.
- It threatens domestic and international security.
- It retards social and economic development.
- It threatens the sustainability of natural resources.

Get *Banana Republic* from www.benco-boardgames.com/bananarepublicgame.htm. CORIS, Corruption Online Research and Information System: www.corisweb.org.

Are you ruthless enough to attain absolute power?

You are Jomo Amin, rebel leader of the Southern Swamp. You currently have 40 soldiers and 30 rifles, 8,000 voters, and 10,000 bucks.

Question: A famine is killing many people in the province of the president of the nation. Relief agencies want to provide aid to them by transporting it through your province.

Which of these courses of action will you take?

1. You hijack the supply trucks and distribute the food among your own voters.

2. You declare a cease-fire to allow the supplies to reach the people who need them.

3. You refuse to allow the supplies to move through your territory in the hope that this will weaken the president.

...try acting like a dictator

Do you have what it takes to be a dictator?

Find out. Play *Banana Republic*. You will need 2 to 5 other people to play this game with you. Your goal is to become president of your country. Then you have to remain president for long enough to collect enough medals to become president for life.

If you understand the issues, you will be better equipped to fight corruption.

PLANT *another tree*

> *When we plant trees, we plant the seeds of peace and seeds of hope. We also secure the future for our children. One of the first things I did yesterday when I got the extraordinary news about [my Nobel] prize was to plant a Nandi flame tree. It was at the foot of Mt. Kenya, which has been a source of inspiration to me and to generations before me.*
>
> *So, on this wonderful occasion, I call on all Kenyans and those around the world to celebrate by planting a tree wherever you are.*
>
> —Wangari Maathai

Professor Wangari Maathai won the 2004 Nobel Peace Prize for her efforts in planting trees in Kenya through the Green Belt Movement, which she founded.

Experts say that a forest cover of at least 10% is required for a country to sustain life naturally—which will enhance the availability of rain, replenish underground water, improve soil fertility, provide clean air, prevent soil erosion, and beautify the environment. Kenya's forest cover is presently less than 2%.

Wangari Maathai started the Green Belt Movement in 1977, working with local women's groups to plant trees on farms. Each group had a nursery to raise seedlings. Some of the seedlings were planted on their farms, but most were given free-of-charge to nearby communities. Once the trees had been planted, group members would then ensure that the farmers were taking proper care of the trees. The Green Belt Movement paid the women one Kenyan shilling (which is not a lot— around two cents) for each exotic tree they distributed and two shillings for each indigenous tree or fruit tree. Twenty million trees were planted in the first twenty years and have survived.

Since 1997, the Green Belt Movement has focused on planting indigenous trees on public lands in forest catchment areas and in riparian lands (along rivers) to preserve local biological diversity.

Green Belt Movement: www.greenbeltmovement.org.
The Man Who Planted Trees is available from: www.chelseagreen.com.

Do you know...

Riparian areas are the green areas on each side of a stream or a river supporting vegetation. They are very important. They purify water by removing sediments and contaminants; they reduce the risk of flooding and erosion; they increase the available water and stream flow duration by holding water in stream banks and aquifers; they provide a habitat for a diversity of plant and wildlife and for a healthy fish population; they provide water, food, and shade for wildlife; and they provide recreational space for fishing, camping, picnicking, and other leisure activities.

...or 25 million trees

- ⚽ Be inspired by Wangari Matthai's achievement. Also read the classic *The Man Who Planted Trees* by Jean Giono.
- ⚽ Get together with friends and neighbors in your community and plan a campaign to plant 1,000 trees. That will be a start.

16 MARCH

check out the IDEAS BANK

The Global Ideas Bank contains a mixture of weird and wonderful ideas for changing the world. Some have been tested in practice, some are works in progress, others are just good ideas. You can vote on the ideas and add your own comments.

Here are some of the ideas:

Mayor on a park bench. The mayor turns up each week to discuss the city and its problems with local residents.

A web page for every prescription drug, for information and patient discussions. The best advice comes from users rather than experts.

A pig in every neighborhood. People in inner cities have virtually no exposure to animals other than domestic pets. This cuts them off from nature.

Free wireless Internet access. Canada is currently installing wireless access throughout its library network. This idea is a must!

Print statistics on toilet paper. This will grab people's attention, and inform them about an interesting problem they did not know about.

The Global Ideas Bank: www.globalideasbank.org

An idea submitted to the Global Ideas Bank by Dr. G. Caldwell

Committees, decision-making groups, and governments may think they know what they are talking about, but they hide it in fancy language. I suggest that at every meeting of any decision-making group (at 10 Downing Street, the White House, the local pub darts team, etc.), there be a cardboard cutout of an 11-year-old. My boy is called Jack.

Then as the meeting continues, everyone has to check that Jack understands what they are talking about, and if he is getting bored and fidgety. If Jack can understand and is interested, then the meeting is going well, and it is likely that more sensible decisions will be made.

...and contribute a great idea

Send in your ideas to the Global Ideas Bank. There's a prize for the best idea of the year.

Read *The Problem Solving Pocketbook: An introduction to Creativity Techniques for the Budding Social Inventor*, from the Global Ideas Bank, £3.50.

Visit the Enterprise Insight website, which has a manual for turning your ideas into action. The site is aimed at business enterprises but is equally applicable to social enterprises. You can find it on the web at www.starttalkingideas.org.

MARCH 17

WINDUP RADIOS *a lifeline*

How can you listen to the radio if you have no source of power? As well as bringing people pleasure, the radio is a vital source of information and education, but one that is unavailable to the millions of people who have no electricity and cannot easily afford batteries. 🌐 British inventor Trevor Baylis struggled with this problem and came up with the clockwork radio. He proposed that the radios be used for spreading the word about safe sex, as a way of combating the spread of AIDS in Africa.

Clockwork technology can be used for other electronic gadgets, as Chris Staines and Rory Stear realized when they set up the Freeplay Energy Group. As well as radios, the Freeplay product range now includes flashlights, mobile phone chargers, and standby power units.

The Freeplay Foundation was created by Freeplay Energy in 1998, to ensure that the technology reached those who needed it most. Over 300,000 Freeplay radios have been brought into communities in more than 40 developing countries. This has benefited over 6 million people directly (and many more indirectly) by enabling them to listen to radio for pleasure and information.

The foundation created the Lifeline radio in 2003, based on feedback from children orphaned by AIDS and conflict in Kenya, Rwanda, and South Africa. The rugged, self-powered Lifeline radio is the first created specifically for humanitarian projects, especially for children living on their own.

Radio can help children learn. The Zambia Education Project donates radios to community schools, enabling children not having formal schooling to receive primary-level education. 🌐 Radios also bring hours of listening pleasure.

Freeplay Energy Group: www.freeplayenergy.com
Freeplay Foundation: www.freeplayfoundation.org

In Malawi, the ministry of agriculture distributed 9,100 Freeplay radios to farmers' clubs in remote areas throughout the country. Each of the clubs, or listening groups, elected a chairperson who was responsible for the use and care of the radio and for notifying club members of the broadcasts.

In Madagascar, a radio drama series for women's listening clubs has been developed, aimed at improving health education, family planning, and AIDS prevention. Windup radios, funded by the Rotary Club, have been distributed to clubs, who provide regular feedback on the programs.

...around the world

Give the gift of a radio

A gift of just one radio can make a positive difference to a family, a classroom, or a whole community for years to come. Through the Freeplay Foundation, just $55 is enough to bring a radio to a family or a community. Save up the money, and donate it. It'll make a wonderful gift.

18 MARCH

global SISTERHOOD

If you want to know how women's lives are changing around the world, visit the Global Sisterhood Network. This organization monitors electronic and print media for developments likely to have a direct impact on women's lives. These include developments in agriculture, economics, employment, environment, health, law, militarism, politics, technology, trade, and science.

The Global Sisterhood Network (GSN): www.global-sisterhood-network.org

Subscribe to the Global Sisterhood Network List for daily online feminist comment and information: http://groups.yahoo.com/group/GSN

 How does the Global Sisterhood Network describe itself?

GSN provides regularly updated information including critical comment and displays of newspaper and journal articles that reinforce patriarchy/misogyny, but have attracted sparse attention and/or comment as the world moves closer to undemocracy.

—The Global Sisterhood Network

...for a feminist perspective

⊗ **Visit the GSN website** and click on Links and GSN Network to find a list of women's groups worldwide who are doing their share toward making a better world:

Afghan Women's Mission, supporting Afghan women refugee projects: afghanwomensmission.org

Friends of the River Narmada, supporting Narmada Bachao Andolan, India, which is protesting the construction of a big dam: www.narmada.org

Gramya, female infanticide prevention in Andhra Pradesh: home.vicnet.net.au/~gramya

Research Foundation for Science, Technology and Ecology, Vandana Shiva's acclaimed group: vshiva.net

Revolutionary Association of the Women of Afghanistan, Afghan women for human rights and social justice: www.rawa.org

⊗ **Link to the following groups** associated with the Global Sisterhood Network:

Committee on Women, Population, and Environment, Hampshire College, Massachusetts: www.cwpe.org

Feminism on Line, feminist links: home.wanadoo.nl/~vidabo/FeminismOn-Line.html

Feminist Peace Network, ending violence toward women and children: www.feministpeacenetwork.org

International Women's Tribune Center, connecting women globally for social change: www.iwtc.org

Organization of Women's Freedom in Iraq: www.equalityiniraq.com/english.htm

Saidit Online: feminist news, culture, and politics: saidit.org

WINGS, women's voices on radio worldwide: www.wings.org

Women in Black, women against injustice, violence, and war: wib.matriz.net

Women's International League for Peace and Freedom, which is the oldest women's peace organization in the world: www.wilpf.int.ch

MARCH 19

EARTH DAY *needs your pledge*

The one thing we all have in common is our planet. So let's pledge our lives and fortunes to aid the great task of the earth's rejuvenation, and each do our part as a trustee of the earth to take charge and take care of the planet.

—John McConnell, founder of Earth Day

Earth Day is an annual event dedicated to celebrating the wonder of life on the planet and making a pledge to ensure a sustainable future for all its inhabitants. It is held each year at the spring equinox, which falls on March 20 or 21. Earth Day is celebrated around the globe by people of all backgrounds, faiths, and nationalities.

The Earth Day Network was founded by the organizers of Earth Day to promote environmental citizenship and year-round worldwide action. Earth Day Network links up action campaigns in the US and across the world. 🌳 At the network website you can find ideas for action on animals and plants; clean air and water; food and agriculture; forests and wilderness; global warming and clean energy; nuclear and toxic waste; oceans; planes, trains, and automobiles; politics and people; recycling and solid waste; urban growth; and more. If you're stuck for ideas on how to save the world, this would be a good place to start!

Earth Day Network: www.earthday.net
Earth Day site: www.earthsite.org

I Will Not
A poem by a student of class 5 of Karachi High School for Earth Day 1991

Today on Earth Day we are celebrating by making promises, but I will not:
    I will not stop throwing paper on the ground.
    I will not stop using plastic bags
    I will not go to clean the beaches
    I will not stop polluting
I will not do all these things because I am not polluting the world
    It is the grown-ups who are dropping bombs
    It is the grown-ups who have to stop
One bomb destroys more than all the paper & plastic that I can throw in all my life
    It is the grown-ups who should get together and talk to each other
    They should solve problems and stop fighting and stop wars
    They are making acid rain and a hole in the ozone layer
I will not listen to the grown-ups!

...promise to help the planet

Sign the pledge at the Earth Day website:

I will act as a Trustee of the Earth by
    Promoting actions to preserve peace and planet
    Conserving nature and its resources
    Encouraging environmental stewardship, and
    Asking others to do the same.

learn the art of NONVIOLENCE

Many computer games involve zapping the enemy and other terminator tactics. Ivan Marovic, a founder of the Serbian student resistance group Otpor!, has developed a game—called *A Force More Powerful*—which teaches the tactics of nonviolence rather than shoot-to-kill.

You will learn how to defeat real-world adversaries without using laser guns and AK-47s, but by nonmilitary, nonviolent tactics, including leafletting, protests, strikes, boycotts, mass action, civil disobedience, and noncooperation. The game features scenarios inspired by recent history—conflicts against dictators, occupiers, colonizers, corrupt regimes; and struggles to secure political and human rights of ethnic and racial minorities and women—to demonstrate the effectiveness of the "weapons" of nonviolence.

A Force More Powerful **is a game of strategy** that focuses on abstract ideas and planning, rather than depending on reflexes, coordination, and quick thinking. Players learn strategic planning, formulation of goals (such as ensuring free elections or the resignation of a dictator), as well as the appropriate tactics to use to achieve success.

A Force More Powerful, a game of nonviolent strategy:
www.aforcemorepowerful.org/game/index.htm
Otpor!, the Serbian resistance movement:
www.unesco.org/courier/2001_03/uk/droits.htm
International Center on Nonviolent Conflict, advocating and promoting
nonviolence to achieve social and political goals: www.nonviolent-conflict.org

Otpor! (Resistance!) was a pro-democracy Serbian youth movement that started at Belgrade University in October 1998 as a response to repressive university and media laws that were introduced that year. Following the NATO airstrikes against Yugoslavia during the Kosovo war, Otpor! started a political campaign against the Yugoslav president, which resulted in almost 2,000 Otpor! activists being arrested. During the presidential campaign in September 2000, Otpor! launched its "He's finished" campaign, which galvanized discontent and resulted in Milošević's defeat.

...play the computer game

Learn how to change the world using nonviolent means.

Play *A Force More Powerful.*

The game has been produced in partnership with the International Center on Nonviolent Conflict. It costs $19.95, and 10 or more copies are $9.95 each.

Individuals working overseas to promote freedom and secure human rights who cannot afford the full sales price should e-mail Miriam Zimmerman at mzimmerman@yorkzim.com with information about their work and resources, and a request for a discount.

MARCH 21

HARVEST *the rain*

Rainwater comes direct to you whenever it rains. If your house sits on a tenth of a acre plot and a storm dumps 0.75 inches of rain, you've just received 1,750 gallons of water on your house and garden. This water is largely clean and chemical-free. ♣ Most people don't utilize this rainwater, they just let it drain away. But in countries where rain comes seasonally or where there is simply not enough of it, communities will set up elaborate water-catching systems to collect rainwater and stop it from running off into the sea.

This is called rainwater harvesting. It can include storing and utilizing the water that falls on roofs; building dams, ponds, and other systems for containing the water; and using the rainfall to recharge the groundwater. Harvesting rainwater and using water sensibly are crucial in a world running short of water.

Two good sites dedicated to rainwater harvesting are Harvest H2O: www.harvesth2o.com and the Rainwater Harvesting Network: www.rainwaterharvesting.org.

A how-to guide, complete with simple drawings and a photo gallery of rainwater harvesting projects: www.dot.co.pima.az.us/flood/wh/index.html

Think of others on World Day for Water

Anytime we need water in the rich world, we just turn on a tap. You probably give little thought to the amount of water you use, or to how all this clean and drinkable water is brought to your home. But for billions of people around the world, getting enough clean water to meet their daily needs is a major struggle. Women and children may have to walk hours every day to get to their local water source—which might be a lake or a pond. They may have to make several trips just to meet their family's daily water needs, and this water is not always clean.

...catch that water

♣ **Design a rainwater-catching system** to harvest all the water that falls onto the roof of your house. Spend as little as possible. What materials will you need? What will it look like? How much will it cost? If you had to purchase a domestic rainwater-harvesting system, it would cost around $4,000.

♣ **Build your rainwater-catching system.** Use the rainwater to water your garden and your pot plants and to wash your dog and your car. You would need to filter it, if it is to be drinkable.

♣ **Produce a simple design manual** and circulate it to your friends. Your ideas might even help solve the water crisis around the world!

face up to GLOBAL WARMING

Climate change poses a bigger threat to the world than terrorism.
—David King, UK government chief scientific adviser

Since the beginning of time, the earth has been warmed by sunlight, which penetrates the insulating atmosphere of carbon dioxide, water vapor, ozone, methane, and nitrous oxide. This atmosphere traps heat on the earth, creating the greenhouse effect and keeping the climate stable enough to sustain life. Without it, the earth would be too cold for living creatures.

Since the Industrial Revolution, the burning of fossil fuels has increased greenhouse gas emissions. These gases trap more and more heat, which would otherwise escape into space. As a result, the planet's temperature is rising. Unless something is done, the world will become too hot for life as we know it.

Log your energy use at http://fp.arizona.edu/khirshboeck/nats101gc/energy_log.htm

Two scenarios for 2050

The best scenario: New Year's Eve 2049 is being celebrated around the world with great gusto. It's the biggest party since the start of the millennium. The year 2050 was the deadline set by the United Nations for the global economy to switch away from burning fossil fuels. And to the surprise of everyone, especially the cynics, the target has been met—but only just in time.

The real breakthrough was the 2025 International Climate Treaty, negotiated after the final breakdown of the Kyoto agreement. Under this treaty, the populations of countries declared uninhabitable by the UN were offered residence in Europe and North America because of their role in causing global warming—reversing decades of harsh immigration policies designed to keep environmental refugees out of rich countries.

The worst scenario: With a global temperature now 5°F higher than at the turn of the century, the world is now a very different place. Millions have already fled from the low-lying Pacific atolls of Tuvalu, Kiribati, and the Marshall Islands because of a close to 3 foot rise in sea levels.

In Europe, the Alps finally lost their snow and ice. Only the biggest glaciers remain, and the ski industry collapsed 20 years ago. The Himalayas have also lost about a third of their remaining ice cap, and last year the Ganges ran dry for the first time. Panic swept through India and Bangladesh, and in the biggest migration in human history, nearly 300 million people are currently moving toward Europe.

—Adapted loosely from www.outtherenews.org May 2001

...and do your bit

🌳 **Make a 24-hour personal energy log** to see how much you are consuming.

🌳 **Plant one tree.** It will consume more than enough CO_2 to offset the CO_2 you are exhaling.

🌳 **Live light.** Go on a carbon diet. Change your lifestyle to cut down on your emissions.

CIVIL LIBERTY *is precious*

We hold these Truths to be self-evident,
That all Men are created equal,
That they are endowed by their Creator with certain unalienable Rights,
That among these are Life, Liberty and the Pursuit of Happiness.

This is the central credo of the Declaration of Independence.

The ACLU—the American Civil Liberties Union—was founded in 1920 to fight to preserve the liberties enshrined in the US Constitution, especially

⊗ The First Amendment rights: freedom of speech, association, and assembly, and the freedom of the press and freedom of religion supported by the strict separation of church and state.

⊗ The right to equal protection under the law and equal treatment regardless of race, sex, religion, or national origin.

⊗ The right to due process—being given fair treatment by the government whenever the loss of liberty or property is at stake.

⊗ The right to privacy—which means freedom from unwarranted intrusion into personal and private affairs.

In the face of the internment of 110,000 Japanese Americans during World War II, the spying, blackmail, and harassment of Americans by the FBI during the McCarthy era, the civil rights movement, the so-called War on Terror and homeland security today, the ACLU has been fighting to defend the basic rights and freedoms of every US citizen.

American Civil Liberties Union: www.aclu.org

Shami Chakrabarti is the director of Liberty, the UK equivalent of the ACLU. At the end of 2005, she was selected as one of the ten most influential people in the UK by a leading radio program. Shami is often seen on TV, promoting the cause of civil liberty. This is what the rock group the Dastards has to say:

"Shami Chakrabarti," by the Dastards

I turn on my TV.
The only one I want to see Is Shami Chakrabarti.
Speaking with such bravery. ...
She's a fighter for liberty, for kindness and decency.
She champions dignity. Defending humanity.
I'm not getting paranoid. But human rights have been destroyed...

Download the song from www.dastards.com/mp3_down.html

...defend it to the death

⊗ See and sign the Declaration of Independence. Put your signature alongside those of the founding fathers: www.archives.gov/national-archives-experience/charters/declaration.html

⊗ Join the ACLU. Become a card-carrying member. Government power needs to be checked, liberties upheld, privacy ensured. Play your part in seeing that all this happens. Join the more than 400,000 members and supporters of the ACLU. Make a commitment to civil liberty. The cost: $20. The value: it's the future of civil liberty that's at stake.

24 MARCH

become a ZOO CHECKER

An adult lion's roar can be heard up to five miles away. One of the few places you can still hear the sound is at your local zoo. There are approximately 1,500 zoos around the world, providing an invaluable opportunity for people (and especially children) to experience the diversity of animal life on our planet. But if you think the lions and tigers and bears living in zoos are happy campers, you are wrong.

Some zoo animals are kept in appalling conditions. It's a tragedy when creatures are treated badly, and animal abuse may also be occurring in circuses, magic shows, dolphin shows, and other tourist attractions where performing animals are used. Many establishments do not provide their animals with adequate living conditions. A lion's roar of distress may not bother some zookeepers, but if you care enough, you should try to do something.

Sign up to be a zoo checker: www.bornfree.com/zoocheck/zoo20.htm

Did you know?

An albatross can sleep while it flies. It apparently dozes while cruising at 25 miles per hour.

Clams can change sex. All start out as males, but some decide to become females later in life.

Elephants have a gestation period of over 20 months.

Mockingbirds can imitate any sound from a squeaking door to a cat meowing.

Sharks are apparently the only animals that never get sick. Current research suggests they are immune to every known disease, including cancer.

The kiwi can't fly, lives in a hole in the ground, is almost blind, and lays only one egg each year. Yet it has survived for 70 million years.

The poison-arrow frog has enough poison to kill about 2,200 people.

You can see all these animals and many more in a zoo.

...blow the whistle on animal abuse

The Born Free organization has set up the Zoo Check and Travelers' Alert systems for reporting maltreatment of animals.

🌳 **If you see animals being badly treated** or kept in appalling conditions at your local zoo or at a tourist attraction (at home or abroad), take photographs or make video evidence of the conditions in which the animals are being kept.

🌳 **Send your evidence to Zoo Checker,** and a campaign will be started to improve the treatment of these animals.

MARCH 25

DESIGNER *ambitions*

Architecture for Humanity is a nonprofit organization founded by Cameron Sinclair, a London-trained architect. It promotes architectural and design solutions to global, social, and humanitarian problems and brings design services to communities in need.

Architecture for Humanity runs design competitions, open to everyone. These competitions don't focus on designing the next Trump hotel. The aim is to obtain designs of low-cost structures for international communities in crisis. ✹ Entrants are provided with a list of materials and costs local to the area where the winning project will be built. They are then asked to formulate a design, taking into consideration factors such as how to get water, what resources are available locally, whether there is electricity, and the budget. If your design is selected, they build it.

Architecture for Humanity: www.architectureforhumanity.org

Some Architecture for Humanity projects:

2004: A competition to design a soccer field in Somkhele, an area in South Africa with one of the highest rates of HIV in the world. The field had to offer a place for young people to play soccer, and to host the first-ever girls' soccer league in the area. It also had to offer a place to learn about HIV/AIDS and a mobile health-care facility. The design by second-placed finalists David Mathias and Tim Denis is shown here.

2004 and ongoing: Rebuilding Bam in Iran. Architecture for Humanity is collaborating with Relief International to provide permanent housing for the many thousands of residents left homeless by an earthquake that killed over 41,000 people.

2002: A design competition for mobile health clinics to provide basic health care, health education, and AIDS/HIV testing in sub-Saharan Africa.

Architecture for Humanity is also working on land mine clearance, playgrounds in the Balkans, and refugee housing on the borders of Afghanistan.

...architecture for humanity

✹ **See if there is an Architecture for Humanity group near you.** There are 132 groups in cities around the world, some with memberships of over 300 (and some with just one member looking to find some architectural soul mates). Meetings are held on the first Tuesday of each month at 7 p.m. to discuss design and development issues. Everyone is welcome. If there *is* a local group that meets near you, why not go along?

✹ **Check out the latest competition.** Your design could be featured in a top architectural magazine and exhibited in international design shows, not to mention help to solve a humanitarian crisis and save thousands of lives.

✹ **Go to the People We Like section** of the Architecture for Humanity website. It offers information on interesting people and organizations promoting socially responsible design.

protest through SONG

Songs are enormously important for peace or protest. They create a sense of unity and purpose. They bring people together. They make you feel good. Here are some songs for peace and for protest:

Songs of peace
  Bob Marley & The Wailers "War" (from the album *Rastaman Vibration*, 1976)
  Faithless "Mass Destruction" (from the album *No Roots*, 2004)
  Boogie Down Productions "Stop the Violence" (from the album *By All Means Necessary*, 1988)
  Curtis Mayfield "We've Got to Have Peace" (from the album *Roots*, 1972)
  Spearhead "Piece O'Peace" (from the album *Home*, 1994)
  Basement Jaxx (featuring Yellowman) "Love Is the Answer" (from the album *Peace Songs*, 2004)

Songs of protest
  Public Enemy "Fight the Power" (from the album *Fear of a Black Planet*, 1994)
  Levellers "Liberty Song" (from the album *Levelling The Land*, 1992)
  Johnny Cash 'I Shall Not Be Moved' (from the album *My Mother's Hymn Book*, 2004)
  Chumbawumba "Enough is Enough" (from the album *Anarchy*, 1998)
  The Pogues "Streets of Sorrow/Birmingham Six" (from the album *If I Should Fall from Grace with God*, 1987)
  Jimmy Cliff "Viet Nam" (from the album *Wonderful World, Beautiful People*, 1970)

Antiwar songs: www.lacarte.org/anti-war/index.html
Peace songs: www.newsongsforpeace.org and www.songs4peace.com

Producers of songs for peace and protest

The Smithsonian Institution publishes a wide range of folk songs, some of which are classics of peace and protest, including Pete Seeger's *Songs of Protest and Struggle*, Woody Guthrie's *Struggle, Good Morning Vietnam* and *Poems for Peace*. www.folkways.si.edu

Amaze Me: Songs in the Key of Peace is a peace CD featuring female musicians from across the US who care about their country and want to see it become a leader for peace. All of the album proceeds are being donated to organizations working for peace, such as Women against Military Madness, DemocracyNow, and CodePINK. For more information, go to www.rubberneckrecords.com/bio.

...call for a better world

Be inspired.
  ♥ Download the above songs onto your iPod, listen, and be inspired.
  ♥ And if you'd like to, write your own song or poem for peace and post it on the 365 Ways to Change the World website: www.365act.com.

MARCH 27

HUMAN MANURE *what to do*

We take the disposal of human waste for granted. We just flush the toilet and watch it disappear. Most human waste is disposed of through the sewerage system. But there are a number of problems with this. ♣ Raw sewage starts to break down, using oxygen dissolved in the water. But once the oxygen is used up, microorganisms continue the process anaerobically (without oxygen). This produces a nutrient-rich effluent (which could be used as fertilizer) and methane gas (which could be used as a fuel). But the untreated effluent is often left to run into rivers and ends up in the sea. The nutrients cause algae to bloom, and when they die, they decompose, which uses up dissolved oxygen in the water. The reduction of oxygen in the water kills marine animals.

To ensure sustainability, everything taken from the land needs to be put back. If this doesn't happen, the natural fertilizers contained in the soil diminish and have to be replaced with chemical fertilizer. These chemicals run off into rivers and lakes and pollute the water table. ♣ Clean water is piped to us, often over hundreds of miles, and around 40% of it is flushed straight down the toilet. There has to be a better way. Composting toilets are the answer.

Composting Toilet World, which describes itself as "the official website of composting toilets": www.compostingtoilet.org

Composting toilets

Composting toilets use little or no water; they are not connected to an expensive sewage system; they cause no environmental damage; and they produce compost as a by-product, which you can use in your garden—or sell.

There are two ways of composting. The batch system uses a container, which is filled, then replaced with an empty container. The composting process is completed inside the filled container. In a continual process system, the waste moves downward and is harvested as compost after about six months.

If your carpentry skills aren't good enough, then think about buying a composting toilet. There are lots of models to choose from. Go to the Composting Toilet World website for advice and information.

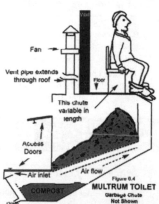

Figure 6.4
MULTRUM TOILET
Garbage Chute
Not Shown

...with all that poo

♣ *The Humanure Handbook.* This is a guide to composting human manure. The authors claim that "after reading this book, you will never flush a toilet with indifference again." Buy *The Humanure Handbook* at www.amazon.com.

♣ **Build your own composting toilet** using wood and sawdust. A simple design will cost you only $30 to build. Get the plans from www.jenkinspublishing.com/sawdustoilet.html

You are six... You are not allowed to go to school because you are a girl. You are nine. You are forced to go to work instead of school. You are fourteen. You have never been to school at all.

You are seven... and you are not safe. You are one of millions of children who live and work on the streets of the world's cities. You ran away from home to escape violence. Now, on top of your daily struggle to survive, you have to contend with insults, beatings, and sexual abuse, both on the streets and when you are frequently arrested and imprisoned.

You are eight... and you work ten hours a day at a brick kiln. You are one of an estimated 250 million child laborers working worldwide. Because you are forced to work, you cannot go to school. Without an education, you'll be trapped in a life of poverty. You'll lose your childhood and your future.

You are a child... You are one of an estimated 300,000 boys and girls under the age of 18 fighting in armed conflicts around the world. In 2000, the UN adopted an Optional Protocol to the Convention on the Rights of the Child that prohibits forcibly recruiting children under 18 or allowing them to participate in armed conflicts. But child soldiers are still serving in more than 30 countries.

Earth Action: www.earthaction.org

Of course, your life is not nearly as bad as this. You've never had to live on the street, you've never been a child laborer, you've not fought as a child soldier, you *did* go to school. But there is something you can do for those children who are being denied their rights.

The UN Convention on the Rights of the Child (CRC) commits all governments to prevent all these abuses of children's rights. But most of them aren't delivering. We need real public pressure from as many people as possible to say that this situation must be dealt with.

...postcards for a fairer world

Join Earth Action.

Then several times a year you'll receive a Planet Postcard by e-mail or regular mail about one critical issue about the environment, social justice, peace, or human rights. Each postcard will give you everything you need to send a strong, clear message to a government or corporate leader requesting that they take action. You can order more postcards from the Earth Action website if you want to send lots.

Earth Action is a worldwide movement for social justice. Join, and you'll be joining with thousands of people around the world who are speaking up. And send lots of postcards.

HITCHHIKE *to Morocco*

Imagine a classroom, but take away the books, desks, chairs, and windows. Remove the roof as well for good measure. Next put an undertrained teacher in charge of too many children—some of whom have walked 3 miles to school or had no proper breakfast or both. ◤ These are the conditions in which many children in the world today are trying to get an education. It is not their fault that they were born in a country without the resources for a decent educational system.

Without education, it is hard for any community to escape from poverty. But things can be done. ◤ Link Community Development is based in South Africa and also works in Ghana and Uganda. It supports head teachers in implementing development plans for their schools. It trains teachers, helps schools raise money for improvements, and provides educational electives for teachers to share their expertise with an African school.

Link has helped improve education for over 500,000 children. Only 700 organizations like Link would be able to improve education for all Africa's children.

Link Community Development: www.lcd.org.uk
Morocco Hitch: www.icd.org.uk/events/hitch
Camfed, extending girls' access to education in Africa: www.camfed.org
Information on girls' education: www.educategirls.org

Dance classes in Morocco

While working as a Peace Corps volunteer in Morocco, I noticed that instead of going to school, young girls were required to stay at home to take care of the household chores while their mothers wove carpets to sell at the weekly market. I wanted to give young girls an opportunity to be themselves, express their creativity, and most importantly have fun! I started a series of dance classes. Wrapped in headscarves and long skirts, we twisted, turned, and let loose. This increased the girls' self-esteem and gave them something to look forward to.

—Kari Detwiler, New York

...give children a chance

Hitchhike to Morocco

◤ **Travel in a group of two or three people,** and get to Morocco however you can.

◤ **When you get to Morocco,** you might even visit a school or two.

become a SOCCER FAN

In the UK, Street League uses the power of sports to transform people's lives—people from underprivileged, poorly educated, socially excluded, and conflicting communities. Players include the homeless, people participating in drug and alcohol rehabilitation projects, refugees and asylum seekers, long-term unemployed, and others. 🏠 Founder Damian Hatton says, "As well as the structure given to their lives through practice and match timetables, players might be motivated to make positive changes in their lifestyles through a desire to improve their sporting performance." Anyone can participate, regardless of their ability. There are weekly training sessions with qualified coaches, monthly match days, and a cup competition.

Street League was founded in 2001 by Dr Hatton (while doing a stint on an infectious disease ward in a London hospital). The idea grew. There are now more than 850 players in Street League teams across the UK, in cities as far apart as London and Glasgow. A year ago there were just 260 players. 🏠 Graz 2003, Gothenburg 2004, New York 2005: The Homeless World Cup brings together teams from national Street Leagues and homeless soccer projects in 26 countries. It is organized though the International Network of Street Newspapers. The World Cup provides a shared international goal, and also great publicity for the homeless football movement.

Homeless World Cup: www.streetsoccer.org
Street League: www.streetleague.co.uk

These organizations promote antiracism soccer tournaments:
www.mondialiantirazzisti.org
www.progettoultra.it
www.farenet.org

And these promote soccer among young people in developing countries:
globall.streetfootballworld.org
www.playsoccer-nonprofit.org

Jose's story

Drug dependency lost 42-year-old Jose everything—his job, his family, his home. After seven years of sleeping rough and watching friends die from AIDS or go to prison, he started rehab. Now he's got an apartment, attends college, and is reconnected with his children. The credit "goes to God—and to soccer." Jose was a member of the US team that competed in the first Homeless World Cup in 2003. He didn't actually get to Austria, as he had to complete his rehab. But the months of exercise and practice helped him clean out his body and open his mind.

...the action's on the street

Become a soccer fan.

Adopt a side in a local street league and turn up to see them play. This will provide real encouragement.

MARCH 31

APRIL *fool*

"April 1…the day upon which we are reminded of what we are on the other three hundred and sixty-four."

—Mark Twain

Today is April 1, All Fools Day, otherwise known as April Fool's Day. It is a day to play practical jokes on your friends and colleagues. Tradition has it that the practical joke should be performed before noon. To work, an April Fool's joke needs to seem credible and perhaps appeal to the vanity or snobbery of the person being fooled.

April Fool 1957: The respected and normally rather stuffy BBC TV news show *Panorama* carried a feature on the spaghetti harvest in Europe. The mild winter had led to a bumper crop. The program showed Swiss family farmers harvesting strands of spaghetti from the trees, rather than the vast spaghetti plantations of the Italian Po valley. Huge numbers called up to find out more about spaghetti growing and where to buy spaghetti trees.

April Fool 1977: The British newspaper *The Guardian* published a special 7-page supplement to mark the tenth anniversary of the independence of San Serriffe, a former British colony in the Indian Ocean. The geography and culture of this obscure nation was described using puns on typographical terms, such as *serif* for the country, *upper and lower case* for its two main islands, Upper Caisse and Lower Caisse. Its capital was Bodoni, and its leader General Pica. It seemed an idyllic holiday spot. Several days later, button badges began to appear saying, "I've been to San Serriffe."

About April Fool's Day: http://en.wikipedia.org/wiki/April_Fool's_Day
Top April Fool hoaxes of all time: www.museumofhoaxes.com/hoax/aprilfool/
View the spaghetti harvest: http://news.bbc.co.uk/onthisday, then go to April 1.
Find out more about San Serriffe: http://en.wikipedia.org/wiki/San_Serriffe

Testosterone is the world's most dangerous chemical. It fuels aggression, and this can lead to war. There is too much aggression in the world. We should be making love not war. You can't love others without loving yourself first. So here's what to do: masturbate for peace. Masturbate for Peace says that it is an international movement for peace, with over 17,000 petitions from 91 countries and all 50 states of the US. You can sign their petition and in your own words say why making love (even if it's with yourself) is better than making war. Join this movement. Focus your thoughts and energy toward love and peace. Encourage others to do the same. And think about these slogans: "Fighting for peace is like raping for virginity" and "War is expensive; peace is priceless."

…love yourself

Become a prankster.

Devise a great April Fool's joke that will highlight an issue such as creationism versus evolution or that will take a pompous politician down a peg, and which will fool the media. Now organize it.

guerrilla GARDENING

Armed with trowels, seeds, and vision, you can garden everywhere. Anywhere.

—Guerilla Gardeners

Our cities are a sad concrete mess. More parking lots than parks. More traffic signs than trees. While you're looking at the cityscape, ask yourself: does it have to be like this? Guerrilla Gardeners are people who anonymously plant herbs, flowers, and vegetables on vacant land, in cracks in the pavements and by the sides of roads and footpaths.

Planting-as-protest began in the 1970s with a New York group called the Green Guerrillas. These urban horticulturalists lobbed seed grenades (Christmas tree ornaments filled with soil and wildflower seeds) into hundreds of abandoned, debris-filled building sites, which eventually became hundreds of beautiful flower and vegetable-filled community gardens. Their slogan was "Resistance Is Fertile."

Why not become a guerrilla gardener? Start to sow the seeds of change. Start to reclaim the urban environment for nature. All you need is

    Some seeds and a small bag of soil

    A trowel and a watering can

    Used packaging—recycled of course

    Some friends (doing it with others is always more fun)

    As much creativity as you can muster.

Primal Seeds, a network protecting biodiversity: www.primalseeds.org
Guerrilla gardening and reclaiming public space: www.publicspace.ca

Plant for Peace, Toronto Peace Gardeners Mission Statement, May 2003

The most revolutionary action is to plant in a spirit of peace. Join us as we reclaim Ecology Park beside the subway as a place for community and peace. Community includes all the birds, the sky, trees, people, little animals, stones, plants, and insects. Peace means a place to sit, smile, breathe, and enjoy all the treasures of the present moment. Guerrilla Gardening is a revolutionary idea—the way to peace.

...sow the seeds of revolution

🏠 **Walk around and look for good places to start planting.** Derelict front gardens, buildings awaiting redevelopment, car parks, traffic circles and medians, beneath trees—these are just a few places where you might find a crack in the concrete where you can start planting.

🏠 **You can plant seeds and cuttings in spring and summer,** and bulbs in the autumn. You can plant flowers, vegetables, shrubs, trees. If you're planting seeds, sprout them at home and allow them to grow for four to eight weeks before transplanting them at your chosen site.

🏠 **Protect your new plants for the first few days;** cut the tops and bottoms off plastic water bottles and put these over the plants.

🏠 **Design a wonderful garden.** Label the plants. Take photos as they grow.

LOCKS *of love*

Alopecia aresta has no known cause or cure, and many children suffer from it. Locks of Love provides hairpieces to children in North America aged 18 or younger who are suffering any form of medical hair loss and who are in financial need. Other recipients are cancer patients undergoing chemotherapy. Wigs restore self-esteem and helps children have better relationships with their peers.

Wigs made from human hair are not always an option for cancer patients. There are two main reasons. The wigs are made to order, and this can take two months, but most people don't know two months beforehand that they are going to have chemotherapy. They want their wig a bit sooner. Human hair wigs are expensive; if your hair is going to grow again, it may seem a bit of a luxury.

Anyone can donate their hair to Locks of Love from anywhere, provided these conditions are met:

10-inch (25-cm) minimum hair length (tip to tip). Pull curly hair straight to measure its length.

Hair supplied bundled as a ponytail or braid. Layered hair may be divided into multiple ponytails for donation.

Hair clean, dry, placed in a plastic bag, and then in a padded envelope.

Hair can be from men as well as women, young and old, all colors.

Hair may be colored or permed but must not be bleached or chemically damaged (if unsure, ask your stylist).

Hair swept off the floor is not usable.

Hair cut years ago is usable if it has been kept in a ponytail or braid.

Hair that is short, gray, or unsuitable for children will be separated out and sold at market value, which will offset the cost of manufacturing.

Most hair donated to Locks of Love comes from children wishing to help other children.

Locks of Love: www.locksoflove.org

What happens to your donated hair:
1. Ponytails and braids are sorted by length and sent to the wig manufacturer.
2. Short, unusable hair is removed by a hackle machine, to leave only full-length hair.
3. Each hairpiece requires up to 10 ponytails because the shorter hair can't be used. Different colors of hair are blended and sent with a foam head block to the factory in Indonesia.
4. A surgical silicone skullcap, colored to match the child's skin tone, is made from the head block.
5. Some 150,000 pieces of hair are individually injected by hand into the skullcap using a special needle. The hair is sealed into the base with a layer of silicone. Two inches of hair is lost during this process, which takes about eight weeks.

...donate your hair

Grow your hair to more than 10 inches.

Then get it cut off. Send it to Locks of Love.

emulate GANDHI

Apply the following test: recall the face of the poorest and the weakest man [or woman] whom you may have seen, and ask yourself if the step you contemplate is going to be of any use to him. Will he gain anything by it? Will it restore him to a control over his own life and destiny?

—Mahatma Gandhi

Your reading this book means that you are a very fortunate person. Seriously. You have the resources to buy it. You can take the time to read it, even if you are just flipping through it. You are literate, so you can understand what the words mean. And you can see with your eyes, helped perhaps by contact lenses or glasses. All this makes you one of the world's more fortunate people.

Every single day you probably walk past people down on their luck. Your natural instinct, most likely, is to ignore the people who are sitting in the street begging for a few pennies. For you, this is a moment of discomfort that you shrug off when you get round the next corner.

There are many reasons why people are living rough. But it is always hard and often lonely. A small act could transform their whole day—an act of kindness, a smile, a little conversation, a coin or two from your pocket that you can well afford. For you this could be insignificant; for them it could mean everything.

Find out about Gandhi, his life and his ideas from the
Mahatma Gandhi Foundation: web.mahatma.org.in
Gandhian Institute: www.mkgandhi.org
Kamat's Mahatma Gandhi album: www.kamat.com/mmgandhi/iink.htm

Who was Mahatma Gandhi?

Mahatma means "Great Soul," a title given to Gandhi as a mark of respect. Mohandas Gandhi was born in 1869 in western India. He went to London to study law and qualified as a barrister in 1891. He then went to South Africa, where he was appalled by the conditions and lack of human rights of immigrant Indians, and he set out to change their lives, developing the idea of nonviolent resistance as a protest tool.

He remained committed throughout his life to religious tolerance and to improving the lives of the very poorest.

...do something today

Practice the Gandhi principle. Gandhi believed that no day was worth living unless by the end of the day you could say that you had done something to improve the plight of someone less fortunate than you.

Today, when you are out doing whatever you do, stop when you pass someone begging. Take them out for a pizza. Ask them how their day is going. Listen to their dreams for the future. Share ideas about the state of the world.

SPEED DATING *for change*

Use social occasions with your friends not just to gossip about who is dating whom or how much so-and-so is earning. Not just to discuss the problems of the world and moan about politicians, but to focus on a particular problem that you are interested in and to discuss solutions and practical ideas for actually doing something.

Adapt the speed dating dynamic to discuss ideas for changing the world:
> **Fill a room with people** who are eager to change the world.
>
> **Get people into pairs** with five minutes to share their ideas.
>
> **Each fills in a score out of ten,** based on how interesting the other person's idea is, whether they think it feasible and whether they would like to join with that person in taking the idea forward.
>
> **A whistle is blown after five minutes,** and everyone moves to another pairing.
>
> **The process continues** until the end of the evening.

Or have a dinner party discussion. Ask seven people to dinner. Every guest is invited to think of a practical idea to change the world that they could do with a group of people. Over dinner or after eating, each person is invited to talk about their idea for 2–3 minutes, followed by discussion. At the end of the evening, the best idea is chosen—by consensus if possible—and everyone is then invited to work on it.

Speed dating for crickets

To determine whether male crickets were attractive or unattractive, Australian researcher Megan Head organized "dating tournaments" where pairs of male and female crickets were timed to see how long it took them to have sex. Males that got the females interested quickly were labeled "attractive." Megan then looked at what happened afterward.

Females who mated with attractive males died earlier and had slightly fewer children. But they had a greater number of attractive sons and their grandchildren were born much sooner. This means that their genes are more likely to be passed down into future generations.

Megan's work has implications for the long-term consequences of human mating choice. It's the quality of the offspring that's important, not just the quantity.

...a transforming event

Revive your love life and make new friends.

- **Organize a** Change the World dinner party or Speed Dating to Save the World party.
- **Do this by candlelight** for a romantic atmosphere and to save electricity. Then see what happens!

5 APRIL

Genocide occurs, and we say "Never again." But we always seem to allow it to recur. So, with Rwanda, Kosovo, and Darfur fresh in our minds, with communal violence between Hindus and Muslims on the rise in India, it's a good time to act. The Rwandan genocide started on April 7, 1994. One million people were massacred in 100 days. We must do our best to stop anything like this from ever happening again.

The first step in preventing genocide is awareness. Educate yourself about what is happening on the planet. Often major media sources do not cover the atrocities that are happening. Know where injustice is occurring. Mary Kayitesi Blewitt, originally from Rwanda, founded SURF (the Survivors Fund) after losing 50 family members herself during the Rwandan genocide. SURF helps survivors deal with and recover from the tragedies of 1994. ❧ Remember Rwanda preserves the memory of the Rwandan genocide by remembering its victims and those who tried to aid its victims, and through public education on the Rwandan and other genocides.

The Elie Wiesel Foundation for Humanity creates forums for the discussion and resolution of urgent ethical issues. It is particularly concerned with hate, intolerance, injustice, and indifference. It organizes an annual essay contest for undergraduates in US colleges. Read what they have to say.

www.preventgenocide.org
SURF: www.survivors-fund.org.uk
Elie Wiesel Foundation: www.eliewieselfoundation.org

Assumpta's story

I was 18 at the time of genocide. I lost my mother, father, brothers and sisters, and 30 other relatives, and suffered rape and beatings. My surviving sister went back to my home village after the genocide and was attacked again with machete by the killers of my family, who feared that she would denounce them to authorities. She was in a coma for months and slowly gained consciousness. She lost her hearing ability and she lives with constant headache and mental problems. I have tried to commit suicide twice but failed to die. I live in the shadow of genocide. Sometimes I imagine meeting my mother on the street. Sometimes I see people wearing similar clothes like my dead relatives, and I follow them and tap on their shoulders...

...stop genocide

Learn about the tragedies of Rwanda.

❧ **Download** the personal testaments of Rwandan genocide survivors, adults and children, being collected by the Memory and Remembrance Project of the Survivors Fund (SURF) at www.survivors-fund.org.uk/remember/index.htm.

❧ **Print out** and frame the photos at the Remember Rwanda website collected as a 10th anniversary memorial:
www.visiontv.ca/RememberRwanda/main_pf.htm.

❧ **Create** your own mini-exhibition to remember Rwanda.

POLIO *let's make it history*

:)

Polio is one of a very few diseases that can be totally eradicated: the disease only affects humans, an effective and inexpensive vaccine exists, and immunity is lifelong. Polio will die out through mass immunization. ☺ In 1988, the Global Polio Eradication Initiative was launched, spearheaded by the World Health Organization, Rotary International (who have provided volunteers and fund-raised all over the world), Centers for Disease Control and Prevention (CDC), and UNICEF. The effort has so far galvanized more than 200 countries, 20 million volunteers, and an international investment of $3 billion. The number of polio cases worldwide has decreased from 350,000 in 1988 to fewer than 800 in 2003.

An estimated 5 million people are able to walk thanks to this initiative. These people would otherwise have been paralyzed. The campaign has also helped strengthen health delivery in many countries. Hundreds of thousands of health workers have been trained, and millions of volunteers have been mobilized to support immunization campaigns.

Polio is endemic in only six countries: Afghanistan, Egypt, Niger, Nigeria, India, and Pakistan. And they have all publicly pledged an all-out effort to end the disease. The ultimate success of the world's largest public health campaign is now within reach. ☺ If the world seizes the chance to end polio, no child will ever again experience the crippling effects of this devastating disease. And drug companies could play a stronger role in helping combat malaria and the spread of HIV, and in extending the lives of those living with AIDS.

World Health Organization: www.polioeradication.org
Rotary International: www.rotary.org/foundation/polioplus/

Sanofi-Pasteur, the vaccines business of the Sanofi-Aventis Group, which is the world's third-largest pharmaceutical company, had donated 120 million doses of their polio vaccine to the polio eradication program by 2005.

Chiron Vaccines provided more than 20 million doses of polio vaccine between 1997 and 1998. In 2002, it made a second donation of 9.5 million doses.

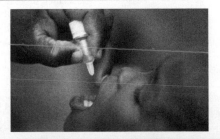

...through global eradication

Write to the chairs of Sanofi-Aventis and the Chiron Corporation. Congratulate them on the support they have given to the global initiative, and request that they continue this support until polio is eradicated. Ask that they also make a similar commitment to address other important health issues in the developing world.

Jean-François Dehecq, Président-Directeur Général, Sanofi-Aventis, 174 Avenue de France, 75013 Paris, France. www.sanofi-aventis.com

Howard Pien, President, Chief Executive Officer, and Chairman of the Board, Chiron Corporation, 4560 Horton Street, Emeryville, CA 94608-2916. www.chiron.com

consider TITHING

Tithing means giving away 10% of your annual income to charity. The idea of giving a proportion of your income to charity, and the idea of this specific amount—10%—comes from the Old Testament. But many religions encourage tithing.

There are lots of good reasons for giving to charity:
   If you have more than enough money, you can help others who don't.
   If you have more than enough things, buying more is a waste.
   Using your money creatively to help others or to change the world can be a lot of fun.

You might not be willing to give 10% just now, in which case give a smaller proportion of your income. And increase your level of giving as your income rises and as you start to enjoy what you are achieving with your money. And you don't have to be limited to 10%. You can give more!

If you feel already overcommitted financially, you might consider donating your time or talents to a charitable cause instead.

To calculate how much a tithe is per annum, per month, per week, or per day, put in the figure for your annual income and use the tithe calculator at www.nacba.net/tithe.htm.

If you want to give your money away, there are a number of decisions to make.

How much of your income to give away. Decide whether this is to be a certain proportion of your income, or a fixed annual sum, or some other amount.

Whether to plan your giving, by setting aside a monthly or annual sum into a separate bank account.

How to give tax-effectively, so that you benefit from the tax reliefs that are available.

...give 10% to charity

Start giving a portion of your income or of your time to charity.

♦♦ **Calculate** how much money you actually need to live at the standard you want. Then donate everything in excess of this.

♦♦ **Tithe your time** instead of your money. Cash may be tight, so you may be able to give your time instead. Ten percent of your work time equals four hours a week. Donate that by volunteering.

♦♦ **Tithe your talent** instead of your money. Do you have a skill or an expertise or a talent which you can donate?

♦♦ **Donate a valuable item** that you don't really want or no longer need. Whatever the item, it will have value. Donate this as your contribution. Or sell it on eBay and donate the proceeds.

♦♦ **Get a part-time job** specifically to donate your earnings from it. You could babysit, work as a bartender, or mow someone's lawn through the summer.

APRIL 8

WHISTLE *blowing*

Speaking out takes courage. If you witness wrongdoing at work or elsewhere, you must choose whether to remain silent or to bear witness and speak out. It is easier after the event to say that "we should have spoken out." But at the time, it can be a difficult personal decision.

But whistle-blowing should be approached wisely. Is the wrongdoing substantial enough to warrant the risks of reprisal and the investment of time and resources to expose it? If you do decide to pursue the matter, then you should do so in a planned way, making a commitment to see it through, and not be put off by bureaucracy and stonewalling.

How to blow the whistle:

Before taking any irreversible steps, talk to your family and close friends.

Find out if there are other witnesses and if they are upset about the wrongdoing.

Consider first if you are able to make an effective complaint within the system.

If you do decide to blow the whistle, decide whether you want to "go public" or do it anonymously.

Develop a plan of action, so you are in control of the process.

Keep a careful record of events as they unfold.

Identify and copy all necessary supporting documents before anyone has suspicions about you.

Get the support of potential allies, such as elected officials, journalists, activists, and whistle-blower networks.

Do it on your own time and with your own resources, not your employer's.

Invest funds to get a legal opinion from a competent lawyer.

Tell the truth; never exaggerate your charges. You may find yourself and your own life investigated. Make sure you have nothing to hide.

Government Accountability Project: www.whistleblower.org
National Whistleblower Center: www.whistleblowers.org

Blowing the whistle on tobacco

Jeffrey Wigand was vice president for research and development at Brown & Williamson, a Big Tobacco company. In 1995 he blew the whistle on the tobacco industry, which had been minimizing the addiction and health issues of cigarette smoking, despite having evidence of the dangers. A huge settlement was awarded to victims of smoking, and this led to a complete change in the way tobacco was marketed. Dr. Wigand has now set up Smoke-Free Kids to educate children on the harmful impact of tobacco.

Jeffrey Wigand inspired the Hollywood film *The Insider*: www.jeffreywigand.com
Make an evening of it. Also watch *Erin Brockovich*, starring Oscar-winning Julia Roberts as a whistle-blower on toxic waste: www.erinbrockovich.com

...and expose wrongdoing

Speak out!

If you see wrongdoing, have the courage and commitment to speak out.
Blow the whistle.

9 APRIL

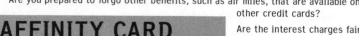

ethical **FINANCE**

Choose where to put your savings and whom to borrow from. Your choice can have an impact not just on the banks, but also on the companies they choose to invest and not to invest in. Financial companies such as banks rely on your money to keep them in profit. Many people bank with a regular commercial bank, such as Citibank (the world's largest) or HSBC (which advertises itself as "the world's local bank").

An alternative is to use a bank that is a co-operative. This means the bank doesn't have to pay out dividends to its shareholders and so has more commitment to invest locally and uphold socially responsible values.

Websites for socially responsible investors:
Social Investment Forum: www.uksif.org
Ethical Investment Research and Information Service (with free online magazine): www.eiris.org

Affinity cards

Your credit card provides another opportunity to do good with your money. There are hundreds of different credit cards available. Some are issued by a financial institution in partnership with a charity, which gets an upfront fee for every new customer plus a small percentage of the amount spent on the card. These are known as affinity cards.

If you are interested in an affinity card, think about four things:
Are you prepared to forgo other benefits, such as air miles, that are available on other credit cards?

AFFINITY CARD

Ethical Bank

Are the interest charges fair?

Does the card give enough to the charity? Some give more than others.

Do you believe enough in the cause to want to support it through an affinity card?

if the answers are yes, this is a painless way of supporting a charity.

...invest to make it work

Swap your credit card for an affinity card, and bank with an ethical bank.

If you have stocks and shares (or a pension fund), think about investing ethically—putting your money in companies that do not degrade the planet or exploit their workers or make dangerous products.

There is a good deal of advice available on ethical investing. There are specialist unit trusts for the ethical investor.

NEEM *the village pharmacy*

The neem tree is known as the "village pharmacy" in India because of its many healing properties. It is the source of a large number of natural medicines. It helps protect crops against insect pests and people against disease-carrying mosquitoes. Its twigs are used as a toothbrush and toothpaste all in one.

The neem tree was largely unknown to the rest of the world until 1959, when a German scientist witnessed a locust swarm in Sudan. After the swarm had passed by, the only tree left untouched by the locusts was a neem tree. On closer investigation it was concluded that the locusts did indeed land on neem trees, but they always left without feeding.

There has been worldwide scientific interest in neem since this discovery, and intense research into its many properties. We now know that the neem tree contains many natural active ingredients that make it resistant not only to locusts but also to more than 300 different types of insects, as well as to fungi, bacteria, and even viruses. These chemical defenses are not only useful in protecting neem trees but can also be used as the basis for natural medicines.

The Neem Foundation promotes the growing and use of neem:
www.neemfoundation.org

Properties of the neem tree

Healing and soothing
Leaves from the neem tree can be used to ease a variety of skin conditions, complaints, and wounds. In India, neem leaf poultices and infusions and neem oil are widely used in the treatment of skin and nail complaints.

Insect repellent
Neem is also a powerful insect repellent. The oil was extensively tested in Scotland on the Highland midge by a team of leading experts. Neem seed extract, the highly concentrated extract from neem seeds, is an extremely powerful way of eliminating insects, particularly head lice.

Economic fuel
Neem has a huge potential for solving global agricultural, public health, population, and environmental pollution problems. The demand for neem products, especially the seed as the basic raw material, is set to increase by leaps and bounds, and with it income generation and job opportunities.

...a tree for global problems

Go neem! Buy neem soap, neem shampoo, neem mosquito and insect repellent, and neem treatment for head lice.

Big drug companies have become interested in identifying the active ingredients of neem and patenting them. But the neem tree is part of India's indigenous knowledge base. For biopiracy issues around the attempts to patent neem, go to www.american.edu/TED/neemtree.htm

visit the world's HERITAGE

Heritage is our legacy from the past, and what we pass on to future generations. Our cultural and natural heritage are both irreplaceable sources of life and inspiration. Places as unique and diverse as the wilds of East Africa's Serengeti, the Pyramids of Egypt, the Great Barrier Reef in Australia, and the baroque cathedrals of Latin America make up our world's heritage.

What makes the concept of world heritage exceptional is its universal application. World heritage sites belong to all the peoples of the world, irrespective of the territory on which they are located.

The naming of world heritage sites encourages the preservation of cultural and natural heritage around the world. This concept is embodied in an international treaty called the Convention Concerning the Protection of the World Cultural and Natural Heritage, adopted by UNESCO in 1972.

The UNESCO World Heritage Center: whc.unesco.org

World Heritage Sites in the US

Mesa Verde
Yellowstone National Park
Everglades National Park
Grand Canyon National Park
Independence Hall, Philadelphia
Kluane/ Glacier Bay, Alaska
Redwood National Park
Mammoth Cave National Park
Olympic National Park
Cahokia Mounds
Great Smoky Mountains
La Fortaleza and San Juan Historic Site
Statue of Liberty
Yosemite National Park
Chaco Culture Historical Park
Hawaii Volcanoes National Park
Monticello and the University of Virginia
Pueblo de Taos
Carlsbad Caverns National Park
Waterton Glacier Peace Park

...contribute to conservation

Plan a visit to a world heritage site.

- **Prepare a picnic.** No preprepared foods; no packaging; no plastic bags; no cans, no plastic water bottles. Just good friends, real food, proper plates and cutlery. Make sure that everything but the food is reusable. Have a great day out.

- **Visit every world heritage site** in your region of the country.

- **Go on a conservation holiday** with Earthwatch to help save world heritage sites. No experience is necessary—only a thirst for adventure and a passion to make a real contribution to heritage conservation.

APRIL 12

MUSLIMS *in the West*

Islamophobia is currently a problem throughout the world. Since 9/11 and the start of the "War on Terror," there has been a growth in Islamophobia (hatred of Muslims) in North America and Europe. This has increased following the bomb blasts in London (on July 7, 2005).

Young Muslims now feel vulnerable. They feel that people are thinking, "If you look like a Muslim, you must be a terrorist." They feel they might be picked up in a dawn raid, or be imprisoned indefinitely for nothing, without having any right to a hearing. They feel that the society they live in doesn't want them any more—that it wants them to hide their faith and become less visible. ✖ In France, the government passed a law that banned people from wearing religious symbols in state schools. So schoolgirls can't wear a *Hijab* even if they feel strongly that they should as a matter of modesty.

Muslims from all over the world have come to our country and been offered citizenship. Their children have been born and educated here and English is their mother tongue. ✖ We will be better able to understand the terrorist threat and what to do about it if we better understand how young Muslims see the world.

muslimyouth.net: www.muslimyouth.net

Comments from young Muslims in the West:

 How hard can it be to live as Muslim in the West?

To accept that with every tick of the clock, things change. Fashion changes and just as long as none of it clashes with the Islamic rulings on clothing, then we can change with it. Because sometimes we have to.

Personally speaking, I like to mix and match. I love wearing Indian sequined tops with flare-bottom trousers. I like to get the best of both worlds.

It is clear that the events of 9/11 have had a major impact on the world and on Muslims in particular. And so practicing Islam freely in Britain has become a lot harder. This has caused many Muslims to value their religion a lot more and their citizenship a lot less.

...deal with Islamophobia

Take a look at muslimyouth.net, produced by and for young Muslims. It is a good antidote to the way Muslim issues are being reported in the press.

- ✖ **Find out about Nasim Ali,** who set up Camden United, an antiracist football project in Fitzrovia in central London, and who is now, aged 28, Deputy Mayor of Camden and adviser to the police and the Prince's Trust.

- ✖ **Hear about Hannah Al-Rashid,** who won a European gold medal for pencat silat, a Malaysian martial art.

- ✖ **Hear positive stories of these and other young Muslims** who are changing the world for the better.

- ✖ **Read it regularly.** Find out about the views of young Muslims on cultural identity, religious observance, the war on terror, and a whole lot more.

13 APRIL

plant a TREE

Trees renew our air supply by absorbing carbon dioxide and producing oxygen. Just two mature trees can provide enough oxygen for a family of four.

One tree produces nearly 260 lbs of oxygen each year.

One acre of trees removes up to 2.9 tons of carbon dioxide each year.

Shade trees can protect against fierce sunlight and make buildings cooler in the summer.

Trees cool the air by evaporating water in their leaves.

Tree roots stabilize the soil and prevent erosion.

Trees improve water quality by slowing and filtering rainwater, as well as protecting aquifers and watersheds.

—Adapted from Fun Facts on the Trees Are Good website of the International Society of Arboriculture

Trees are Good has information on trees and caring for them: www.treesaregood.com

Trees for Cities: www.treesforcities.org

Tree charities plant trees for you

Charities such as Trees for Cities plant trees in cities in return for donations of around $25 a year. They also have a partnership with Ben & Jerry's, whereby they supply free tree-planting kits (in a Ben & Jerry's ice cream tub, of course).

Trees for Cities also works overseas. You can plant banana, lemon, or avocado trees somewhere exciting such as Addis Ababa.

Trees for Cities runs a number of interesting training courses, including How to Operate a Chain Saw, and How to Hang from a Tree.

Tree Aid runs tree nurseries, plants trees, and manages woodlands in Ethiopia, Mali, Burkina Faso, Niger, and Northern Ghana, all in the arid zone of central Africa. Help regenerate the desert by getting Tree Aid to plant a tree.

...improve air quality

Grow your own trees

🌳 **Go to your local ice cream shop** and ask them for some large empty cartons. Find some seeds (acorns if you want to plant oak trees), and plant the seeds in the cartons. Put the tubs in a sunny window, water from time to time, and add some plant food if you feel that your trees are getting hungry. Transplant into a bigger pot as your trees grow.

🌳 **Find a suitable spot** to plant your trees: on a bit of waste land, along a road, at the edge of an existing grove of trees.

🌳 **Visit your trees.** Look after them. Take pride in what you have done.

IN AID *give 0.7%*

Today is tax day. Not a day to celebrate, but the last day to file your tax form. Perhaps also a day to think about the plight of the poorest of the world's citizens.

In 1970, rich nations promised 0.7% of their gross national income for development. The intention was to raise the level to 1%. By 2003, only six of 19 OECD countries had managed to achieve more than half the 0.7% target. ● The US was giving just 0.15%, the UK 0.34%. But Sweden, the Netherlands, Luxembourg, Denmark, and Norway were all exceeding 0.7%. ● In 2005, a pledge was made by the European Union that member states would achieve 0.56% by 2010 and reach the 0.7% target by 2015. This is too little and too late.

The Millennium Goals were agreed on by the international community in 2000 to address poverty, hunger, universal primary education, health care, access to clean water and proper sanitation—all problems that the people of the rich world do not have to face, but which are part of the daily struggle for most of the people living in the poor world.

An immediate annual injection of at least $50 billion per year is required. This figure would ensure progress towards the Millennium Development Goals. For the goals to be met, $94 billion a year is needed.

Global Call to Action against Poverty: www.whiteband.org
Organization for Economic Cooperation and Development (OECD): www.oecd.org

Living on less than $1 a day

While you drink a cappuccino at Starbucks, consider that one-sixth of the world's population are having to live on just a dollar a day.

Meanwhile, in Europe every cow receives a subsidy of more than $2 per day (which is more than the income of half the world's population).

...tax yourself to end poverty

Put your money where your mouth is. Build on the goodwill shown by the Make Poverty History campaign and Live8 in July 2005, when 2 billion people worldwide tuned into, or attended, concerts aimed at raising awareness of global poverty.

● **Shame your government** into moving toward the 0.7% commitment much more quickly by setting up your own 0.7% campaign.

● **Pledge to give 0.7% of your own annual income** as development aid. Ask your friends to do the same, and use the Pledge Bank to challenge others to join with you: www.pledgebank.com

Some projects require too much computing power to solve, so much that it is impossible for any one computer or any one person to solve them in a reasonable amount of time. Using a large number of small computers via the Internet in a distributed network is a way of overcoming this problem.

ChessBrain was the first distributed network to play a game against a single human opponent. On January 30, 2004, ChessBrain earned an official world record for the largest networked chess computer in history. One chess grand master competed against 2,070 PCs from over 50 countries. The game ended in a draw.

Besides playing chess, projects include:

Prime numbers: Finding larger ones—now with more than 10 million digits
Extraterrestrial radio signals: The search continues.
Exploring protein folding: To try to find treatments for diseases such as Alzheimer's and Huntington's chorea
Finding new and more effective drugs to fight cancer and AIDS
Mapping the World Wide Web at grub.org

Choose the project that interests you the most. Go to distributedcomputing.info/projects.html.

Monkey business

Help test the Shakespeare monkey theory: if you have enough monkeys banging randomly on typewriters, they will eventually type the works of William Shakespeare.

The current record is the first 24 letters of *Henry IV part 2*, which was typed after 2,737,850 million billion billion billion monkey-years, on January 3, 2005.

To participate in this effort, display the project web page in your web browser.

A Java applet generates random pages of text and compares them to all of Shakespeare's plays, and displays any matches between the first however many characters of your random page and a Shakespeare play.

If you beat the record, you press the Submit Record button. www.aardasnails.com

...join a distributed network

Join a distributed network. You will need to visit a website and download some software while keeping your computer connected to the Internet. After that you won't notice a thing. Your computer will be using its unused storage and processing capacity to solve some of the world's big problems, which are either too large or too expensive for a supercomputer to manage on its own.

AIR MILES *donate them*

Today, more than 120 million people worldwide belong to airline loyalty schemes. The air miles scheme awards air miles as a customer loyalty bonus in other retail sectors. Air miles have been called "a new global currency."

Frequent flier schemes started in 1981. Almost 14 trillion frequent-flier miles have been accumulated. 👫 Each mile is worth between two and ten cents. The total stock of air miles issued is worth more than $700 billion, which is more than the value of all dollar bills in circulation. 👫 You can spend air miles on travel and other benefits. Some schemes allow you to donate them for use by a charity.

The Make-A-Wish Foundation grants wishes to children who have a life-threatening medical condition. Children over the age of two and a half, and under the age of eighteen at the time of referral, are potentially eligible to have their wish granted. The foundation contacts the doctor treating the child to determine if the child is medically eligible for a wish (based on the foundation's medical criteria), and that the child has not received a wish from another wish-granting organization.

Most wishes fall into one of these categories:

I wish to go somewhere.
To a favorite theme park or an exotic beach, on a cruise, to see snow for the first time, or to attend a major sporting event or concert.
I wish to be somebody.
To be someone for a day—a fireman, a police officer, a model.
I wish to meet someone famous.
To meet a favorite athlete, recording artist, television personality, movie star, public figure.
I wish to have something.
A computer, a shopping spree, something special the child has wanted for ages.

To donate air miles, go to www.wish.org/home/giving/airmiles.htm.

Beat cancer with a video game

Ben Duskin was diagnosed with cancer at age five. His mother used a video-game analogy to explain what was going on inside his body. Ben asked Make-A-Wish to create a video game to help other people battle cancer. In the game, Ben whizzes around on his skateboard killing bad cancer cells. The game is based on the idea that attitude is what gets you through cancer. Play the game at www.makewish .org/ben.

...make a wish come true

👫 **Help make a child's wish come true.** Put a smile on his or her face. Help the child's recovery. Go to Make-A-Wish Foundation: www.worldwish.org.

👫 **Donate your air miles to the foundation.** Participating airlines include America West, American, British Airways, Continental, Delta, Northwest, Southwest, United, and US Airways.

use recycled TOILET PAPER

Reducing the amount of paper you use and increasing the amount that is recycled can help reduce the pressure on the world's timber resources. This saves energy as well as trees, as recycled paper manufacture only uses half the energy and water required for new paper.

Toxic wastes, including dioxins and other substances, are discharged from pulp mills. Yet until recently there was little control of these discharges. Even though paper can be recycled and the amount being recycled has been increasing, more than half of all paper used is still thrown away. ♣ One in five of the world's trees is used to make paper. Check out your own wastebasket. On average 30% of your waste is paper and cardboard. That's two trees' worth each year just caused by you!

Paper facts and lots of other information
www.wildlifewatch.org.uk/helpingwildlife
http://es.epa.gov/techinfo/facts/recypapr.html

ShitBegone toilet paper

ShitBegone is 100% recycled, because who wants to flush trees down the toilet? Why buy something made of trees when you don't need it?

ShitBegone toilet paper is nonembossed. Instead of being puffed up with air, ShitBegone is wound tightly on the roll. This makes ShitBegone rolls smaller and harder than the rolls that other companies sell. But ShitBegone is just as soft, just as long-lasting, and cheaper too!

ShitBegone expresses hope and belief that a better world is possible!

—Adapted from the ShitBegone
website: www.shitbegone.com

...and roll back waste

- ♣ **Use recycled toilet paper.** It is available from many supermarkets and also from eco-shopping services.
- ♣ **Buy some now.** And just for a challenge, see if you can cut down on the number of squares you use.
- ♣ **Start to use other recycled paper products**—for instance, tissues and paper towels.

APRIL **18**

CYBERSPACE *connecting up*

The Internet creates all sorts of opportunities for connecting people. Some intriguing projects have been developed with this aim.

The 1000 Journals project consists of 1,000 journals, which travel at random through the world. Each person completes a page, and then sends it to another person. The first 700 journals were sent to people who asked for them, who then passed their journal to a friend. People add whatever they like to the journal that is in their possession before passing it on—writing, painting, bits and pieces. Sightings of all 1,000 journals are logged on the website. The first journal to return had traveled to 13 US states and also to Brazil and Ireland. The completed journal was exhibited on the 1000 Journals website.

The Degree Confluence Project's aim is to visit each point on the surface of the earth where a degree of latitude and a degree of longitude intersect, and for the person visiting each location to take a photo. The pictures and stories from that location are then posted on the website. So far 3,430 points have been photographed in 155 countries. There is an intersection point within 49 miles (79 km) of everyone, and a total of 12,737 intersection points on dry land. Anyone can participate in this project.

1000 Journals: 1000journals.com
Degree Confluence Project: www.confluence.org
PhotoTag: www.phototag.org

PhotoTag—releasing cameras into the wild

This fun, not-for-profit venture captures the chance wanderings of disposable cameras, which are labeled and sent out with instructions for those who find them to take one picture and then pass the camera on. A prepaid and addressed envelope is included with the camera so that it can be mailed back to PhotoTag when all the film has been used up.

People who stumble upon a camera can log on to the PhotoTag website to update the progress of their particular camera. And when the camera is returned (if it ever is), then the photo images are posted on the website. Forty cameras have been released since 2000, of which only six have so far been returned.

...see what can happen

- **Visit these websites** and find out as much as you can about these projects.
- **Let this be a spur to your imagination.** Think up a project that will connect people in your community or across the world.
- **Take the first crucial step** in developing your idea.
- **Keep going** until your project is out there.

link up with SLUMS

There are 923 million people around the world living in slums: 554 million people in Asia, 187 million in Africa, 128 million in Latin America and the Caribbean, and 54 million in the rich world. This represents nearly one-third of the world's urban population and 43% of people in developing countries. 🌐 In the next 30 years, the number will increase to 2 billion if no action is taken.

The UN defines a slum as a household lacking

Access to sufficient and affordable water.

Access to a private or shared toilet.

Secure tenure without threat of eviction.

A permanent and adequate structure in a nonhazardous location.

Sufficient space—with not more than two people sharing a room.

Most slum dwellers live in homes of less than 150 square feet with no amenities or services. When people begin to feel more secure, they will often build brick walls, put a better roof on their house, and consider themselves the owner. Instead of rent, they will be paying money to a local boss, who will protect them from being evicted by the authorities or the landowner. 🌐 Sometimes a slum community will be resettled, with the city authorities providing a site and services, and the people building their own homes. More often, they will be evicted with nowhere to go, and have to find somewhere to live all over again.

Shack/Slum Dwellers International: www.sdinet.org
UN Habitat, the United Nations Human Settlements program: www.unhabitat.org

Shack/Slum Dwellers International provides a forum for slum dwellers all over the world to report on what they are doing to improve their housing. The success stories include accounts of how they are

Advocating their needs, and obtaining basic rights.

Obtaining land, designing and building their own housing.

Developing income-generating activities.

You can read the good news about how the government in Thailand has approved a $470-million plan to upgrade and develop housing in 2,000 communities in 2005–2008. The people living in the communities will be the key actors and owners of the project, and will develop it collectively.

Or you can keep up to date with darker developments in the slum-clearing in Zimbabwe.

...help upgrade homes

Contact one of the slum-dwellers associations listed on the SDI website and set up a link between them and your own community.
Organize fund-raising on the theme of housing. Here are some ideas:

🌐 **Hold a mass sponsored sleep-out** on your street or in someone's garden, under homemade shelters.

🌐 **Raise sponsorship** to spend 24 hours with no water supply, collecting all your water from a neighbor at least 100 yards away.

🌐 **Try making some "Shack Chic" objects** (see Craig Fraser's photographs on www.quivertree.co.za) and selling them on the street.

SLOW *down*

Most people agree that modern life is lacking something. Life in the fast lane means stress, worries about status and money, and a feeling that you are somehow missing out. Here are two interesting reactions to an ever-faster world:

Downshifting: swapping a high-octane, high-earning, stressed-out career for a more relaxed existence. In other words, going slow and enjoying it. One source estimates that 16 million people in Europe will have downshifted by 2007. ♞
In the UK, broadcaster and journalist Tracey Smith organizes an annual National Downshifting Week in the last week of April in order to highlight ways in which people can live simpler and happier lives, while being kinder to the environment. Among her suggested activities are

Schedule half a day off work to spend entirely with someone you love.

Cut up a credit card.

Eliminate three nonessential purchases a week.

Slowing down: The Society for the Deceleration of Time campaigns for slowness. Its 1,000 members undertake to contribute to a general process of deceleration and to pause for reflection wherever appropriate. The society was founded in 1990 and is based in Klagenfurt, Austria. It organizes talks and workshops, and an annual symposium. It also organizes stunts to get publicity for the idea of deceleration. For example:

Gold medals for the slowest competitor in Olympic events—an idea they put to the International Olympic Committee.

Pedestrian "speed traps," which time people over 50 meters. If pedestrians take under 37 seconds, they are pulled over and asked to explain their haste. As a punishment they are then asked to walk a tortoise puppet along the same 50-meter stretch.

Society for the Deceleration of Time: www.zeitverein.com (An English-language version of this website is being created at a snail's pace!)

Tracey Smith's downshifting website: www.frenchentree.com/fe-downshifting

The National Downshifting Week website has lots of good links: www.downshiftingweek.com

In Praise of Slow by Carl Honore has chapters on slow food, slow cities, slow mind and body, slow medicine, slow sex, slow work, slow leisure, and slow child rearing. The author writes
> *I am a speedaholic, and so this book is also a personal journey. I want to be free of the constant itch to go faster. I want to be able to read to my son without watching the clock. I want to find a way to live better by striking a balance between fast and slow.*

www.inpraiseofslow.com

...enjoy being relaxed

Sign up to the idea of slowing down. Think of ten ways in which you could slow down your own lifestyle. Make a pledge today to do all of these.

21 APRIL

be a backyard BEEKEEPER

Bees are essential to life on earth. They transfer pollen from the male parts to the female parts of flowers. Without this process, many garden plants would not be pollinated and so would fail to produce the fruits, vegetables, and flowers that we need and enjoy. Around 80% of the food we eat comes from crops that have been pollinated by bees.

Beekeeping can be a lot of fun. The bees will do most of the work. To collect 1 lb. of honey, bees will need to visit over 2 million flowers. This means a journey of around 55,000 miles—the equivalent of more than twice round the world. A worker bee will visit up to 100 flowers each trip and make up to 15 trips each day.

To get started you will need

a hive
some basic equipment
protective clothing
and, of course, some bees.

A typical hive will produce around 25 lbs. to 30 lbs. and possibly as much as 60 lbs. of honey each year.

Backyard Beekeeping—notes on keeping bees in urban and suburban neighborhoods: outdoorplace.org/beekeeping/citybees.htm

Where to put your bees

You don't even need your own garden. You can do it on your rooftop. Or you can arrange with a park or a landlord or ask a local community garden to put your hive on their land. Your bees will be doing a useful job for them, so they may welcome you.

You will need to put in around half an hour per week per hive from mid-April to August to look after your bees. You can buy a complete hive of bees, or you can obtain a swarm, when a bee colony divides into two, with half leaving to form a new colony elsewhere; or you can buy a nucleus and grow a colony.

...pollinate the world

Become a beekeeper!

Even if you live in a concrete jungle, you can do it. You'll be a friend of the earth, a pollinator, and a food producer.

You can sell the honey you produce to earn an income. Or you can distribute it among your friends.

APRIL 22

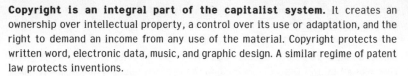

COPYRIGHT *and copyleft*

Copyright is an integral part of the capitalist system. It creates an ownership over intellectual property, a control over its use or adaptation, and the right to demand an income from any use of the material. Copyright protects the written word, electronic data, music, and graphic design. A similar regime of patent law protects inventions.

Copyright has a value. It may be owned by the original author, or it can be assigned or sold to another person. For example, Michael Jackson purchased the copyright to a large number of Beatles songs, and the copyright to *Peter Pan* was donated by J. M. Barrie to the Great Ormond Street Hospital for Sick Children, for which it has produced a steady stream of income over the years.

Copyright lasts for 70 years from the original publication date or the author's death, whichever is later, according to international conventions. After this time, the work goes out of copyright and can be used freely by anyone without payment.

The GNU General Public License project: www.gnu.org/copyleft/gpl.html
Free Software Foundation Copyleft site: www.gnu.org/copyleft/copyleft.html

There is an alternative to copyright: "copyleft." This has been developed by the Free Software Foundation. It asserts the author's ownership over the work but allows it to be distributed free, while at the same time preventing anyone else from claiming copyright over it.

Copyleft should be used by anyone wanting to promote free and wide dissemination of any work, both to set out the terms for dissemination and as a statement of commitment to the idea of sharing. In a world where genetic sequences and traditional medicines and foods (such as basmati rice) are being patented, the idea of copyleft shows that there is an alternative.

...property is theft

Add the following to anything and everything you write:

This work is "copyleft" as part of the author's commitment to a fair and sharing society. This means you are free to publish any part or all of it under the following license:

Copyright © year of publication, author's name.

Permission is granted to anyone to make or distribute verbatim copies of this work, in any medium, provided that this copyright notice and permission notice are preserved, and that the distributor and any subsequent distributor grants the recipient permission for further redistribution as permitted by this notice.

Modified versions may not be made except with the permission of the author.

Failure to comply may result in legal action to obtain financial compensation for the illegal use of the intellectual property.

hug a TREE

Almost everybody understands the value of trees, whether they just enhance the landscape or are essential to one's life and livelihood. And people do some weird and wonderful things to protect them.

When a 400-year-old giant oak tree in Southern California was threatened by the widening of a highway for a new housing development, John Quigley came to its rescue. With the support of other tree lovers, he ascended into the leafy heights of Old Glory, as the beautiful oak tree was named by local children, and stayed there for 71 days during the winter of 2002–2003. Eventually he was removed by police and the highway was built, but the tree was carefully removed and replanted on a new site where it is now thriving.

The Chipko Movement became world famous in the 1970s and 1980s. It showed the power of ordinary people to stand up to the rich and powerful. Local people on India's border with Tibet had used the forests in the foothills of the Himalayas in a sustainable way for many years. The forest had provided them with food, materials for shelter, medicines, and fodder for their animals. Then the government restricted their access and sold licenses to fell the trees to the highest bidder. 🌳 When a sporting goods manufacturer arrived to fell the trees, local people, including many women, went out and hugged the trees to prevent their being chain-sawed to destruction. This was the birth of Chipko Andolan (Hindi for "Movement to Hug"). 🌳 The movement leader, Chandi Prasad Bhatt, declared their aim: "Let them know they will not fell a single tree without felling one of us first. When the men raise their axes, we will embrace the trees to protect them." The loggers withdrew. Over the next few years, many forests were saved through what became the Chipko Movement.

Embrace the trees and
Save them from being felled;
The property of our hills,
Save them from being looted.   —Poem for Chipko

Read about Old Glory: www.landscapeonline.com/research/article/5502
For more information on the Chipko Movement:
www.unu.edu/unupress/unupbooks/80a03e/80A03E08.htm
National Arbor Day: www.arborday.org

Celebrate Arbor Day: In 1872, J. Sterling Morton proposed to the Nebraska Board of Agriculture that a special day be set aside for the planting of trees, a day to be called *National Arbor Day*. The idea was launched by planting 1 million trees in Nebraska.

The date of local Arbor Days varies, so that the day falls on around the best tree-planting date. In each state there are Tree Cities where the mayor proclaims Arbor Day, and urges citizens to plant trees to *"gladden the heart and promote the well-being of this and future generations."*

Each US state has a different state tree, from the *Sitka spruce* in Alaska to the *Cottonwood* of Wyoming.

...and gladden your heart

🌳 **Go out and hug a large and lovely tree** in your local park or wood. Think about the heroism of the Chipko pioneers and about what you can do to preserve trees and woodlands.

APRIL 24 *Arbor Day is during the last week of April*   118

BOYCOTT *bad companies*

As a consumer you are in a powerful position. You can support companies that behave ethically, but you can also exercise your buying power to boycott companies who are behaving in unethical ways. Taking action then involves doing nothing other than *not* buying products from suppliers you disapprove of.

Boycotts work. Canadian forests, Mexican salt marshes, whales, and the seabed have all benefited from boycott activity in the past. Animal rights campaigners have also been sophisticated users of the boycott technique, with successes in the fields of live animal transport, hunting, pet shops, and animal testing. Last but not least, human rights boycotts have also made a string of gains, most notably perhaps over corporate activity in Burma.

See the boycott list and contact details at Ethical Consumer: www.ethicalconsumer.org

Find out about company practice at www.responsibleshopper.org.

Co-op America's boycott and action site includes a downloadable guide to organizing a consumer boycott: www.coopamerica.org/programs/boycotts

Some ongoing campaigns:

Boycott Coca-Cola is supported by the Colombia Solidarity Campaign and India Resource Centre following environmental and human rights abuses in both countries. In Colombia, Coca-Cola stands accused of complicity in the assassination of eight trade union leaders since 1990. Many other leaders have been imprisoned, tortured, forcibly displaced, and exiled. In India, the company has depleted and polluted groundwater in Kerala. Show your solidarity by checking out www.colombiasolidarity.org.uk and www.indiaresource.org.

Boycott De Beers has been called by Survival International in support of the Bushmen of the Kalahari in Botswana, who claim they have been forcibly evicted from their ancestral land to make way for future diamond mining, and continue to be persecuted. Seven claimed to have been tortured by wildlife officials for hunting to feed their families. Support the Bushmen at www.survival-international.org.

Boycott Nestlé is another long-running campaign, called by Baby Milk Action, originally in response to the irresponsible marketing of breast-milk substitutes for babies. It's estimated that 1.5 million babies die each year because they are not breast fed. Recently, the group has broadened its focus to include information about Nestlé's water extraction exploits at historic Sao Lourenco, Brazil. Find out more on www.babymilkaction.org.

...the power of not buying

Boycott those companies and products you strongly disapprove of.

Your actions can make a difference. Make an effort to withdraw your financial support from immoral organizations, and stop buying their products.

main street DIVERSITY

Starbucks is one of just a few big corporations that are taking over our Main Streets. It may serve good coffee, support fair trade, and donate some of its profits to good causes, but it also drives local shops out of business and creates a uniform look to shopping centers in whichever city or country they are in.

Space Hijackers opposes the way that public space is being eroded and being replaced by corporate profit-making space. They want to reclaim public ownership for these spaces.

A particular target of Space Hijackers is Starbucks. 🏠 In 1997, a 25-year-old Houston-based computer programmer called Winter started a quest to visit every Starbucks in the world and drink an espresso or a black coffee at each. By 2005, he had visited 4,765 Starbucks in North America, and 213 elsewhere. This was possible only because Starbucks is opening, on average, 25 new outlets each week...

Starbucks Musical Chairs: www2.spacehijackers.org/starbucks/index.html
Space Hijackers: www.spacehijackers.org
Starbucks: www.starbucks.com

Starbucks Musical Chairs

You're sitting down in your local Starbucks. The people who sit next to you keep moving away to other seats. So you sniff yourself to check you don't smell. Suddenly, a girl stands up at the far end of the cafe and screams at the top of her voice, "I've been Starbucked!"

Everyone else in the store simultaneously sighs with depression. The next thing you know, everyone in the store starts laughing; they all get up and leave the café at once. You and the staff are the only ones left, and they look as stunned as you...

Everyone has been playing Starbucks Musical Chairs!

...give cities a human face

Get together with a group of friends to play Starbucks Musical Chairs. The rules are:

🏠 Players separately make their way to a Starbucks and sit down.

🏠 Each player smuggles in a drink of their choice disguised as a Starbucks beverage. (If players purchase anything from Starbucks, they are disqualified.)

🏠 Players move chairs each time two songs have been played on the in-store stereo.

🏠 Points are awarded, based on where the person is sitting (on the floor 5 points; sole occupant of an armchair 20 points).

🏠 The first player to reach 100 points stands up and says "I've been Starbucked." He or she is the winner.

🏠 Other players curse themselves for losing and leave the store.

APRIL 26

PETITION *the world*

> *Words without actions are the assassins of idealism.*
>
> —Herbert Hoover

An effective way of getting attention and gathering support for an issue is a petition. The days of knocking on the doors in residential neighborhoods begging for signatures have passed. Not only is this hard work, it's only really appropriate for a neighborhood campaign, when everyone has a vested interest in the subject. Nowadays, the advent of the Internet has given us a fast and easy mechanism for collecting thousands of signatures.

What makes for a good petition? Explain exactly what the issue is, and what you are asking people to sign up for. Do your research. Present the reader with concrete facts. Be brief. Don't write more than half a page.

How to collect more signatures than you ever dreamed possible:

Send e-mails to your friends asking them to sign.

Post links on relevant discussion boards.

Contact relevant writers and journalists and tell them about your petition.

Send out a press release announcing your petition.

Talk about your petition in online chat rooms.

Add a link to your petition in your e-mail signature and your website.

Ask special interest groups to add a link on their website or in their newsletters.

Submit your petition page to search engines (it usually takes between three and four weeks to be indexed). Type into Google "submit search engines" to find a way of reaching a lot of search engines for free.

Here are two websites where you can set up and distribute your petition for free:
The Petition Site: www.thepetitionsite.com/create.html
PetitionOnline: www.petitiononline.com/petition.html

Some petitions on the PetitionOnline website:

Al-Sistani For 2005 Nobel Peace Prize
To: the Committee for Nobel Prize for Peace

Get softball back into the 2012 Olympics
To: the International Olympic Committee

Property rights in animals
To: the US Congress

Please Lindsay, eat!
To Lindsay Lohan, teen actress

> Metal fans against Sharon Osbourne - Signatures
> http://www.petitiononline.com/mod_perl/signed.cgi/mad
>
> Metal fans against Sharon Osbourne
>
> We endorse the Metal fans against Sharon Osbourne Petition to Sharon herself..
>
> Read the Metal fans against Sharon Osbourne Petition
>
> Sign the Metal fans against Sharon Osbourne Petition
>
> *Use the Reload button in your web browser to see new signatures*
>
> Name   Comments
>
> 1934 Total Signatures

...a mouse click and it's done

Create your petition online. It's free!

After you have collected signatures, don't just let your petition sit and rot. Send it to politicians, companies, and leaders—whoever can help you work toward getting the change you want.

try experimental TRAVEL

Feeling like a day out? A long weekend away? A vacation of a lifetime? Why not do something really different, and at the same time, save energy, reduce your carbon emissions, and see the world in a completely new perspective?

In 1990, Joel Henry started experimenting with travel as a form of conceptual art. He invited people in Strasbourg, France, to travel to Zurich, Switzerland, view the city as a serious tourist, and then bring back some memento of their visit. Each person paid his or her own costs and traveled independently. They met up on their return to discuss their visit. ♣ This was the start of Latourex, the laboratory of experimental travel.

Latourex: www.latourex.org
The Lonely Planet Guide to Experimental Travel:
www.lonelyplanet.com/experimentaltravel

Guide to Experimental Travel

Joel Henry teamed up with Rachel Antony to compile the *Lonely Planet Guide to Experimental Travel*. Here are some of the 40 ideas in the book:

A-to-Z travel: Find the first street in a town that starts with the letter A and the last that starts with the letter Z, draw a line between the two. Walk as close to your line as the roads will allow you. That's your route for exploring the city.

Backpacking at home: Go to the airport dressed as a backpacker. Take public transport back to the center of the city, check into a hostel, and spend a few days doing backpacker things.

Chance travel: Every time you come to a crossroads, flip a coin. If it's heads, you turn left; if tails, you turn right. See where chance will take you.

Eros-tourism: Discover a city while looking for love. Arrange to take a holiday with your partner, but travel to the city independently with no plans for meeting up. Your task is to find your loved one.

...for a very different holiday

♣ **Become an experimental traveler.** You can use Rachel and Joel's book to give you ideas for what to do. But come up with your own ideas too. Do it by yourself, or make it a group thing. Why not set up your own Experimental Travel Group, and plan one experimental tour each month?

♣ **Spend a day at the airport:** enjoy the shopping, pray in the chapel, have a meal, wash and brush up, meet up with others waiting for their flight. And remember Merhan Karimi Nasseri, a stateless refugee from Iraq who has been living at Paris Charles de Gaulle airport since 1988, and whose story formed the basis of the Hollywood film *Terminal*, starring Tom Hanks.

APRIL 28

PRISON *put yourself in*

Please, use your liberty to promote ours.

—Aung San Suu Kyi, opposition leader in Burma and Nobel Prize winner

Burma is ruled by a brutal dictatorship, which uses murder, torture, and rape to keep 50 million citizens under its thumb. Hence its nickname, the Prison without Bars. ❧ The Burmese government has incarcerated over 1,000 political prisoners, 38 of whom are elected members of Parliament. Millions of people have been forced into slave labor. Living conditions are horrendous. Yet the borders are sealed, and no citizen can leave.

Aung San Suu Kyi is the face of hope for the Burmese people. She is a renowned advocate for democracy. She is also the world's only Nobel Peace Prize recipient to be kept under house arrest. ❧ For decades she has been campaigning for liberation for the Burmese people from the Burmese government. She is the leader of the National League for Democracy, the legitimately elected leader of Burma, and she is being held prisoner.

Aung San Suu Kyi's website: www.dassk.com
US Campaign for Burma: www.uscampaignforburma.org

Aung San Suu Kyi's father, General Aung San, led his country's fight for independence from the UK in the 1940s and was killed in 1947. She studied at Oxford, married, and had two sons, but returned to Burma in 1988 to tend her critically ill mother. She became involved in the prodemocracy movement, which was gaining momentum, despite the murder of thousands of demonstrators by the State Law and Order Restoration Council (SLORC). In the 1990 general election the party she headed, the National League for Democracy, won 80% of the vote, but the SLORC refused to recognize the result and arrested her. Since then, she has been under almost constant house arrest, speaking in public on only a few occasions. She was awarded the Nobel Peace Price in 1991.

...campaign for Burma

Arrest yourself and your friends in your own house for 24 hours to draw attention to the situation in Burma. Why not ask everybody to give $10 and use the party to raise money for the international struggle for freedom for the people of Burma? Have a great time, but make sure that you also tell the local media what you are planning.

adopt NONVOTERS

All of us know people who don't vote at election time. Are they the kind of people who give long-winded speeches about how little difference their one vote will make? Are they completely fed up with politics and politicians of all parties, seeing them as corrupt windbags who promise a lot and then deliver nothing? Or are they just so lazy that they can't be bothered to get off the sofa?

Voting is the most direct route we have to our politicians. When someone doesn't vote, one less voice is heard and the democratic process is weakened. It is our opportunity to back someone we trust and whose ideas we like, someone whom we believe will do their best for the community they represent.

We have the chance at election time to engage with politicians. After they have been elected, hold them accountable to all the promises they made and ensure that they make their best efforts as our representatives. If they are performing poorly, then we can vote next time for someone better. ⸮ You accomplish all of these things and more when you vote. The actual voting process only takes a few minutes.

The Orange Revolution in Ukraine: orangeukraine.squarespace.com
A guide to the Iraqi election:
www.motherjones.com/news/update/2005/01/01_402.html
Find out about elections around the world: www.electionworld.org

Democracy

Democracy is the recurrent suspicion that more than half the people are right more than half the time.

—E. B. White

Many societies do not have true democracy. Fair elections are something that people fought hard and even died to get—for example, in Ukraine in 2004 when the protests of millions on the streets achieved a second election after the first was rigged.

...drag them to the polls

Your vote can make a difference.

- ⸮ **If you are over 18,** make sure you are registered to vote and that you vote on Election Day.
- ⸮ **Drag all your nonvoting friends to the polling station**, no matter how much they protest.
- ⸮ **Pledge here and now that you will vote** at the next election. Also pledge that you will take five people to the polls who wouldn't otherwise vote.
- ⸮ **After they have voted, do something that's fun.** Take them out to lunch, have a voting party on election night just for people who have voted. Do whatever it takes!

APRIL 30

CAR *pooling*

Commuting to work? Driving your children to school? Going shopping? Going to town? Going to a baseball game? Driving abroad for business or pleasure? The chances are that there will be empty seats in your car. But other people might want to travel to roughly the same place at roughly the same time and could share the journey with you. Can you find them?

It makes financial sense to share the costs of a journey. It also makes good environmental sense, as it results in one less car trip, though it'll always be better for the environment if you walk, cycle, or use public transport. ♣ If you're traveling by car, think about carpooling. The Internet is a great mechanism for linking up people who want to share a journey. ♣ You could also consider car sharing, whereby people join together to jointly own and run a car.

The benefits of sharing a journey:

> **Saves money**
> **Reduces the number of cars** on the roads—less congestion, less pollution, and fewer parking problems
> **Is especially beneficial** for people in rural areas
> **Makes an enjoyable journey** out of that boring slog to work in the morning
> **Provides an alternative** to owning your own car

World CarShare Consortium: www.ecoplan.org/carshare

Here are some simple rules for Internet carpooling:
Decide if you are prepared to travel with a member of the opposite sex.
Exchange telephone numbers and make arrangements over the phone, even if the first contact is by e-mail.
Meet in a well-lit public place.
Give someone else your journey details plus contact details of who you are traveling with.
Take basic safety precautions. Ask for car details—make, model, color, and registration number. Ask the driver to bring along a driver's license plus proof of insurance and an inspection certificate.

...halve the impact

♣ **Just for the fun of it, go traveling.** Log in to a carpooling website, and find somebody who is going somewhere interesting. Share a ride with him or her.

♣ **Start carpooling.** Next time you have a spare seat in your car or want to go somewhere, offer to share the ride.

urban LETTERBOXING

Letterboxing combines orienteering and treasure hunting with craftsmanship and inventiveness. Traditionally, it has been a countryside rambling activity.

A funky way of exploring your city. A letterbox is a weatherproof box that contains a unique rubber stamp and a log book. 🏠 The box is hidden somewhere interesting. Letterboxers exchange clues to the location of the boxes. They then find and stamp the box's log book with their own personal stamp (to show that they've been there), and stamp their log book with the box's stamp (to show how many letterboxes they've hunted down).

All about letterboxing: www.letterboxing.info
Website for urban letterboxing: www.spacehijackers.org/letterboxing
The US letterboxing website (for rural letterboxing): www.letterboxing.info

Letterboxing: a short history

Letterboxing began in southwest England in 1854, when a Victorian gentleman named James Perrott hid his calling card in a jar in a remote area by Cranmere Pool on the moors of Dartmoor. Perrott was a guide on the moor, and he encouraged his clients to leave their cards in the jar as well.

Eventually, visitors began leaving a self-addressed postcard or note in the jar, hoping for them to be returned by mail by the next visitor (thus the origin of the term "letterboxing"). This practice ended in time, however,

and the current custom of using rubber stamps and visitors' log books came into use.

By the 1970s there were 15 boxes on the moor. In the 1980s, letterboxing exploded on Dartmoor (literally, on occasion, since part of the park is used as an artillery range by the British army!). Today, there are more than 3,000 letterboxes in the 365 square miles of Dartmoor National Park.

www.letterboxing.info

...get to know your city

Go urban letterboxing.

🏠 **Make a personal stamp, construct your letterbox, and find somewhere interesting to hide it.** Put your letterbox somewhere that enhances people's perception of the urban (or rural) environment. Be careful where you put it, though; you don't want it to be control-exploded as an unidentified suspect object.

🏠 **Enter its location** on the Urban Letterbox database on the letterboxing website.

🏠 **Then start letterboxing**, using the locations and clues listed for other people's letterboxes.

MAY 2

STAND UP *for press freedom*

Today is World Press Freedom Day. This may not seem important if you have a free press. But more than a third of the world's people live in countries where there is no press freedom, where journalists are persecuted for telling the truth, and where politicians would rather their people did not know the truth.

Reporting can be a dangerous job: 42 media professionals lost their lives in 2003 for just doing their job. Around the world, 184 journalists, media assistants and cyber-dissidents are in prison, some simply because they used the "wrong" word or photograph.

Reporters Without Borders is an international network of journalists working to uphold press freedom by

> **Monitoring press freedom** around the world via a network of over 100 correspondents.
>
> **Publishing regular reports** on press freedom. This includes an annual World Press Freedom Ranking. In 2003 at the bottom of the list were Burma, Cuba, and North Korea.
>
> **Defending journalists** who have been imprisoned or persecuted for doing their work, and providing legal aid to get torturers and murderers of journalists brought to trial.
>
> **Campaigning to reduce censorship** and oppose laws that restrict press freedom.
>
> **Working to improve the safety** of journalists around the world, particularly in war zones.

Reporters Without Borders: www.rsf.org

Persecuting journalists in Eritrea: In September 2001, the Eritrean government ordered all the country's privately owned publications to close down. In the following days, police arrested more than 15 journalists. They were accused of having published interviews with political leaders who had been publicly calling for democratic reforms in the country. Those leaders were also arrested. Today, ten journalists remain behind bars in Eritrea.

Shutting down a website in China: When state security police came to arrest Huang Qi at his home on June 3, 2000, he just had time to send this e-mail: "Goodbye everyone, the police want to take me away. We've got a long road ahead of us. Thanks to all those helping to further democracy in China." Huang, founder of the website www.tianwang.com, waited nearly three years before finding out he had been sentenced to five years for "subversion" and "incitement to overthrow the government." Huang has been tortured in prison. His website was closed down, and the domain name is for sale. Why not buy it and create a memorial to Huang's bravery?

...support its defenders

- ♪ **Visit the Reporters Without Borders website.**
- ♪ **Find out about abuses** of press freedom around the world.
- ♪ **Sign and send petitions** to try to free some of the world's imprisoned journalists. Just click and send. It will remind the oppressors that their victims have not been forgotten.

Books can change the world. Perhaps the most influential political tract ever was *The Rights of Man* written by Tom Paine, which fueled both the American and the French revolutions. Alexander Solzhenitsyn brought the world's attention to Stalin's prison camps in *The Gulag Archipelago*, which was an important step in the collapse of Communism.

This is why people ban books and burn them. But banning and burning books will not stop the flow of ideas. Even in the repressive Soviet Empire, people copied by hand and passed on these copies through a process known as samizdat publishing.

Here are six titles in search of an author.

1 *How to Be a Guru:* to inspire activists all around the world and build a movement that will change the world
2 *The Layman's Guide to the Indian Highway Code:* a humorous look at behavior on Indian roads and an insight into the Indian psyche. An instant best-seller.
3 *101 Ways to Rig an Election:* which will become the standard work in teaching good governance
4 *Twenty-five Ways to Say NO:* a practical manual for dealing with bureaucracy
5 *How to Bribe an Official:* You never know when you might need to
6 *Ten Things to Do with Coca-Cola Other than Drink It:* a fun look at a global brand and its impact on the world

Reports on anti-Coca-Cola campaigns in India:
www.indiaresource.org/campaigns/coke/2004/cokespins.html

Some things to do with Coca-Cola:

The Centre for Science and Environment in Delhi has claimed that the top 12 soft drink brands of Pepsi and Coca-Cola in India contain pesticides and insecticides in excess of limits set by the European Commission. Other Indian campaigners claim that Indian cola bottling plants are extracting so much water that local wells are running dry as the water table falls, and that solid and liquid waste discharged by factories is polluting local groundwater.

Some farmers in India are using Coca-Cola as a pesticide, spraying their cotton and chili fields with the Real Thing. Gotu Laxmaiah, a farmer from Andra Pradesh, sprayed several hectares of cotton and observed that "the pests began to die after the soft drink was sprayed on my cotton."

Guardian Unlimited reports that "the properties of Coke have been discussed for years. It has been reported that it is a fine lavatory cleaner, a good windscreen wipe and an efficient rust spot remover. Uncorroborated reports from China claimed that the ill-fated New Coke was widely used in China as a spermicide."

...then write the book!

Write your own book to change the world. Recognize the power of the written word.

♟ First think up a great title (the fun part), then write your book.
♟ Once it's written, put it on the web, publish it yourself, or find a publisher.

SPEED *dating*

☺

Every year, nearly 600,000 women die from complications during pregnancy and childbirth. That's the equivalent of a ship the size of the *Titanic* sinking every single day with no survivors. Maternal deaths account for 25% to 30% of all deaths among women of reproductive age. There are huge differences across the world: for example, a woman in Somalia is 700 times more likely to die as a result of pregnancy or childbirth than a woman in the UK.

Safe Motherhood protects women throughout pregnancy and childbirth. It means ensuring that all women everywhere receive the care they need to be safe and healthy. This goal can be achieved by providing high-quality maternal health services to all women during pregnancy, childbirth, and the postpartum period. These include:

Care by skilled health personnel before, during, and after childbirth.
Emergency care for life-threatening obstetric complications.
Services to prevent and manage the complications of unsafe abortion.
Family planning and health education.

Millennium Goal 5 aims to improve maternal health. The target for 2015 is to reduce by three-quarters the chance that a woman will die in childbirth (currently one in 48).

Safe Motherhood, an international campaign: www.safemotherhood.org
Maternity Worldwide: www.maternityworldwide.org

According to Marie Stopes International, every minute of every hour of every day

380 women become pregnant; half of these pregnancies are unplanned or unwanted.
110 women experience pregnancy-related complications.
40 women have an unsafe abortion.
One woman dies from complications during pregnancy. More than 99% of these deaths occur in developing countries and most could be avoided with improved obstetric care.

...to save mothers

Organize a speed dating evening to raise money for Maternity Worldwide. They will tell you what to do, and every $23 you raise will sponsor a safe birth.

☺ **You need about 25 single men and 25 single women** in the same room, seated male/female. Each person gets a few minutes to talk to the person next to him or her.

☺ **Every three to five minutes a buzzer rings,** and the men change seats.

☺ **Each person is given a Speed Dating card** and checks the names of people he or she would like to see again. If interest is mutual, then they get sent their new friends' e-mail addresses. What happens next is up to them...

plant your BIRTH TREE

Each day of the year has a particular tree associated with it. The tree for the day you were born is known as your birth tree. Don't just plant any tree. Plant your birth tree. Or commemorate someone else's birthday by planting his or her birth tree.

Some people believe your birth tree confers a set of characteristics on you. For example, if you were born on July 10, your birth tree is a fir. You are likely to have all of the following characteristics: taste, dignity, cultivated airs, a love of anything beautiful, modesty, ambition, and many friends.

To find out about your birth tree:
www.geocities.com/Athens/5341/tree.html
www.artistic.fadingwhispers.org/cornucopia/birthtree.html

Jan 02 to Jan 11	**Fir**	May 01 to May 14	**Poplar**
Jan 12 to Jan 24	**Elm**	May 15 to May 24	**Chestnut**
Jan 25 to Feb 03	**Cypress**	May 25 to Jun 03	**Ash**
Feb 04 to Feb 08	**Poplar**	Jun 04 to Jun 13	**Hornbeam**
Feb 09 to Feb 18	**Cedar**	Jun 14 to Jun 23	**Fig**
Feb 19 to Feb 28	**Pine**	Jun 24	**Birch**
		Jun 25 to Jul 04	**Apple**
Mar 01 to Mar 10	**Weeping Willow**		
Mar 11 to Mar 20	**Lime**	Jul 05 to Jul 14	**Fir**
Mar 21	**Oak**	Jul 15 to Jul 25	**Elm**
Mar 22 to Mar 31	**Hazelnut**	Jul 26 to Aug 04	**Cypress**
Apr 01 to Apr 10	**Rowan**	Aug 05 to Aug 13	**Poplar**
Apr 11 to Apr 20	**Maple**	Aug 14 to Aug 23	**Cedar**
Apr 21 to Apr 30	**Walnut**	Aug 24 to Sep 02	**Pine**
		Sep 03 to Sep 12	**Weeping Willow**
		Sep 13 to Sep 22	**Lime**
		Sep 23	**Olive**
		Sep 24 to Oct 03	**Hazelnut**
		Oct 04 to Oct 13	**Rowan**
		Oct 14 to Oct 23	**Maple**
		Oct 24 to Nov 11	**Walnut**
		Nov 12 to Nov 21	**Chestnut**
		Nov 22 to Dec 01	**Ash**
		Dec 02 to Dec 11	**Hornbeam**
		Dec 12 to Dec 21	**Fig**
		Dec 22	**Beech**
		Dec 23 to Jan 01	**Apple**

...for a greener world

🌳 **Use the table to identify your birth tree.**

🌳 **Plant your birth tree** to commemorate your next birthday. Do it yourself in your own garden, or on a plot of vacant land, or in a clearing in a wood or forest. Find somewhere that desperately needs a tree. Then plant one.

MAY 6

WATER *fetching*

Millions of people worldwide lack piped water. Many also live far away from a safe water source. Women and girls have to walk long distances every day to collect their family's water needs from a nearby dam, lake, or river. ● The traditional way of collecting water is using a bucket or pot carried as a head load. Most women can manage to carry around 5 gallons, girls less. Collecting water is time-consuming, and more than one trip may need to be made each day. Some women spend two to three hours every day of their life just collecting water. It is hard work and can cause serious health problems. But there is a simple answer.

Instead of carrying water on your head, why not roll it along the ground? The Hippo Water Roller carries 20 gallons of water. It has a clip-on steel handle for pushing it along the ground. Water purification tablets can be added; the rolling motion ensures these fully dissolve in the water. ● The drum is manufactured from polyethylene and can easily withstand typical rural conditions such as uneven footpaths, rocks, and even broken bottles. If it happens to meet a land mine, the water will absorb most of the blast.

Children and older people can easily push a full roller over most terrains, because the low center of gravity makes the effective weight around 22 lbs. But the really good news is that approximately five times as much water can be collected in less time and with far less effort. Someone who has been spending two hours a day fetching water would save more than ten hours a week. ● Think what she could do with this extra free time—grow vegetables, milk a cow, do handicrafts. Think of how much extra money she will be able to earn. The Hippo Water Roller and water purification products for one year cost ZAR 1,075 (about $150).

The Hippo Water Roller is an Operation Hunger project: www.operationhunger.co.za

Did you know?

The average American uses between 80 and 100 gallons of water every day.

The average person in a developing country uses $2^{1}/_{2}$ gallons of water every day for their drinking, washing, and cooking. This is the same as an average flush of a toilet.

Around 40 billion working hours are spent carrying water each year in Africa. Maybe half of these could be saved by using the Hippo Water Roller.

...made slightly easier

Spread the word about the Hippo Water Roller.

Hundreds of millions of women all over the world would benefit if there was an easier way of fetching water. Tell NGOs in Africa and Asia to go to the Water Hippo website to find out more: www.hipporoller.org.

send FLOWERS

I, Woodrow Wilson, President of the United States of America, do hereby direct the government officials to display the United States flag on all government buildings and do invite the people of the United States to display the flag at their homes or other suitable places on the second Sunday in May as a public expression of our love and reverence for the mothers of our country.

—President Woodrow Wilson, 1914

Mother's Day started with the Greeks. Their spring festival honored Rhea, who was mother of many gods. The Romans had a similar festival honoring Cybele. ⚫ Christians honored Mary, mother of Christ, on the fourth Sunday of Lent, which also occurred at around the same time of year.

In the US, the idea of Mother's Day was started by Anna Jarvis. Anna was an Appalachian housewife who decided to campaign about the poor health of her community. To focus on this, she organized a "Mother's Work Day." After Anna's death, her daughter continued to campaign for a day dedicated to mothers. ⚫ In 1913, the US House of Representatives adopted a resolution calling for officials of the federal government to wear white carnations on the second Sunday in May, which began to be called "Mother's Day." Then in 1914, Woodrow Wilson formally created Mother's Day as we now know it.

Organic Bouquet: www.organicbouquet.com
NORD: www.rarediseases.org
Order Charity Flowers through Practical Action:
www.practicalaction.org/?id=flowers_by_post

Say it with flowers. Make a difference.

Order flowers via *Organic Bouquet*. Their growers are small businesses, and each is given a page on the website to tell you about their family and farm. A proportion of the proceeds is donated to nonprofits working for the environment and human and animal rights. If you have your own website, create a link to Organic Bouquet. They will give you a 15% commission on any sales you generate.

Order flowers via NORD, the National Organization for Rare Disorders. Click on the link to "From You Flowers" and 20% of your order cost will be donated to NORD. Search their database and find out about cerebellar agenesis, Chagas disease, Cochin Jewish disorder, Coffin-Siris Syndrome, Colorado tick fever, and more than 1,150 other rare diseases that we hope you haven't got. And if you have, then NORD has a list of more than 2,000 patient organizations that can help you.

...with a difference

On Mother's Day, send your mom some flowers. But send flowers with a difference—flowers which will also contribute to a better world.

MAY 8 *Mother's Day is the second Sunday in May*

TRADE *fair*

Many farmers now have to work harder and longer for less money. Prices paid for agricultural commodities produced in the southern countries have not risen in real terms over the last 40 years. At the same time, the cost of fertilizers, pesticides, and machinery (imported from the rich countries) have all increased substantially. ⚫ If the market price of commodities falls below the actual cost of production, as it can do, millions of small farmers are forced into crippling debt, some losing their land and homes.

What farmers need is a fair price for their products that covers the cost of production, and an assurance that they will be able to sell what they produce. This is the basis of the fair-trade movement. ⚫ Fair-trade certification was launched in the 1980s in the Netherlands. A consumer label, the FAIRTRADE mark, was awarded to products that met fair-trade standards. You can buy over 1,000 FAIRTRADE products from coffee, chocolate, and tea to fresh fruits. Products are available in supermarkets, independent shops, and cafés, and sales are growing by 40% each year.

Fair Trade Federation: www.fairtradefederation.org
Fairtrade Labeling Organizations International: www.fairtrade.net
International Fair Trade Association: www.ifat.org
World Fair Trade Day: www.wftday.org

Fair-trade Towns
In 2000, Garstang in Lancashire declared itself "The world's first Fair-trade Town." The idea has spread. To be a Fair-trade Town, five goals must be met:

1   The local council must pass a resolution supporting fair trade, and serve fair-trade coffee and tea at its meetings and in its offices and cafeterias.
2   A range of fair-trade products must be readily available in the town's shops, local cafés, and catering establishments.
3   Fair-trade products must be used by some local workplaces and community organizations.
4   The campaign should have popular support.
5   A committee must be formed.

Campaign to get your town declared a Fair-trade Town.

Four facts about fair-trade

1   Out of every $100 generated by world exports, only $3 goes to low-income countries.
2   For every dollar given to poor countries in aid, $2 are lost because of unfair trade. This costs the poor world $100 billion a year.
3   If Africa, East Asia, South Asia, and Latin America increased their share of world exports by just 1%, 128 million people would be lifted out of poverty.
4   Rich countries spend $1 billion a day on agricultural subsidies.

...make yours a fair-trade Town

⚫ **Look for the FAIRTRADE** on products. Go out now and buy fair-trade chocolate and fair-trade tea or coffee.

⚫ **Make a commitment to buy fair trade** whenever you can.

be a virtual VOLUNTEER

Virtual volunteering means that you can give practical help without leaving your home. Anyone who has the time available and wants to change the world, who has regular, reliable access to a computer and the Internet, and has skills and experience that others might need is a great candidate for online volunteering. 👫 Your skill could be computer programming, writing, fund-raising, project management, fluency in another language, or simply the time you can offer to help get a task done.

You can even help an organization halfway round the world. More than 15,000 people have registered on the United Nations online volunteering website as being interested in doing something. They work on anything from translating documents, editing press releases, and conducting research, to creating web pages, designing brochures and newsletters, giving professional expertise and advice, and much more.

What it takes to be a good online volunteer:
Attention to detail
Commitment to answer e-mails quickly
Commitment to stay with a project through to its completion
Enjoying working independently
A desire to learn, and a willingness to be flexible
Having a clear definition of what you want out of it
Being enthusiastic about the goals of the organization you are helping

Online volunteering: www.onlinevolunteering.org

Raising the visibility of volunteer organizations in Egypt

Carlos Jiménez from Spain has been the driving online volunteer force behind the website of the Volunteer Network Egypt, a portal aimed at increasing the awareness of volunteerism in Egypt.

The portal was launched on International Volunteer Day (December 5) in 2004. Its successful launch can be attributed to a considerable degree to Carlos's skillful and committed coordination of a team of 11 online volunteers from seven countries, spread over the Arab region, Asia, Europe, and North America.

Online volunteering gives us the opportunity to contribute—from our homes, from our workplaces—much more than a donation. We can actively participate, as protagonists, in sustainable development.

...with a click of your mouse

Become an online volunteer today.

👫 **Go to www.onlinevolunteering.org and register** (the website used to be called NetAid).

👫 **Or if you could use an online volunteer** to help you change the world, then post your volunteering assignment on the website.

LESS *is more*

Imagine having enough money to meet all your needs. Now think about a society and economy operating without any of the problems caused by money and its unfair distribution: poverty, exploitation, homelessness, unemployment, fear, and stress. A world where everyone can afford what they need, where they can all work and have the time and facilities to play.

This is the dream of an "open money economy," where people within a community can freely exchange goods and services. 🏠 LETS (Local Exchange Trading System) is a working example of an open money system. With LETS, members exchange goods and services with each other. People receive credits for all the goods and services they provide. These can then be used to purchase other goods and services from within the LETS community. 🏠 A credit cannot be exchanged for cash. A bookkeeper records all the transactions and keeps accounts for members, showing whether they are in credit or debit.

LETS relies on trust and cooperation among the community. If someone builds up a substantial credit and there is nothing they wish to purchase, then they will probably lose interest. If they go into debt because they have been on a spending spree or because they can't provide things that other people want, then the LETS community has to sort the matter out with the person concerned. 🏠 LETS really works. LETS has a particular relevance for people who are out of work either through lack of employment opportunities, disability, or retirement. LETS enables them to participate in economic life when they don't have a means of doing this within the formal economy.

All you need to know about LETS: www.gmlets.u-net.com
International LETS groups network: www.lets-linkup.com

Travel without money

James Taris traveled the world without money for 400 days. This is the website he created with free tips for living on LETS: www.travelwithoutmoney.com

...let's stop using money

If you get hooked on the idea, then set up a LETS group. Start by organizing a street party. Ask everyone to write all the things they think they might need on one set of cards, and all their skills and other things they could offer on another set of cards. Put these up on a notice board. Then see what happens.

say no to # BILLBOARDS

Mobile billboards drive around the city but don't actually go anywhere. They are those trucks you see being driven through the streets where you live and work, with an advertising billboard on the back. They take up road space and contribute to gridlock. They spew out pollution and greenhouse gases but ignore the fact that that they're inconveniencing everybody else.

Mobile billboards are a good indication of a selfish and wasteful society. They are completely unnecessary. If people really want to advertise in the streets, they could use the sides and backs of buses as an alternative.

Here are two Canadian websites which should spur you on in your own battles with mobile billboards in your own country:
Stop Mobile Billboards: www3.sympatico.ca/alwaysweb/mobile_billboards.html
überculture's Montreal campaign: www.uberculture.org/projects/bad_trucks.html

Say NO to mobile billboards!

Ad Trucks are Bad Trucks. They're bad for the environment, bad for driving, and pretty much illegal.

—Überculture, Montreal, an organization campaigning to reclaim public space.

Downtown Montreal has over 30 billboard trucks each day, traveling 1.45 million miles a year, burning over 100,000 gallons of gas and emitting 2 million pounds of carbon dioxide.

Mobile Billboard
Live Display Area. 10' 5" x 22' 8"
Truck Length: '93' • Height 12' 5"

Skyline
OUTDOOR ADVERTISING

...and save our air

Campaign against mobile billboards:

🌳 **Make a note of any mobile billboard you see.** Write down where you saw it, its registration number, the company advertising, and the date and time. If you have a camera, photograph it.

🌳 **Write to the company to complain.** Tell them to be more environmentally sensitive. Tell them that you will stop buying their products if they don't change their policy. And tell them that you will tell all your friends to do the same. Make sure the company knows that thanks to its advertising policy, it has lost a customer, not gained one.

🌳 **Try to get some really bad PR for the advertiser.** Think of a creative and powerful way of getting media coverage for a Say NO to Mobile Billboards! campaign.

🌳 **Don't buy from any company that advertises on mobile billboards.** Don't vote for any politician or political party that uses a mobile billboard for campaigning.

MAY 12

GUTENBERG *project*

Michael Hart set up Project Gutenberg in 1971 when he was a student. His goal was to make available free electronic copies of out-of-copyright books and books whose copyright had been donated. Project Gutenberg became the world's first digital library. Michael himself typed in the first hundred books. With the emergence of the Internet in the mid-1990s, the project took off. It is now truly international.

A book is scanned into an electronic copy. This is then proofread and any corrections made. If the original is in poor condition, as with very old books, the book has to be typed in manually word by word. There are now a thousand volunteers all over the world who help with these processes. The books are produced in text format, so as to minimize the size of the file. ✋ Any title can be downloaded for free from the Project Gutenberg website and then sent on to people who might be interested in reading it. ✋ Software on the website (which is still being tested) will allow users to convert books into other formats and eventually into Braille and voice.

The number of books available reached 11,000 by the start of 2004, and 350 new titles are added every month. Most titles are in English, but there are now books available in 25 languages, and the target is to extend the library to at least 100 languages. Michael's dream is to have one million titles available by 2015.

Project Gutenberg: www.gutenberg.net

Become a Distributed Proofreader

Go to the Project Gutenberg website, to the book you want to work on. Pages of the book appear side by side in two forms: one the scanned image and the other the text produced by OCR (optical character recognition). You compare the two and make corrections. OCR is around 99% accurate, which makes for about ten corrections a page. Save each page. You can then either stop work or do another page.

All the books are proofread twice (the second time by an experienced proofreader) before the final version is ready for distribution. If any

further errors are noted by readers after the book has been distributed, they can then be corrected. Proofreaders aren't given a quota to fulfil, but it's suggested that you do at least one page a day. This is a small contribution toward creating a library of a million books.

...bringing people books

✋ **Read a Gutenberg book tonight.**

✋ **Send people books** they might be interested in as a virtual birthday present.

words without BORDERS

The smuggler passed the slope and walked on toward the minefield, measuring each of his steps with increasing care. Bluebells bloomed and blades of grass, flattened by the wind, spread across the ground, trying to hide themselves in the stone-filled meadow that ran up to the hilltop in a gentle slant, beyond which lay the cliffs and the pass. No minesweeper had come to this place; there were no barriers, no warning signs…

—the opening paragraph of *At the Borderline* by Sherko Fatah

Storytelling is as old as the human race. Cavemen illustrated their stories with rudimentary paintings on cave walls. Today we communicate our stories through newspapers, magazines, the Internet, television, radio, and CDs. Even airplanes sometimes write messages in the sky. 💡 Storytelling gives pleasure, stimulates thinking, connects us to real and imagined worlds, enlarges our vision, and generates understanding. In a world full of ignorance about other peoples and cultures, writing produced by other cultures has an especially important role to play.

If a book is written in your own language, it is increasingly easy to access it via the Internet. But if it is written in another language, it must first be translated. Today, 50% of all books translated are translated from English, but only 6% are translated *into* English. This disproportionate flow of information is a great loss to English readers.

> Words without Borders: www.wordswithoutborders.org
> The International Storytelling Center: www.storytellingcenter.com

Words without Borders is trying to address this problem. They are translating some of the world's best writing—selected and translated by a distinguished group of writers, translators, and publishing professionals—and publishing these translations on the Internet.

> *Our ultimate aim is to introduce exciting international writing to the general public— travelers, teachers, students, publishers, and a new generation of eclectic readers— by presenting international literature not as a static, elite phenomenon, but as a portal through which to explore the world.*

The International Storytelling Center sees storytelling as a vehicle for social change. They have a resource pack to show how to use stories and storytelling in preventing conflict, reconciling differences, and building peace.

...read books in translation

Sign up to Words without Borders to get their free e-newsletter.

Find a story from their library. Read it by yourself, or read it to somebody else. Hear about life in Africa, the Americas, Asia, Europe, the Middle East, and the Pacific Rim.

Soon Words without Borders will be setting up online reading group discussions—something to look forward to.

AIDS ORPHANS *in South Africa*

The struggle against global AIDS is one of the great challenges of our time. And the suffering of children affected by AIDS is one of the issues that most demands our attention. ✎ Nowhere is the problem more evident than in South Africa, where it is estimated that there are nearly 1 million AIDS orphans. This is close to the number of children aged under five in the entire state of New York. Soon there will be 2 million AIDS orphans.

Africa's AIDS orphans have been described as "an army in search of a leader." Brought up without the protection of adults, without their basic material needs' being met, and without moral guidance, these children are the most dispossessed.

Heartbeat works with 5,000 children in more than a dozen areas of South Africa. Home-based care workers serve as surrogate parents for AIDS orphans and other children who head a household. ✎ Heartbeat provides food, clothes, school fees, and basic medicines to these children, and, just as importantly, supplies nurturing, attention, and counseling. The care workers provide protection from sexual and physical abuse.

Find out about Heartbeat at www.austincommunityfoundation.org/?nd=invisible. Find out about Nkosi's Haven at nkosi.iafrica.com.

Nkosi Johnson died from AIDS in 2001 aged only 12. During his short life, Nkosi saw that not enough was being done to protect children from being born with HIV or to care for those who were born with HIV and to provide for orphans. He also saw AIDS discrimination at work when he was refused entry to school. Nkosi, with his foster mother, set about doing something. Nkosi himself became the human face of AIDS orphans in South Africa, gaining enormous media attention for the cause.

Nkosi and his foster mother, Gail, set up Nkosi's Haven, which is a hostel accommodating 11 mothers who are HIV positive or with full-blown AIDS, and 27 children (of whom ten are HIV positive). The next-door property has also been purchased, which will double the capacity of the hostel, and plans are being made to purchase a 12-acre farm and a property with 13 self-contained cottages and flats to set up residential communities for mothers and children living with AIDS.

...one million and rising

✎ **Organize a dinner of hope.** Host a dinner at your home. Book a restaurant. Have a picnic. Throw a party. Invite as many people as you can.

✎ **Ask your guests to make a contribution.** Every dollar raised will help AIDS-orphaned children in South Africa. Find out more from www.starfishcharity.org, which supports Heartbeat.

A netizen is a citizen of the Internet, a member of a worldwide community. All netizens should have rights, freedom, and equality. But in order for the cyberworld to be a place for good, we need responsible netizenship.

Citizens Coalition for Economic Justice in Korea has drawn up the following charter for good netizenship. Netizens should

Voluntarily develop the cyberworld as an open and sound space for everyone.

Respect and protect the human rights and privacy of others, valuing them as their own.

Try to respect the work of others while having access to unlimited information.

Protect the private information of others as if it were their own.

Refrain from using vulgar or foul language.

Use their real names, and take responsibility for their actions and comments.

Not produce or disseminate incorrect information.

Not engage in illegal actions, such as spreading a virus or cracking passwords.

Participate positively in the cyberworld by watching out for and commenting on irresponsible actions.

Contribute toward creating a positive Internet culture by keeping and practicing these principles.

One in five children is sexually solicited online every year. Online sexual solicitation is an unprovoked, uninvited, unwanted request to engage in sexual activity, engage in a sexually explicit conversation, or give personal sexual information with someone first met online. The Internet allows people to masquerade behind a false identity, name, age, and even gender. Go to www.cybertipline.com to learn more.

Cybertipline: www.cybertipline.com
Citizens Coalition for Economic Justice: www.ccej.or.kr

A Worm exploits the tsunami to spread a virus

A mass e-mail sent out in January 2005 posing as a plea for aid to help the victims of the December 26, 2004, Asian tsunami disaster was in fact a vehicle for spreading a computer virus. The worm appeared with the subject line: "Tsunami donation! Please help!" and invited recipients to open an attachment "tsunami.exe." If opened, this would then forward the virus to other Internet users. Another worm said the tsunami was God's revenge on "people who did bad on earth."

...ensure Internet safety

♪ **Be a responsible netizen.**

♪ **Sign the charter.** Do what you can to promote its principles.

♪ **Encourage others to do the same.**

MAY 16

HELPLINE *volunteers*

Helplines provide comfort and sometimes direct assistance to those in real need. Samaritans was started in 1953 by Chad Varah, a young London vicar. Chad had buried a 14-year-old girl who had taken her own life, having mistaken her periods for a sexually transmitted disease. He recognized the distress caused by having nobody to talk to about confidential issues and decided to take action. ♛ Chad organized a network of people who would be at the other end of a telephone and could be asked anything. Around 4.6 million calls are now received each year by Samaritans.

The idea of telephone helplines has now spread around the world. The Befrienders International network, now run by Samaritans, is a network for suicide lines, and Child Helpline International is for children's helplines. The use of the Internet, cellphones, and broadcast television are all being explored as additional mechanisms for providing advice.

Some hotlines and helplines in the US

Al-Anon/Alateen (alcoholism): 1-888-4-AL-ANON
The Alcohol Hotline (alcohol and drugs): 1-800-ALCOHOL
Childhelp USA (child abuse): 1-800-4-A-CHILD
CyberTipline (reporting child pornography): 1-800-843-5678
Gay and Lesbian National Hotline: 1-888-THE-GLNH
National AIDS Hotline (AIDS/HIV): 1-800-342-AIDS
National Center for Missing and Exploited Children: 1-800-THE-LOST
National Herpes Hotline: 919-361-8488
National Domestic Violence Hotline: 1-800-799-SAFE
National Hopeline Network (suicide): 1-800-SUICIDE
National Sexual Assault Hotline: 1-800-656-HOPE
National Runaway Switchboard (missing children): 1-800-RUNAWAY
National STD Hotline (sexually transmitted diseases): 1-800-227-8922
National Suicide Prevention Lifeline: 1-800-273-TALK
NineLine (crisis intervention for youth and parents): 1-800-999-9999
Poison Help (poison emergencies): 1-800-222-1222
Victims of Crime Help Line: 1-800-FYI-CALL

Child Helpline International: www.childhelplineinternational.org

E-mail received by the Muslim Youth Helpline:

hi my name is youssef and i am a heroin addict and i need some help, i chase about 0.5 of a gram a day. if u can help me phone me on this number. A.S.A.P. cos am suffering every min of every hour of every day. salamo alaikum.

Muslim Youth Helpline was set up by 17-year-old Mohammed Mamdani in 2001. Young Muslims contact the helpline by phone or e-mail. www.myh.org.uk

...it's good to talk

Volunteer on a telephone helpline. Whether it is physical abuse or mental distress, the fear of dying or the problems of living, dealing with a crisis or just giving advice, there is a helpline that needs you to talk to people in distress.

naked BIKE RIDERS

When I see a person on a bicycle, it gives me hope for the human race.

—H. G. Wells

There are so many reasons to cycle rather than drive: You save a lot of gas. You aren't giving your hard-earned cash to an evil oil company. Biking produces no harmful emissions. You will get a healthy heart and body, not to mention great legs. You can't get stopped for driving under the influence. You can laugh and make faces at all the poor fools stuck in traffic as you sail past them. Your maintenance costs are close to zero. ♣ The bottom line is that cycling benefits both you and the earth.

See how many more calories you burn when you cycle:

Activities	Number of minutes	Calories burned
Cycling (15 mph)	30	360
Walking	30	144
Watching TV	30	32
Driving	30	71
Sex (vigorous)	30	53
Kissing	30	36
Sleeping	30	27

World Naked Bike Ride: www.worldnakedbikeride.org

The World Naked Bike Ride is an annual global event. People ride as naked as they dare around town to protest against oil dependency and celebrate the power of the human body.

Every group has its own approach to cycling naked. Some focus on body painting. Some participate within the context of ancient cultural celebrations. Some use the day to promote cycling and a cleaner environment. Some use their body to call attention to political issues. Some ride at night. Some during the day. Some skip the bicycles altogether and rollerskate or skateboard.

...go as bare as you dare

Take part in your nearest World Naked Bike Ride.

♣ **Date:** Early June. Check the website for the exact date.

♣ **Dress code:** As bare as you dare.

♣ **What to do:** Sign up at the World Naked Bike Ride website, then tell your friends to tell their friends that it's time to take off their clothes and hop on their bikes!

MAY 18

GOOGLE *bombing*

A Google bomb is an attempt to get a site ranked first when people search for it on Google. This is quite easy if you understand the way the Google search engine works. The key factors are the number of links and the use of particular words or phrases on many linked webpages.

The first Google bomb to get publicity was in 1999. Typing in the words "More evil than Satan" led to the Microsoft Home Page. Such was the interest in this phenomenon that now typing in this phrase gets you to several articles on the discovery of Google bombing.

Google bombs come and go. Many get too well known, and mentions in popular web journals gets these journals to the top spot. Google bombing can be used to get your organization or issue to the top of the search results, which should be an important goal for your PR.

Try Google bombing at www.google.com

These Weapons of Mass Destruction cannot be displayed

In 2004, by typing in "Weapons of Mass Destruction" and clicking I'm feeling lucky, you got to www.coxar.pwp.blueyonder.co.uk. This came up on your screen:

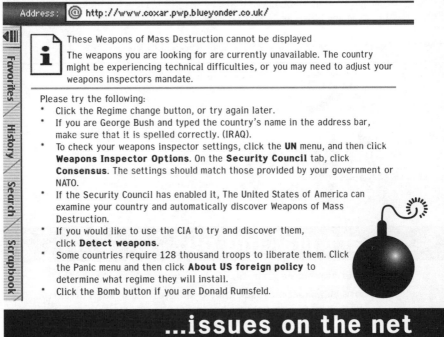

Address: @ http://www.coxar.pwp.blueyonder.co.uk/

These Weapons of Mass Destruction cannot be displayed

The weapons you are looking for are currently unavailable. The country might be experiencing technical difficulties, or you may need to adjust your weapons inspectors mandate.

Please try the following:
* Click the Regime change button, or try again later.
* If you are George Bush and typed the country's name in the address bar, make sure that it is spelled correctly. (IRAQ).
* To check your weapons inspector settings, click the **UN** menu, and then click **Weapons Inspector Options**. On the **Security Council** tab, click **Consensus**. The settings should match those provided by your government or NATO.
* If the Security Council has enabled it, The United States of America can examine your country and automatically discover Weapons of Mass Destruction.
* If you would like to use the CIA to try and discover them, click **Detect weapons**.
* Some countries require 128 thousand troops to liberate them. Click the Panic menu and then click **About US foreign policy** to determine what regime they will install.
* Click the Bomb button if you are Donald Rumsfeld.

...issues on the net

Google bombing will get your message out.

Try typing in a slogan, and see what comes up. For example:

👫 **End Third World Debt** gets you to an article on third world debt on the Socialist Workers Party website.

👫 **Education, Education, Education** gets you to the UNESCO website.

👫 **Make Love Not War** gets you to political posters from the Sixties Project.

promote veggie SEX

Try a veggie burger in the kitchen for a whopper in the bedroom! What could be more of a turn-on than snuggling up to someone who's both passionate and compassionate.

—Bruce Friedrich, director of vegan campaigns,
People for the Ethical Treatment of Animals (PETA)

In August 2004, PETA launched its Make Out Live campaign. On a popular Los Angeles corner, a couple made out all afternoon on a bed in plain view of everyone who walked by. They wanted to raise awareness for vegetarianism by proving their claim that "vegetarians make better lovers." Supporters held a banner next to the bed and handed out free vegetarian starter kits to passers-by. It's debatable how many people converted to vegetarianism, but they certainly got a lot of attention for the cause!

Do vegetarians have an advantage in the bedroom? Yes. They are likely to be more fit and have more stamina than people who stuff themselves with fat-laden meat, dairy products, and eggs. They don't have to rely on chemical potions like Viagra to be up for any task: the cholesterol in meat and other animal products causes hardening of the arteries, slowing the flow of blood to all the body's vital organs, not just the heart. 🚶 And there's nothing sexy about someone who turns a blind eye to the daily suffering of the billions of animals who are raised and killed for food each year.

Read about the case for vegetarianism at www.peta.org.

PETA was founded in 1980, and now has more than 800,000 members. It subscribes to the basic principle that animals are not ours to eat, wear, experiment on, or use for entertainment. It campaigns on factory farming, laboratory use of animals, the fur trade, and the use of animals in the entertainment industry.

...start making out

Instead of organizing a sit-in, stage a make-out:

🚶 **Choose an important issue that is not getting enough attention.** Get together some friends. Set up a bed in a very public place. Have a couple make out like mad while volunteers hold up signs and hand out leaflets to people gawking as they walk by. If you want to make it really spicy, get a dozen couples to make out at the same time.

🚶 **Ask people to sign a petition.** Suggest a simple action they can take.

🚶 **Don't get too carried away.** The police will arrest you if your spectacle turns hard-core. You will find yourself in the news but for the wrong reason.

SPEAK to a *Thai farmer*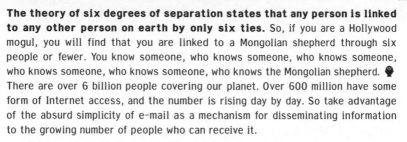

The theory of six degrees of separation states that any person is linked to any other person on earth by only six ties. So, if you are a Hollywood mogul, you will find that you are linked to a Mongolian shepherd through six people or fewer. You know someone, who knows someone, who knows someone, who knows someone, who knows someone, who knows the Mongolian shepherd. ♣ There are over 6 billion people covering our planet. Over 600 million have some form of Internet access, and the number is rising day by day. So take advantage of the absurd simplicity of e-mail as a mechanism for disseminating information to the growing number of people who can receive it.

If you can reach hundreds of people, and they can reach hundreds of people, and they can reach hundreds of people, and they can reach hundreds of people, and they can reach hundreds of people, and they can reach hundreds of people (that's six degrees of separation), then your message can speak to a Mongolian shepherd, or a Thai chicken farmer, or the president of a country.

Change can start with a simple message. This is like planting a seed. Put forward an idea and give one or two key facts and figures, and it could get people thinking about the world in a slightly different way. Changing people's attitudes is a first step in creating change.

End Hate has a message to get your neurons moving: www.endhate.org

Ending hate with e-mail

What if we all decided, starting right now, that the color of our skins didn't matter?

—or religion?
—or nationality?
—or ideology?

What if we stopped being afraid? Think about it for a minute. Maybe it wouldn't be that hard to live in peace. Maybe it's just that simple.

It's estimated that there are 605,000,000 people on earth with Internet access. If 100,000,000 see this message, can they make a difference? Forward this. Maybe it's just that simple. Maybe—its—that—simple@endhate.org

...spread the word by e-mail

♣ **Compose a clear, simple message that promotes positive change.** It can be about racism, sexism, war, peace, sex, inclusion—whatever inspires or infuriates you.

♣ **Create a simple weblink for people to access the message.** Or just put it in an e-mail.

♣ **Forward this to everyone you know,** everyone in your address book. And ask them to forward it to everyone they know. Your message could reach the four corners of the globe in a single day. Who knows what its impact will be?

save endangered SPECIES

Some animals and plants are so sought-after that they are at risk of extinction. The World Wildlife Federation (WWF) compiles an annual Top Ten most wanted list of species threatened by unsustainable trade and consumer demand. For 2004, these were:

Humphead wrasse: a bulbous-headed, coral-reef fish caught and displayed live in tanks for diners in East Asian restaurants.

Ramin: a tropical hardwood grown largely in peat swamp forests in Indonesia and Malaysia, used for mass-produced moldings, doors, and picture frames.

Tigers: Over the last 100 years, tiger numbers have been reduced by 95%— with perhaps fewer than 5,000 tigers left in the wild. They are poached for their skins, and for bone used in traditional Chinese medicines.

Great white sharks: The largest of the predatory sharks, they are poached for their jaws, teeth, and fins, which are in demand worldwide.

Irrawaddy dolphins: These are entangled in fishing nets and injured by explosives used for dynamite fishing. They are also in demand for display in zoos and aquaria.

Asian elephants: They are poached for ivory and meat in many Asian countries. There are now only 35,000–50,000 Asian elephants in the wild, with an additional 15,000 in captivity.

Pig-nosed turtles: a giant freshwater turtle with a protruding snout, found in Papua New Guinea, northern Australia, and Indonesia, in demand by the international pet trade. Nests are robbed of eggs, which are either eaten or sold.

Yellow-crested cockatoos: Fewer than 10,000 of these exotic-looking birds remain. They are in high demand by the international pet trade.

Leaf-tailed geckos: These lizards found in Madagascar, with their barklike appearance, are also in high demand by the international pet trade.

Trade in these species needs to be regulated and well managed. Don't even think of getting a pig-nosed turtle or a yellow-crested cockatoo as a pet.

International office of WWF: www.panda.org
US office of WWF: www.worldwildlife.org

Save our trees: Over 8,000 tree species, 10% of the world's total, are threatened with extinction. These include the monkey puzzle tree, the Nubian dragon tree and the Clanwilliam cedar. Find out about these and other threatened trees at Global Trees Campaign: www.globaltrees.org.

...greed leads to extinction

Campaign for wildlife conservation from your desktop.

🐼 **Get a Panda Passport from www.panda.org.** You will be asked to post letters or send e-mails, petitions, or faxes to decision makers.

🐼 **You may be asked to make a personal commitment,** such as buying wood products made only from FSC-certified wood or switching to renewable energy.

SUSTAINABLE *development*

"Sustainable development" is jargon commonly used by development experts. But what does it really mean? The most widely used definition appeared in the 1987 Brundtland Report *Our Common Future*, which was endorsed at the 1992 Earth Summit in Rio: "Development that meets the needs of the present without compromising the ability of future generations to meet their own needs."

Visit the UN's Division for Sustainable Development at www.un.org/esa/sustdev/index.html.

There are five types of "capital" we can exploit for society's benefit. We need to nurture all of them and ensure that they are used prudently and effectively:

Natural capital is the basis of life on earth. It includes renewable and nonrenewable resources.

Human capital consists of people's health, their well-being, their knowledge and skills, their creativity, and their motivation to actively make things better. Education, training, and sharing of ideas all help build human capital.

Social capital consists of those institutions that enable people to work together in common cause, including families, communities, businesses, trade unions, schools, and voluntary organizations.

Manufactured capital includes tools, machines, and buildings, which are all needed for production. Invention and advances in technology extend the impact of manufactured capital.

Financial capital is the money needed to make things happen, including investment funds, grants, loans, and microcredit.

...nurturing the future

Enhance your own human capital.

👫 **Think about the skills you lack and the training you need.** These might include creative thinking, project planning, financial planning and budgeting, communication and media, IT, fund raising, public speaking, leadership and assertiveness, teamworking; it's a long list. Most of these skills can be learned on the job, but there are also good training courses that will meet your needs.

👫 **Learn from other people.** Whom can you talk to? What projects could you visit?

👫 **List the things you might do to enhance your own human capital.** Select five things that you will do over the coming year. Make sure you do all of them.

23 MAY

try VEGETARIANISM

Producing meat requires a huge amount of resources compared to growing fruit, vegetables, and grains. This is a fact that nobody can refute. Whether you give a damn about animal cruelty or not, you cannot deny the enormous drain that meat eating has on the world's limited supply of fertile land and water.

Here are a few facts:

Twenty vegetarians can live off the same amount of land that one meat eater would require.

If Americans reduced their meat consumption by 10%, it would free 13 million tons of grain—enough to feed 60 million people (the population of the UK).

An average $2^1/_2$ acre field will yield 412 lbs. of beef or 50,000 lbs. of potatoes.

It takes 30 gallons of water to produce 1 pound of wheat, and 3,000 gallons to produce 1 pound of meat.

The water used to produce 11 lbs. of steak is equivalent to the average consumption of water for an entire household for an entire year.

Cows breaking wind and belching are estimated account for 35% of Ireland's greenhouse gas emissions, thereby being a major cause of global warming.

Here are some good websites for vegetarian recipes. There are lots of others.
VegWeb: www.vegweb.com
Nava Atlas's Vegetarian Kitchen: www.vegkitchen.com
The Vegetarian Resource Group: www.vrg.org

An incredible double green hummus
For this recipe, you need:
  1 bunch fresh coriander
  1 bunch fresh dill
  Juice from half a lemon
  4 garlic cloves (more or less to your taste)
  Half cup of tahini

2 cans chick peas
Quarter teaspoon chili powder
1 teaspoon salt

Using a blender, blend everything together except the chick peas. Add the chick peas and blend until smooth. Adjust the amounts to taste. This hummus is great on sandwiches with tomato or cucumber or onion slices.

—contributed to the VegWeb site by
Elizabeth Rosegunn

...to save resources

Commit to eating a vegetables-only dinner once a week. This is a start. It will be even more effective and much more fun if you do it with all your family.

Not only will you be doing your bit for the environment, you will be opening up your taste buds to a whole new range of foods and flavors. If you still hanker after meat, there are excellent meat substitutes available.

MAY 24

GOAT *revolving*

Giving poor families an animal is a good starting point for helping them out of poverty. It used to be cows, but now it's other animals as well. Very poor people, with little land and few resources, sometimes find it difficult to manage a dairy cow.

Send a Cow has launched a new program called StockAid. This scheme provides the poorest of the poor with smaller stock, such as goats, pigs, or poultry. They are thus able to begin rearing livestock even where they are unable to provide the shelter or fodder needed for a cow. This is particularly helpful to families suffering the impact of drought, AIDS, and conflict.

Send a Cow: www.sendacow.org.uk
Christian Aid: www.christianaid.org
Goats for Peace: www.goodgifts.org
Heifer International: www.heifer.org

Christian Aid runs a revolving goat scheme. Here's how the scheme works:

Step 1. Goats are given to a goat bank.
Step 2. The goat bank lends a female goat to a family, possibly a widow and her children.
Step 3. The goat grazes on scrub land or eats up waste, and produces milk.
Step 4. The children have nutritious milk to drink, and any surplus is sold.
Step 5. The goat produces manure. If the widow has a plot of land, this fertilizes the soil and the crop yield goes up. This represents more to eat or more money for the family.
Step 6. The goat gets pregnant and produces more goats.
Step 7. One female is returned to the goat bank to pay off the loan, and the widow keeps the others.
Step 8. A goat is lent to another widow, and so the process of getting families out of poverty will go on.

It takes £60 for Christian Aid to provide four goats for a goat bank in Bolivia or Burundi, and £25 for Send a Cow to send a goat.

Goats for Peace is a scheme run by the Good Gifts Catalogue, which gives goats to widows and families in several countries, including to genocide survivors in Rwanda. £15 pays for one goat.

...help a family out of poverty

Buy a goat for a family, and help the family take a first step toward self-sufficiency.

You won't have to go to the pet shop to buy it. You won't have to gift-wrap it; you won't need to feed it. You won't have to clean up its mess. You just provide the money, and someone else does what's necessary. Your bright new goat will be delivered to its proud new owner.

Provide a hand up to someone who needs it. You won't even notice the $120 it costs.

25 MAY

start your own AID AGENCY

Many people go it alone and choose to run their own aid agencies. Often they are just ordinary people, motivated by what they see abroad. This may not be a perfect way of getting aid to the neediest, but it is direct, it involves no highly paid professionals with Land Cruisers and professional jargon, and it is done with a good heart.

The first step is to find out about local problems and needs. As an outsider it isn't always easy to know who or what to support. Ask around. Talk to a teacher or the village head. Work through existing community institutions.

> **Support** obvious immediate need: medicines for eye and ear infections can save sight or hearing.
>
> **Set up** a hardship fund for distributing small grants to those in need after you've gone.
>
> **Support** people with no source of income, such as widows.
>
> **Help** build facilities of obvious community benefit, such as a classroom, toilets, or village well.
>
> **Use** your support to add to the energies and efforts of local people.

100 Friends Project: www.100friends.com

I am Marc Gold. I started the 100 Friends project in 1989. The idea is simple. Every year about 100 people contribute to the project, and I take the money to Third World Countries and look for the neediest people I can find. I then put the money to work in the most compassionate, appropriate, culturally compatible, constructive, and practical manner possible. I pay for my own travel expenses.

The project began when I visited India for the first time. I met a Tibetan woman in the Himalayas who had a terrible ear infection. I was able to save her life with antibiotics that cost about a dollar. For another $30

I purchased a hearing aid that restored her hearing. I was shocked to see that something so important could be accomplished with so little.

Over 15 years Marc has made nine trips: to India, Thailand, Cambodia, Tibet, Nepal, Vietnam, Afghanistan, Bangladesh, South Africa, Mozambique, and Turkey. He now collects and distributes $18,000 a year. Marc says. "Ultimately you have to ask yourself: Is it better to sit around doing nothing, or to do something, however imperfect?"

...and travel helpfully

Resolve to make a difference by

🌐 **Becoming one of Marc Gold's 100 Friends.**

🌐 **Doing it yourself.** Change the world while traveling.

MAY 26

CANCER *survivors*

The Big C can strike anyone anywhere. One in three people will be diagnosed with cancer during their lifetime. Cancer is the second most likely cause of death, coming a close second after heart failure. The main types of cancer are bladder, breast, cervical, colonic and rectal, endometrial (lining of the uterus), esophageal (throat), kidney, leukemia, lung, lymphatic (Hodgkin's disease and other lymphomas), melanoma (skin), multiple myeloma (bone marrow), oral (mouth cavity), ovarian, prostate, testicular, and uterine.

Over the last 50 years, deaths from cancer have not been reduced. But death from heart disease has halved. ☺ For men the most common cancers are lung, prostate, and colo-rectal; for women, lung, breast, and colo-rectal. Together these account for more than half the incidence of cancer. ☺ The overall survival rate for all cancers is 63%. The highest levels of survival are prostate (98%), melanoma (90%), breast (87%), and urinary tract (82%).

The Live Strong website: www.livestrong.org
Find out more about cancer from CancerFacts: www.cancerfacts.com

Lance Armstrong's story

Lance was 25 when diagnosed with testicular cancer. This is treatable if detected early. But Lance ignored the warning signs, and the cancer spread to his abdomen, lungs, and brain. Once diagnosed, Lance immediately declared himself a cancer survivor rather than a victim, and was determined to live, not die. He underwent two surgeries (one to remove a cancerous testicle and the other to remove two cancerous lesions on the brain) plus four chemotherapies.

Lance survived the treatment, and went on to become the most successful cyclist ever, winning the Tour de France a record seven times in a row from 1999 to 2005.

...live strong with Lance

☺ **Wear yellow and live strong** to salute a cycling legend and support his efforts to promote cancer survival. Nike launched the Wear Yellow campaign to support the Lance Armstrong Foundation. Nike donated $1 million and is helping raise an additional $5 million through the sale of yellow wristbands with the words "Live Strong."

☺ **Buy a wristband.** They can be purchased for $1 each in quantities of 10, 100, or 1,200 from the foundation's website. These wristbands created a trend for wristbands for other causes in other colors.

☺ **Keep healthy.** Stop smoking, eat five portions of fruit and vegetables daily, live healthy, and go for cancer screening as recommended by your doctor.

fight BIO-PIRACY

Bio-pirates exploit patent and trademark laws for profit. Patents and trademarks exist to protect tangible property, such as inventions or brands. But in some cases they are used to make amoral proprietary claims. Examples include ripping off indigenous knowledge, monopolizing genes, patenting plants, or even trademarking a patron saint.

Examples of bio-piracy include the following Captain Hook Awards:

🌐 **The greediest:** Genetic Technologies (Australia) patented noncoded DNA (known as 'junk DNA') of all living creatures, including humans. This DNA was believed to be unimportant biologically, but scientists have now realized that junk DNA plays a crucial role in switching particular genes on and off.

🌐 **The worst corporate offender:** Monsanto holds a European patent on a soft-milling, low-gluten wheat that is derived from a traditional Indian wheat variety. Monsanto's patent covers not only the low-gluten wheat plant, but also the flour, dough, and edible products (cookies, cakes) produced from it!

🌐 **The worst nano-pirate:** Mr. Yang Mengjun (China), secured 466 patents on nanoscale versions of traditional Chinese medicinal herbs by turning the plants into fine powders and claiming a new invention with increased solubility and bio-availability. Yang has patents on barks, roots, fruit, and leaves that have been used in Chinese medicine since ancient times. Nano-piracy is a new way to monopolize traditional knowledge.

Nominate someone for a Captain Hook Award for bio-piracy: www.captainhookawards.org

RiceTec

By patenting similar or superior basmati grains outside India, RiceTec has ended India's ownership of the basmati brand. Basmati rice is no longer a product unique to the specific climate and soil conditions of the Himalayan foothills (unlike sherry, which can only be made in Spain, or scotch whisky, which can only come from Scotland).

Today, the world is on the brink of a biological diversity crisis. We here in India are working towards increasing awareness of the importance of conserving our valuable genetic heritage, while challenging and opposing the forces responsible for its rapid erosion and usurpation. Join us in the struggle and research for sustainability and justice in these turbulent and uncertain times.

—Vandava Shiva

Vandana Shiva has been fighting the theft of indigenous knowledge by multinational companies and has run a vocal campaign against RiceTec for securing US patents on basmati rice, which is a major contributor to the Indian economy. www.navdanya.org

...for the real owners

Bring the bio-pirates to justice. Shower RiceTec with rice.

Buy basmati rice from India. Write to John Nelsen, CEO, RiceTec, Inc., P.O. Box 1305, Alvin, TX 77512, enclose some rice, and ask him to hand back the basmati brand to its indigenous owners.

MAY 28

PEACEMAKERS *are stars*

The Nobel Peace Prize has been running since 1901, when Henry Dunant, the founder of the Red Cross, shared the prize with Frédéric Passy, a leading international pacifist. The prize honors individuals and organizations for the exceptional contributions they have made to peace and justice.

There is now an'alternative Nobel Peace Prize, known as the Right Livelihood Award. This award was established in 1980. The idea of "right livelihood" is an ancient one. It embodies the principle that each person should follow an honest occupation which fully respects other people and the natural world. It means being responsible for the consequences of our actions and taking only a fair share of the earth's resources. The prize honors individuals and organizations who uphold these ideals.

These people should be the stars in our human cosmos. But their work often entails huge personal sacrifice and being opposed or persecuted by powerful forces around them. The Right Livelihood Award now has over 100 laureates from 48 countries.

For Nobel Peace Prize Winners, go to nobelprize.org/peace.
The Nobel Peace Prize has developed an online museum. Go to www.nobelpeacecenter.org.

For Right Livelihood Winners, go to www.rightlivelihood.se.

Nobel Winners in recent years have included:

2003: **Shirin Ebadi**, an Iranian human rights activist.

2002: **Jimmy Carte**r, who since relinquishing the US presidency has devoted himself to peace and conflict resolution through the Carter Institute.

1999: **Médecins sans Frontières**, for their medical work in areas of conflict.

1998: **John Hume** (with David Trimble), who was the architect of the peace process in Northern Ireland.

1997: **The International Campaign to Ban Landmines.**

1996: **Carlos Belo** and **Jose Ramos-Horta,** for their efforts to bring a peaceful conclusion to the conflict in East Timor.

1995: **Joseph Rotblat** and the **Pugwash Conference** for their efforts to ban nuclear weapons.

Right Livelihood Award Winners in 2003 and 2004 included:

Walden Bello and **Nicanor Perlas** (Philippines), for their outstanding efforts in educating civil society about the effects of corporate globalization and how alternatives can be implemented.

The Citizens' Coalition for Economic Justice (South Korea), for its efforts to bring social justice and accountability to South Korea, and for promoting reconciliation with North Korea.

Bianca Jagger (Nicaragua), for her human rights campaigning.

Memorial (Russia), for prompting civil society and revealing the truth about the past.

...know their work

Find out about these and other award winners.

Be inspired by them. Learn from what they have done.

imagine PEACE

John Lennon imagined peace in his song "Imagine." Those who died fighting for the US through many wars were probably also imagining peace but did not live to see it. Memorial Day celebrates their sacrifice. ☺ Imagine peace. Think about what peace means to you.

Here are some ideas to reflect on:

If soldiers fought for peace instead of going to war, what would they be doing?

If all guns were replaced with flowers, what would the world look like?

How can we get rid of hate and violence in the world? In your neighborhood?

Listen to the song "Imagine" by John Lennon. Make a drawing of what you imagined.

What animal represents peace? What animal represents violence? Why are they different? How are they similar?

If peace grew from a tree, what would it look like?

What ingredients would you use to make a "peace meal"? Write a recipe for this.

If peace could be embodied in a person, who would that person be?

Read the full text of "Imagine" at
www.merseyworld.com/imagine/lyrics/imagine.htm.

Art for peace

Young people can teach us a lot. As future adults and even future leaders of the world, they have important visions of the future and ideas for dealing with the world's problems.

Enabling young people to express their ideas for peace through art is a step toward making peace a reality. It can inspire young people to share their dreams, and even to take action for a better world.

Focusing on peace creates optimism. Focusing on the terrorist threat only makes us more afraid.

...a world without war

Organize a local art show on the theme of peace. Why not do it to commemorate those who died in a conflict or a violent event that has touched your community?

❀ **Contact** schoolteachers and afterschool program organizers.

❀ **Find a venue** to exhibit the work—ideally, a centrally located space such as a library, grocery store, shopping mall, or town hall.

❀ **Have an official opening.** Ask the young artists to bring their family and friends to admire the show.

❀ **Get a sponsor** and offer prizes for everyone.

The young people can express their views in a variety of media (drawing, painting, sculpture, an installation, a happening). Ask the young artists to use their imagination. It is important to remove the idea of competitiveness from the event, as the purpose is to promote peace and cooperation, which means respecting everyone's views and ideas.

TOBACCO *sucks*

Two giant corporations dominate the world cigarette market. They are Philip Morris (owned by Altria) and British American Tobacco (BAT). ☺ They stand accused of promoting a product that is addictive and injurious to health, and of doing little to discourage underage smoking (which may create a lifetime addict). ☺ Passive smokers (those who breathe in smoke-polluted air) are also at risk, as are fetuses if the mother-to-be is a smoker.

Public attitudes are changing fast. Banning smoking on public transport (including airlines) and in public places (such as restaurants and bars) and having smoking restricted to designated areas at the workplace are all becoming much more common. ☺ Tobacco advertising has now been banned throughout the European Union, including motor racing sponsorship.

Smoking has more than 50 ways of making you ill and more than 20 ways of killing you. In general, smokers endure poorer health than nonsmokers. An estimated 8.6 million people in the US have at least one serious illness caused by smoking. ☺ Half the teenagers who smoke will die from diseases caused by tobacco if they continue to smoke; those dying before 70 will lose an average 21 years of life. Between 1950 and 2000, 60 million people worldwide died from tobacco-related diseases.

American Lung Association: www.lungusa.org
Big Tobacco Sucks, the California campaign against the tobacco industry: www.bigtobaccosucks.org

Passive smoking

Increases the risk of heart disease to about one-quarter of that faced by an active smoker.
Increases the risk of lung cancer by 20 to 30%.
Aggravates asthma and other existing respiratory complaints.
Increases coughing, wheezing, and phlegm.

...reclaim clean air

Get a sensible smoking policy introduced at your workplace.

This will benefit smokers and nonsmokers alike, and productivity could even increase by as much as 3% in a clean-air environment.

A workplace smoking policy should state the following:
☺ The principles guiding the policy, such as the rights of nonsmokers and compliance with government legislation.
☺ Where and when smoking is permitted, and if there are designated smoking areas.
☺ What the arrangements are for visitors or members of the public.
☺ Any contractual obligations, such as time off allowed for smoking breaks.
☺ What support is available for smokers who wish to quit.
☺ What physical improvements are needed, such as improved ventilation.
☺ Procedures for reviewing the policy, ensuring compliance, and resolving disputes.

go UNSHOPPING

In a throwaway convenience world, we buy so many things we don't need: things that are often overpackaged and stuffed with poisons. The principle of *unshopping* involves *unlearning* all the bad habits of our consumer society, shopping more responsibly and thinking about the future of the planet.

Co-op America has come up with a list of ten things you should never buy.

Styrofoam cups: Polystyrene is forever: it's not biodegradable. Americans use enough styrofoam cups each year to circle the earth 436 times. *Don't be a mug. Use a mug.*

Paper towels: They waste forest resources and your money. *Use a dishcloth.*

Bleached coffee filters: The dioxins used in the bleaching contaminate groundwater and are linked to cancer. Find a better way of making coffee. *Use a cafetière.*

Overpackaged food: One-third of what we put in the rubbish bin is packaging. This is a complete waste of resources. *Buy in bulk; buy things with less packaging; take your own shopping bag with you.*

Hardwood products: Every year 27 million acres of tropical rainforests are being destroyed. *Use products made from sustainably harvested timber or salvaged wood.*

Chemical pesticides: They poison the soil and contaminate the groundwater. *Grow native plants and use organic pest-control techniques.*

Household cleaning fluids: Many of these release volatile organic compounds. *Buy biodegradable nontoxic cleaners and washing powders, or make your own with simple ingredients such as vinegar and soap.*

Higher octane gasoline than you need: The higher the octane, the more hazardous the pollutants. *Drive less, drive a smaller car, and use lower-octane fuel.*

Toys made with PVC: Chemicals used to make PVC are known carcinogens; dangerous additives are often used; and PVC is the least recycled plastic. *Use toys made from natural materials; tell manufacturers to stop using PVC.*

Plastic forks and spoons: They are not biodegradable. *Carry your own utensils and food containers.*

Co-op America: www.coopamerica.org
The Ecologist: www.theecologist.org

...10 things never to buy again

❦ **Make a commitment not to buy any of these items.** It's a start toward creating a better world. You'll find that once you get into the swing of things, you won't even notice the difference.

❦ **For more ideas, read the following books:**

50 Simple Things You Can Do to Save the Earth and *The Next Step: 50 More Things You Can Do to Save the Earth* by Earthworks Group.

Save Cash AND Save the Planet by Andrea Smith and Nicola Baird.

Go M-A-D: 365 Daily Ways to Save the Planet published by *The Ecologist*.

GREEN *funerals*

Funerals are environmentally unfriendly. Think of the wood used for the coffins, the land used for burial, the access roads on the site, and the embalming chemicals that can leach into the soil. ♣ Funerals are a $30 billion industry and the third-largest personal expense after a house and a car.

There is an alternative to using the funeral industry—a green burial in a field or in woodland. Natural burial grounds decompose very quickly; and then you're left with an area of regenerated flora not cluttered up with marble or granite memorial stones. ♣ Green burial grounds are often not consecrated, but priests can bless individual plots. Each grave can be marked with a shrub, tree, or even an electronic chip. Cardboard coffins with strap-down lids cost as little as $75; both they and their contents rot rapidly. ♣ In Connecticut, Indiana, Louisiana, Nebraska, and New York, the law requires the involvement of funeral directors. In other states, you can get a permit to handle the body yourself. Burials on private property are problematic in cities and require zoning approval in rural areas.

Along with a green burial, why not have an alternative funeral? Celebrate the life of the deceased, rather than mourn the passing. ♣ Find out what to do by reading the *Natural Death Handbook*, which is a mine of ideas and practical advice.

The *Natural Death Handbook* from the Natural Death Centre:
www.naturaldeath.org.uk
Final Passages, supporting home and family-directed funerals:
www.finalpassages.org

What about a bamboo coffin?

The SAWD partnership is a UK company producing bamboo eco-coffins in Hunan Province, China. The bamboo is grown and cut under license from the government. Pandas do not live nearby. The coffins are handwoven and then transported by sea Russian-doll-style (one inside another) so as to minimize transport costs. The coffin received a best coffin award from the Natural Death Centre. www.bamboocoffins.co.uk

...dying to save the world

Express a wish to have a Green Funeral. Suggest the idea to your parents.
The *Natural Death Centre* has information and inspiring ideas.

let them eat CAKE

Hunger exists all over the world. The United States is the world's second-wealthiest nation, yet 12% of the population lives below the poverty line, and the numbers are rising every year.

Right now, there are 13 million American kids living in households where people have to skip meals or eat less to make ends meet. That means 10% of households in the US are living with hunger or are at risk of hunger.

Research indicates that children who are undernourished may suffer long-term damage in both their physical growth and their brain development. Not only are these kids suffering today, but the stunting of their growth and brain development will hinder their ability to improve their lives in the future.

www.hungerday.org

A hunger-free world

More than 800 million people in the world go hungry. But we have the means to end hunger. The costs are not big. The United Nations estimates that the basic health and nutrition needs of the world's poorest people could be met for an additional $13 billion a year. Animal lovers in the US and Europe spend more than this on pet food. What sort of world is it where there is enough food to feed the world, yet people are still going hungry? Bread for the World is an international campaign to end hunger: www.bread.org

One woman's campaign

Carmel McConnell is a woman in a hurry. For one in four children in England, the school meal is the only hot meal they are getting. And many children arrive at school in the morning too hungry to learn. Magic Breakfast provides enriched bagels and cereal to children. Carmel wants to make sure that every child starts the school day properly fed. She wants to see this happen within two years. www.magicbreakfast.com

...feed the hungry

Hold an old-fashioned bake sale to support National Hunger Awareness Day.

Recruit your friends, colleagues, the family dog, anyone and everyone, and have them bake something tasty.

Set up a table in your office, in school, or on the street and sell the baked goods. Make sure you clearly mark your table so that people know that their money is going to alleviate hunger.

☺ **The Great American Bake Sale,** for instructions on how to hold the bake sale and where to donate your money after you rake in the dough: www.greatamericanbakesale.org

☺ **America's Second Harvest.** Every dollar you raise at your bake sale will help them bring 15 meals to the table. Now, that's efficient spending! www.secondharvest.org.

CHILD *prostitution must end*

In every continent, and in developed and developing countries alike, poverty, lack of education, and parental pressure are forcing children into the sex industry. Some are sent by their families into what they believe is domestic service, but the children are then kidnapped, trafficked across borders, and forced to work as sex slaves.

Commercial sexual exploitation of girls and boys exists in three main forms:

Prostitution (which includes child sex tourism)

Pornography

Trafficking for sexual purposes

Commercial sexual exploitation of children is a multibillion-dollar industry. Over 1 million children worldwide are involved. Most are aged between 13 and 18, although some are as young as five. In Vietnam, 30% of the 185,000 prostitutes are under 16. ➤ A large proportion of child prostitutes catch sexually transmitted diseases; 70% of child prostitutes in Thailand are HIV positive, and many girls have abortions. Most children suffer serious psychological problems.

Article 34 of the Convention on the Rights of the Child requires countries to act to prevent the inducement or coercion of a child to engage in unlawful sexual activity, and to prevent the exploitative use of children in prostitution, pornography, or other unlawful sexual activities. Article 35 requires countries to act to prevent the abduction of, sale of, or traffic in children for any purpose or in any form. Despite these measures, child prostitution persists.

Child prostitution, like child slavery, should simply not be tolerated. It is a gross abuse of the human rights of those who are least able to do anything. Whoever you are and whatever you do, you must do something about it.

End Child Prostitution, Child Pornography, and Trafficking of Children for Sexual Purposes (ECPAT): www.ecpat.net

Anti-Slavery Society: www.antislavery.org

The Hearth

Many Albanian girls are being trafficked across the Adriatic to Italy, where they are forced into prostitution. In 1997, Vera Lesko founded the Hearth of Vlora Women to try to put an end to this abuse, and to deal with related problems of drug abuse and child abuse in the family. The Hearth raises awareness of the problem, and it provides counseling and medical and legal assistance. The Hearth opened the first shelter in Albania in 2001 for trafficked women and girls. it provides secure accommodation and an opportunity for the young women to find a way out of trafficking and rebuild their lives.

...imagine it were your child

Raise public awareness. Use the Internet to do some research. Then write, design, and print a simple leaflet, which could include facts and figures, case studies if you can find them, and a call to action. Print off 100 copies of this leaflet, and hand them out in the street or put them through people's mailboxes.

help the ENVIRONMENT

When it comes to saving the environment, every bit helps. Even turning the tap off when you brush your teeth or putting a bird house in your garden is a worthwhile contribution.

World Environment Day www.unep.org/wed

Visit the New Dream Foundation to see the impact of your actions: www.newdream.org/tttoffline

A few of the ideas:

Clean air

Drive intelligently: accelerate gradually, obey speed limits, combine several errands in one trip.

Limit how long your car engine runs when you stop.

Use a car with a three-way catalytic converter.

Wildlife

Put out a bird feeder or nesting box.

Build a pond in your garden.

Take part in a local tree planting.

Buy products made from sustainably produced wood.

Water

Take showers instead of baths.

Limit use of garden sprinklers or hoses.

Collect rainwater to water your plants.

Put a bag of water in your lavatory cistern to reduce the water flushed.

Turn off the tap when brushing your teeth.

Use full loads in your dishwasher and washing machine.

Repair dripping taps and turn off taps properly.

Use environmentally friendly cleaning products.

Energy use

Buy local produce or grow your own.

Fly less frequently.

Use thermostats that switch off the heating when you're out.

Insulate your home.

Use a fan instead of air conditioning.

Turn off appliances and lights when not needed.

Use energy-efficient lightbulbs.

Heat small meals in a microwave.

Insulate your hot water tank properly.

Dry your clothes on a clothesline.

Waste

Use a doorstep recycling scheme.

Choose products with recyclable packaging.

Make compost.

Reuse plastic shopping bags or use cloth bags.

Use rechargeable batteries.

Print and photocopy on both sides of paper.

Reuse envelopes.

Find people to use the things you no longer want.

Use a cloth hankie.

Use the front of greeting cards to create postcards or gift tags.

Cook fresh food, which has less packaging.

Drink tap or filtered water, not bottled.

...60 ways to save the world

Pledge to do at least 10 of these—20 if you want to be a superhero—and tick them off as you go.

CREATE *a lifeline*

A man pulled a gun on his girlfriend and threatened to kill her if she left him. Fearing for her life, the woman fled with her two young children. They ran to a nearby strip mall to try to find a safe place to hide until she could locate a safe place to stay for the night. She called the Domestic Violence Hotline from a restaurant, while watching her abuser search for her in every store. She was rescued and taken to a local shelter.

Domestic violence is a largely hidden but serious problem all over the world. In the US, the National Domestic Violence Hotline has found that

❧ While women are *less likely* than men to be victims of violent crime overall, women are 5 to 8 times *more likely* than men to be victimized by their partner.

❧ Some 31% of women report being physically or sexually abused by a husband or boyfriend at some point in their lives.

❧ Most domestic violence occurs within a current or former relationship; 76% of women who reported being raped and/or physically assaulted since the age of 18 were victimized by a current or former husband, a cohabitating partner, a date, or a boyfriend.

❧ A child's exposure to the father's abusing the mother is the strongest risk factor for transmitting violent behavior from one generation to the next. Studies show child abuse occurring in 30–60% of those family violence cases that involve families with children.

National Domestic Violence Hotline: www.ndvh.org
Call to Protect: www.wirelessfoundation.org/CalltoProtect/index.cfm

Donating phones to victims of violence

Call to Protect collects wireless phones for the benefit of victims of domestic violence. Some of the phones are sold, and the proceeds used to fund agencies fighting domestic violence. Others are refurbished and donated to victims of domestic violence and could be a lifeline if the victim is again threatened by her abuser.

Nasra Ismail, who was a student at George Washington University in Washington, DC, organized a campaign campaign with Call to Protect to build awareness of domestic violence and do something to help prevent it.

The students managed to collect over 100 phones, which were then sent to Call to Protect to be given out to women so that they would be able to call for assistance when faced with an emergency. If 100 or more phones are collected, Call to Protect will pay shipping and handling costs.

...prevent domestic violence

Help address the problem of domestic violence.

Organize a campaign at your school or office, or locally in your community. Collect used cellphones. You too could collect over 100 phones, which could make over 100 women feel more secure.

My name is Talana Shabera. I'm an Ethiopian. I'm fourteen years old. I was promised in marriage when I was three years old, betrothed at ten years old, and pregnant at twelve. After three days of labor I was carried on a stretcher to a hospital, where my baby died two hours later. The obstructed labor left me incontinent. I smell and I feel so ashamed.

Talana is suffering more than any women in the world should have to suffer. Her problem is fistula—a tearing of the soft tissue between the vagina and the bladder—which occurs during a lengthy and complicated childbirth. Over 9,000 women and girls in Ethiopia suffer this painful and undignified condition. But exact numbers are impossible to obtain, as women with fistula are often hidden away or abandoned.

As long as poverty continues, so will fistula. Many expectant mothers in Ethiopia, perhaps as many as 70%, live over two days' walk from the nearest hospital. They need access to obstetric care and a skilled attendant to be with them during the birth. ● While women in the West are having liposuctions, implants, and cosmetic surgery to hide the signs of ageing, perhaps as many as 2 million women in the developing world are having their bodies destroyed, simply as a result of the lottery of where they happen to have been born.

Safehands for Mothers: www.safehands.org

The Fistula Foundation, supporting the fistula hospital in Addis Ababa: www.fistulafoundation.org

Two feisty women

Dr. Catherine Hamlin decided to do something about fistula. Forty years ago, she set up the Fistula Hospital in Addis Ababa. This has become a world center of excellence. As well as trying to repair the damage in women with fistula, the hospital provides training for obstetricians and gynecologists from all over the world.

Nancy Durrell McKenna is a photographer who has taken some wonderful photographs of pregnancy. She has founded Safehands for Mothers to do something for mothers who don't have access to proper obstetric care. Safehands will produce and distribute training materials for health professionals.

...a hidden problem

● **Participate in the Fistula Hospital's Love-a-Sister program.** Help one woman obtain free, safe surgery to repair her devastating injuries of fistula and rebuild her life. A $450 contribution will pay for surgery and postoperative care. This is not much to repair a life. If you don't have the money, go out and raise it.

● **Celebrate your fund-raising success by** downloading some of Nancy's wonderful photos from the Safehands website. Frame them and hang them on your wall.

OCEAN *clean up*

June 8 is World Ocean Day, a chance each year to celebrate the world's oceans and their rich diversity of life, to highlight the problems and action being taken to promote a healthy and productive ocean, and to conserve marine resources for future generations.

Oceans cover 70% of the planet's surface. Everybody on the planet is affected by the oceans—from the Gulf Stream, which warms the European Atlantic seaboard, to the El Niño and La Niña temperature fluctuations, which create climate change in the southern Pacific, and the Indian monsoons, in which moist ocean air condenses to water the otherwise dry land.

But ocean environments around the world are under severe stress due to rising sea temperatures, overfishing, destruction of coral reefs, the impact of cruise ships, entangled animals, marine debris, pollution, mercury contamination, offshore drilling, unsustainable coastal development, and many other factors. The basic problem is humankind's greed and unconcern for what is a common resource.

International Coastal Cleanup: www.coastalcleanup.org
World Ocean Day: www.theoceanproject.org
The Ocean Conservancy: www.oceanconservancy.org

Endangered fish: The **stellar sea lion,** the largest sea lion in the world, is found in Alaska and the Aleutian Islands. Once numbering 300,000, they are now threatened by many factors including loss of food due to overfishing, entanglement, and pollution. They are in serious decline. **The manatee** was once mistaken for a mermaid by lonely sailors. Found mainly in Florida, only 3,500 survive. About 300 die each year, many run into by speedboaters. Get to know these beautiful marine mammals and other endangered species, including Beluga whales, bocaccio, bottlenose dolphins, Goliath groupers, gray whales, Hawaiian monk seals, lingcod, harbor porpoise, right whales, sawfish, sea otters, sea turtles, and sharks. They are all very special. They all have a right to life. Find out more about them and what you can do to help at the Ocean Conservancy website.

...take a day at the seaside

Clean up the beach.

The International Coastal Cleanup takes place in September each year. On a single day, 300,000 volunteers in 90 countries—from Argentina to Vietnam—help clean up over 11,000 miles of shoreline.

Cleanup Day is also about pollution prevention. Volunteers record the different types of marine debris, and analyzing the debris leads to a better understanding of the sources of pollution. Ocean Conservancy then uses this information to educate the public, business, and government officials about the problem. Understanding the problem is the key to finding long-lasting solutions.

Bangladesh needs BEES

Bees and honey played an important part in ancient civilizations. The founder of the kingdom of Sparta in ancient Greece took ideas from bee colonies, especially regarding discipline, organization, and administration. 🐝 Modern beekeeping in the Indian subcontinent (as opposed to collecting wild honey in the forests) started during the Gandhian self-reliance movement in the 1940s. Some of the Bangladeshi refugees in West Bengal learned how to keep bees in wooden hives during the war of liberation in the 1970s, and they took their expertise back to Bangladesh after the war had ended. 🐝 The importance of honey is stressed in many religions. Prophet Hazrat Mohammad told his companions that honey is the best among all the drinks. The Bible mentions honey and the honeybee 60 times. In ancient Hinduism, bees were considered the companion of a holy god.

Bee products have important medicinal and dietary uses. The symptoms of colds, typhoid, constipation, and dysentery can be reduced by eating or drinking honey; the immune system can be strengthened. Honey is used to beautify skin and hair of the human body. Royal jelly is used as a tonic. Bee venom is used in many pharmaceutical applications.

Beekeeping does not require land (hives can be placed on a roof) or a big investment. It is something that anyone can do in their leisure time, through which they can generate additional income for their family. Besides being a source of extra money, it can also improve the nutrition of those poor families who decide to keep bees.

Bees for Development helps people worldwide to create sustainable livelihoods with bees: www.beesfordevelopment.org

Hunger-Free World Bangladesh: www.hfwbd.org

Hunger-Free World, in Bangladesh, is one of many NGOs around the world now promoting beekeeping as part of a strategy to raise the income levels of rural people. They provide farmers and families with
> **The hives:** three bee boxes and three iron stands, together with a colony of bees.
> **All the equipment needed:** a division box, knife, musk, uniform, net, gloves, feeder, smoker, queen excluder, and a honey extractor machine.
> **Sugar** to feed the bees in the off-season.
> **Training** in beekeeping.

...for a better future

🐝 **Support a rural community** in the developing world to start beekeeping to generate livelihoods and improve health.

🐝 **Go on a beekeepers' safari.** Bees for Development organizes safaris in countries such as India, Trinidad and Tobago, and Tanzania. They combine travel with adventure, learning, making new friendships, and tasting exotic cuisine. Nonbeekeepers as well as beekeepers are welcome.

OBESITY *a growing problem* ☺

The growing waistlines of Americans are eating into the profits of the airline industry. A study by the US Centers for Disease Control calculated that $275 million has to be spent each year on 343 million more gallons of fuel needed to carry the extra 10 lbs. that the average American gained during the 1990s. This increase adds an extra 3.8 million tons of carbon dioxide to annual greenhouse gas emissions.

Obesity is a major cause of disease, primarily heart disease and diabetes. And it is becoming a global problem. ☺ In the rich world, obesity is largely caused by lifestyle (increasing calorie intake and lack of exercise). The increasing quantity of processed foods means that fat and sugar now account for more than half the caloric intake, and consumption of refined grains has largely replaced that of whole grains. Snacking between meals is also becoming routine. ☺ In the developing world, the trend toward urban living and a westernized diet is a significant factor. ☺ There are also cultural factors at work. For example, being overweight may be seen as a sign of power and success in countries where many people go short of food. In China, the one-child policy has created a generation of "little emperors," spoiled rotten by their parents.

Check the shape you're in by using the calculator at www.worldheartday.com/aheartforlife/Obesity.asp.

In the US 28% of men and 33% of women are obese, and 64% of the adult population is overweight. Obesity levels are rising sharply, and are also increasing in Australia, Canada, and Europe, although they are still lower than in the US.

In South Africa (urban areas) 10% of men and 33% of women are obese.

In Brazil (urban areas) 8% of men and 33% of women are obese, more than double the rate 22 years ago.

In Mexico people now drink more Coca-Cola than milk.

In China 70 million people are overweight. In Beijing, 20% of children are obese.

...that needs reducing

If you are overweight or obese, here are some ways to get into better shape:

At work:
    Get off the bus or train a few stops earlier and walk the rest of the way.
    Go for a walk at lunchtime.
    Use the stairs instead of the elevator.
    Go and speak to colleagues instead of using the phone or e-mail.
    Stand while on the phone.
    Schedule exercise time into your day.

In your leisure time:
    Plan outings and holidays that include exercise: walk, run, swim, or fly a kite.
    Dance for fun.
    See the sights in a city by walking, jogging, or cycling.

prisoners in GUANTÁNAMO

I can recognize the conditions that prisoners are being kept in at the US camp at Guantánamo Bay because I have been there. Not to Cuba's Camp X-Ray, but to the darkened cell in Beirut that I occupied for five years. I was...denied all human rights and contact with my family, and given no access to the outside world. Because I was kept in very similar conditions, I am appalled at the way we—countries that call ourselves civilized—are treating these captives. Is this justice or revenge?

—Terry Waite

International law requires that people who are detained be formally charged, informed of their rights, and permitted access to legal counsel. This was not done for the Guantánamo detainees.

The prisoners are being denied due process of law. The law provides no basis for circumventing these requirements by labeling such persons "enemy combatants."

Human Rights Watch says that three categories of prisoners at Guantánamo should be released:

Taliban soldiers detained in the now-concluded war between the US and the government of Afghanistan, unless they are being prosecuted for war crimes.
Civilians with no meaningful connection to Al-Qaeda or the Taliban, who probably should never have been sent to Guantánamo in the first place.
Suspected terrorists whose detention had nothing to do with the war in Afghanistan. They should be charged with a crime and prosecuted.

Cageprisoners.com is a website raising awareness of Guantánamo, run by Muslim volunteers. Watch their video: www.cageprisoners.com/downloads/why.swf

Wikipedia has good background information: en.wikipedia.org/wiki/Camp_X-Ray

Amnesty International says:

Allegations of abuses such as arbitrary arrests [and] ill-treatment...are raised each year in the US State Department reports on human rights practices in other countries. Now they are being made against the US government in the context of its War on Terror.

...in limbo, but not forgotten

Prisoners are detained without charge as part of the War on Terror, held without any indication of a release date. These detainees are in a legal limbo.

- Show them that civilized nations should respect human rights, even when fear of terrorist attack is running high. Engage in discussion with them, and learn about their perspective.

- Do this by writing an occasional letter to a prisoner. The Cage Prisoners website tells you how to do this and gives their addresses.

LETTER *writing*

Dear Forest Service staff,

I am deeply concerned about the Forest Service's plans to remove Yellowstone's grizzly bears from the endangered species list. As the Forest Service revises the plan, I strongly urge you to select Alternative 4, which would protect important wildlands, restore degraded habitat, and maintain habitat within and between grizzly bear ecosystems. Please choose Alternative 4 and do everything possible to ensure Yellowstone's grizzlies remain adequately protected.

Yours faithfully…

If you feel strongly about something bad that is being planned or already taking place, you need to make your views known to those who are causing the problem or who can help with a solution.

Letter writing is one way. It's not the only way. Demos, marches, stunts, publicity campaigns, and lobbying are other things you might do. But sending a letter will let you get your views across and make it clear that you care. One letter may not make much of a difference. But lots of letters show that lots of people care.

Protecting grizzly bears may not be your passion. Perhaps what you really care about is protecting areas of outstanding beauty, ancient monuments, heritage sites, other wildlife, or campaigning against superstores and shopping malls, SUVs…

These two letter-writing websites are small ones run by committed individuals:
Global Response with 5,500 members from 92 countries: www.globalresponse.org
Earth Action Network campaigning in the US: www.earthactionnetwork.org

ActionNetwork with over 750,000 activists taking action on mainly US issues: www.actionnetwork.org

Earth Action Network was started by Dr. Mha Atma Singh Khalsa, a Los Angeles chiropractor. He wanted to do something to help the planet, and read in an activist guidebook that a single letter received by a government or company was considered to represent the views of 100 to 1,000 people. As a result, he began writing letters to influential people, based on information he got from environmental newsletters and reports. A friend pointed out to him that there were many others who felt as strongly as he did and who would love to have a chance to do the same, and Earth Action Network was born.

…make your views known

Rapid-response letter writing has developed with the Internet. All the big campaigning organizations encourage it, whether the issue is human rights, conflict, or the environment.

- **If you are concerned about an issue,** then join a Rapid Response Network of your choice. Sign up and start writing.
- **Write your own letters** in your own words.

buy local EAT LOCAL

Food is traveling farther and farther, often hundreds or even thousands of miles from where it was produced to where it is consumed. Long-distance transport pollutes the atmosphere with greenhouse gases and other harmful emissions and clogs up the highways with semis. But there are other problems too:

The local food chain is fast disappearing. Family farms, local slaughterhouses, small processing plants, local food distribution systems, and small shops are all finding that they are unable to compete in today's global market.

Centralization of food distribution has meant the loss of local distinctiveness—traditional varieties and a sense of belonging to the community.

Money leaks out from the local economy—and into the bank accounts of distant multinational food businesses.

Much of this shift is our fault. As consumers we always have a choice. If we use our choice positively to buy local, then shops will put more effort into stocking local produce.

Local Food Works: www.localfoodworks.org

Farmers' markets are markets where farmers and other producers from the local area sell their own produce directly to the public. All products sold will have been grown, reared, caught, brewed, pickled, baked, smoked, or processed by the vendor. Freshly picked fruit and vegetables are offered, though not necessarily organic produce. Stalls usually offer meat, fish, cakes, pies, jams, chutneys, cheeses, flour, soups, drinks, and other fare. Plus a chance to talk to the vendor.

...reduce food miles

Some simple things to do that will reduce food miles and help regenerate the local food chain:

🌳 Buy local whenever you can.

🌳 For food that cannot be grown in your region, such as tea, coffee, bananas, or chocolate, buy fair-trade products where these are available.

🌳 Buy seasonal fresh produce as it becomes available.

🌳 Wherever possible, buy from small, local shops and markets.

🌳 Avoid products that have been air-freighted in.

🌳 Write to your supermarket's head office—to the managing director—asking them to stock more locally grown and made produce. Ask smaller retailers to do the same. Ask local restaurants to feature local produce on their menus.

🌳 Consult a local food directory to see who's growing or producing what in your locality. If there isn't one, why not produce one yourself?

🌳 Grow your own food—organically, if possible—in your back garden, in a community garden, or even in window boxes and on the roof.

🌳 Write to your representative asking for a clearer labeling system that shows the distance food has traveled and the country or countries of origin.

🌳 Ask publicly funded cafeterias (such as in schools, hospitals, government offices, and prisons) to make a point of buying more local, seasonal, and organic food.

JUNE 13

FLAG *day*

"I pledge allegiance to the flag of the United States of America and to the Republic for which it stands, one Nation under God, indivisible, with liberty and justice for all." People usually recite the pledge by standing at attention facing the flag with their right hand over their heart. When not in uniform, men remove their hats with their right hand and hold them at the left shoulder, the hand being over the heart. Persons in uniform remain silent, face the flag, and render the military salute.

Flag Day **honors the adoption of the Stars and Stripes** as the US national flag by the Second Continental Congress on June 14, 1777. This new flag symbolized the new nation, the United States of America, and all that it stood for. The first national Flag Day was observed on June 14, 1877, one hundred years after the original flag resolution.

Pause for the Pledge of Allegiance: Americans everywhere are invited to pause for a moment on June 14 at 7:00 p.m. Eastern Daylight Time to say simultaneously the 31 words of the Pledge of Allegiance to the Flag. This ceremony is recognized by Congress as part of National Flag Day ceremonies (Public Law 99-54).

Freedom and the Constitution: the First Amendment states that *"Congress shall make no law respecting an establishment of religion, or prohibiting the free exercise thereof; or abridging the freedom of speech, or of the press; or the right of the people peaceably to assemble, and to petition the government for a redress of grievances."*

The US Constitution: www.usconstitution.com
Amendments to the US Constitution:
www.law.cornell.edu/constitution/constitution.table.html#amendments
American Civil Liberties Union: www.aclu.org

Flag burning

In demonstrations all over the world, enemies of the USA burn the US flag as a symbol of protest. But when US citizens burn the US flag in protest against their government, is this an un-American activity or is it an exercise of freedom of speech?

Does the First Amendment allow the government to punish individuals who mutilate flags, burn draft cards, or engage in other acts deemed disrespectful of patriotic symbols? Or should we be celebrating the fact that we can do this, as we seek to promote freedom and democracy across the world?

You decide. For information on flag burning, see
www.esquilax.com/flag
www.law.umkc.edu/faculty/projects/ftrials/conlaw/flagburning.htm

...know what the flag means

If you are a US citizen, then pause for the Pledge of Allegiance at exactly 7:00 p.m. EDT wherever you are. Use this day to reflect on two things:

♟ **Liberty and justice for all.** Is this a dream or a reality for the US? And what can *you* do to ensure liberty and justice for all?

♟ **Freedom of speech.** Are our freedoms being curtailed too much in relation to the actual threat of terrorism? If so, how can we speak out?

donate SMART CLOTHES

Imagine you are down and out or simply very poor. All the clothes you own are shabby. But you've managed to get a job interview, and you want to look your best. You've got a problem. You've got nothing nice to wear for your interview. This makes it less likely that you'll get the job. This is the catch-22: no smart clothes, no job; no job, no money to buy smart clothes.

Dress for Success is an organization that addresses this very problem. Women are referred to it by government agencies and other organizations, including homeless shelters, domestic violence shelters, immigration services, and job training programs. ⌂ Each client receives one suit for a job interview and a second suit when she gets the job. The Dress for Success Professional Women's Group then provides ongoing support to help clients build a successful career.

Dress for Success: www.dressforsuccess.org

A story of success
Nancy Lublin used a $5,000 inheritance from her great-grandfather to start Dress for Success, putting a great idea into practice.

Dress for Success now provides interview suits, confidence boosts, and career development to more than 45,000 women in over 73 cities each year.

...help to dress for success

⌂ **Dress for Success needs a supply of clothes.** Donate new or nearly new (and clean) office clothes. There is a particular need for clothes in larger sizes:
Coordinated, contemporary, interview-appropriate skirt and pantsuits
Beautiful, crisp blouses
Gorgeous blazers and jackets
Professional shoes

If you've got the time and energy, why not start a Dress for Success branch in your town or city. Their website tells you how.

⌂ **Thrift stores would love the things that Dress for Success can't use.** Donate your old clothes, jewelry you no longer wear, decorative items you are fed up with, and unwanted presents. The stores will convert these into cash for a good cause.

⌂ **Buy as many of your clothes as possible at thrift stores** and become the new home for someone else's perfectly good clothes. You'll be saving money and supporting a charity. And you'll also be dressing distinctively rather than being a boring old follower of fashion!

JUNE 15

POVERTY *can be conquered*

One day our grandchildren will go to museums to see what poverty was like.

—Muhammad Yunus

Muhammad Yunus, a banker from Bangladesh, had an idea for eradicating poverty. He would lend money to really poor people using a simple formula. People would save regularly for a period of time, and then they would be able to get a loan. Each borrower would join a group of borrowers who would be jointly responsible for the loan. This would create peer pressure on the borrower to repay the loan, and would make defaults less likely. No collateral would be needed from the borrower.

Grameen, the organization that Yunus set up, now works in 43,000 villages across Bangladesh and gives loans to 2.8 million borrowers, 96% of whom are women. Over the years, it has lent more than $4 billion to these borrowers, of which $3.6 billion has been repaid. The recovery rate is 99%. Borrowers own 93% of the bank; the remaining 7% is owned by the government. The idea of the Grameen Bank led to the development of a "microcredit" industry around the world, which lends to poor people to help them escape poverty.

International Year of Microcredit 2005: www.yearofmicrocredit.org
Grameen Bank: www.grameen-info.org
Start Talking Ideas: www.starttalkingideas.org

Good Gifts, supporting small businesses in the developing world:
www.goodgifts.org

Aruma is a widow in Ethiopia who was struggling to feed her family. She was offered a loan to buy a goat, which then provided milk for her family plus some to sell. The goat produced some kids, and these were sold. Soon Aruma had saved enough money to buy a cow, which produced even more milk and money for her. She was a proud mother when her eldest son got a place at college. Without the original loan, he would almost certainly have had to drop out of school to start earning money.

Didier is a young tailor in Benin. He could not get hold of the funds he needed to set up a tailoring workshop. He managed to get a microloan of $850, which took his equipment as security. Only a week after getting the loan, he was offered a contract to make ready-to-wear shirts. He has recruited two employees, and is well on the way to becoming a successful local entrepreneur.

...a small loan is the first step

- **Support someone in the developing world** to start a microbusiness. It might be taxi driving, brewing, tailoring, vegetable growing, livestock. You choose: just go to the Good Gifts website.

- **Go to the Start Talking Ideas website** and find all the information and ideas you need to become an entrepreneur.

- **Start your own business with a $200 loan.** You come up with the business idea. You lend yourself the money. Find four friends who will all do exactly the same. You have 365 days to see who can make the most profit from their enterprise.

16 JUNE

transform ARID LANDS

Semiarid land in Africa is turning to desert, in part because of poor land and water management. ⊕ In areas where electricity is simply not available, the only fuel for cooking is wood. The daily search for wood is taking people further and further afield and is resulting in whole areas being stripped of what meager vegetation they had. Once the trees and scrub have gone, there is nothing to hold the topsoil in place. Any rain that falls quickly evaporates, the soil dries off and the wind simply blows it away.

Water needs to be carefully managed. In much of Africa rainfall is highly erratic. It is always possible that seasonal rain will just not arrive at all. And when it does arrive, much of it simply drains off into rivers, and flows out to sea. ⊕ If only that rainwater could be retained, it could be used during the dry season to increase food production. It would also have a positive impact on people's daily lives, as they would no longer have to walk long distances to fetch water, and the water itself would be cleaner.

One answer lies in small-scale "sand dams," which an organization called Excellent Development has been helping to build for over 20 years. Started in 1984 by 18-year-old Simon Maddrell, it has worked with communities in East Africa to construct 50 dams, and aims to make that 300 by 2010.

Excellent Development: www.excellentdevelopment.com

UN Convention to Combat Desertification: www.unced.int

A sand dam is a reinforced concrete wall, 2 to 4 yards high, built across a seasonal river bed. A pipe is laid through the dam, and extended 65 feet back upstream. When the seasonal rains occur, sand is washed downstream and collects behind the dam. It traps water within it, which seeps out and runs through the pipe long after the soil in neighboring valleys has dried up.

As well as helping to construct the dam, local people work to improve the land behind it, terracing the hillsides to improve water and soil conservation. The extra water enables them to grow vegetables, which improve their diets. They also grow trees in nurseries, eventually replanting them to further rehabilitate the semiarid land.

...help build a sand dam

Join Excellent Development on a four-week expedition to Southeast Kenya to help local communities build sand dams and plant trees. You can spend the final four days relaxing on safari or at the beach!

RECHARGE *batteries*

Batteries are so much part of our daily lives that we rarely think about them until they need replacing. And that's precisely the time that we do need to think about them, because we have to address the problem of what to *do* with them, and what to replace them with. ♣ Most of us just chuck them in the wastebasket without thinking about it, but we need to get into the habit of recycling them.

Worldwide, more than 300,000 tons of batteries are sold annually, and almost all of them end up in a landfill site. Many batteries contain some very nasty chemicals, such as cadmium, which can poison the environment. They also include zinc, which could be reused if the battery were recycled. ♣ Battery use is increasing, which means that battery waste is becoming an ever-bigger problem.

Many children's toys and games are battery powered, which is why it is great to hear of schoolchildren campaigning to have collection points for used batteries in all the schools in their area. If they can do it, so can you.

Find out everything you need to know about batteries at www.batteryuniversity.com.

The different types of rechargeable battery:
Lead-acid: heavy but cheap; used for car batteries and for equipment where weight is not an issue, such as wheelchairs.
Nickel-cadmium: long-life, used for power tools; contain toxic matter. Avoid if possible.
Nickel-metal-hydride: used in mobile phones and laptops; contain no toxic matter.
Lithium-ion and Lithium-ion-polymer: high-energy and low-weight; used in lightweight laptop and notebook computers and for mobile phones.
Reusable alkaline: cheap rechargeable batteries used for flashlights and other consumer devices.

...don't let energy go to waste

♣ **Reduce the environmental impact of battery use:**
Use rechargeable batteries wherever possible. Some batteries can be recharged up to 1,000 times. But you will need a battery charger.
Purchase Nickel Metal Hydride (NiMH) batteries in preference to Nickel Cadmium (NiCd) batteries, as these are much less toxic.
Never throw used batteries away with your household rubbish, as some of their ingredients, especially cadmium, are highly toxic.
Recycle used batteries instead.

♣ **Ask your employer or your school or college to provide a battery bin** for collecting and recycling used batteries. If they won't, then build one yourself. Make it bright and colorful; produce a leaflet alongside it, explaining why it is important to recycle batteries. The battery bin should be situated in a prominent place.

♣ **Find out if your local government does anything about battery recycling.** Some do. But if yours doesn't yet, then use your lobbying skills to persuade them that they should.

18 JUNE

emancipation of SLAVES

On January 1, 1863, Abraham Lincoln issued his Emancipation Proclamation proclaiming the abolition of slavery in the US. The war was won on May 26, 1865.

News of the Emancipation Proclamation finally reached the last remaining slaves in Galveston, Texas, on June 19, 1865, and this day, June 19 (known as *Juneteenth*), commemorates the freeing of the last slaves.

Juneteenth commemorates African-American freedom. According to the Juneteenth website, "it is a day, a week, and in some areas a month marked with celebrations, guest speakers, picnics, and family gatherings. It is a time for reflection and rejoicing. It is a time for assessment, self-improvement and for planning the future. It is a time to emphasize education and achievement."

Juneteenth is also a day for those whose ancestors did not suffer the pain and indignities of slavery to celebrate in solidarity with those whose ancestors did.

The Sankofa Experience, Dallas, Juneteenth 2005: A reenactment of our African ancestors' journey from Africa to America. Participants were able to feel the excitement of living in an African village, the horrors of being kidnapped and placed on a slave ship, the shame of being sold on an auction block, the brutality of working on a plantation, and the fear and anticipation of escaping to freedom on the Underground Railroad. The event was held on sacred black-owned land, purchased in 1876 by former enslaved Africans.

Juneteenth: www.juneteenth.com

The story of Charlie Aarons: Uncle Charlie, as he is known among his own color and the white people who know him, told the writer he was born at Petersburg, Virginia, and his parents, Aaron and Louisa, were owned by a Mr. J. H. White, who had a store in the city, but no plantation. His parents had three children, two boys and a girl, and when Uncle Charlie was about ten years of age, he was sold by Mr. White to a speculator named Jones who brought him to Mobile. He recalled being placed on the block at the slave mart on Royal and State streets, and the anxiety of hearing different people bidding for him, and being finally sold to a Mr. Jason Harris, who lived near Newton Station in Jasper County, Mississippi.—Contributed to the Federal Writers' Project by Mary A. Poole in 1937.

...celebrate Juneteenth

- ♩ **Organize an event for Juneteenth**. Or participate in someone else's event. Go to the Juneteenth website, and look for what's happening where you are. Or go down to Texas where Juneteenth originated. You'll find a lot that will inspire you.

- ♩ **Read more about Charlie Aarons** and the stories of other slaves at *Born in Slavery: Narratives from the Federal Writers' Project*, Library of Congress: http://memory.loc.gov/ammem/snhtml/snhome.html.

REFUGEES *seeking asylum*

Everyone has the right to escape persecution in his or her own country and to seek asylum in another. That principle is enshrined in the Universal Declaration of Human Rights (1948) and was reinforced by the 1951 Geneva Convention. Today 19 million people are estimated to be living in another part of their country, or in a different country entirely, because life became unsustainable in their homeland. Many have fled from conflict, suffering rape, torture, and the deaths of family members. But instead of finding the personal and economic safety they sought, they are destitute and relying on the support of international agencies.

Some people migrate because they are unable to find work in their own country. Where there is no welfare state, no work means no food. Often they become illegal immigrants—hidden from sight and open to exploitation. Some hand over a large amount of cash to pay for travel arrangements and work permits and are then shipped illegally to the country of destination, where they may be kept as debt slaves and forced to work for low wages. Girls and women may arrive thinking they will be domestic servants but end up working as prostitutes. ‡ As parts of the world become uninhabitable though climate change and pressure on natural resources, the number of environmental migrants is bound to increase.

The main countries from which people have sought refuge are Afghanistan (2,084,900), Sudan (730,600), Burundi (488,000), Democratic Republic of Congo (462,200), Somalia (389,300), Palestine (350,600), Vietnam (349,800), Liberia (335,500), Iraq (311,800), and Azerbaijan (250,500).

Amnesty USA's Refugee Program: www.amnestyusa.org/refugee/index.do

Forced Migration Online, information on human displacement: www.forcedmigration.org

UNHCR: www.unhcr.org

The United Nations High Commission for Refugees (UNHCR) tries to safeguard the well-being of refugees. It compiles detailed statistics, available on their website.

The richer nations stress the need to curb the inflow of migrants, but in reality, it is the countries least able to afford it who are receiving the highest proportion of immigrants in relation to their own populations.

Distribution of refugees and asylum seekers (2004)		Numbers of refugees per 1,000 inhabitants (2002)	
Asia	6.9 million	Armenia	70
Africa	4.86 million	Congo	40
Europe	4.42 million	Yugoslavia	38
North America	.85 million	Djibouti	37
Latin America	2.07 million	Zambia	27
Australasia	.08 million	US	2.5

...support them

Do something positive to help people who have fled to your country.
The very least you can do is to challenge the negative attitudes sometimes expressed toward refugees, asylum seekers, and immigrants.

build a SOLAR COOKER

A few years ago, I woke up to the fact that half of the world's people must burn wood or dried dung in order to cook their food. It came as quite a shock to me, especially as I learned of the illnesses caused by breathing smoke day in and day out, and the environmental impacts of deforestation—not to mention the time spent by people (mostly women) gathering sticks and dung to cook their food.

And yet, many of these billions of people live near the equator, where sunshine is abundant and free. As a University Professor of Physics with a background in energy usage, I set out to develop a means of cooking food and sterilizing water using the free energy of the sun.

—Steven E. Jones, Brigham Young University

Using a solar-powered cooker in a land where the sun shines nearly every day has to be a win-win situation.

Here are some of the reasons why a solar cooker is a good thing:

It helps prevent deforestation and desertification. In developing countries, the majority of rural people cook over wood fires or stoves. The year-round removal of so much vegetation contributes to soil erosion.

It saves the time of the women whose job it is to collect the firewood, and might even free up young girls so that they can attend school.

There is no smoke pollution, reducing the risk of the respiratory disease that affects women and their children who spend so much of their time breathing in the smoke from open fires.

It reduces injuries from burns.

It reduces carbon dioxide emissions and makes a small contribution to the reduction in greenhouse gases.

It can be used to produce safe drinking water as well as to prepare food, thus reducing the risk of disease.

The sun's energy is free.

Plans for building a solar cooker are available at solarcooking.org
Steven Jones: http://en.wikipedia.org/wiki/Stephen_E._Jones

There are three types of solar cooker:

Box style, which works like a mini-greenhouse.

Panel style, which directs sunlight into the cooking area using reflecting panels.

Parabolic, which focuses an intense beam of sunlight on the bottom of the cooking pot.

All can be made using simple materials: aluminium foil, cardboard, polyethylene, or, in the case of the one shown here, an inflated car inner tube, a sheet of wood, an aluminium saucepan and lid painted black on the outside, and a sheet of glass.

...cook your dinner for free

- **Build a solar cooker yourself.**
- **Organize a solar-cooked lunch party** for your friends on a sunny day.
- **Become a passionate advocate for solar cooking** and do what you can to spread the word.

GLOBAL *warming*

Our house is burning down and we're blind to it.... The earth and humankind are in danger and we are all responsible. It is time to open our eyes. Alarms are sounding across all the continents.... We cannot say that we did not know! Climate warming is still reversible. Heavy is the responsibility of those who refuse to fight it.

—Jacques Chirac, president of France

Peter Sweatman writes,

Three years ago I met a successful lawyer who told me about the enormous problems we are creating through our reckless abuse of the environment. He said that the situation was as serious as a huge meteorite directly colliding with the earth sometime during the lifetime of our children or grandchildren. 🌳 I set out to find out more. I talked to people and read a number of books. I now believe that the single biggest issue humankind faces is global warming. The issue is not the amount of warming but the speed of the change, which will lead to massive species loss, population migration on a global scale, increased weather disasters, and rising sea levels—if nothing is done now.

I decided that individual action was vital, and set about planting trees and "greening" my life. But I also felt that there were many people who did not have enough information and were not being offered things to do about it. With four friends, I then founded Catalyst Climate Change Trust to pool our resources and research, lobby, and inform people about global warming.

Our first step was to commission research into how European companies, which are regulated to reduce their CO_2 emissions, can sue companies that are operating in non-Kyoto signatory countries: that is, those that are competing in the global market but are able to produce CO_2 freely. This research was launched at the international climate talks. It received huge media attention. 🌳 We then arranged for 450 of our friends and colleagues to listen to a group of the best-informed climate specialists talk about global warming at a seminar we held at the Royal Geographical Society. Many have subsequently offered to give money, take individual action, or join CCCT to help us take the next steps. 🌳 All of the above was achieved with minimal funds, but with lots of energy and passion. If five of us can do this, what could 50 or 500 people do? Maybe save the world?

Peter Sweatman: www.ctt.org
www.marklynas.org
www.climateark.org

www.heatisonline.org
www.earthday.net/footprint/index.asp
www.co2.org/calculator/index.cfm

...must be reversed

🌳 **Read *High Tide* by Mark Lynas.** Mark visits some of the climate change hotspots around the world: the Peruvian Andes to examine the glaciers melting, northwest China to inspect desertification, the Pacific to watch islands sinking, the US East Coast to see the impact of hurricanes. And he reports the situation as it is. If you've got the time, go and see for yourself.

🌳 **And if you are now convinced by the seriousness of global warming, do something.** Join with your friends and start campaigning.

Merlin Matthews was such a genius at fixing everyone's bikes when he was at college in the UK that he earned the nickname "Dr. Bike." He would fix bikes in exchange for beers on Friday evenings. He was even approached for advice about starting up a bike factory in Haiti. This made him realize that there are lots of bikes being thrown away that could be fixed. 🌐 He decided to find a way of collecting old bikes and sending them to Haiti, thinking that he would be able to spend most of his time in Haiti's sunshine running a bicycle repair workshop. Sadly, he realized that his time would be better spent doing the fund raising, sorting out the bikes, and shipping them. 🌐 He linked up with Institute for Transportation & Development Policy, International Bicycle Fund, and Bikes Not Bombs in the US, which had similar ideas, and as a result decided that, since US organizations are better able to help in Latin America, he should to focus on supplying bicycles to Africa.

The charity he started, Re-Cycle, has so far donated over 14,000 bikes to Africa. Many people there have to trek hours every day just to get drinking water, or walk miles to get to school—and more miles to get back home. A bicycle can make the difference between life and death, or between a child gaining an education or not. The charity also works with local African groups, teaching people how to repair and maintain their bicycles.

Check out these bike recycling groups:
Re-Cycle: www.re-cycle.org

Bikes for the World and Bikes Not Bombs both donate bikes from the US to the developing world: www.bikesfortheworld.org and www.bikesnotbombs.org

Afribike, a South African organization providing South Africans with bicycles: www.afribike.org

And these organizations promoting sustainable transport solutions globally:
International Bicycle Fund: www.ibike.org

Institute for Transportation & Development Policy: www.itdp.org

Can you provide any of the help needed to recycle bikes internationally?
Storage space for collected bikes—needs to be 100% secure, but infrequent access required.
Contacts in the haulage industry and the shipping world—to get good discounts.
Containers (40-ft. or 20-ft.) at the end of their seaworthy life—donated to be used for secure storage or turned into a cycle repair workshop in Africa.
Secondhand bikes, parts, and tools (all donated, of course).

...send it to Africa

Allow your old bicycle to improve someone's life in Africa or Latin America. Go and dig it out from behind the broken fridge and donate it. Someone in need will be very grateful.

JUNE 23

SLOW FOOD *now*

☺

The Slow Food movement was founded in 1988 by Carlo Petrini, an Italian journalist and activist. He was protesting against the opening of a McDonald's next to the Spanish Steps in Rome, seeing it as part of a rapidly spreading global fast-food culture. He believed that the world was forgetting the joys of good food and leisurely dining.

Eating something delicious will help sustain biodiversity by preserving food plants now under threat from a food industry demanding mass production of foods that look good (rather than taste good) and which have long shelf lives. The pleasure we take in eating good food is itself a small but meaningful political act.

Eco-gastronomy isn't going to save the world, but if you can bring food politics and the pleasure of eating together, the Vesuvian apricot and Delaware Bay oyster won't be the only species to benefit.

Slow Food: www.slowfood.com

The Slow Food Manifesto

Our century, which began and has developed under the insignia of industrial civilization, first invented the machine and then took this as its life model. We are enslaved by speed and have all succumbed to the same insidious virus—Fast Life—which disrupts our habits, pervades the privacy of our homes, and forces us to eat Fast Foods. To be worthy of the name, *Homo sapiens* (Latin for "thinking man") should rid himself of speed before it reduces all of us to a species in danger of extinction.

A firm defense of quiet material pleasure is the only way to oppose the universal folly of Fast Life. Suitable doses of guaranteed sensual pleasure and slow, long-lasting enjoyment should hopefully preserve us from the contagion of the multitudes who mistake frenzy for efficiency.

Our defense should begin at the table with Slow Food. Let us rediscover the flavors and savors of regional cooking and banish the degrading effects of Fast Food. In the name of productivity, Fast Life has changed our way of being and threatens our environment and our landscapes. So Slow Food is now the only truly progressive answer. It guarantees a better future. But it is an idea that needs plenty of supporters in order to turn this (slow) motion into an international movement, with the little snail as its symbol.

...make it last

Organize a dinner party for your seven best friends.

☺ Ask them all to prepare and bring something delicious using only the best ingredients plus a bottle of something special. Plan the menu together or leave things to chance.

☺ Linger over your dinner, the longer the better. Have a really great time. Repeat as often as desired.

put theories to THE TEST

If you saw someone pouring $1.4bn into encouraging people to eat apples, which is the amount McDonald's spends in a single year on radio, television and print advertising, you'd see apple sales go through the roof. Suddenly, you'd have Justin Timberlake on TV going: "Man, I love apples! You should eat some apples too! Look at me—I'm running, and I'm eating apples."

—Morgan Spurlock

Morgan Spurlock, a 33-year-old New York filmmaker, was watching the news at his parents' home in West Virginia in November 2002 when he saw that two teenagers from New York were suing McDonald's for making them obese. He decided to test out the teenagers' claim that eating fast food could seriously damage your health, and film the process. ☺ For a whole month he would eat nothing but McDonald's food: for breakfast, lunch, and dinner. There were three ground rules:

1 He had to eat every item on the McDonald's menu at least once.

2 He could only eat what was available over the counter (no special orders).

3 He had to order a SuperSize meal whenever a counter assistant offered him this option.

He would record the state of his health prior to this new diet and afterwards. The outcome was *Super Size Me*, an award-winning 98-minute film.

In the first week he put on 9 lbs. After a month he'd added a total of 24 lbs. His cholesterol level rose by 65 points and was 33% higher than when he started. His doctor also suggested that this diet of fast food was causing serious liver damage. It took Spurlock 14 months to return to his former physical condition.

Spurlock's film challenges the power of the huge food corporations to determine what we eat. It is not just their menus but their marketing clout, and the impact that this has on lifestyles and attitudes, that seems to be leading to an epidemic of obesity.

Super Size Me: supersizeme.com

Industry response
Since the first showing of the film *Super Size Me,* McDonald's has phased out its SuperSize meals and is testing a Go-Active Happy Meal with a salad, bottle of water, and free pedometer!
But consumer demand seems insatiable. Hardee's has launched its Monster Thickburger with 1,420 calories and 107 grams of fat per portion. It consists of 2 slabs of Angus beef (664 calories) and 4 strips of bacon (150 calories) with 3 slices of processed cheese (186 calories) and mayonnaise (160 calories) in a sesame seed bun (230 calories) spread with butter (30 calories). Throw in a portion of fries and a carbonated drink, and it's a day's calorie intake on a plate—a "monument to decadence" and "not a burger for tree-huggers," says Hardee's.

...wise up, don't fatten up

☺ **Complain to the FCC** (which oversees advertising to make sure it is "legal, decent, honest and truthful") if you see any advertising **on TV** that is obviously untrue.

☺ **If there is something that you feel needs testing,** test it out and see what happens.

JUNE 25

TORURE *is endemic*

If we fail to do anything about torture, we condone it.

—Michael Palin

Beatings, electrocutions, being suspended for hours, mock drownings, sleep deprivation, rape... The ingenuity of humans to think up ways of torturing their fellow humans is limitless. ♪ Room 101 was dreamt up by George Orwell for his novel *1984*, as the place where each person confronted his or her own worst nightmare. For Winston Smith, the hero of the novel, it was rats. In Room 101, Smith had a cage containing starving rats strapped to his face until he "confessed" that he loved Big Brother. ♪ Would you have been able to hold out? Or would you, like Smith, have "confessed"? What would be your breaking point?

Horrendous stories are published almost daily about people being tortured. Don't run away from them. Often, people have had to go through a second form of torture, just to recount and relive their story. As a tribute to the courage they have shown in standing up for what they believe in, we can at least do them the honor of listening to them.

World Organization Against Torture, an international coalition fighting arbitrary detention and torture: www.omct.org

The Wikipedia article on torture, with lots of information on torture methods: en.wikipedia.org/wiki/Torture

Elizabeth is a 21-year-old student from Zimbabwe. Early in the morning, a group of men, some in Zanu-PF T-shirts, barged their way into her house. A black hood, drawn tightly at the neck, was placed over her head, and she was taken away, detained for two days, beaten and raped, and questioned about her political activities. All she had done was to participate in the youth section of a prodemocracy movement opposing the president.

Edwin, from an English-speaking area of Cameroon, was 15 when he was caught participating in a student demonstration protesting against plans to scrap the Anglo-Saxon system of education. He was held for three weeks, beaten, kicked, and whipped with the buckled end of a belt. Undeterred, Edwin joined an opposition group and cofounded the Student Parliament. His university branded him a dissident and refused to let him do postgraduate studies. At one protest he was arrested by paramilitary gendarmes, had his skull split by a rifle butt, and was dragged naked along the ground. Beatings have left him deaf in one ear.

...do something about it

The Medical Foundation for the Care of Victims of Torture helps over 3,000 people a year with practical assistance, medical treatment, and psychotherapeutic support.

Support the foundation by torturing yourself. Identify your worst fear and resolve to face it head on. You might, for example, be afraid of heights. Arrange to do a charity parachute jump to raise money for the foundation. They'll provide an action pack telling you how to do it.

start your own SCHOOL

If you are planning for one year, plant rice. If you are planning for ten years, plant trees. If you are planning for 100 years, plant education.

—old Chinese proverb

Only 37 out of 155 developing countries have universal primary education and have managed to enrol all school-age children in a school, and to keep them at school until they have received a rudimentary education. This advance is helping to meet Millennium Development Goal 3: to ensure that, by 2015, children everywhere, boys and girls alike, will be able to complete a full course of primary schooling. Another 32 countries look likely to achieve this goal by 2015. But in 70 countries, more needs to be done.

Ethiopia is a country that is still trying to address the problem. Nearly two-thirds of Ethiopians cannot read or write. But with more than half the people in the country under 15 years old, there is an opportunity to rectify this problem. Primary school is free, and is supposedly mandatory, but fewer than half of all children ever begin school and only one in ten continues to the eighth grade. It is also normal for a class to have up to 100 children, making teaching and learning very difficult indeed.

Asfaw Yemiru believes that education is the only way for the poor to achieve a better life. When still only 14 years old, he opened a school for street children, outdoors under a big oak tree. That was in 1957. Four years later, he built the Asere Hawariat School for 2,000 children (grades 1 to 5). In 1972 he opened the Moya School for 2,000 children (grades 6 to 8), where children learn practical and vocational skills as well as the formal curriculum, and their education is still free of charge. Schoolbooks are also free in Asfaw's schools, and students do not have to wear a uniform.

Asfaw Yemiru won the World Children's Prize in 2001: www.childrensworld.org
School of St. Jude: eol.habari.co.tz/st-jude.htm

After finishing college, a young Australian, Gemma Sisia, traveled to Uganda to teach for three years. On her return, Gemma started taking $10 out of her paycheck each week to sponsor some Ugandan children she had met. Soon her family and friends were also sponsoring children's education.

This was the starting point for Gemma to build and run a school—St. Jude's near Arusha in Tanzania. The 300 students currently range in age from four to ten years old, and each year a new grade is added. Gemma has persuaded people around the world to sponsor pupils by donating money for tuition, books, uniforms, and hot lunches.

...one class at a time

Go to Africa, and help start a school—just like Asfaw and Gemma did. But if you can't do that, then think about supporting the costs of one child. Girls are especially in need as they have fewer opportunities. Why not support a child at Asfaw's or Gemma's school?

RESPONSIBLE *travel*

Responsible travel conserves the environment and improves the well-being of local people. By being responsible you are likely to get a little bit more out of your travels—as well as putting something back.

Here are some suggestions from Responsible Travel on to how to approach travel to foreign countries in a way that will bring benefits to the country, without diminishing the self-respect of its people.

Read up on the countries you plan to visit. The welcome will be warmer if you take an interest and speak even a few words of the local language.

Think small when booking a holiday. For example, stay in bed and breakfasts, village houses, and locally owned accommodation, benefiting local families.

Travel like Gandhi, with simple clothes, open eyes, and an uncluttered mind.

Ask to see your tour operator's responsible travel policy.

Help the local economy by buying local produce rather than imported goods.

Bear in mind that a small amount saved when bargaining to buy an item could be extremely significant to the seller.

Recognize cultural differences. The people in the country you are visiting may have different time concepts and thought patterns from your own. This does not make them inferior, only different. Respect local cultures, traditions, and holy places.

Cultivate the habit of asking questions and discover the enrichment of seeing a different way of life through other people's eyes.

Use public transport, hire a bike, or walk where convenient. You'll meet local people and get to know the place much better.

Use water sparingly. Local people may not have sufficient clean water for their needs.

Find out where locals go when they have time off. Visit the main tourist sites, but get off the tourist trail too.

Don't discard litter; take it home with you. Waste disposal is a major expense in poorer countries.

Ask permission before you photograph people. In some cultures it can cause offense.

Do not buy products made from endangered species, hard woods, shells from beach traders, or ancient artifacts (which have probably been stolen).

Take small gifts from home as gifts for your hosts. Ask your tour operator for suggestions.

Spend time reflecting on your experiences. Try to deepen your understanding. Enjoy the memories.

For a more detailed explanation of sustainable tourism, see www.uneptie.org/pc/tourism/sust-tourism/home.htm.
International Ecotourism Society: www.ecotourism.org
Responsible Travel: www.responsibletravel.com

...a guide to good practice

Next time, travel more responsibly. Why would you want to do otherwise?

don't just SIT THERE

Everybody can be great. Because anybody can serve. You don't have to have a college degree to serve. You don't have to make your subject and your verb agree to serve....You don't have to know the second theory of thermodynamics in physics to serve. You only need a heart full of grace. A soul generated by love.

—Dr. Martin Luther King, Jr.

Do Something provides young people with two-week challenges in three areas: community building, health, and the environment. These can be done after school or as an in-school class project. The Do Something website contains support material that can be downloaded.

Doing something helps young people develop life skills and gives them the chance to lead.

Find out about the Do Something challenges and awards: www.dosomething.org
Youth Venture, grants for young social entrepreneurs: www.youthventure.org

Here are two of the challenges for young people:
Take the "Thanks/Giving" Challenge.
Nearly half of all young children in the US live in poverty or near poverty. These kids aren't from outer space: they live in your town. Be a local hero! Go out into your local community. Go and talk to businesses, neighborhood stores, and local markets. Request a donation of canned goods in exchange for your doing minor tasks to help them. They do the *Giving;* you *Thank* them by doing something in return. Bring the food you have collected to your school or youth project, and help feed hungry kids in your neighborhood.

Take the "Second Hand This!" Challenge.
The Second Hand This! Challenge offers a mechanism for young people to encourage their family, neighbors, and peers to quit smoking. The objective is to galvanize youth to take a proactive stance on creating a smoke-free environment. Young people will write letters, hand out lollipops, write poetry, and engage in other creative activities designed to get people to sign a pledge to quit smoking.

...do something

Once you have had a taste of doing something, you will probably want to do a lot more. Now's the time to think about starting your own project to address an important problem or need where you feel that you can do something and make a lasting impact. There are a number of steps to take:

- **Think of a problem,** then come up with a solution. Your idea for a project should be practicable as well as creative.
- **Plan what you want to do,** and what you will need to do it. Make a plan. Draw up a budget.
- **Get some friends together** whom you'd like to work with. It's easier and can be a lot more fun to work as a group.
- **Then get going.** Do your best. But learn from your mistakes. You are on the way to becoming a young social entrepreneur, a change maker who will change the world!

JUNE 29

WATER *purification*

> *The human right to water entitles everyone to sufficient, safe...*
> *accessible and affordable water for personal and domestic uses.*
>
> —*The Right to Water*, 2002

About 1.1 billion people do not have access to safe drinking water: that is at least a third of people in developing countries. Two-thirds of these people live in Asia. In sub-Saharan Africa, 42% of the population does not have access to a clean, safe drinking-water supply. ☺ This lack of clean water, together with a lack of proper sanitation facilities, causes serious health problems. The main dangers are diarrhea and cholera. Together these kill 1.8 million people each year, 90% of whom are children under five years old.

One of the UN's Millennium Development Goals is to halve, by 2015, the proportion of people who do not have access to safe drinking water and basic sanitation. The UN has declared 2005–2015 as the International Decade for Action, in order to provide a greater focus on water-related issues under the slogan "Water for Life."

There is a simple practical technology for purifying water in emergencies (such as the post-tsunami period) as well as for everyday use. It's called SODIS, which stands for solar disinfection, and it is being promoted by Fundación Sodis in Latin America and by the Solaqua Foundation in other parts of the world. ☺ SODIS is a simple alternative to boiling water (which consumes firewood) and chlorination (which requires the availability of chemicals and also adversely affects the water's taste).

Solaqua Foundation: www.sodis.ch/Text2002/T-Howdoesitwork.htm
UNESCO Water Portal: www.unesco.org/water

This is how SODIS works:

Get hold of a transparent plastic bottle. Wash well before first-time use. Use Polyethyleneterephtalate (PET) plastic bottles rather than polyvinylchloride (PVC). Whereas PET bottles smell sweet when burned, PVC bottles often have a bluish tinge, and produce pungent smoke.

Fill the bottle three-quarters full with water from a local water source such as a stream or river. The water should not be too muddy. Shake to aerate the water: the dissolved oxygen helps in the purification process. Then fill completely and screw on the cap.

Place the bottle on a corrugated metal roof in strong sunlight for one full day. The heating of the water and the ultraviolet (UVA) radiation together destroy the microorganisms that cause waterborne diseases.

Pour into a cup and enjoy!

...do it yourself

☺ **Try the SODIS process for yourself,** as an act of solidarity with those who have no alternative.

☺ **Share the technology** with anyone you think might be interested.

In 1844, 28 craftsmen in Rochdale, England, pooled their money to open a store that sold basic commodities such as flour, oatmeal, butter, sugar, and candles. These "Rochdale pioneers"—Miles Ashworth (a flannel weaver), James Bamford (a shoemaker), John Bent (a tailor), and the others— were the founders of the cooperative movement. They wanted to achieve fair prices for the essential goods they needed, and they wanted to ensure that the products they were buying were not being adulterated, which was common practice at the time.

Cooperatives involve people working together, using the economies of scale for mutual financial benefit. Cooperatives belong to the members, who control trading practice and distribution of any profits (as a dividend), and are run democratically—one member, one vote. ✋ Today there are producer cooperatives jointly marketing members' products, consumer cooperatives through which members jointly purchase what they need, credit unions in which members pool their savings and obtain cheaper credit, giving cooperatives through which members pool their charitable donations to give bigger amounts to the causes they wish to support, housing cooperatives that build and manage housing on behalf of owner-tenants, school-run cooperatives that hire a minibus for the journey to school, and even babysitting cooperatives whereby young parents share babysitting. ✋ These cooperatives can be formally constituted, or they can be run informally.

Co-op On Line: www.cooponline.coop
International Cooperative Information Center: www.wisc.edu/uwcc/icic
Amul, an Indian milk-processing plant: www.amul.com
The National Dairy Development board: www.nddb.org

Milk cooperatives in India

Dr. Verghese Kurien is known as the "father of the white revolution" in India. He started a milk processing plant so small producers could get a decent price for their milk. This has now grown into Amul, which collects, processes, and sells 5 million liters of milk a day on behalf of 2.36 million producers. The National Dairy Development Board was set up under Dr. Kurien's leadership to spread the principles of cooperation in the dairy industry across India. Dr. Kurien has done more to transform rural livelihoods in India than almost anyone else.

...people working together

Start your own cooperative. It only needs three of you to get started. Decide what you want to do. Here are two simple ideas:

✋ **A dog-walking cooperative,** with each person taking a turn walking everyone's dogs.

✋ **A food cooperative,** with each member going to the wholesale market once a week to purchase fresh fruit and vegetables.

Work out your rules. These set out what members are going to get out of the co-op and what they are going to put in (time, skills, money, membership fee), as well as how it is going to operate (membership, meetings, responsibilities). This constitution should be signed by all the members.

MAD*pride*

Mad Pride was formed in 1997 and is comprised of ex-psychiatric patients and enlightened others. Sick of the "loony" tag, outraged by increasing stigma and legislative attempts to nab us and jab us, we campaign for urgent issues, risking our necks and the wrath of our shrinks.—Mad Pride website

First there was Black Pride; then there was Gay Pride; now there's Mad Pride. All have in common the idea of people celebrating who they are and their differences, and campaigning for justice and equal human rights.

MindFreedom is at the center of the psychiatric survivors' liberation movement. They have declared July as Mad Pride Month, when events are organized in Canada, France, the UK, and the US to promote self-determination for those deemed "mad," and to highlight human rights abuses of people diagnosed with psychiatric disabilities.

MindFreedom is campaigning to put an end to involuntary electric shock and drug treatment. It seeks a voice for mentally ill people in shaping the treatments and services provided for them. It documents the oral histories of survivors, in order to assist others and to act as a clarion call for change.

For Mad Pride Month 2005, Oregon activists screened people for normality. They dressed in white coats with rubber noses and silly hats, and ushered people through something similar to an airport screening door. People were invited to answer absurd but friendly questions or make animal noises and strange dance moves. No matter how people responded, they were all classified as "normally free" and given a certificate, on the back of which was information on government plans to make mental screening common practice.

MindFreedom: www.mindfreedom.org
MadNotBad: www.madnotbad.com

According to the Mental Health Foundation,

1 in 5 women and 1 in 7 men have some sort of mental problem (mostly anxiety, depression, or some sort of phobia or panic attacks).

1 in 100 will suffer manic depression or schizophrenia.

The total cost of mental health in the US is estimated at $79 billion per year (which includes $63 billion in lost productivity).

..."mad" patients with attitude

☺ **Keep sane.** Reduce the stress in your life. Do the ten simple things suggested by the "Ways to Look after Your Mental Health" poster from the Mental Health Foundation. Download this from the publications section of their website.

☺ **Understand those who suffer mental illness.** Read their personal testimonies on the MindFreedom and MadNotBad websites.

☺ **Wear a Mad Pride T-shirt,** to show solidarity with the Mad Movement and find out what's happening for Mad Pride week this year.

☺ **Go to the Mad Market section of the MindFreedom website,** and buy a hypodermic highlighter for $3. This popular novelty stationery item also *highlights* the human rights issues in mental health. Buy lots, and give them to all your friends.

bombard the GUN LOBBY

There are 639 million guns in the world and 16 billion rounds of ammunition are manufactured each year: that's two bullets for every person on the planet. Every year throughout the world roughly half a million men, women, and children are killed by armed violence. That's one person every minute of every day of every year. ✷ Weapons fuel violent conflict, state repression, crime, domestic abuse, the slaughter of schoolchildren, and accidental death. If arms continue to spread, more lives will be lost, and more human rights violations will take place.

The first week in July is the annual Global Week of Action to Control Arms. The week culminates with International Gun Destruction Day, at which guns are publicly destroyed across the world.

The International Action Network on Small Arms (IANSA), together with Amnesty International, are campaigning for tougher arms control: www.controlarms.org

Brandon's Arms, an organization committed to reducing deaths caused by firearms: www.brandonsarms.org

Brandon's battle to save lives

When he was seven years old, Brandon Maxfield was shot in the face and paralyzed while staying with friends. Someone in the house had heard a noise outside and started to load a gun, which accidentally went off. The gun, manufactured by Bryco Arms, had a faulty design that required the safety catch to be turned off before ammunition could be loaded. Brandon sued the manufacturer and was awarded $24 million in damages.

However, the company declared itself bankrupt, and got permission from the court to sell its assets, including its gun-making factory near Los Angeles, equipment, and a stock of 75,000 unassembled guns. Just one bid was received—of $150,000 from the plant's manager. But the Court allowed 20 days for other bids to be made. Brandon, now aged 17, raised $505,000 and submitted a rival bid, determined to "melt down all the guns to keep them off the street and to keep kids from getting hurt." Unfortunately, the plant's manager topped this with a bid of $510,000, and Brandon's bid to save lives failed.

...for a safer world

Take action to control arms.

Sign the Million Faces petition. This is the largest visual petition in the world. It will create a gallery of 1 million people who are prepared to take a public stand on gun control. You will be asked to submit a photograph of yourself plus personal details and to choose a slogan. How about:

Get tough on arms.
It's time for an arms trade treaty.
Make me safe from armed violence.
No more arms for atrocities.
Stop gun running.
Stop the terror trade.

Change often happens when people band together in common interest. In the summer of 1776, independence from England was the issue. And on July 4 the Second Continental Congress adopted the Declaration of Independence, which was signed by 56 representatives from 13 colonies. In 1977, two other communities declared their independence from England.

The 120 residents of Freston Road in London were threatened with eviction to make way for a giant factory complex. They held a referendum on declaring independence from the UK: 95% were in favor. They applied for membership in the United Nations. Everyone could be a minister. The education minister was a two-year-old, and the foreign minister was a dwarf, who wore a T-shirt saying "Small Is Beautiful." There was no prime minister.

There was media attention from around the world. The *Daily Mail* printed a lead story and a report "from our Foreign Correspondent in Frestonia." Busloads of tourists were shown the borders and received passport stamps. Frestonia applied to join the International Postal Union, and printed its own postage stamps. Frestonia was eventually rebuilt to a community design with several million pounds of foreign aid from the UK.

The King of Hay and Hay Peerage: www.haypeerage.ukhome.net
Frestonia: www.globalideasbank.org: search on Frestonia

The king of Hay declares independence. The booktrade in Hay-on-Wye was started in 1961 by antiquarian bookseller Richard Booth, who lived nearby. Hay was situated on the mountainous, underpopulated mid-Wales border. Richard wanted to create a town full of bookshops and an international reputation.

On April 1, 1977, Richard declared "Home Rule for Hay" and appointed himself king. This started as a joke but was taken seriously by the media and was given worldwide publicity. Richard's bookshop is now the biggest secondhand bookshop in the world. Hay's population is just 2,000, but there are 30 bookshops and an important annual literary festival. Hay has become the "book capital of the world."

On Independence Day, the king ennobled two small boys who were in the crowd watching the ceremony. This marked the beginning of the Hay peerage. Following the success of Hay-on-Wye, 20 other book towns have been created in areas facing economic decline.

...declare your independence

- 🏠 **Sign the Declaration.** Add your name alongside Thomas Jefferson, John Adams, and others in quill pen, American, Colonist, or Patriot style. Sign online and download the printed declaration: www.archives.gov/national-archives-experience/charters/declaration.html.

- 🏠 **Purchase a Hay hereditary title:** knight $45; baron $65; earl $75; duke $85. You get a certificate and a Hay passport. Bed and breakfast with the king costs $95. You can talk to him about the benefits of independence and declaring independence for your own community.

in Kenya STREET CHILDREN

Jonathan and Flick Hart support schools and children in Kisumu, on the shores of Lake Victoria, Kenya. Both retired teachers, they are able to visit Kisumu several times a year. Their work really does make a difference. Here is their account of what they do:

We help an orphanage for street children that houses 45 children aged between 6 and 18. The home consists of a large dilapidated house with a steeply sloping concrete yard. There are several crowded bedrooms; the oldest boys sleep in a leaky garage. There is no water supply, and every drop has to be paid for and collected by handcart. Food is basic, and cooked by the children on an outdoor wood stove. The children have to do everything and have organized a rota.

Health is a big problem. A pile of rags on a bed turned out to be a child suffering from TB. This took days to sort out. TB treatment is free, but all other medicines are expensive. One problem is convincing people to keep taking the TB medication once they feel better. We found malaria, including cerebral malaria which can kill in days, malnutrition, worms and all sorts of infections. Two children had dangerously infected sores on their legs. We managed to clean them up and prevent potentially crippling conditions. The concept of keeping wounds clean is simple, but is difficult to explain and achieve, particularly with no clean water supply.

We are also supporting links between schools in the UK and Kisumu. With money we have raised ourselves, and donations from the UK schools, we had 140 desks made for three schools where previously children had been sitting on the earth floor to do their lessons. Each desk seats 3–4 children. They are made by the local "fundi" and cost $20 each. We also bought four new, top-of-the-range computers locally, for two schools, and these cost $2,400 for all four.

Find out about street children and the organizations working for them:
www.streetchildren.org.uk

A young man called James works with the street children. When we were introduced, we asked him where his office was. He replied, "On the street, with the children." That was music to our ears! He deals sensitively with the children, who call him "teacher." He also works to create a life for them off the streets. Some of his ex-street boys work on a market stall, making and selling sandals from recycled tires. The sandals are made in a variety of styles and imaginatively decorated with beads and studs. We purchased 85 pairs for the children in the Juvenile Remand Home that we also visit.

...making sandals just for you

Draw an outline of your foot on a piece of paper. Send this with $50 in cash or a money order and your address to Hart Foundation, 196 Icknieldway, Letchworth SSG6 4AE, UK.

In return you will get a great pair of beaded sandals (either flip-flops or proper sandals—you can choose which), made for you by ex-street kids of Kisumu. Your support will create work for them, pay for postage anywhere in the world, and provide a bit more to support James's work with street children.

CHEMICAL *soup*

Toxic chemicals can be found in virtually all creatures and in every environment. Manufacturers are making enormous quantities for agricultural use, for industrial use, and for the products we buy and use in our lives. Most of these will be released into the environment, and once there they can travel great distances, persist for years, and become concentrated in living things that we may end up eating.

An estimated 1,000 new chemicals are created every year, in addition to the tens of thousands already in commercial use. Very few have been tested properly for their effect on wildlife and humans. There is growing evidence that some of these chemicals can alter sexual and neurological development, impair reproduction, cause cancers, and undermine immune systems. 🌳 If we can reduce the amount of chemicals that pass through our hands and bodies, we will make a small contribution to a safer world.

www.worldwildlife.org/toxics/you_do.cfm

WWF recipes to help make your home toxin-free:

All-purpose cleaner
3 tsp. liquid soap / 1/4 cup vinegar /
1/4 cup lemon juice / 1/4 cup borax
(per gallon of water)

Window cleaner
1/4 cup vinegar
1 gallon warm water

Stain remover
Soak fabrics in water mixed
with borax, lemon juice,
hydrogen peroxide, or white
vinegar.

Oven cleaner
Baking soda, vinegar, salt, steel wool.

Clean grease with rag and vinegar.
Sprinkle salt on spills. Let it sit for a few
minutes, then scrape the spill and wash
the area clean. For stubborn spots, use
baking soda and steel wool.

Controlling cockroaches and ants
Combine powdered sugar and borax in
equal parts and sprinkle
where they crawl.

...stop poisoning yourself

Reduce the chemicals in your life. The World Wildlife Federation has created a list of actions you and your family can take to reduce your consumption of toxic chemicals at home and in your life. Do some or all of them:

Buy organic. Organic products include cotton clothing, fruits, and vegetables.

Thoroughly wash fruits and vegetables, and peel them whenever possible.

Stop using pesticides. Green up your garden using natural methods:
   Traps and biological controls such as parasites and natural predators
   Disease- and pest-resistant plants
   Plants, such as basil, chives, mint, marigolds, and chrysanthemums, that repel insects
   Compost and mulch to improve soil health and to fertilize

Use environmentally friendly cleaning products in your home:
   Don't buy or use chlorine bleach.
   Use simple and inexpensive cleansers such as soap, vinegar, lemon juice, and borax.
   Avoid air fresheners and other perfumed products: freshen your air by opening windows or using baking soda, cedar blocks, or dried flowers.

slow CITIES

All cities now seem to look and feel much the same. This is partly as a result of globalization. Everywhere you go, you will now find a McDonald's and a Starbucks, and everyone is always in a hurry. ♣ Inspired by the success of the Slow Food movement, 32 Italian towns and cities joined together in 1999 to create the Slow City movement to try to reverse this trend.

A Slow City is a place where people care about their town or city, enjoy living and working there, and value the things that make it special. Over 100 cities in 10 countries have now joined the movement. Ludlow in England was the first city in the English-speaking world to join. ♣ The Slow City program involves

Enlarging parks and squares and making them greener.

Outlawing car alarms and other noise that disturbs the peace.

Eliminating ugly TV aerials, advertising billboards, and neon signs.

Promoting recycling, alternative energy, and cleaner greener transport.

These are specific things that can be done to improve the quality of life in a city. Appreciation of the seasons, purchase of local produce, and a slower and more reflective pace of life are some of the less tangible aims of the Slow Cities movement.

For a town to become a Slow City, the mayor has to make an application to the Cittàslow Committee in Italy, submitting a presentation about the town or city, giving reasons for wanting to apply, identifying goals that have already been met, setting out steps that will be being taken to meet the other goals, and giving details of who is involved in the project. ♣ Towns and cities that subscribe to these ideals, and with a population under 50,000, can apply to join. Larger cities are considered to have become just too big to slow down.

Find out more about Slow Cities from www.cittaslow.net

Slow City principles

Encouraging diversity not standardization

Supporting and encouraging local culture and traditions

Working for a more sustainable environment

Supporting and encouraging local produce and products

Encouraging healthy living especially through children and young people

Working with the local community to build these values

...where the living is easy

♣ **Write a simple manifesto for slowing down** the town or city where you live—even if the population's bigger than 50,000.

♣ **Try to get a debate going locally.** Write a letter to your local newspaper asking people to contact you if they are interested. Tell your local representatives about the movement you are starting. And if your town or city is small enough, float the idea of it joining the Slow City movement.

HELP, *disaster*

Every year there are natural disasters (these seem to be increasing as climate change makes the weather less predictable). There are also man-made disasters largely as a result of technological failure or conflict.

Disasters come in all shapes and sizes; most affect humans; some affect wildlife. Here are some major disasters from recent years:

The Bhopal chemical spill (India, 1984)

The Ethiopian famine (Ethiopia, 1984)

The Chernobyl reactor meltdown (Ukraine, 1986)

The Exxon Valdez oil spill (Alaska, 1989)

The Rwandan genocide (Rwanda, 1994)

The destruction of the Twin Towers (New York, 2001)

Hurricane Katrina (New Orleans, 2005)

The Asian Tsunami (Indonesia, Thailand, India, Sri Lanka, Maldives, 2004)

The Kashmir earthquake (India, Pakistan, 2005)

The response to a disaster usually happens in four phases: *rescue* (saving lives from the rubble or floods), *relief* (providing food, clean water, and temporary shelter), *rehabilitation* (restoring roads, homes, and livelihoods), and longer-term *community development.*

The Disaster Center provides information on disasters and links to disaster relief organizations: www.disastercenter.com

The tsunami wave that came from "out of the blue" in 2004 and wrecked whole coastlines and communities that inhabited them in the countries of the Indian Ocean led to an outpouring of generosity. Public donations from the US alone totaled $1.6 billion:

1. American Red Cross $567 million
2. World Vision $246 million
3. Catholic Relief Services $159 million
4. US Committee for UNICEF $137 million
5. Save the Children USA $132 million
6. Care USA $56 million
7. Habitat for Humanity $50 million
8. Americares Foundation $45 million
9. Mercy Corps $33 million
10. Oxfam America and Samaritan's Purse $30 million each

The magnitude of the disaster, the idea that on a quiet sunny morning the sea could suddenly turn into a wall of water, and the fact that it happened the day after Christmas created a "tsunami of aid" all around the world. If you couldn't send things or rush there as a volunteer, at least you could give money. And that's what millions did.

...a tsunami of aid

Next time there is a disaster, give generously, because people really need your help. If possible give to a local appeal (if you have information on who is doing what) or to a diaspora appeal (for example, the Indian community in the US responding to the Gujarat earthquake in 2001), as the money will go more directly to the affected communities.

But remember, the Asian tsunami killed perhaps 300,000 people, but many more than that die *every week* from AIDS, TB, malaria, poverty, and conflict. This is the real tsunami in today's world. So pledge to do whatever you can to fight for a fairer, better world.

paint a MURAL

Does your local park need brightening up? Your office, or even your own garden? Why not paint a mural? You could paint an outdoor mural on a blank wall or a door, or an indoor one—anywhere there's a wall that's crying out "Paint me!"

Murals can brighten up the environment. They can also assert the culture of a minority group or promote a social or political message. 🏠 People painted murals during the Great Depression in the 1930s as public art projects. Murals today are being painted on housing estates, in parks, and in playgrounds. They can be painted indoors as well as outdoors. Murals can be painted by people from the community working together, or by a single artist as a piece of outdoor art.

If you're going to paint an indoor mural, why not do it with natural paints? Normal paints give off volatile organic compounds (VOCs), which can cause respiratory disease and are suffused with toxic chemicals and heavy metals. It is estimated that each household has gallons of leftover paint, and much of this will end up in the household trash, and then be dumped in landfill and leach out into the soil.

Natural paints are made with citrus-oil solvents rather than petrochemicals. They get their colors from minerals and clays. They may not be as bright, and mostly they are for indoor use. But they are eco-friendly. 🏠 A green mural will show that you care about the environment in two different ways—artistically and chemically.

For information on eco-paints, go to www.ecopaint.net.
And go window shopping at www.ecomall.com.

Be inspired! To see some great examples, visit these two archives of mural paintings:
Social and Public Art Resource Center: www.sparcmurals.org
New Deal Mural Archive: newdeal.feri.org/library

...so long as it's green

🏠 **Find a wall** that needs painting. It could be inside or outside.
🏠 **Draw a design** for the mural you would like to paint. Do this with a group of friends, and discuss it with the local community where the mural will be painted. The theme could be something relevant to your neighborhood and community. It could celebrate a person or event. Or it could simply be a public work of art.
🏠 **Get permission,** if you need it.
🏠 **Buy the paint.**
🏠 **Draw an outline** of your design on the wall.
🏠 **Paint it!**
🏠 **Admire your efforts.**
🏠 **Have a party** to celebrate. Drink organic wine, of course.

BOMB *for peace*

Thailand has suffered decades of intermittent violence from Muslim separatists. In February 2004, the separatist movement in the nation's three southernmost provinces stepped up attacks on police, government buildings, and other symbols of the mainly Buddhist Thai state. The government responded with force and declared martial law in the region. Around 450 people were killed.

On December 5, 2004, the government of Thailand dropped an estimated 100 million origami birds as an attempt to promote peace, in a campaign devised by Prime Minister Thaksin Shinawatra. ✄ The crane is a widely recognized Thai symbol for peace, so people across the country folded paper cranes and wrote peace messages on them. ✄ The "peace bombing" was scheduled to coincide with the 77th birthday of revered King Bhumibol Adulyadej. About 50 military planes and helicopters lifted off from three air bases and released the paper birds at low altitude. The airdrop took all day but was completed by sunset after more than 150 flights.

As the birds fell to their targets in the provinces of Narathiwat, Yala, and Pattani, schoolchildren rushed out to collect them and read the notes inside. Some students constructed giant nets stretched across schoolyards to capture birds. There was great interest in finding the bird that the prime minister himself had signed. Mr. Thaksin promised that any student who found it would win a scholarship. ✄ Local officials responded with creative ideas for preventing a massive litter pileup. The governor of Narathiwat offered to exchange ten paper birds for an egg and 30 collected birds for a kilogram of rice.

There were critics of this campaign, who said that it would not solve the complex problems causing the violence. However, it was a creative way of highlighting the need for a resolution of the conflict in the region.

Peace Pals has instructions for making a simple peace dove: members.aol.com/pforpeace/ peacepals/project2.htm

For more information on how to create an origami bird and lots of links: www.paperfolding.com/diagrams

Livio de Marchi, an Italian artist, has created a huge floating dove of peace: www.liviodemarchi.com/ukmain3.htm

...with an origami bird

✄ **Create a flock of paper birds** with your own peace messages and display them around your workplace or school. Or hang them from trees in your neighborhood.

✄ **Recruit as many friends as you can to help you with the project.** You can make your bird display more eye-catching by using an array of colored paper.

ecological FOOTPRINTS

An ecological footprint is the area of productive land required to produce the food, energy, and materials consumed by a person or a country, and to absorb the waste they produce or cause to be produced. 🌳 The organization Redefining Progress has produced a table of footprints for each nation, measured in hectares (about 2.5 acres) of land per person.

10 largest footprints		10 smallest footprints	
US	9.57	Pakistan	0.67
United Arab Emirates	8.97	Ethiopia	0.67
Canada	8.56	Tajikistan	0.65
Norway	8.17	Malawi	0.64
New Zealand	8.13	Burundi	0.63
Kuwait	8.01	Congo, Dem. Rep.	0.62
Sweden	7.95	Haiti	0.62
Australia	7.09	Nepal	0.57
Finland	7.00	Mozambique	0.56
France	5.74	Bangladesh	0.50

Selected others: UK 4.72, Russia 4.28, Germany 4.26, Japan 3.91, South Africa 3.52, China 1.36, Nigeria 1.10

A large footprint indicates a higher standard of living but also a lifestyle that wastes resources. Differences between countries are also caused by factors such as the climate and the need to travel. Rich countries can mostly be found at the top of the list and poor countries at the bottom. 🌳 The total footprint for all of humanity was 13.2 billion hectares. It continues to increase with the world's population and rising living standards, although growth is mitigated to some extent by technological advance.

Measure your ecological footprint by taking the Ecological Footprint Quiz at www.myfootprint.org

Redefining Progress: www.rprogress.org

Facts and figures on the ecological footprint: www.redefiningprogress.org/newprojects/ecolFoot.shtml

Big feet

Average footprint per person: 2.18 hectares
Average area of productive land available per person: 1.89 hectares
Global deficit per person: 0.29 hectares

The global footprint exceeds the Earth's capacity. This sustainability gap must be addressed, as the human race cannot continue indefinitely to take more from nature than nature can provide.

...keep yours small

See what you can do to reduce your footprint:

🌳 Walk and cycle whenever you can.

🌳 Share car journeys and use public transport.

🌳 Downsize your car and go electric or hybrid.

🌳 Avoid air travel.

🌳 Eat less meat and buy fresh food locally.

🌳 Reduce, reuse, and recycle as much as you can.

🌳 Insulate your home and turn the thermostat down.

DOCTOR *yourself*

I am a district pastor in Ghana with churches in 26 towns and villages. I started using the book Where There Is No Doctor *during my visits to these communities. With the help of the book, ailments such as headaches, diarrhea, dysentery, skin diseases, convulsion, toothaches, constipation, and dehydration have been treated at little or no cost at all.*

In the 1970s, a group of health activists in Mexico compiled a notebook of treatment information for some of the common medical problems they found in their village. This grew into a much bigger healthcare manual covering almost every common health problem villagers were facing, and giving advice on what to do about the problem in the absence of a doctor. ☺ The manual was aimed largely at village health workers. It was initially published in Spanish as *Dónde No Hay Doctor*. Through the Hesperian Foundation this book has now been adapted and translated into 90 languages from Amharic to Urdu, and used all around the globe. ☺ The Hesperian Foundation has now developed a range of other health materials, all of which are published cheaply and distributed worldwide.

The distribution of low-cost health information helps people and communities deal with their urgent health problems and take preventive action. Providing good information that is appropriate to the health needs and living conditions of local communities is an extremely cost-effective way of improving health.

Hesperian Foundation: www.hesperian.org
Hesperian's Gratis Book Program: www.hesperian.org/projects.php
Teaching Aids at Low Costs (TALC): www.talcuk.org

Gratis Books

The Hesperian Foundation has developed a Gratis Book Program to provide books free to those who can't afford them. Donate $15 to pay for one book plus shipment. Around 1,500 free books are distributed this way every year.

Where There Is No Doctor helps people to treat their health problems and to recognize problems that need to be referred to an experienced health worker.

Where Women Have No Doctor helps women and girls to identify common medical problems and treatments. It covers sexual and mental health, diseases, pregnancy and childbirth, nutrition, disabilities, and injuries.

Where There Is No Dentist helps people care for their teeth.

...books to save lives

☺ **Buy a copy** of *Where There Is No Doctor* either direct from Hesperian, or from TALC. Use it yourself as a self-help health manual.

☺ **Make a donation** to the Hesperian Gratis Book Fund.

☺ **Or if you are traveling abroad** to a poor country, buy a copy of one of the books in the local language. Donate it to a village library or information center. It may help save someone's life.

fight MALARIA

If you ever think you're too small to be effective, then you've never been in bed with a mosquito.

—Wendy Lasko

Malaria is one of the world's major killers, up there with HIV/AIDS and TB. Malaria causes over 1 million deaths a year, and it's on the increase. The majority of victims are children under five and pregnant women. Half the human race is at risk. The Roll Back Malaria Partnership, coordinated by the World Health Organization, aims to halve the impact of malaria by 2010, but it's going to be a struggle.

Malaria is caused by a parasite and transmitted to humans through bites by the anopheles mosquito. Here are some worrying facts about the disease:

Every year 300–500 million people suffer from malaria, which is around 7% of the global population.

Africa has 90% of reported cases, and these account for around 10% of hospital admissions, 25% of doctor visits, and 40% of public health spending.

Someone dies from malaria every 29 seconds.

There are four types of malaria, all of which produce a severe fever. But the most common can cause death and is becoming increasingly resistant to antimalaria drugs.

Medicines for Malaria Venture has been set up to discover, develop, and distribute new and affordable antimalarial drugs for treatment and prevention. MMV is developing a new drug, ACT, based on an herbal Chinese remedy, which could be the biggest breakthrough for a generation.

Malaria Foundation International has information and lots of useful links: www.malaria.org

Medicines for Malaria Venture: www.mmv.org

Antimosquito software download: www.thaiware.com

How to prevent the mosquito bites that may carry malaria:

Screen windows and doors.

Use mosquito nets on beds.

Use biological control: some fish in small ponds and water tanks reduce the larval mosquito population.

Stop mosquitoes from breeding by closing off or removing stagnant water.

Use insect repellents, including body lotions and mosquito mats and coils.

Treat interior walls and bed nets with insecticide.

...through your computer

Antimosquito software has been developed by a Thai computer programmer. It generates sound waves through the computer's speakers that repel the mosquitoes, cockroaches, and rats within a 2-meter radius. Fortunately the frequencies that annoy rats and cockroaches are undetectable by humans. By 2005, there had been over 400,000 downloads with an 85% approval rating. This was one small step to dealing with malaria!

JULY 13

MONKEY *around*

Kids need to relax and have a good time like everyone else. Play is not just monkey business. It leads to more focused learning, healthier physical development, and better social skills.

Yet there are not nearly enough safe areas for kids to play. Every year in the US over 200,000 kids go to the emergency room because of a playground-related injury. Play doesn't have to be dangerous.

But there is something even worse than unsafe play, and that's no play at all. A lot of schools are now cutting out recess from the school curriculum, thereby reducing a child's opportunity to play. Imagine if companies banned coffee and watercooler breaks: employees would go ballistic!

KaBOOM! has an answer to this. It has done all the hard work. And it has laid out all the steps that need to be taken to make it as easy as A-B-C for you to build a safe playground in your community.

The first KaBOOM! playground was constructed in Washington, DC. There are over 400 all over the US, and more are being built every month.

Here are some fun KaBOOM! facts:
- The most popular playground colors are red, then blue and yellow.
- The most popular playground pieces are swings, then spiral slides and rocky ridge climbers.

KaBOOM!: www.kaBOOM.org
The last weekend in April is National Playground Safety Week: www.playgroundsafety.org/safety_week

Ways to say thank you to sponsors, donors, and the community:
1. The #1 way to say thank you is simply go up to the person, pat them on the back, shake their hand, give them a hug, and say a big *thank you!*
2. An inscribed plaque dedicating the playground to all who helped build it.
3. A time capsule: everyone who helped chooses an item that is special to them, and these are buried a time capsule.
4. A newspaper ad: take a full-page ad in the next day's local paper to thank everybody. List all their names.
5. A skywriting message for the whole town to see.
6. Banners: have a local business donate printed banners with the names of everyone who helped. Or have the children make them!
7. An awards ceremony, when you can give out small trophies to those who truly earned them.
8. T-shirts with the names of all your sponsors and donors.
9. Hold a postconstruction barbecue to celebrate your new playground.
10. Brainstorm an even better idea!

—adapted from KaBOOM!'s "Top Ten Ways to Say Thank You"

...build a playground

- **Monkey around with KaBOOM!** Volunteer. Get your hands dirty; take part in one of the hundreds of KaBOOM! buliding initiatives that are happening all over the US.
- **Start a playground initiative in** your own community. Download a "KaBOOM! Playground Planner" from their website. This will tell you everything you need to know to do it.

Solar electric power has become a realistic possibility, and not just for pocket calculators. Solar power can change lives in parts of the world that are beyond the reach of the conventional electricity network, and it doesn't produce any greenhouse gases or damage the environment.

Greenstar, an organization working to deliver solar power to villages in the developing world, has designed a portable community center that uses solar power to operate a water purifier, a classroom, a small clinic with a vaccine cooler, and a digital studio with satellite or wireless Internet connection. ♣ Greenstar then works with local people to develop a website that the villagers can use to conduct trade.

Greenstar plans to install 300 similar centers around the world. It uses "virtual volunteers" on assignments such as researching online sources of books on solar power, which will be used to create a solar bookstore.

Light Up the World Foundation uses solar-powered light-emitting Diode (LED) lighting to light up the lives of the world's poor. The lighting is safe, healthy, environmentally responsible, and affordable, and is four times brighter than other solar lighting.

Greenstar: www.greenstar.org

The Barefoot College: www.barefootcollege.org

Light Up the World Foundation: www.lutw.org

Purchase solar energy devices for use in the developing world: www.sustainablevillage.com

The Barefoot College in Tilonia (near Ajmer in northern India) has set up a "barefoot solar engineers" program. It trains unemployed young people and women with low literacy skills to install and maintain home solar-lighting systems in their villages. These solar engineers have electrified 300 adult education centers in India, 521 night schools, and 1,475 houses in Ladakh, which is 2 miles high in the Himalayas. It has saved 3,000 liters of kerosene and diesel a year.

The college also runs training courses for participants from all over the world on the use of solar systems in sustainable development. All the electricity for their two-acre training center is supplied from a 40 kw solar unit. This project has received international acclaim and is well worth visiting—if you happen to be passing by...

...use solar power

♣ **Find out as much as you can about solar energy:** how much it costs; how much it will save; where to get it; and how to install it.

♣ **See if you can get a solar unit installed** at home or your workplace. Or why not run a campaign to get solar power installed in your school or college? Louise Ng is a 17-year-old in London who convinced her school that solar energy was both realistic and feasible. She raised enough funds to install a solar sun-station that provides power for the school and feeds surplus electricity back into the national grid.

♣ **Get started in solar energy.** Buy a solar flashlight ($19) and a solar mosquito guard ($10) from the Real Goods Catalog: www.realgoods.com

SUDAN *take a stand*

After the Holocaust in Nazi Germany, the world said that it would never
be allowed to happen again. But it has happened, repeatedly and with no sign
of ending. ❧ Over the past few years in Sudan, millions of people in Darfur have
experienced a daily hell that we can hardly fathom.

The first thing we can do to help is conquer our ignorance about what is
happening. A snapshot of the crisis in Sudan:

The Janjaweed Militia are perpetrating atrocities against African farmers. They
burn down entire villages, raping and killing everyone they can reach.

There is a severe water shortage that leaves people lined up at pumps,
waiting for up to ten hours to get enough water to survive.

Women are afraid to leave their homes for fear of being raped by the
pillaging militias.

With the onslaught of torrential rains, malaria will ravage the population.

Over 1.2 million people have been made homeless.

Southern Sudan news site: www.gurtong.org
Join the Million Voices campaign: www.millionvoicesfordarfur.org
Darfur Peace and Development: www.darfurpeaceanddevelopment.org

Who is Magboula?

When people ask you about your arm band, tell them
about Magboula Khattar, a 24-year-old Sudanese
woman. The Janjaweed Arab militia burned her
village, murdered her parents, and finally tracked
her family down in the mountains. Magboula hid, but
the Janjaweed caught her husband and his brothers,
who were only four, six, and eight years old, and
killed them all. She escaped with her baby girl to a
refugee camp in Chad. She is just one of the 1.2
million people who have been left homeless by the
Janjaweed.

Remember that when Sudan is old news, there's
bound to be somewhere else where atrocities we
can barely imagine are taking place.

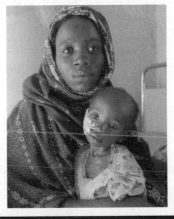

...on genocide

Make and wear an armband in support of the people in Sudan. This is what
you need to do:

❧ **Take an old sheet** and a thick marker pen. Cut the sheet into strips the
width of your thumb and length of your forearm.

❧ **Write "Ask me about Magboula"** on the center of the strip.

❧ **Prepare a short information sheet** on Magboula and a brief overview of
the situation in Sudan.

❧ **Wear the armband** to work or school, or just around town. Bring extra
armbands with you. Give them out to people you meet during the day, and ask
them to wear the bands to show their support.

And tomorrow, think about designing a T-shirt to reinforce your campaign.

16 JULY

Pets require a lot of care and attention, but they can be a fantastic addition to your life.

If you want a pet, there is no reason to go to a pet shop. Many puppies and kittens sold in pet shops come from pet breeders. Sometimes the animals are inbred and are not used to living in a home environment. ♣ Why not take care of an unwanted pet instead? Go and find a pet at your local animal shelter. Greyhounds, for example, make wonderful pets. Yet many are killed as soon as they are too old to race.

Find the pet that's just right for you. Understand the responsibilities of owning a pet (and the cost involved). And give your new pet a warm home and a lot of tender loving care.

If you don't want a pet, you can still do something to help an animal. Go to the Animal Rescue website, and click on the icon. Your simple click will provide food for an animal in need. ♣ In 2004, over 4 million people clicked each month. This raised enough to fund 31.5 million bowls of food. Visitors who shopped at the on-site store funded an additional 3.1 million bowls of food. As at other click-and-donate sites, your click costs you absolutely nothing. It simply triggers a donation by one of the site's sponsors.

The Animal Rescue Site: www.theanimalrescuesite.com
Cats & Dogs Online: www.catsdogsonline.com
The Humane Society: www.hsus.org
Adopt a pet through Petfinder: www.petfinder.com

An online matchmaking service

Cats & Dogs Online was created when Jacqueline Holstead had to find homes for her three cats—BB, a lovely, lively little black cat; Rusty, a big cuddly teddy bear of a cat; Beatie, the talkative Tonkinese cat. The process of finding new homes was logistically and emotionally difficult. It became clear that adopting an animal is not an easy task, and finding the right new home for your pet is even more difficult.

Cats & Dogs Online brings animal-loving people together—people who wish to adopt a pet and people who find that they need to rehome their pet. The website helps provide new homes and happy endings.

...from an animal shelter

♣ **Next time you want a pet, get it from your local animal shelter or rescue center.** You'll be making a poor animal very happy.

♣ **Make sure your pet is neutered;** otherwise you could end up with ten pets instead of the one you planned for. As a matter of course, many animal shelters will vaccinate, neuter, and give a full battery of tests to your new pet in order to ensure that you take home a healthy animal. You won't get this five-star service if you buy a pet at the local store.

PLANT *diversity*

The total number of plant species in the world is estimated at around 300,000. Many are in danger of extinction, threatened by habitat transformation, alien invasive species, pollution, and climate change. Their disappearance would lead to a loss of biodiversity. Maintaining plant diversity is a challenge the world needs to deal with: plant life may contain untapped secrets with the potential to meet present and future needs of humankind. 🌳 The terms *native* and *nonnative* are used to distinguish between those species we believe would have been found growing in our country or region if no human beings had ever lived there and those that have arrived or been developed with a helping hand from humans.

Planting native species in your garden is one simple way of safeguarding them—as well as providing a perfect habitat for native wildlife. 🌳 However, global warming is changing the climate so that native species in some areas no longer thrive. To protect native species for the future, we need to be aware of the bigger picture.

The United States Botanic garden: www.usbg.gov
The Brooklyn Botanic Garden: www.bbg.org

Native species are considered preferable by conservationists because they are a product of the natural habitat and ecosystem. Species of plants, animals, fungi, and microorganisms within any habitat are highly interdependent, and the introduction of a new species from outside can destabilize what exists naturally. For example, a nonnative sycamore tree would take up a space that would otherwise have been occupied by a native oak. Compared with an oak, the sycamore supports only a limited variety of leaf-eating insects and small mammals. This, in turn, would affect the number and even the viability of other species, such as insectivorous birds or mammals. Although native species may not always support more biodiversity than an equivalent nonnative, it is true in most cases, as native species have had much more time to develop stable links with each other.

...protect native species

- 🌳 **Find out what species are native to your area.** Find out where you can buy seeds; these won't cost much. There are native species of wild flowers, pond plants, shrubs, and trees to suit all tastes.
- 🌳 **Take an inventory of your garden** to see what native species you already have and what nonnative species are taking up space but not providing resources for wildlife.
- 🌳 **Designate areas of your garden for native species** (especially trees and shrubs). Plant one native species each month. Over time you will turn your garden into something both you and the local wildlife can enjoy.

18 JULY

try out a WHEELCHAIR

The best way to understand the frustration that people with mobility problems face in their everyday lives is to experience it for yourself. You can do this easily by getting into a wheelchair for a day. The steps you did not notice become insurmountable barriers, the public transport you got around on is suddenly completely inaccessible to you, and there are no disabled toilets at the meeting you are attending.

Your day will become dominated by all the things you can't do, by finding all the opportunities that the rest of the population takes for granted denied to you. But for those who need a wheelchair all the time, this is what their whole life consists of. ✖ Only when all of society comes to realize the importance of disability access as a basic human right—and at whatever the cost of provision—will conditions begin to change.

Learn more about disability rights and disability issues from these websites:
The Disability Network: www.disabilitynetwork.com
Disabled Peoples International: www.dpl.org

There are lots of "wheelchair for a day" projects to promote accessibility awareness. Here is one that took place in Vermont in 2002:

On the first day of the Wheelchair for a Day campaign, 16 biology students and four faculty members spent the day in 20 wheelchairs, which the students had obtained for the event. For the second and third days of the campaign, the wheelchairs were made available to staff and other faculty at five points on the campus. Those who were interested signed up to use the wheelchair at a specific time.

All participants received a free T-shirt designed by the students. It had the image of a person in a wheelchair at the foot of the hill leading up to the college chapel. The slogan was "Accessibility: It's an Uphill Battle."

The week also included a panel discussion and a forum on the final day at which participants discussed their experiences as wheelchair users and decided what to do as a result.

...for greater understanding

✖ **Borrow a wheelchair for a day.** Get in it and go for a day out. Make a diary of your experience. Take a camera to photograph what you find most aggravating.

✖ Join with disabled people to campaign for better access throughout your neighborhood or city.

JULY 19

GUERRILLA GIRLS

Florynce Rae Kennedy, prominent civil rights activist and pro-choice campaigner, once famously said, "If men could get pregnant, abortion would be a sacrament." Maurice and Charles Saatchi, advertising gurus, sprang to public notice with a poster of a pregnant man, saying, "If this could happen to you, you'd be more careful."

The world looks different from male and female perspectives—not least when it comes to aggression and warfare. The architects of the Iraq war on both sides were practically all men. Would the situation have been different if the hormones coursing through their bodies had been estrogen rather than testosterone?

Since 1985 the Guerrilla Girls have been reinventing feminism. Still going strong in the 21st century, they're a bunch of anonymous females who take the names of dead women artists as pseudonyms and appear in public wearing gorilla masks. ✖ Guerrilla Girls have produced over 100 posters, stickers, books, printed projects, and public demonstrations to expose sexism and racism in politics, the art world, film, and the culture at large. They use humor to convey information, provoke discussion, and show that feminists can be funny. They wear gorilla masks to focus on the issues rather than their personalities. ✖ Dubbing themselves "the conscience of culture," they see themselves as feminist counterparts to the mostly male tradition of anonymous do-gooders like Robin Hood, Batman, and the Lone Ranger.

Guerrilla Girls, fighting discrimination with facts, humor, and fake fur since 1985: www.guerillagirls.com
Life of Florynce Kennedy: rwor.org/a/v22/1090-99/1095/flo_kennedy.htm

Guerrilla Girls on Feminism

We believe feminism is a fundamental way of looking at the world and recognizing that half of us are female and all of us should be equal. It's a fact of history that for centuries women have not had the rights and privileges of men and it's time for that to end.

Despite the tremendous gains of women over the last hundred years, misogyny—the hatred or hostility towards women as a whole—is still rampant throughout our culture and in the larger world. We think that is the number one reason women need feminism.

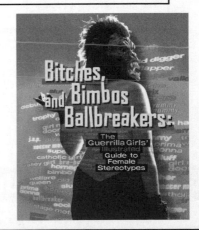

...reinventing the F-word

Fight testosterone power and make politicians more peaceful. Got any leftover estrogen pills? Send an "Estrogen Bomb" to Bush, Cheney, and Rumsfeld, white men in power, with your own message suggesting a more feminine way of governing the US and the world. Address: The White House, 1600 Pennsylvania Avenue, Washington, DC 20500.

20 JULY

campaign for **BHOPAL**

At five minutes past midnight on the night of December 3, 1984, the Union Carbide pesticide plant in Bhopal in central India exploded, releasing a toxic gas that caused 8,000 deaths within a few days, and more than 20,000 in the years since. An estimated 150,000 people have suffered serious health problems. ♣ On the night of the disaster, six safety measures designed to prevent a leak were either malfunctioning, shut down, or otherwise inadequate. The refrigeration unit was deliberately turned off, in order to save a measly $40 a day.

The site of the closed factory remains a toxic hot spot, with concentrations of carcinogenic chemicals and heavy metals. Chemicals continue to seep into the water supplies of an estimated 20,000 people who are living in surrounding communities. These people have no choice but to drink, wash, and cook with this water every day.

The Indian government charged Union Carbide's CEO with negligent homicide, but Warren Anderson has not been extradited from the US to stand trial in India. Dow Chemical purchased Union Carbide in 2001 but has refused to take responsibility for the Bhopal cleanup. ♣ In 1999, 15 years on, Bhopal survivors filed a class action suit against Union Carbide in the US courts, asking that the company be held responsible for violations of international human rights law and for cleaning up the environmental contamination in Bhopal. This case will test the limits of a corporation's ability to use the laws of one nation to escape responsibility in another.

Read the stories and reports about Bhopal at the Greenpeace archive: www.greenpeace.org/international/footer/search?q=bhopal
The Bhopal People's Health and Documentation Clinic: www.bhopal.org
The International Campaign for Justice in Bhopal: www.bhopal.net

Compare the compensation figures:

For the victims of 9/11: Congress authorized a $5.9 million compensation fund for the 2,963 deaths and about 4,400 injury claims arising from the disaster. The average death payment is just above $2 million, while the largest death payment to date has been $7.1 million.

For the victims of Bhopal: Five years after the disaster that claimed 8,000 deaths and an estimated 150,000 seriously injured people, Union Carbide agreed to a compensation fund of $470 million. Victims each received less than $350 for injuries they are likely to suffer all their lives. The world's largest industrial accident cost Union Carbide just 48 cents a share.

...victims of Union Carbide

♣ **Support the Bhopal People's Health and Documentation Clinic,** which is treating 1,000 victims each month and is documenting toxic deaths in the community. The clinic is funded entirely by donations. It was awarded the Margaret Mead Centennial Award in 2002 for its outstanding work.

♣ **Join the International Campaign for Justice in Bhopal.** The campaign aims to bring justice to Bhopal survivors by keeping world attention focused on Dow Chemical's liability for the Union Carbide disaster.

JULY 21

SHOP *ethically*

Every time you go shopping, you have the power to make a difference to the world. Every dollar you spend is a vote for the company that makes the product that you're buying. Buying ethical products sends support directly to companies working to improve our world, while at the same time depriving others that abuse it for profit. ⚽ Ethical consumerism means that when you go shopping, you take into account the issues that are important to you and favor companies whose policies and activities you'd prefer to support.

Ethical shopping also means avoiding or boycotting companies whose policies and activities you disagree with. All too often, companies are involved in unethical practices, such as exploiting workers in the developing world, dumping toxic chemicals into the environment, or producing items that involve the exploitation of animals. ⚽ Awareness of global poverty, animal welfare, and green issues are at an all-time high. If we can carry this awareness into our shopping basket, we can all work together to help make the world a better place and make sure that companies start treating it, and us, with more respect.

A small number of multinational companies own a large proportion of Americans' favorite brands, but there are still plenty of alternatives out there, and a range of smaller companies who are as concerned with treating the world with more respect as with making money. The Ethical Consumer Research Association researches the companies behind the brands so that you don't have to be a super detective to be an ethical consumer. This information is published in the bimonthly *Ethical Consumer* magazine.

See www.ethicalconsumer.org and on the www.ethiscore.org website.
Other ethical consumerism websites include www.responsibleshopper.org.

Ethical shopping list

Everyone has his or her own priorities when they go shopping, but consumers are beginning to take ethical issues into account as well as price and quality, and companies are responding accordingly. We all go shopping, and so ethical consumerism is an easy way of using your money to try and make a difference.

Fairly traded products
Local produce
Organic produce
Fridge with energy efficiency A rating
Secondhand shirt from thrift shop
Pay money into cooperative bank
Drop off recycling

...make your money talk

What else can I do?
⚽ **Write to companies** whose policies you disagree with, telling them why you are avoiding them.
⚽ **Join consumer campaigns** targeting companies whose activities you disagree with.

22 JULY

create an AXIS OF EVIL

Axis: a main line of direction, motion, growth, or extension
Evil: something morally reprehensible, causing harm

In 1982, President Reagan referred to the Soviet Union as the "Evil Empire." In his 2002 State of the Union speech, President George W. Bush echoed this idea when referring to North Korea, Iran, and Iraq as constituting an "Axis of Evil" with respect to the war on terror:

> *North Korea is a regime arming with missiles and weapons of mass destruction, while starving its citizens....states like these, and their terrorist allies, constitute an Axis of Evil.*

Whether or not you agree with President Bush's sentiments regarding the war on terror, one very real evil is the denial of human rights in North Korea. More than 4 million people have died of starvation since 1995, despite the fact that North Korea receives more food aid than any other nation in the world. Article 3 of the Universal Declaration of Human Rights states that everyone has the right to life.

US Committee for Human Rights in North Korea: www.hrnk.org
Human Rights Watch's North Korea page: hrw.org/doc/?t=asia&c=nkorea
Free North Korea: www.freenorthkorea.net
North Korea Freedom Coalition: nkfreedom.org

The Korean paradox

Article 5 of the Universal Declaration of Human Rights states that no one shall be subjected to torture or to cruel, inhuman, or degrading treatment or punishment. According to *The Hidden Gulag: Exposing North Korea's Prison Camps*, published by the US Committee for Human Rights, North Korea has three types of labor camps, where "the injustices and cruelty these prisoners suffer is almost unimaginable...a starvation diet, torture, beatings, inhumane living and working conditions..." The report describes

 conditions in North Korea's six political penal labor camps, known as Kwan-Li-So, where tens of thousands of political prisoners work as slaves in mining, logging, and farming enterprises.

This is the sort of future that a human rights activist in North Korea could face, while those conforming with the regime celebrate the birthday of Kim Jong Il with this felicitation:

> *Our Dear Leader, you are a guardian star of the Korean people and a benevolent teacher....In our undivided heart, we repeat our pledge of unbending loyalty to the President and the Dear Leader...*

...fight for what's right

Identify your own "Axis of Evil" around an issue that you care passionately about. The issue might be nuclear proliferation, child labor, greenhouse gas emissions, manufacture and sale of land mines, execution of juveniles, censorship of information...

- **Identify the "baddies,"** those countries (perhaps including your own) that remain out of line.
- **Find out all the relevant facts.** Create a league table from the best to the worst. Find out about the organizations that are doing something about the issue.

JULY 23

BIG BROTHER

Government agencies and private companies are increasingly violating the privacy of people everywhere. Enormous amounts of personal data are being collected, stored, and processed—often illegally—in the pursuit of more efficient marketing, greater social control, and more powerful mechanisms for monitoring of the citizen.

—Privacy International

Google uses a cookie that expires in 2038. This places a unique ID number on your hard disk. Any time you land on a Google page, you get a Google cookie if you don't already have one. If you have one, they read and record your unique ID number.

▲ About 75% of searches are done on Google. For all searches they record the cookie ID, your Internet IP address, the time and date, your search terms, and your browser configuration. Google retains this data indefinitely, and they won't say why they need this data or if they have ever been subpoenaed to disclose it.

In many countries, people are able to trace how you have voted. In the UK, for example, the number on your voting slip is recorded on the electoral roll used by the polling station to note down who has voted. It is then possible to find out the names and addresses of everyone who has voted for a particular party. A complete list of people voting for extremist parties could easily be compiled and handed over to the internal security services as a list of "subversives." The fear of being traced could deter people from expressing their true voting intentions.

Your mobile phone will show where you have made calls from, and soon satellite tracking systems for road tolls will record where your car has traveled. Your shop loyalty card and credit cards show what you have been purchasing. Video cameras are everywhere recording you walking in the street. You are being watched.

Privacy International: www.privacyinternational.org
Privacy.org, a news site established by Privacy International and the Electronic Privacy Information Center: www.privacy.org

Privacy International runs its Big Brother Awards in Australia, Austria, Bulgaria, Denmark, Finland, France, Germany, Hungary, Japan, the Netherlands, Spain, Switzerland, the UK, and US.

Big Brother Awards are given to government agencies, private companies, and individuals who have done something that significantly violates our privacy. The panels of judges worldwide consist of lawyers, academics, consultants, journalists, civil rights activists, and others.

...is watching you

Think about how your privacy is now increasingly being threatened.

▲ Is there is any person or any institution invading your privacy you would like to propose for an award?

▲ Tell Privacy International. Nominate someone for a Big Brother Award.

24 JULY

open source COLA

The ethos of the Open Source Software movement allows the free copying and modification of software while crediting the ownership of the original idea. It enables a piece of software to be continually improved through the input of others.

Opencola uses the same principles. It is a brand of cola for which the instructions for making it are freely available and modifiable. Anybody can make the drink, and anyone can modify and improve on the recipe. ⚽ It was originally designed as a publicity stunt to promote the Opencola software design company in Toronto and its services. But the drink took on a life of its own. It sold 150,000 cans, and the company became better known for the drink than for the software it was intended to promote. The cola website is now run from Japan. ⚽ The success of Opencola partly stems from its being a quirky idea and partly from a widespread mistrust of big corporations. Opencola provides you with a great opportunity to create a no-logo, no-brand product and use it to explain the benefits of open source sharing and the issues of globalization.

Opencola background and recipe:
www.colawp.com/colas/400/cola467_recipe.html

Find out more about open source software and copyleft from the Wikipedia encyclopedia: en.wikipedia.org/wiki/Open_source and en.wikipedia.org/wiki/Copyleft

Opencola recipe

7X (Top-Seekrut™) flavoring formula:

Mix the following oils together in a cup: 3.5 ml orange oil, 1 ml lemon oil, 1 ml nutmeg oil, 1.25 ml cassia oil, 0.25 ml coriander oil, 0.25 ml neroli oil, 2.75 ml lime oil, 0.25 ml lavender oil. Add 10 g gum arabic. Add 3 ml water and mix well in a blender. Keep in a sealed glass jar in the fridge or at room temperature.

Opencola syrup:

2 tsp 7X formula
3 1/2 tsp 75% phosphoric acid or citric acid
2.25 l water

2.25 kg plain granulated white table sugar
1/2 tsp caffeine (optional)
30 ml caramel color

In a 4-liter container, take 5 ml of the 7X mixture and add the acid. Add the water and then the sugar. While mixing, add the caffeine (optional), and make sure it dissolves completely. Then add the caramel color. Mix thoroughly.

To prepare the drink:

To finish, take 1 part syrup and add 5 parts carbonated water.

This recipe is licensed under the GNU General Public license. It is open source cola, or, if you prefer, "free" cola. You're free to use this recipe to make your own cola, or to modify it. If you distribute modified colas, you're expected to send an e-mail to the recipe's author, Amanda Foubister at amanda@opencola.com with your modifications.

...it's almost the real thing!

Make your own cola. Drink it at home, at parties, or at festivals and fairs where you can promote the idea of open source sharing.

JULY 25

GUIDE DOG *training*

Dogs can become canine superheroes. Guide dogs are the eyes of the blind and hearing dogs are the ears of the deaf. ❌ These dogs are not born knowing hundreds of commands. They need to be trained. This is something you can help with. So why don't you help train a guide dog? ❌ The rewards will be enormous. The animal you help train will dramatically improve the quality of life of a disabled person. You will be giving that person a constant companion, a best friend, and the freedom to live in a more enabled way.

Guide dogs are generally from one of the following breeds:
Labrador retriever
Golden retriever
German shepherd
Labrador/golden retriever cross

Guide dogs have to be trained to lead their partner in a straight line between two points and around any ground or overhead obstacles. The dogs can't read traffic signals, so are trained to stop at the curb while their human partner listens for oncoming cars. But if the human partner begins walking and a car approaches, the dog is trained to stop. The dogs are trained to ignore all outside stimuli such as strange smells and sounds, other dogs, and humans.

Guide Dogs of America: www.guidedogsofamerica.com
Dogs for the Deaf: www.dogsforthedeaf.org

Puppy walking is an important part of developing a future guide dog. A volunteer puppy walker takes a puppy aged around six weeks into his or her home and nurtures it for the first year of its life—teaching it basic commands and getting it used to as many different environments as possible. This is done under the guidance of a puppy walking supervisor.

...walk a puppy

Become a puppy walker. Help turn Fido into a Florence Nightingale.

Puppy walkers have to meet certain criteria. To take on this role you need to
❌ **Be at home** most of the day (puppies cannot be left for more than three hours).
❌ **Be over 18 years old.**
❌ **Live in a ground-floor dwelling** with a securely fenced garden or yard that has speedy access to a "spending" area (where the pup can relieve itself).
❌ **Not have children under three.**
❌ **Have regular access to car travel.**
❌ **Be willing to take the puppy out** as part of your daily routine—to the supermarket, for example.

CASTEISM

cast out

Discrimination is often discussed on the basis of race, ethnic background, gender, age, and sexuality. But discrimination on the basis of caste is a hugely important and worrying issue that is often ignored.

Casteism is most evident in Hinduism, which has four "castes," based on occupation and ancestry. At the top are the priestly caste of the Brahmins; next the soldiers or Kshtriyas; then the merchants and farmers (the Vaishyas); finally those that serve them (the Shudras). ✖ Beyond these come the Dalits—who are completely outside the caste system ("out-castes" or "untouchables"). Dalits are right at the bottom of the social hierarchy. In Hindu societies, many Dalit communities suffer extreme discrimination.

Dalits get the poorest shelter, often having to live in huts outside the perimeter of the village; they may be denied access to water for fear of their polluting it; they often have the worst, lowest-paid jobs, which also means that their nutrition and health are poor and that their children have to work and are therefore denied an education. ✖ Hinduism even denies Dalits advancement in the next life. Dalits are condemned to return to the world over and over again as "polluted" and "outcast" people. A Dalit can never escape the oppression of the caste system. ✖ There are 160 million Dalits in India and 260 million in Asia as a whole.

National Campaign on Dalit Human Rights: www.dalits.org
International Dalit Support Network: www.idsn.org
A Dalit website with lots of links: www.ambedkar.org

Martin Macwan is a Dalit. He began life as a child farmhand. He then worked his way through school and went to college, graduating in psychology and then getting a law degree. In 1983, he started to work with tribal children and Pakistani refugees in Gujarat.

Macwan wanted to do more than just provide a social service. He started to work on Dalit rights and caste discrimination. In 1986, four of his friends were shot dead, 18 more

wounded, and several villages set on fire in an attack by feudal landlords. The landlords resented what they saw as "uppity Dalit activists" and wanted to "teach them a lesson." Macwan escaped death only because he had gone home sick earlier that day. Macwan held a dead friend's body and vowed, "He died and I escaped. I swore with his corpse in my arms: your death will not be in vain."

In 1989, Macwan started Navsarjan Trust in Ahmedabad to mobilize and empower the Dalits. Since then, Navsarjan ("New Creation") has grown into one of the most effective Dalit advocacy groups in India. In 1996, he launched the National Campaign on Dalit Human Rights, which is working for the abolition of "untouchability."

...it's as bad as racism

Support the Dalits in their campaign for human rights.

✖ Send Martin Macwan a letter of support: martin@icenet.net

✖ And why not raise some money for the Dalit rights movement?

There are equivalents to caste discrimination in other societies and cultures. Any discrimination based on the accident of birth should be fought against.

ACT *for love*

Act for Love is an online dating service for activists, leftists, news junkies—people with brains who actually care about the world. This is the place to take action AND get action. Get started now!

The idea is simple. Everyone wants to meet his or her perfect match; many people use online personals services to do so. So why not create a place where activists can meet other activists? At least they will have something in common. And why not let people make the world a better place while they're finding their perfect match?

Act for Love helps make the world a better place by

1. Donating a portion of its proceeds to good causes and activist efforts.
2. Featuring campaigns on its website, and starting campaigns for causes without champions.
3. Building a network of activist singles—and turning them into activist doubles!

www.actforlove.org

Featured campaigns have included:

Tobacco-Free Kids: Philip Morris changed its name but not its deadly tobacco products. Calling itself *Altria* won't prevent a single child from starting smoking or save a single life. Or change the fact that the company is still spending millions of dollars a day on marketing and promoting cigarettes that hook kids. Protect kids, not Big Tobacco. Tell President Bush, *"Don't pardon Big Tobacco!"*

Undo It, campaigning to reduce greenhouse emissions in the US. The earth is heating up, thanks to heat-trapping greenhouse gases produced by burning fossil fuels, and the damage is already appearing. Send the message that global warming demands action. Add your voice to over 333,000 others on the Emissions Petition to support the Climate Stewardship Act, a bipartisan bill to reduce greenhouse gas pollution in the US. Cut the emissions. Sign the petition.

Greenpeace, campaigning to protect forest wildernesses. US national forests are coming under greater threat. The Roadless Area Conservation Rule, which protects 58.5 million acres of forest land, is in imminent danger of being undermined. Tell the Forest Service that our last remaining wild forests need protection.

And also these:

Working Assets: to encourage voter registration

NARAL Pro-Choice America: to stop antichoice legislators from banning emergency contraception

The American Civil Liberties Union: campaigning to improve the Patriot Act

...date for change

Find the action

If you share these views and values and are a single, then join the Act for Love network. Take action by supporting these and other campaigns.

Get action by registering your personal details as a first step in finding your perfect match. You never know. Today might just be your lucky day!

donate YOUR CAR

For some people, a car can be the difference between working and not working. For a charity, a car can be the difference in how well it performs.

Cars 4 Causes is a charity to help charities, a saint for the saints. The organization accepts car donations and then relays cash from the sale of the car or the car itself to organizations or individuals who are in need.

Cars 4 Causes is a great success story. Two people started with an idea in 1997 of selling a 1982 Nissan Maxima, and now they have created a thriving charity with close to sixty employees. They have donated over $22 million to over 7,000 charities. And they say that they are just getting started!

How Cars 4 Causes works

Step 1: A donor completes a donation form on the website or contacts Cars 4 Causes by telephone, giving general information on the vehicle and selecting a charity. Most intact vehicles are taken, running or not.

Step 2: Vehicles are towed away and all paperwork completed at no charge. Vehicles are prepared for sale by having minor repairs and maintenance work done.

Step 3: Donors are informed of a fair market value for the vehicle and given a thank-you letter and a donation receipt (to gain a tax deduction).

Step 4: The vehicle is sold through advertising, a Cars 4 Causes retail lot, on eBay, or through a live auction. The revenue is then distributed to the chosen charity.

www.cars4causes.net

Trivia on the Cars 4 Causes website

- Americans eat enough ice cream each year to fill the Grand Canyon.
- Rabbits can't walk. They always hop or leap.
- An alligator will go through as many as 3,000 teeth in its lifetime.
- The average pencil will draw a line 35 miles long.
- Goodyear once made a tire completely out of corn.
- The average adult has four dreams a night and one nightmare a year.

...and choose your cause

Donate your car.

If you, your family, or a friend are spending a lot of your free time visiting car lots to try to get a deal, then the chances are that there is an old car rotting in a driveway somewhere. Donate it. This is entirely tax-deductible, and Cars 4 Causes makes the process easy as pie. They are looking for any sort of vehicle. The only criterion is that the car be intact. The newest car ever donated was just one year old; the oldest, seventy-five.

As you tearfully part from your beloved old clunker, Cars 4 Causes will be towing your car away. They will either sell the car for cash or donate it to a nonprofit. If they sell it for cash, you can even stipulate which organization should receive the donation. Suddenly your old car that was only causing you grief will be transformed into a vehicle of great worth.

LOVE *your neighborhood*

Your neighborhood is special. Even if it's not perfect, you can learn to love it. Look around you and think about the things you really like. And do what you can to resist the way in which everything is becoming more and more uniform—the same shops, the same undistinguished new buildings, the same ways in which cars and parking are given precedence over people.

What's special could include parks and playgrounds, with people enjoying themselves, statues, architectural details such as a crazy chimney or interesting doorway, shop signs, road names, front gardens, trees and flowers...

Common Ground, with rules for local distinctiveness:
www.commonground.org.uk/rules.html

Some rules for local distinctiveness (adapted from Common Ground)

Change things for the better—not just for the sake of change.

Let the character of the people and place shine through. Kill corporate identity before it kills our main streets. Give local shops precedence.

Defend detail. Respond to the local and the vernacular. New buildings or developments need not be bland, boring, or brash.

Enhance the natural features of the area—the rivers and shore, the hills and valleys, the woods and plains.

Get to know your ghosts. The hidden and unseen stories and legends of the area are as important as what is visible.

History is a continuing process, not just the past. Don't fossilize places. Celebrate time, place, and the seasons with feasts and festivals.

Jettison your car whenever you can and use public transportation. Places are for people and nature, not cars.

Know your place. Facts and surveys are not the same as knowledge and wisdom.

Buy things that are locally distinctive and locally made—such as food and souvenirs. Resist the things that can be found anywhere.

Names carry resonances and secrets. Respect local names and add new ones with care. It is not good enough to call a new development Applewood when all the apple trees have been destroyed.

Reveal the past. Decay is an important process. Don't tidy things up so much that the layers of history and reclamation by nature are obliterated. Let continuity show.

Use old buildings again. Find new functions for them.

...make your locality unique

🏠 **Take a camera** and photograph the 25 things that most please you about your neighborhood.

🏠 **Prepare a virtual exhibition.**

🏠 **Contact your local paper** and offer to e-mail your exhibition to anyone who is interested.

population PRESSURE

There were 6,465,035,104 human beings alive on the planet on September 7, 2005, at 13:09 GMT precisely, according to the US Census Bureau estimates. 🌐 The world's population has doubled since 1963 and increased by 74.4 million during 2005. By mid-2050, the population is estimated to rise to 9.22 billion. 🌐 Our planet has a limited supply of land, water, and natural resources. Will it be able to support its increasing human population? What will be the environmental consequences? Will technology come to the rescue?

In the 1970s the world's two most populous nations took action to curb their growing populations. China instituted a one-child policy, and India introduced sterlization camps and forced vasectomies. The side effects ranged from human misery to female infanticide. 🌐 It is now recognized that since poverty and gender inequality are key factors in population increase, the best way of slowing the rate of increase is by creating a social climate receptive to messages about family planning.

Providing a decent education for girls, so that they develop into women who have a much clearer idea of the options open to them, is an effective way of reducing the birth rate. Literate women are in a better position to act on information about how to limit their family and protect their children from disease. They are more likely to generate extra income to bring up a smaller family in greater prosperity.

World population information: www.census.gov/ipc/www/world.html
World Population/Overpopulation Awareness: www.overpopulation.org
United Nations Population Fund: www.unfpa.org

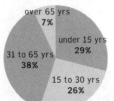

over 65 yrs
7%

under 15 yrs
29%

31 to 65 yrs
38%

15 to 30 yrs
26%

Population trends

Children under the age of 15 currently make up a large proportion of the world's population.

With birth rates falling, and people living longer, children will decline as a proportion of the population.

...help to relieve it

Whether you have a large family or a small family will not make much of a difference to the world's population. But you can make a difference by helping families and communities to get out of poverty. Your financial support will help meet basic community needs (such as health and sanitation), provide a better education, and help families find ways of increasing their income. You can

🌐 **Sponsor a child,** where your support will help a family and the wider community. Organizations such as ActionAid and Plan International specialize in child sponsorship. It costs around $1 a day.

🌐 **Adopt a village.** The Adopt-a-Village Registry aims to create a register of villages that would like to be adopted, and then to link these with individuals and agencies that would like to adopt them. Set up after the 2004 tsunami to create a "tsunami of kindness," this project is still under development: www.adoptavillageregistry.com

LEMONADE *for Alex*

We have heard people say that Alex lost her battle with cancer. We believe that this could not be farther from the truth. Alex won her battle in so many ways...by facing her cancer every day but still managing to smile; by never giving up hope; by living life to the fullest; and by leaving an incredible legacy of hope and inspiration for all of us.

—Jay and Liz Scott, Alex's parents

Alexandra Scott was an extraordinary eight-year-old. When she was only one year old she was diagnosed with neuroblastoma, an aggressive form of childhood cancer. At the age of four, she decided to set up a lemonade stand to raise money for her treatment. And then her goal became to raise $1 million for pediatric cancer research, one glass of lemonade at a time. Now there are hundreds of lemonade stands all over the US, raising money for Alex's pediatric cancer fund. Alex's fund has so far raised over $1.4 million.

Alex died on August 1, 2004. Her story is told in a book, *Alex and the Amazing Lemonade Stand*.

Childhood cancer facts:

One in every 600 children develops cancer before the age of 15.

Leukemia and brain tumors account for more than half the cases.

The causes of most childhood cancers are unknown. At present, childhood cancer cannot be prevented.

Childhood cancer occurs randomly and spares no ethnic group, socio-economic class, or geographic region.

Alex's Lemonade Stand: www.alexslemonade.org
Children's Cancer Web, information on childhood cancer: www.cancerindex.org/ccw

How to make your own lemonade (sufficient for 50 glasses):

1   **Make a syrup.** Add ten cups of sugar to ten cups of water in a saucepan. Bring slowly to the boil, stirring until the sugar completely dissolves. Allow to cool. Refrigerate.
2   **Juice 50 lemons.** Make sure you remove the pips. Add the lemon juice to the syrup.
3   **Dilute to taste** with still or sparkling water. Add approximately three times the quantity of water to syrup.

...fight childhood cancer

Set up a lemonade stand in Alex's honor. Send the profits to Alex's Lemonade Fund at the Philadelphia Foundation: www.philafound.org/Alexslemonade.html

You will need

☺ **A table,** lots of lemonade, a jug, and plastic cups.

☺ **A sunny day** (hopefully).

☺ **A cheerful friend** to keep you company.

☺ **Posters and banners** that say what you are raising money for.

☺ **A cash box.**

Would you like to own Microsoft? When you buy a share in Microsoft, you become a co-owner of the company, along with all the other shareholders. You get these benefits:

A share certificate, proclaiming your ownership

An annual report of the company's performance

Share dividends

The right to attend the company's annual general meeting and to vote on the resolutions put to the meeting. These include appointing company directors and agreeing on their remuneration.

When you decide to sell your shares, you might even make a profit if the value of the shares has increased.

As a shareholder, you can vote against the appointment of a director or against his or her proposed remuneration. Of course, your share of the company is tiny, so this vote will only have an impact if it is part of a wider campaign. 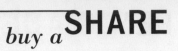 At the AGM, there will also be an opportunity to ask the chair a question. You might ask about

Child labor: does the company use it?

Waste disposal: does the company dispose of its waste safely?

Global warming: is the company doing enough to address global warming?

Whatever your particular concern, you can ask the company for a response in front of a large audience with lots of journalists present.

Some companies find their shareholder meetings become a forum— sometimes a battleground—where social and environmental issues are raised: such companies include Nestlé (which markets formula milk in the developing world) and Exxon (which is not doing enough to counter global warming). All you need is one share in order to have the right to attend.

Information and ideas on shareholder activism:
www.coopamerica.org/socialinvesting/shareholderaction

Isabel Losada was campaigning with the Free Tibet Movement. They arranged for her to attend the AGM of BP to raise the issue of BP's investment in PetroChina, which was planning to build a pipeline through Tibet. Once she was in the meeting hall, Isabel changed into the costume of a Chinese soldier. Every time the chair mentioned Tibet, she clapped and cheered. Every time her fellow Free Tibet protesters got to ask a question, she hurled abuse at them. And she congratulated the chair on not letting terrorists disrupt the profits of the company. Humor is an excellent way to make a point. Read Isabel's book, *For Tibet with Love.*

...and have your say

Is there a company you would like to confront over an issue?

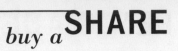 Buy one share in that company—through an online trading service or a stockbroker.

 Go along to the AGM. When the chair asks for questions, stand up and have your say.

HELLO *peace*

If only we could achieve peace in the Middle East, then we would stand a much better chance of creating peace in all of the world.

The purpose of the Hello, Peace! project is to get large numbers of Israelis and Palestinians to connect up and talk about peace, and to put pressure on both governments to move toward dialogue and away from violence.

The project enables any Israeli or Palestinian simply to pick up the phone at no charge and talk with someone on "the other side" about peace.

Hello, Peace! is based on an automated telephone system, using interactive voice response (IVR). When people call *6364, they identify themselves as Israeli or Palestinian, perhaps indicate the age of the person they wish to talk to, and say whether they want to talk now or later. A computer automatically connects them to someone who fits the profile and has expressed a willingness to talk.

Since October 2002, over 230,000 calls have been placed through this system. This is an extraordinary level of response—and real evidence that many Israelis and Palestinians in fact *do* want to talk with each other about peace.

Hello, Peace! is an initiative of the Parents Circle—Families Forum, a group of over 200 Israeli and over 200 Palestinian parents, each of whom has lost children or close family members in the conflict.

www.hellopeace.net
www.theparentscircle.com

Cut and paste this message...

Hello, Salaam! Hello, Shalom! Hello, Peace!

If you're in Israel, the West Bank, or Gaza, now you can just pick up your phone at no cost and talk to someone on the other side about reconciliation, tolerance, and peace.

Just dial *6364 from any Bezeq or mobile phone and listen to the instructions. Call as many times as you want—more is better! More details at www.hellopeace.net.

And even if you're not in the Middle East, you can help by sending this e-mail to everyone you know there or who may have connections there. Every call makes the message grow stronger: it's time to stop the killing and start talking again.

...and good-bye war

Hello, Peace! wants to get its phone number to the entire Israeli and Palestinian populations through a large-scale messaging campaign—including radio spots, the Internet, billboards, targeted phone calls, and an e-mail and text messaging campaign.

🕊 **Send the Hello, Peace!** phone number and instructions to family, friends, colleagues, or organizations you know of in Israel, Gaza, or the West Bank.

🕊 **E-mail a paragraph** about Hello, Peace! to online discussion groups, newsletters, and any group you can think of with an interest in the Middle East.

books not BOMBS

At age 16 Ramsey Jammal became aware of the need for school supplies in Iraq. He decided to do all he could to help. With the help of his mother, he started a collection, and in just two months, the collection barrels he set up at his church were overflowing. Now Ramsey is planning to collect sports equipment.

For the first time in a long while, kids in Iraq have the chance to a decent education. The problem is, they have no school supplies. Obviously, without pencils and books it is difficult to learn how to read and write. This is a countrywide problem that you can help solve.

Operation Iraqi Children was launched by actor Gary Sinise *(Forrest Gump, Apollo 13)* and author Laura Hillenbrand *(Seabiscuit: An American Legend)* to get a basic school supply kit to children in Iraqi schools.

"Imagine sending your child to a school in which there are virtually no books, no pencils, no paper, no blackboards," says Hillenbrand. *"This is the reality for Iraqi children. The future of the Iraqi nation is being squandered for lack of basic school supplies."*

Operation Iraqi Children provides a standard pack for children, comprising

- small pencil sharpener
- large eraser
- box of colored pencils (crayons melt!)
- package of notebook paper
- composition book

- 3 folders with inside pockets
- zippered pencil bag
- 12 new pencils with erasers
- pair of blunt-end scissors
- 12-inch ruler with metric markings

Don't include anything else. Operation Iraqi Children aims to supply children in 1,500 schools. They need your help.

For more information: www.operationiraqichildren.org

You can also send sports equipment or stuffed animals. Appropriate sports equipment includes soccer balls, jump ropes, and Frisbees. Please send all balls deflated for air transport and include a small hand pump for reinflating.

When choosing what to send, avoid items that are religious, depict war or conflict, or are strongly gender- or age-specific. You are asked to be sensitive to the fact that you are sending items into a culture less exposed to television and video games, and which is under some emotional strain.

...send school supplies to Iraq

Put together a school kit for an Iraqi child. Even better, get some friends to do it alongside you. Pack only the listed supplies in a backpack or in a 2-gallon-sized zipper-seal plastic bag.

On the outside of each package, clearly write "SCHOOL KITS, OPERATION IRAQI CHILDREN," the number of kits included in the box, and the name and address of yourself, your school, or your organization.

Address the package to Fast Pace Distribution, c/o Operation Iraqi Children, 6200 E. St. John Ave., Kansas City, MO 64123. By sending it to Kansas City, you avoid the hefty cost of postage to Iraq. They will send your kit to Iraq, where American soldiers help distribute it to local children.

COMPOST *your waste*

Composting decomposes organic matter into a growing medium full of nutrients. It takes place when organic matter is kept warm and dry for some months. It can be speeded up by using worms—called "vermicomposting."

A third of all household refuse could be composted, as well as most garden waste: grass mowings, hedge trimmings, and plants that have flowered (but not weeds). 🌳 Homemade compost makes an excellent soil conditioner and a rich source of plant food. The compost can be used in your garden and for your window boxes and potted plants. It cuts down on the need to buy peat-based products, thus saving the now nearly extinct peat bogs.

Detailed instructions on composting: www.mastercomposter.com

For worm towers, worm condos, worm farms, and other wonderful vermicomposting systems where the worms do all the work: www.composters.com

Do compost

Kitchen waste—fruit and vegetable peelings, tea bags, coffee grounds, crushed eggshells
Garden waste—grass cuttings, hedge clippings, old flowers
Crumpled or shredded card and paper; avoid heavily colored paper
Wood ash
Human hair and animal fur
Autumn leaves; put large amounts in garbage bags to rot down for mulch
Old clothes—pure wool and other natural fabrics
Sawdust, bedding and manure from vegetarian pets such as rabbits

Don't compost

Cooked food, meat, and fish
Droppings from meat-eating animals
Magazines and heavily inked cardboard
Diapers
Coal ash and soot
Diseased plants
Roots of persistent weeds such as bindweed or couch grass
Synthetic fabrics
Glass, plastic, and metal (to be recycled separately

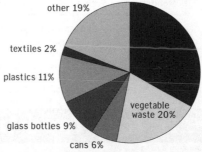

paper & cardboard 33%
other 19%
textiles 2%
plastics 11%
glass bottles 9%
cans 6%
vegetable waste 20%

A rough breakdown

...it's fun and easy

- 🌳 **Build a compost bin and recycle your waste.** If you have a garden or a yard, build a bin from old pallets or wood posts and wire-mesh netting, lined with old carpet or thick cardboard. Cover with a wooden lid or old carpet to keep the rain out and heat in.
- 🌳 **Check out the desktop wormery.** This is an educational toy, artwork, and desktop paperweight all in one. The kit contains bedding, drainage chips, sand, and 12 worms, which you assemble in a small glass-fronted case. Give it to your green friends or worst enemies: £40 from www.wigglywigglers.co.uk

The McLibel trial in the UK was a landmark court case between McDonald's on one side and Helen Steel and Dave Morris, a gardener and a postman from London, who represented themselves in court. McDonald's issued writs against the "McLibel Two" on September 20, 1990, alleging that the pair had libeled the company in the London Greenpeace factsheet "What's Wrong with McDonald's?"

The trial began in June 1994, and three years later, after 314 days in court, Mr. Justice Bell ruled that McDonald's marketing "pretended to a positive nutritional benefit which their food (high in fat & salt, etc.) did not match"; that McDonald's "exploit children" with their advertising strategy; that McDonald's were "culpably responsible for cruel practices regarding the rearing and slaughter of animals"; and that they "pay low wages, thereby helping to depress wages for workers in the catering trade." ⚽ However, the courts ruled that the McLibel Two had still libeled McDonald's over other points (starvation in the third world, destruction of the rainforest, and knowingly selling food injurious to health) and ordered them to pay £40,000 ($76,000) damages. They refused. McDonald's knew better than to pursue the matter.

In 2005, the McLibel Two won a ruling from the European Court of Human Rights that they had been denied basic human rights by being refused legal aid to defend the case. This denial had left them at a real disadvantage, confronted as they were by a barrage of highly paid corporate lawyers and an extremely complex case.

McLibel has been described as "the worst corporate PR disaster in history."

McInformation Network: www.mcspotlight.org

The McInformation Network is run by volunteers from 22 countries on four continents. It aims to compile and disseminate factual, accurate, up-to-date information, encouraging debate about the workings, policies, and practices of the McDonald's Corporation. It also provides fun and games on a McDonald's theme, and we're not just talking Ronald McDonald

...is fast food turning sour?

Go out and buy a Big Mac and fries. Wash it down with a Coke. Enjoy! Become a restaurant critic and rate your Big Mac and fries for taste, appearance, ambience, affordability, and enjoyment. Then think about the wider issues:

⚽ Nutrition. Is a burger and fries healthy?
⚽ Advertising. Did the product live up to the image?
⚽ Employment. What about pay and working conditions for the staff?
⚽ Environment. What happens to all that litter?
⚽ Animal welfare. Do you think the animals enjoyed feeding you?
⚽ Globalization. Do you think McDonald's, and fast food generally, is a good thing or a bad thing?

If you feel strongly about the global food industry and its impact on our lives, visit the McInformation Network website. Volunteers are welcome.

AUGUST 6

CHICKEN *farming*

Every working day in the US more than 25 million chickens are killed for their meat. Five companies account for 56% of US chicken production: Tyson, GoldKist, Pilgrim's Pride, ConAgra, and Perdue Farms, producing each week 370 million pounds of ready-to-cook chicken. ♆ The average egg-laying hen lays 338 eggs per year and is kept for 70 weeks. Every year 100 million spent chickens are slaughtered, mostly for pet food, although some do enter the human food chain. ♆ Most of these birds are on factory farms living in cages stacked in huge sheds containing upwards of 20,000 birds. There are usually four or five birds per cage, and each cage will measure just about 20 inches square.

This is not just cruel to the birds but dangerous for humans. Intensive chicken rearing makes diseases such as salmonella more likely. ♆ There are alternatives:

Better:
Barn hens, with 25 birds per square yard on raised platforms.
Deep litter, part-solid cage and just 7 birds per square yard.

Much better:
Free-range, with access to the outdoors, allowing 400 birds per acre.

Best:
Your very own backyard chickens. The birds are not only decorative and entertaining but provide delicious fresh eggs. This is your chance to change the world—one egg at a time!

www.goodbyecitylife.com/chickens.htm
United Poultry Concerns, campaigning for compassionate and respectful treatment of domestic fowl: www.upc-online.org
Read the story of Viva, the chicken that started United Poultry Concerns: www.upc-online.org/winter0405/viva.htm

The Eglu is a chicken coop for the 21st century, featuring spacious open-plan living for two medium-sized chickens or three bantams. It is a stylish and practical addition to any garden. Designed to be comfortable for the chickens, and effortless for you, the Eglu makes keeping chickens rewarding and fun. It is fitted throughout with wooden roosting bars and an integrated nesting box with privacy screen to preserve your chicken's modesty when laying an egg. The chickens are kept warm in the winter and cool in the summer, thanks to modern twin-walled insulation. To make collecting your eggs easy, the Eglu has an eggport, which gives access to the nesting box. Available in three fantastic colors.

—from the Eglu sales blurb

Every Eglu comes complete with its own private secure area, enclosed with animal-proof wire netting to keep hungry foxes away from your chickens. You also get two chickens, well suited to domestic gardens, friendly, organically reared to Soil Association standards, and at "point of lay." You can start getting eggs and turning them into omelettes right away. www.omlet.us

...free-range in your garden

♆ **Become a backyard chicken farmer.** Find out about raising your own chickens and building your own coop. Download this book and get a list of hatcheries and a book of egg recipes all for $14.77: www.goodbyecitylife.com/chickens.htm

♆ **Adopt a chicken** and find out about trade injustice in Ghana. Click on each chicken and hear their stories on this hilarious Christian Aid website: www.mailorderchickens.org

GIVE IT UP

Giving it up is good for your soul. Hindus go in for renunciation. Christians give it up for Lent (the 40-day period before Easter). Muslims have the holy month of Ramadan (a month when they fast from dawn to sunset). Jews have Yom Kippur (a fast which lasts about 25 hours).

But here's another take on the idea of giving up: There must be things you could give up that would make only a tiny difference to your life. But using the time or money you save, you could then make a big difference to the world. Here are some ideas for what to give up:

Give up drinking bottled water. Drink tap water instead. There's nothing wrong with it, and it's free. And it doesn't involve semis thundering down the highway to bring it to you, or empty bottles to dispose of.

Give up purchasing a cup of coffee on the way to the office each morning. Why? There are cheaper ways of getting your morning caffeine fix. Buy a thermos flask (one of those aluminium designer ones if you care about looking cool) plus a really nice cup and a teaspoon. Make your coffee at home and add milk and sugar as you wish. Use only the finest ingredients—the best coffee, freshly ground, fair-trade of course. Take the thermos with you to work. Then enjoy.

Give up smoking. This is the single most sensible thing you can do for a healthier life. And it will make a huge difference to your finances.

Whatever you think you can give up, do! Then think of something creative to do with all the money you save.

H2G2 is a website inspired by *The Hitchhiker's Guide to the Galaxy*. It is a guide to "life, the universe and everything." It is an open source guide, with visitors to the website contributing, adding to, and amending content. You can contribute your ideas on how to give it up and how to get a life.

Here are some more ideas for things to give up:

Replace things with logos with things with no logo (read Naomi Klein's book *No Logo*).

Give up deodorant, and smell like yourself rather than a perfume factory (and save the world from volatile organic compounds).

Be alcohol-free at least one day a week.

...and get a life!

Answer these two questions:
  1. What can I give up that I will barely even notice?
  2. What will this then enable me to do?
Give it up. And do it!

AUGUST 8

FAIR-TRADE *tea*

A community of forest dwellers in southern India has challenged the bastion of colonial rule and embarked on tea growing. The people are *adivasis*— indigenous forest dwellers. They live in forests about 5,000 feet up in the Nilgiri Hills. Over the years, the adivasis lost their rights over the forest lands, because of enclosure by powerful people who wanted to settle the land and fell the trees, and the Forest Department, who wanted people out of the forests for conservation reasons. ● The tribal community organization (AMS) encouraged settled agriculture in order to make the adivasis economically independent and to protect tribal land rights. It came up with the idea of tea cultivation. This made sense because it was the predominant crop of the area, it would generate a regular income, and planting tea would provide evidence that the adivasis had tenure of the land. ● Over the last ten years, more than 1,000 families have each planted tea on plots of up to one acre, and are now enjoying a steady income.

Tea growing provided the tribal community organization with a base for building a number of other enterprises:

A tea nursery to supply tea plants

Cooperative tea marketing to negotiate a better price with the factories that cure the tea

A 300-acre tea estate owned and operated by the community.

These initiatives led to the Just Change project, which promotes barter trading between communities of poor people in India, and markets the produce made by these communities to affluent consumers in India and overseas.

Just Change: www.justchangeindia.com
AMS, the tribal community organization: www.adivasi.net

Fair-trade Tea

Unlike fair-trade coffee, which is produced by cooperatives of small farmers, fair-trade tea is produced mostly on large privately owned plantations in India, Sri Lanka, and East Africa. To become fair-trade-certified, a tea estate has to provide its workers with fair wages and good working conditions, and ensure adequate housing and health care. Certified estates encourage sustainable farming, they prohibit child labor, and the workers and managers together decide how the fair-trade premium will be used to benefit the workers—for housing, health care, education, or income-generating projects. There are around 50 fair-trade-certified tea estates in India, employing more than 120,000 workers.

...sell it to your friends

Package and market tribal tea from the Nilgiris.

● **Sealed bags** containing 25 tea bags can be purchased from Just Change for 90p. Design nice packaging and leaflets showing where the tea comes from.

● **Sell as much as possible** to friends and colleagues. Make a good profit. Set up a thriving tea business.

● **Organize a Mad Hatter's Tea Party** as a fund-raising event.

make YOUR CASE

Listen Up! is a youth media network that connects young video producers to resources, support, and projects with the aim of creating an authentic youth voice in the mass media. Their America's Youth Speak Out campaign invited young people to produce public service messages that dealt with issues that were important in their lives and in their communities.

These 30-second video messages spoke out about smoking, mental health, domestic violence, literacy, the arts, and many other topics in a voice that other young people could relate to, understand, and respond to.

Hear what these young people have to say. Go to www.pbs.org/merrow/listenup/psacampaign/index.html.

Are you looking for ideas to make a difference?

UNICEF asked young people (under 25) to make a one-minute video telling the world how young people are speaking out, taking action, and making a difference. www.unicef.org/voy/takeaction

Educational Video Center, New York City. The EVC is a media arts center where youth can learn about producing documentary video focused on diverse social issues of concern to the community. EVC's mission is to use documentary video as a means to promote literacy, research skills, and community involvement in at-risk youth.

Street-Level Youth Media: Chicago. Street-Level Youth Media is dedicated to teaching the media arts and emerging media technology as a means of self-expression, communication, and social change to inner city youth. The programs are designed to make young people conscious of community issues and information technology. www.street-level.org

...with a public service message

Take any issue that you care deeply about. Write a storyboard in words (this will be your script) with still pictures (these will indicate the video pictures that you will shoot, so as to give an idea of the movie) for a 30-second public service ad. About nine pictures will be sufficient. If you've the time and the equipment, now shoot your public service ad.

CIVILIAN *casualties*

We don't do body counts.

—General Tommy Franks, US Central Command

War has distressing consequences for civilian populations. Even if civilians are not directly killed or maimed as a result of military action, they may suffer long-term injury or illness as a result of radiation, postconflict contact with unexploded munitions, or pollution caused by the spillage of toxic materials. Populations become displaced and many people suffer deep psychological trauma. ❧ Documenting and assigning responsibility for the side effects of war is a hard task, requiring long-term on-the-ground resources. But direct deaths and injuries from military strikes can be much more easily identified, both in place and in time, and responsibility can readily be attributed to the weapon that caused that death or injury. ❧ Despite this, the military forces operating in Iraq, predominantly from the US and the UK, make no attempt to keep a tally of the civilian deaths caused by their actions.

The Iraq Body Count project has been created "to record single-mindedly and on a virtually real-time basis one key and immutable index of the fruits of war— the death toll of innocents." It aims to promote public understanding, engagement, and support for the human victims of the 2003 Iraq war by providing reliable, up-to-date documentation of civilian casualties.

For every American death there have been 14 Iraqi deaths:
  American servicemen killed in Iraq (August 2006): 2,567
  Iraqi civilians reported killed by military intervention in Iraq (calculated by Iraq Body Count, early August 2006): 39,284–43,744
  Journalists killed bringing the news to you: at least 87

See also the Iraq coalition casualty count: www.icasualties.org/oif
Iraq Body Count: www.iraqbodycount.org
To find out about the cost of the Iraq war to the US ($300 billion as of August 2006) and what the money could have been spent on, go to costofwar.com.

IRAQ BODY COUNT	Min	Max
Reported civilian deaths	24508	27718

...counting war deaths

Start creating a dossier of facts and figures on an issue that particularly concerns you. Save press clippings and read official reports. Use the Internet to help you in this research. Very quickly, you may find yourself becoming an expert on the subject.

if you're YOUNG

These are ways in which young people can link together to change the world:

The Freechild Project was set up to advocate, inform, and celebrate social change led by young people around the world. Their website is a great resource list for youth action and many of the important issues being addressed by young people.

Free the Children is an international network of children helping children at a local, national, and international level through representation, leadership, and action. It was founded by Craig Kielburger in 1995, when he was just 12 years old. The primary goal is to free children from poverty and exploitation.

iEARN describes itself as the world's largest nonprofit global network that connects young people and encourages them to collaborate in changing the world. It brings them together from over 20,000 schools and youth groups in more than 110 countries. There are more than 120 iEARN projects, each trying to answer the question "How will this project improve the quality of life on the planet?"

Peace Child International is an international network promoting youth action. Peace Child focuses mainly on the issues of sustainable development and human rights. Every two years, it organizes a World Youth Congress for up to 1,000 young people (Hawaii 1999, Morocco 2003, Scotland 2005, Bangalore 2007). It also runs a Be the Change program to encourage and support local youth-led initiatives for changing the world. You can get involved in Be the Change, attend a World Youth Congress, or volunteer as an intern at their HQ near London, with full board and lodging provided.

TakingITGlobal is a global online community that inspires young people to make a difference. It provides a source of information on issues, opportunities to take action, and a bridge to get involved locally, nationally, and globally. Membership is free of charge and allows you to interact with various aspects of the website to contribute ideas, experiences, and actions. There are profiles of 850 youth projects that TIG members are undertaking all over the world.

www.freechild.org
www.freethechildren.org
www.iearn.org
www.peacechild.org
www.youthlink.org
www.takingitglobal.org

...join up with others

- **If you're a young person** (age 16 to 25), check out all these websites. And become a member of TakingITGlobal.
- **If you once were a young person,** you can still change the world!

SURFERS *against sewage*

Humans produce waste. They create a continuous supply of sewage that requires disposal. In many countries, sewage treatment and disposal methods are primitive: whatever goes down the toilet washes up on the beach or along the banks of rivers. People relieve themselves in a stream at the top of a hill village, and other people wash and brush their teeth in it at the bottom.

Toxic chemicals produced as by-products of industrial processes also require disposal. Most are discharged into rivers and run off into the sea. Products in everyday use at home contain a vast array of chemicals and organic compounds that are flushed, washed away after bathing or showering, or disposed of directly into the drains. There is no regulation of these discharges. ♣ Once in the ecosystem, these contaminants can react with each other, making it hard to predict their impact on the environment. Many substances will remain in the environment indefinitely, either in the water itself or in the flesh and fat of organisms.

Surfers against Sewage has been campaigning against sewage discharge and toxic dumping since 1990, when a wet-suited and gas-masked "SAS hit squad" demonstration took place at the Royal Cornwall Show in England, with beach pollution fact sheets handed out to the public. (*SAS* is not just the acronym of Surfers against Sewage but also the name of the prestigious special forces regiment of the British army.) ♣ From this small beginning, SAS has become a national campaign, highlighting the problem of sewage disposal into the sea, providing information, and monitoring compliance with legislation.

Join Surfers against Sewage: www.sas.org.uk

The recipe for fecal soup: Everything that goes into the drains—bleach, chemicals from domestic products, paint and solvents, oils and fats—and everything that is flushed down the toilet will end up in the sewers. The result is a complex mixture of liquids and solids: a "fecal soup." The ingredients of this soup are

Sewage-related debris
Bacteria and viruses from human intestines
Chemicals and heavy metals from household and beauty products
Nutrients (nitrates and phosphates)
Endocrine-disrupting substances
Oils, fats, and greases

You're making this soup every day. It's lucky you don't have to drink it. Make sure others don't have to swim in it!

...for cleaner waters

Here is a four-point action plan for safer beaches, rivers, and lakes:

♣ Don't flush trash. The only thing going down your toilet should be human waste and toilet paper.

♣ Enjoy your beach, but remember to dispose of your trash properly or take it home.

♣ If you notice a pollution incident, report it immediately.

♣ Buy organic. Once pesticides get into the water cycle, they can persist indefinitely.

build a FLY TRAP

A fly is any species of insect of the order Diptera, some of which can land on food and transmit bacteria to humans. Particularly the housefly (Musca domestica) is common amongst humans and has caused many diseases to spread in the past. Other flies, such as the horsefly (family Tabanidae), can inflict painful bites. The larva of a fly is commonly called a maggot.

—Wikipedia definition

Flies affect almost everybody. They may not be as much of a nuisance as mosquitoes, but they can be just as dangerous.

Trachoma is caused by *Chlamydia trachomatis*, a microorganism that spreads through contact with eye discharge from an infected person. It is transmitted via towels, handkerchiefs, and fingers, and also through eye-seeking flies, taking the infection from one person to another. ☺ After years of repeated infection, the inside of your eyelid may become scarred so severely that the eyelid turns inward and your eyelashes rub on your eyeball, scarring the cornea (the front of the eye). If untreated, this condition will lead to blindness.

Trachoma affects 84 million people, of whom 8 million have become visually impaired. It is responsible for more than 3% of the world's blindness and is especially prevalent in many of the poorest rural areas in the world.

All about eye diseases, from the World Health Organization:
www.who.int/topics/blindness/en

Teaching Aids at Low-Cost (TALC), fly trap instructions:
www.talcuk.org/free/html/flytrap/flytrap.htm

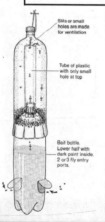

Slits or small holes are made for ventilation

Tube of plastic with only small hole at top

Bait bottle. Lower half with dark paint inside. 2 or 3 fly entry ports.

Build a fly trap
Go to the TALC website and and download instructions on how to build a fly trap. You will need
- Two large clear plastic bottles, preferably identical, one with its screw top.
- One smaller plastic bottle, made of smooth plastic.
- A small quantity of black or dark paint.
- A sharp knife.
- A small piece of string.
- A pointed instrument.
- A candle.

The flies fly into the lower bottle, attracted by bait. They then make their way through a narrow tube into the upper bottle, where they are trapped. Various baits can be used. Chicken entrails are OK but tend to dry up. Flies seem to like the smell of 8 ounces of yeast in a quart of water with 0.2 ounces of ammonium carbonate added two days later. The Masai of Kenya use a mixture of goat dung and cow urine: you could try this!

...for a more comfortable life

We've all seen dying children filmed in refugee camps with flies crawling all over their faces. We've also been infuriated by flies buzzing around us. Here's a chance to address both of these problems.

☺ **Make a fly trap for your kitchen.**
☺ **Choose a country and circulate the instructions** for making a fly trap as widely as possible in that country.

AUGUST 14

GUNS *in the hands of babes*

> *They held a court and found her [a girl presumed to be a spy] guilty. They ordered me to lead her away and shoot her, and at first I hesitated; but then I did it. To [the guerrillas] it was a proof of my loyalty, but to me it didn't prove anything.*
>
> —Gloria, who joined the FARC in Colombia at age 11

> *I killed another child. I did this three times. I felt bad but I knew what would happen if I disobeyed. Now I see dead people and blood in my dreams and I know the spirits of the children are coming to haunt me.*
>
> —Bosco, who was abducted by the Lords Resistance Army from Gulu, Uganda, at age 12

Over 300,000 children are involved in combat, taking part in all aspects of warfare. They are in the front line, carrying AK-47s and M-16s. They go on suicide missions, act as spies, sex slaves, runners, messengers, lookouts, assassins, soldiers, and human mine detectors. Child soldiers are used in more than 30 countries. They are a cheap and expendable commodity, so tend to receive little or no training before being thrust into the front line. They suffer higher fatality rates than their adult counterparts. Some are abducted, some volunteer. The main reason for volunteering is their personal experience of ill treatment by government armed forces.

The Straight-18 Plan: The international community is trying to ratify an international ban on use of child soldiers, setting 18 years as the minimum age for conscription, forced recruitment, and participation in armed conflict.

Coalition to Stop the Use of Child Soldiers: www.child-soldiers.org

The World Revolution, information on child soldiers: www.worldrevolution.org/guide/childsoldiers

Human Rights Watch, stop the use of child soldiers: hrw.org/campaigns/crp/index.htm

Burma has the largest number of child soldiers in the world, according to Human Rights Watch. The national army forcibly recruits children as young as 11. More than 20% of active duty soldiers may be under 18. Armed opposition groups use children as well.

For a copy of HRW's report "My Gun Was as Tall as Me," go to hrw.org/press/2002/10/burma-1016.htm.

...stop child soldiers

Human Rights Watch provides a sample letter for you to e-mail or fax to governments.

- **Let governments know that you care** about the use of child soldiers and that they should sign up or ratify the ban.
- **Encourage Cambodia, Colombia, Jordan, Nepal, and the Philippines** to join the 35 countries that have already ratified the ban.
- **Encourage Algeria, Eritrea, Fiji, Mozmabique, Thailand, and Yemen** to sign up.

anonymous GENEROSITY

The best way to cheer yourself up is to try to cheer somebody else up.
—Mark Twain

God loves a cheerful giver.
—notice seen in Mother Teresa's office

Think about the idea of giving freely to someone, without being asked or being expected to give, without your knowing them or their knowing you.

For example, you are crossing a toll bridge, and you decide to pay not just your own fare but also the fare of the car behind you. You leave a card, saying that this is an act of generosity from a complete stranger. Why don't they then do something that will make someone else happy... and pass the card on. 🚹🚹 They put a $10 note with the card next to an ATM machine, to be picked up by someone who needs the money. 🚹🚹 That person then buys an extra ticket at the cinema for the next customer, who buys a drink in a bar for a person selected at random... and so the process goes on. There will be lots of happy people who have taken pleasure in making lots of other people happy.

It is attitudes and not just acts that can make a difference. Making another person happy could be like a butterfly flapping its wings and causing a hurricane thousands of miles away. Your unattributable act of generosity could be the start of a wind of change.

Give It Forward Today: www.giveitforwardtoday.org

The eight degrees of charity

Charity is a part of every religion. Moses Maimonides was a Jewish sage who lived in the 12th century. He suggested that there were eight degrees of charity:

Bottom level: Giving to a poor person unwillingly. It is better not to give at all.

Seventh level: Giving to a poor person with a glad heart and a smile.

Sixth level: Giving to a poor person after being asked.

Fifth level: Giving to a poor person before being asked.

Fourth level: Not knowing who you are giving to, but allowing the recipients to know who their benefactor is.

Third level: Knowing who you are giving to, but not allowing the recipients to know who their benefactor is.

Second level: Giving to the poor, but not knowing who you are giving to, nor allowing the recipients to know who their benefactor is.

Top level: Investing in a poor person, so that a solution to his or her problem is found.

...a true act of charity

Perform two acts of generosity today.

🚹🚹 **Go to the Give It Forward Today (GIFT) website,** created by 12-year-old Alex Southmayd. He gives lots of ideas, plus you can download GIFT Certificates for the recipients of your generosity.

🚹🚹 **Download two GIFT Certificates** with the message "You have been GIFTed. Your mission (if you accept it) is to GIFT two human beings with an act of kindness. Please pass this on..."

PHOTOGRAPH *a day in a life*

Seeing the world through other people's eyes can be a big shock. Your neighbors may be living next door to you geographically, but your lives could be a million miles apart. Knowing more about their completely different life experiences could help you understand how they feel and even make you see things in a completely new light.

Misunderstanding can foster fear and hatred; unfamiliarity may become an obstacle to peace. The Photographing a Day in Our Life project aims to open your eyes to the perspectives and ideas of your neighbors, through the lens of a camera, and to develop mutual understanding.

Here is how the Photographing a Day in Our Life project works: People from adjoining communities who normally would not interact—or who interact minimally or with some reserve—are grouped into pairs. The two groups could be contrasted by age, gender, religion, race, conflict, sexuality, income and opportunity, domestic situations, disability... whatever. ❧ Each pair is provided with a digital camera. They are charged with the task of "photographing a day in each other's life." ❧ The photographer shadows the person they are paired with and captures images of their daily routine—at work, at play, at home. Then the roles are reversed. The photographer becomes the photographed. ❧ At the end of the project, each pair has to make a short presentation in which they explain what caught their interest in particular, and why they chose to show certain photographs.

PhotoVoice: www.photovoice.org

PhotoVoice: capturing portraits of life at the edge

PhotoVoice, set up by Anna Blackman and Tiffany Fairey, trains socially excluded groups in photojournalism to give them a voice and provide professional skills. PhotoVoice works with homeless people, refugees, street and working children, orphans, disabled groups, and women living with HIV/AIDS in Afghanistan, Democratic Republic of Congo, Nepal, Vietnam, and the UK.

So far, they have trained over 300 people. Their images offer extraordinary insights into how people live, captured by the very people whose lives are a daily struggle.

...how do others see you?

❧ **Organize a Photograph a Day in Our Life project** at your school, community center, or workplace. Or link your church with a mosque, or your Buddhist temple with a synagogue.

❧ **Bring two groups of people together** who ordinarily would not interact or who are divided by conflict. All you need are some digital cameras. After you've finished, upload your photos onto www.fotolog.com.

17 AUGUST

celebrate **CYCLING**

The Revolution will arrive on a bicycle.

—Salvador Allende, President of Chile, 1970–73

Critical Mass is many things to many people, but it is foremost a celebration rather than a protest. It is a bunch of cyclists riding around together, going from one point to another. It is not organized. It is a group of individuals who just happen to be doing the same thing at the same time. And because there's no organization and nobody in charge, no permission needs to be obtained for organizing an event in a public place and there is no organizer to hold responsible.

The phenomenon started in September 1992 in San Francisco as a festive reclaiming of public space. It originally had a less catchy name: "The Commute Clot." The first ride attracted 60 cyclists, and the numbers have grown over the years. The idea has also spread to other cities. Independent Critical Masses have sprung up all over the world. Critical Mass has become a self-propelling global movement.

Critical Mass has a different flavor in every city. Some groups are big, some small. There are different approaches to respecting traffic laws (or lack thereof), interacting with motorists, and relationships with the police. If you want to know more about Critical Mass, you need to find out what it's like locally.

How to start a Critical Mass bike ride: www.criticalmassrides.info/howto.html
How to make a Critical Mass: www.critical-mass.org
How to Not Get Hit by Cars, 10 tips for safer cycling: bicyclesafe.com
A resource site for cycle commuters: www.BikeToWork.com

Liberate London by Bike
Central London Critical Mass ride together monthly
Meet last Friday of each month
6pm Waterloo outside NFT on the southbank
http://www.criticalmasslondon.org.uk

A Critical Mass happening

"What's this all about?" ask amused and bemused pedestrians on Market Street as hundreds of noisy, high-spirited bicyclists ride past, yelling and ringing their bells. There are a wide variety of answers: "It's about banning cars." "It's about having fun in the street." "It's about a more social way of life." "It's about asserting our right to the road." "It's about solidarity."

In riding round the city as part of a Critical Mass, bicyclists find that many important questions come up. Why is there so little open space in our cities where people can relax and interact, free from the incessant buying and selling of ordinary life? Why are people compelled to organize their lives around having a car? What would an alternative future look like?

...create a critical mass

🏵 **Join a Critical Mass ride.** Have fun. Assert the power of the pedaler. Reclaim the streets for the most environmentally friendly (and often the quickest) form of urban transportation.

🏵 **If there isn't a Critical Mass in your city, start one!**

DEMOCRACY *support it*

If democracy is to mean anything, it should express the will of the people, and the ballot box is how the will of the people is manifested. There may not be an election this year or even next. But it is important that you prepare for next time. What issues concern you most? Are the political parties even addressing them, let alone adopting policies you think are sensible?

Now is the time to start getting a group of people together, discussing the issues with them, and planning how, together, you can make an impact when the next election comes. It is never too soon to start a campaign to encourage participation in the political process. Then, when the next election comes, you will be prepared. You will know the issues. You will also know how to get involved in the election campaign.

League of Pissed-Off Voters: www.indyvoter.org

Find out about your congressperson, their voting record, how they stand on the issues.

www.aflcio.org/issues/legislativealert/votes/vr_memb.cfm

EPolitix, online news and discussion of the issues, plus links to MPs' websites: www.epolitix.com

The League of Pissed-Off Voters

This was formed to encourage the younger generation to learn the nitty-gritty of politics and invent fresh ways of playing the democracy game on their terms. The league's intention is to transform thousands of young adults who have never messed with politics before, into savvy political players.

The league publishes the following resources for participating in elections:

A 90-day plan of action

How to host a kickass strategy session

A sample survey for contact collection

The "You get out the vote" toolbox

How to get out the vote in 12 easy steps

...encourage people to vote

Don't leave politics to stiffs in suits. Get out and get active. Do it in your way. Make democracy work—for you!

Organize a Politics 'n' Pizza Brunch. This could also be Politics 'n' Pancakes or Politics 'n' Punk—whatever works for you. Make the invitation simple: "Brunch this wknd?" or "My house Sat." will usually be more appealing than "League of Pissed-Off Voters blah blah blah."

Get together in small groups, and once everyone has had something to eat and drink, make a list of the issues you think are important to all of you and the policies you would like to see implemented. Once candidates have been selected, communicate with them and extract some promises from them.

circles of COMPASSION

A Circle of Compassion is a gathering at which people sit in a circle on the floor. It is also a tool to help people communicate honestly and openly. The circle allows participants to

Listen without judging.

Understand one another, bridge differences, and try to reach a consensus.

Devise and implement creative solutions to problems in a spirit of openess and collaboration.

Settle disputes in a spirit of reconciliation.

The World Conference on Women held in Bejing in 1995 was a milestone in the development of international collaboration among women and women's organizations. Circles of Compassion are being promoted by the Women's World Summit Foundation as a mechanism for discussing some of the critical areas of concern that were identified there. The foundation's target is to achieve one million circles.

Women's World Summit Foundation. Their website has information on organizing a Circle of Compassion: www.woman.ch

The 12 areas of concern

1. The persistent and increasing burden of poverty on women
2. Unequal access to education
3. Inequalities in health and in access to adequate health care
4. Violence against women
5. The effects of armed and other conflict on women
6. Inequality in economic structures, policy making, and production processes
7. Inequality in power and decision making
8. Insufficient mechanisms to promote the advancement of women
9. Lack of awareness of and commitment to women's human rights
10. Insufficient coverage in the media of women's contribution to society
11. Insufficient recognition of women's contribution to managing natural resources and safeguarding the environment
12. The girl child

...address women's inequality

Create your own Circle of Compassion. Take one of the 12 Beijing issues. Invite friends, colleagues, and acquaintances to contribute to the discussion. Think of a positive action you can take together to address the issue.

How a circle is run:

The start and end time for the session are agreed on.

Start the session with a moment of silent reflection.

Each participant shares what is important for them now—a challenge or a joy.

Leadership of the circle is shared by rotation.

Equality is the rule: each person is equal to everyone else.

Ground rules are agreed to and stuck to—e.g., interventions should be in a spirit of observation, never of correction or "setting things right."

One person speaks at a time. She will hold a "talking stick" and pass it on to the person speaking next.

Participants speak from their own experience and from the heart, keeping to the theme of the discussion,

AUGUST 20

COMPUTERS *donated*

More than 600 million perfectly good computers will be discarded by companies worldwide over the next five years. In the UK every year over 3 million computers are decommissioned and 1 million end up filling up landfill sites. ⊕ Fewer than 20% of old computers are recycled. Effective disposal of old computers is becoming increasingly costly, with stricter environmental regulations and declining residual values.

A great many old PCs are in good working order and could continue to be used by someone else. In the developing world, 99% of schoolchildren graduate from high school never having seen or touched a computer in the classroom. ⊕ There are commercial organizations that take old PCs for recycling. There are also specialist organizations that refurbish PCs and then send them to charities, schools, and low-income households in developing countries.

Prices are getting lower and specifications are rising year by year. So the old computers that are being discarded have higher and higher specifications. What you no longer need can be a wonderful opportunity for someone else.

Computer Recycling Center: www.crc.org
Advice for organizations receiving donated computers:
www.digitalequalizer.org/practices.htm

Computer Aid International

This is a nonprofit organization in the UK that renovates and ships computers to developing countries at a cost of around $120 per unit, depending on the quantity shipped. The computers are shipped without a Windows operating system, but Linux can be installed at no extra cost.

Computer Aid International is now shipping 25,000 computers a year, mainly to Africa. These can be used for noncommercial purposes such as

> Computers in schools;
> Setting up an IT skills training project;
> Creating a cyber café to generate income;
> A computer loan scheme for university students;
> distribution to nongovernmental organizations.

...to developing countries

Donate your old computer through a computer recycling scheme.

⊕ **Or you can take an old laptop with you when you** are travelling to countries in the developing world and find an organization or a school and just leave it with them. These will be especially useful in areas where the power supply is irregular.

⊕ **Encourage your employer to donate** all your company's computers when upgrading.

build a TRASH SCULPTURE

We live in a throwaway society:

In the UK alone, 8 million tons of paper are thrown away every year. Making this paper requires 80 million trees.

Each year in the UK 8.5 billion cans, half for food, half for drinks, are produced—enough to reach to the moon and back and halfway there again.

Every year, an average European family with two children throws away 110 lbs. of paper (six trees), 130 lbs. of metal, and 100 lbs. of plastic. That last item may not sound like a lot, but it's equivalent to 13,500 supermarket bags.

Here are three ways to deal with all this trash:

Reduce. Throw away less. Make sure you buy products with as little packaging as possible.

Reuse. Buy a proper bag for your shopping, instead of using plastic bags. Use both sides of a sheet of paper.

Recycle. Eighty percent of domestic trash can be recycled, including paper, glass, metal, and plastic.

See the WEEE Man at www.weeeman.org.

The WEEE man

WEEE stands for Waste Electrical and Electronic Equipment. To highlight the problem of electrical and electronic waste, the British Royal Society of Arts commissioned Paul Bonomini to create the WEEE Man, a humanoid sculpture made out of all the electrical and electronic equipment that one person is expected to consume in a lifetime. It weighs 3.44 metric tons and stands 7 meters high.

To work out its weight, a simple calculation was made. The total electrical and electronic waste for the UK population (938,000 tons in 2003) was divided by the UK population (59,553,000), giving a figure of 15.75 kg per person per year.

Average life expectancy is 78.05 years. A 21-year-old in 2003 will live until 2060. Factoring in an e-waste growth rate of 4%, this person will produce 3.44 tons of WEEE in their lifetime. The same person born in 2003 would live until 2075 and produce 8.36 tons of WEEE. The WEEE Man would have to double its size.

...turn junk into art

🏆 **Make your own sculpture with a message.** Scavenge the local Dumpsters. Make a tour of your neighborhood. See what people are throwing away. Retrieve bits and pieces that look interesting. Use these to build a sculpture in your front garden or a park.

🏆 **Get a picture of your trash sculpture in your local newspaper.** Use the publicity to highlight the quantity of waste being generated. Produce a simple leaflet or poster telling people what to do about this.

AUGUST 22

POSTERS *to download*

Sometimes people are spurred into action by some event. The Sharpeville massacres in apartheid South Africa, the Vietnam war, and now the 2003 US-led invasion of Iraq as part of the "war on terror." All of these have led to an outpouring of protest.

Society may be divided on the issues, but it can produce great poster art!

There are a large number of websites where you can download, reproduce, and distribute some great copyright-free posters that are critical of the Bush-Blair policy on Iraq. Here are some:

Peaceposters: print or e-mail a poster at www.peaceposters.org

Another Poster for Peace: www.anotherposterforpeace.com

Over My Dead Body, with Iraq posters plus a make-your-own educational toy on the G8: www.overmydeadbody.org

Community Reeducation for the Advancement of Patriotism (or C-R-A-P if you prefer): www.c-r-a-p.org/reeducation.htm

The Ronald Reagan Home for the Criminally Insane, also featuring a print-your-own $100 bill from Hallibacon: www.insanereagan.com/graphics.shtml

Insta-Protest—"In a better world I would have never had to make them. The sooner these posters become unnecessary the better": 64.70.140.219/feb15/

...display your protest

Create your own art gallery of posters

- **Visit the websites listed above** and any others you can find.
- **Download those you consider most effective,** print them out (using large-format paper if you can), frame them, and hang them up. E-mail them to your friends. Make and send your own postcards using these designs.
- **Add to your collection by designing and printing your own poster.** The Insta-Protest website features a design-your-own-poster function.

23 AUGUST

Cigarette butts are a major litter problem in our cities. Almost one in three end up discarded on the streets. Globally, 4.3 trillion cigarette butts are littered every year, and in many rich countries they account for around half of all street litter. In the US, more than 250 billion individual butts are discarded each year. In Australia, the smokers of New South Wales throw away enough butts to fill seven Olympic-sized swimming pools. Up to 350,000 butts end up in Port Phillip Bay, Victoria, and the waterways every day.

Indoor smoking bans have led to a dramatic increase in butt litter. What's good for our health can be bad for the environment:

It can take up to 12 years for a cigarette butt to break down.
Cigarette butts can leach chemicals such as cadmium, lead, and arsenic into the water table and the marine environment.

BUTTsOUT is a global campaign on cigarette-butt littering, now active in five countries. It was developed by PlanetArk in Australia. Its goal is to see individual smokers taking financial and personal responsibility for the litter they create and to develop sustainable solutions to the problem of cigarette butts.

The campaign seeks to engage smokers and nonsmokers alike. Nonsmokers can educate smokers to recognize that butts are litter and suggest positive alternatives to stubbing them out in the street. But in the end it is only smokers who can stop the problem by changing their behavior.

BUTTsOUT: www.buttsout.net

Personal portable ashtrays

BUTTsOUT produces a funky, reusable, fire-resistant personal ashtray that can be used outdoors. Some 82% of smokers say they would use them because they are so easy to operate. They trap most smell and smoke, fit into a pocket or clip onto a belt, and are available in a range of colors.

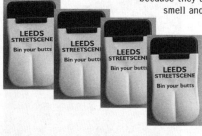

The Leeds City Council in England distributed a customized version as part of a campaign to improve its streets. In the town of Croydon, litter wardens have handed out free personal ashtrays to cigarette litterbugs, and tobacconists are being encouraged to stock them.

...keep your butt to yourself

 If you want to be nice: Buy your smoker friends a BUTTsOUT funky, reusable, fire-resistant personal ashtray. Visit the BUTTsOUT website and select from a range of colors.

A-B-C *make one*

We all tend to take our surroundings for granted. When you have lived or worked in a place for a long time, you cease to see it. You stop noticing the finer details of the architecture or the natural environment.

Your neighborhood has evolved over the years. Understanding what makes it different from everywhere else—what makes it very special to you, what gives it a sense of place, what stories are attached to it, and what makes it the great place that it is—is important. It may be a street sign, a shop front, a carving on the brickwork, a tree or the fruit piled high on a market stall that makes you feel that your neighborhood is special.

Why not celebrate your neighborhood and raise everybody's awareness of their surroundings at the same time by producing an A-B-C: a graphic representation in 26 parts, based on the letters of the alphabet, of what makes your area special.

How to make an A-B-C

Decide the theme of your A-B-C. Will it cover everything, or just focus on one aspect of your neighborhood in particular? Will it have a purpose? Is it for local interest? For tourists? As part of a local campaign? For citizenship education in schools?

Decide on the format. Your A-B-C could take many forms. Some are made entirely from photographs. Others include illustrations, linocuts, engravings, or a mixture of all of these. Some have short captions. Others have longer descriptions.

Identify 26 places, objects, or signs, each one linked to or depicting a particular letter of the alphabet. Take photographs of them. Using the pictures and captions, make these into a small booklet or a large poster.

You can use your A-B-C simply to show what delights you and what you care about—so that others will begin to see the neighborhood in the same positive way as you do. You can use it as part of a campaign to save the area. You can even use it to show what's horrible, abandoned, and in need of a bit of tender loving care.

...of your neighborhood

- 🏠 **Get together a small group of people.**
- 🏠 **Decide on the theme and the format** for your A-B-C.
- 🏠 **Choose an art director** to organize who does what and to create an overall design as well as preparing the artwork for the printer.
- 🏠 **Print and distribute it.** Decide on the selling price. Look out for possible outlets (such as bookshops, cafés, restaurants), and offer a good discount (40% at least) so that it's in their interest to help you sell it.

You need to raise money for a charity. There are a number of options. The usual way is to ask people to donate money, the things that you need, volunteer their time and expertise, or attend a fund-raising event that has been organized to raise money for your cause. But there is another way. You can ask people to donate their skills, or to use their position or contacts to provide you with a "special opportunity"—which you can then auction off to raise money.

There are all sorts of things that you can auction:

Things money alone can't buy, such as
Dinner for two with a famous pop star you know.
A week at someone's fabulous holiday home at the beach.
Watching a football game from the owner's box or on the sidelines.

Things people will agree to do for others, such as
Mow their lawn once a fortnight for three months.
Babysit five times.
Serenade you and your loved one as part of a romantic evening.

All these might be priceless to someone.

The trick is to find things that people really want. Organizing an auction gives you the opportunity to ask people to donate something very special. Getting them to give you something can often be easier than getting them to give you money. Then you turn their donation into cash for your project. This is sometimes called "an auction of dreams."

> For advice on organizing fund-raising events, download How to Be a Fund-raising Champion free from www.millenniumcampaign.org.

Recipe for a successful auction
Ingredients:
Donations of lots of interesting and desirable offers.
Lots of people with money to spend, who are likely to bid for what is to be sold.

Method:
Use a lively outgoing person with a sense of humor to act as auctioneer.
Create an atmosphere that encourages people to feel extra generous.

Result:
Lots of money to use for your project.

...make money from dreams

Organize an auction of dreams to help you change the world.

 Think of some really wacky things that you can ask people to do for you, which you can then auction.
 Persuade lots of people to turn up.
 Have an enthusiastic auctioneer.
 Raise lots of cash.

AUGUST 26

RAISING *water*

How can a children's merry-go-round provide people with water? In rural areas where water is scarce, fetching water will usually be done by women and girls. Water carriers will walk miles, often several times a day, in order to obtain their family's daily water requirements from local dams, springs, rivers, streams, and farm reservoirs. ● Small wells drilled into the ground can provide better access to clean water. These are mainly operated by hand pumps. Although it is hard work pumping the water up by hand, gas or electric pumps are too costly to install, run, and maintain.

The Play-Pump is a South African invention that uses the playful energies of children rotating a merry-go-round to raise water. It can provide up to 370 gallons of water per hour and is effective down to about 300 feet. Water is pumped into a 660-gallon tank, 23 feet above the ground. A tap then provides access to the water. ● Four billboards screen the tank. Two are used for health messages, but two have advertising, which provides money to pay for ongoing maintenance. So far over 400 merry-go-rounds, also called roundabouts, have been installed in villages and primary schools.

Pump Aid, which provides simple but effective pumps in Zimbabwe and Mozambique, also introduces a sense of fun. The pumps it provides outside schools incorporate a "bicycle system." Most of the children have never had the chance to ride a bicycle, so many come to school early to "play" on the pump, thereby helping to fill the school water tanks. ● The job of collecting water, once a tiresome chore, becomes fun, and children no longer have to leave their classrooms to walk miles carrying buckets of water on their heads from a distant muddy pool.

Roundabout Outdoor: www.roundabout.co.za
Pump Aid: www.pumpaid.org

The **Play-Pump** uses the energies expended by the children in making the "roundabout" go round and round to pump the water up from a well. Because the children are having fun, there is never a shortage of volunteers.

...in a roundabout way

Raise money to help African children play, attend school, and keep healthy.

● **A Play-Pump costs $10,000 to install** and provides water for up to 2,500 people. Collect or raise just $200, and Roundabout Outdoor will send you a free handmade wire frame replica of a Play-Pump as a thank-you. This will make a nice collectible for your shelf and will represent one-fiftieth of a continuous supply of clean water for a community.

● **One of Pump Aid's Elephant Pumps costs only $400.** They are made from local materials, use local labor, and are relatively simple to install and maintain. They can raise water from about 65 feet, at 2 pints of water every second.

CREATIVE COMMONS

Jill is a budding photographer who has put her portfolio online. Someday she might want to charge people for copying her photos. But now, when she is still trying to build her reputation, she wants people to copy her work as much as possible. Among her favorite photos are some dramatic black-and-white shots of famous skyscrapers.

Jack is making a digital movie about New York City using his new home computer. He wants to include a still photo of the Empire State Building, but he forgot to take one the last time he was in New York. He searches the Internet for "Empire State Building" and finds a collection of websites, some with photos. But he isn't sure if the photos are copyrighted or not. He uses a search engine that helps him look for files without copyright notices on them. But he knows that even things without copyright notices can be copyrighted. He worries that if he uses the photos he has found online and then posts his movie on the Internet, the people who took the photos will find the movie, get upset, and sue him.

Creative Commons was set up to make it easier for Jack and Jill to find each other online and then to develop the creative collaboration they both seek.

In 2002, Creative Commons released a set of copyright licenses to enable people to dedicate their creative works to the public domain. Their range of licenses covers such things as who can use the material for free, whether it can be adapted or has to remain in its original form, whether the license allows the material to pass to another user under the same conditions (share alike), and the nature of the attribution to the original source. These licenses can all be downloaded for free use. ✋ Creative Commons also wants to increase the amount of source material online, and to make access to that material cheaper and simpler. It provides a space for sharing your works and accessing the works of others.

Creative Commons licenses: creativecommons.org/license
Creative Commons: creativecommons.org

...fostering collaboration

You've created something that you want to share with the world—a photo, a film, a theory, an equation, a slogan, or recipe, a poem, some music.

✋ **Put the best of what you've created online at Creative Commons.** This will get your work distributed, and you can borrow the works of others to use for your website, your newsletters, and your pamphlets.

✋ **Help create a "world bank" of common property** for the benefit of all, instead of tying your work up in copyright restrictions that make it difficult or expensive for others to use.

AUGUST 28

SEED *the world*

It's hard to understand how it feels to live right at the margin, if you have most or all of what you need. Having "nothing" means having absolutely nothing for too many people in many countries. There are lots and lots of reasons why 36,000 people are dying of starvation every day, two-thirds of whom are children: war, drought, overpopulation, AIDS, absolute poverty. But seed shortage is one reason.

The only seeds available to many farmers in some of the poorest countries in the world, where food shortage is chronic, are for varieties of vegetables that do not produce their own seed. There is nothing accidental about this. The varieties, known as F1 hybrids, have been bred to be seedless. Who on earth would do something so unnatural? Why, the companies selling the seed, of course. They claim that such varieties produce higher yields, but it locks the farmers into the need to purchase fresh seed each year, and if they can't afford it, they go hungry.

The mission of the Kokopelli Seed Foundation, which started in France and has now spread around the world, is to create a "community-supported seed fund" to provide poor farmers in poor countries with the seeds they need for their gardens and small farms. Anybody can grow and collect seeds—including you. Gardeners and farmers from all over the world were doing this for thousands of years before the emergence of commercial seed growers—and more recently, the introduction of genetically modified seeds.

Kokopelli's website page devoted to seeds for the developing world:
www.kokopelli-seeds.com/third-world.html

How to become a Kokopelli seed grower

It's not as hard as you might think. Food plants provide plenty of seeds:
A pumpkin or melon contains hundreds of seeds.
A tomato contains around 70 seeds.
A lettuce going to seed may produce up to 10,000 seeds.

A 30 ft. x 30 ft. garden is big enough for 150 tomato plants, which would produce 13 lbs. of seeds, enough to provide 40,000 packets, each containing 30 seeds.

The Kokopelli Seed Foundation will advise you on what seeds to grow and even provide you with starter seeds so that you can start up your "seed factory."

...to feed the world

- **Become a seed donor.** Grow plants, allow some to run to seed, and donate the seeds to the Kokopelli Seed Foundation. Seeds produced by Kokopelli's seed-grower network are sent all over the world. If you haven't got a garden, then do it in containers on your roof or balcony.

- **All seeds for edible plants are welcome:** tomatoes, melons, lettuces, beets, carrots, grains, pulses, peppers. Every species will find a home somewhere.

- **For more details,** read Dominique Guillet's book *The Seeds of Kokopelli*.

29 AUGUST

invest in YOUNG PEOPLE

Children living on the streets need to earn money just to survive. Many do this by begging or ragpicking. But it is difficult for them to keep the money they earn safe, and therefore impossible for them to use it to create a better future for themselves. ✋ In Delhi, a group of street children started their own bank, called Bal Vikas Bank (Children's Development Bank). It is a place to keep their money safe, it encourages them to save for their future rather than just live from day to day, and it makes loans to older children to help them set up a small business.

The bank gives them a chance to do something safer, which will help them earn a better income and get off the streets. For example, two boys started a mobile tea business. They strapped an urn to the back of a bicycle and sold tea to lines of taxi and rickshaw drivers who were waiting to refuel their vehicles.

The amazing thing is that this bank is run entirely by the children. They make the rules, decide the loans, encourage saving, and build the membership. The idea is spreading across India, and children's banks are also being started in Afghanistan, Bangladesh, Nepal, Pakistan, and Sri Lanka. The children now want to spread the idea across the world.

The Bal Vikas Bank program: www.childrensdevelopmentbank.org
Child Savings International, an international network of children's banking schemes: www.childsavingsinternational.org

Taxi driving

A group of seven youths in Kisumu, Kenya, want to become taxi drivers. The "taxis" are bicycles, which have been converted to include a seat over the rear mudguard. This is an accepted form of transport in the town. As taxi drivers, the boys should be able to earn a decent income.

The youths will be offered loans to purchase and modify a bicycle and become taxi drivers. They will repay the loans out of the money they earn, which will enable more youths to take loans to set up in business.

...support their enterprise

Organize a fund-raising event to make a difference to the lives and futures of young people. Set yourself a target of $200. Send all the money you raise to support youth enterprise initiatives, without deducting anything for administration.

✋ Help street children in South Asia set up a children's bank.

✋ Help young people in Kenya become taxi drivers.

✋ Help other young people in other countries set up an enterprise of their own.

AUGUST 30

VEGAN *challenge*

I am a serious meat eater... but I accepted a challenge from a mate and went completely vegan for a week. It was eye-opening to have to think about everything I put in my mouth. I've gone back to eating meat, but going vegan made me think about my choices much more carefully.

—Will Poutney

A vegetarian is someone who abstains from eating any sort of meat or fish. A vegan doesn't consume or use any animal products at all. People become vegetarian or vegan for many different reasons. They may believe it is cruel to kill and eat animals, or that it is a drain on the environment to rear the meat and to dispose of the remains, or simply for health reasons.

Eating a well-balanced diet free from animal products is good for your health. Here are some reasons:

Fat: Vegan diets are cholesterol-free and low in fat.

Heart disease: The risk of developing heart disease among meat eaters is 50% higher than for vegetarians.

Impotence: Meat-based diets can lead to impotence, as fat can clog up the arteries going to all your organs, not just to your heart!

Life-threatening illnesses: Cancer, stroke, diabetes, osteoporosis, obesity, and other diseases have all been linked to meat and dairy consumption.

Unwanted chemicals: Livestock, poultry, and cows are often pumped full of chemicals, hormones, and drugs that are absorbed by your body when you eat these animals.

Toxins in fish: The flesh of fish can accumulate toxins up to 9 million times as concentrated as those in the waters they live in, and the seas themselves are becoming more polluted.

A free Vegetarian Starter Kit: www.vegetarianstarterkit.com
30 reasons to go vegetarian: www.goveg.com/feat/chewonthis

Want some veggie beefcake or cheesecake? "Lettuce ladies" and "broccoli boys," dressed in strategically placed pieces of vegetable, raise eyebrows and open minds as they travel the US, educating people about vegetarianism and serving up delicious veggie food. Apart from repeating all the better-known health benefits of a vegetarian diet, this deliberately non-PC, humorous campaign places a heavy emphasis on the improvement a vegetarian diet brings to your libido.

Choose your favorite pinup, join PETA (People for the Ethical Treatment of Animals), and get a signed photo as part of the membership package.

...try it for seven days

Are you man or woman enough to give up animal products? It will mean a change in your lifestyle and outlook. It's also a great way to see how meat affects the way your body feels.

☺ **Go vegan or vegetarian for a week**—or even a month.

☺ **After that, do what you want.** If nothing else, you will be able to say that you gave it a try.

waste is a BURNING ISSUE

The problem of waste is one of two halves: creating less waste, and then disposing of it in a safe and sustainable way. Most important, we must protect human health and the environment from toxic poisoning. ♣ Safe disposal of waste is as important in the developing world as in the industrialized world. Industrial countries export waste to developing countries for disposal where environmental laws are often softer or not enforced.

"We oppose incinerators, landfills, and other end of pipe interventions." The Global Anti-Incinerator Alliance (GAIA) is an international alliance of individuals, nongovernmental organizations, community initiatives, academics, and others working to end the incineration of all forms of waste and to promote sustainable waste prevention.

GAIA works on municipal disposal, hazardous waste, and medical waste. Each workgroup undertakes projects to prevent incineration and to promote alternatives. GAIA's first global campaign is to stop the World Bank from funding waste incinerators.

We recognize that our planet's finite resources, fragile biosphere, and the health of people and other living beings are endangered by polluting and inefficient production practices and health-threatening disposal methods.

Our ultimate vision is a just, toxic-free world without incineration. Our goal is the implementation of clean production, and the creation of a materials-efficient economy where all products are reused, repaired, or recycled back into the marketplace or nature.

Global Anti-Incinerator Alliance: www.no-burn.org
Recycling fun facts: members.aol.com/ramola15/funfacts.html

How incineration works

The waste is unloaded from a truck into a bunker area, transferred into a hopper, and fed into the furnace.

Combustion of the feedstock takes place in the furnace.

Heat recovery cools the exhaust gases; the recovered heat is reused in the incinerator or used to generate electric power.

A gas cleaning system, typically consisting of a "scrubber" to filter out pollutants, and an electrostatic precipitator or a fabric "bag filter" removes fine particles and some polluting gases.

A fan draws exhaust gases through the system prior to discharge into the atmosphere via a chimney stack.

Solid waste and water residues are removed. Ash and clinker from the furnace fall into a quench tank. This sludge can be highly toxic.

...stop it from going up in smoke

Join in the Global Day of Action.
Here are some actions they suggest:

♣ **Draw the public's attention** to local incinerators, waste facilities, and landfills.

♣ **Picket government agencies** that support or promote "burn" policies.

♣ **Join in the fax and e-mail action** to demonstrate public opposition.

THROW
a public party

Parties are a great way for like-minded people to get together and have some fun. A street party can be a wonderful way for everyone to get together and bring color and laughter into their neighborhood. But what about holding a party in an unexpected place? It will be a memorable occasion!

Partying on the beach: London has its own beach—a small sandy stretch of the river Thames outside the Royal Festival Hall—which is exposed twice a day at low tide. 🏠 Technically the beach belongs to the Port of London Authority, which inherited it from King George IV as payment for his gambling debts. In reality it belongs to all Londoners—an unownable public space.

Reclaim the Beach has been holding free public events on this beach. Everything is done by volunteers, and performers and musicians give their time for free. It all started in 2000, when a group of friends brought a ghetto blaster, a picnic, and a few bottles of wine onto the beach. 🏠 By summer 2001, there were full-scale raves with sound systems, DJs, live bands, lighting, fireworks, and bonfires. Family-friendly daytime events have featured sandcastle competitions, boat rides, and Punch & Judy shows. When the tide rises, everyone goes home.

An underground party: Space Hijackers campaigns for public use of public spaces. In 1999 it "hijacked" a London Underground Circle Line train and turned it into a moving disco. All the equipment was brought in suitcases and transformed on site into a bar, a stereo deck, a snack counter, and a disco light. 🏠 Around 150 people attended, plus all of the passengers who happened to be on the train at the time: all were given free vodka, tequila, and sweets. After one and a half circuits of the Circle Line, the partygoers dashed off to a pub to continue their partying.

Reclaim the Beach: www.swarming.org.uk/recl/recl.htm
A guide to holding a Circle Line party: http://spacehijackers.org
Step-by-step guide to organizing a street party: www.streetparty.net
All about Labor Day: www.dol.gov/opa/aboutdol/laborday.htm

Labor Day

Labor Day celebrates the achievements of American workers and their contribution toward the nation's prosperity and standing. The first Labor Day was held in 1882 in New York City. In 1884 the first Monday in September was fixed as the date for the holiday. The format of Labor Day was spelled out when the holiday was first proposed—a street parade to exhibit the strength and esprit de corps of the trade and labor organizations, followed by a festival for the recreation and amusement of the workers and their families. Speeches by prominent men and women were introduced later.

...in an unexpected place

Organize a public party in an unexpected place.

And have fun!

free SOFTWARE

Free software is a matter of liberty, not price. To understand the concept, you should think of "free" as in free speech, not as in free beer! When programmers can read, redistribute, and modify the source code for a piece of software, the software evolves. People improve it, people adapt it, people fix the bugs. ✋ This can happen at a speed that seems astonishing when compared to the slow pace of conventional software development. Just compare the evolution of the MS Windows operating system (owned by Microsoft) with Linux (which is free and open source).

Free software provides four kinds of freedom for software users:

The freedom to run the program, for any purpose (*Freedom Zero*).

The freedom to study how the program works and adapt it (*Freedom One*).

The freedom to redistribute copies so you can help your neighbor (*Freedom Two*).

The freedom to improve the program and release your improvements to the public, so that the whole community benefits (*Freedom Three*).

Access to the source code—"open source"—is a precondition for Freedoms One and Three.

The free and open source software movement is built on the ideals of collaboration and sharing. It is an idea whose time has come. It is also enabling computer users in the developing world to access software without having to pay an arm and a leg for it or pirate it.

Software Freedom Day is held each September to promote the idea of Free and Open Source Software: www.softwarefreedomday.org

Free Software Foundation has developed free software, created a Copyleft licensing system, and publishes an online directory of free software: www.gnu.org

Open Source Initiative promotes the idea of open source development of software. www.opensource.org

A free software flood...

I'm from Skopje, Macedonia, and Microsoft organized a conference to promote the opening of a Microsoft office in my country. Over 600 IT people attended (managers mostly). This is a lot of people for Macedonia, which has 2 million citizens (only 4% have access to the Internet).

Our organization bought and recorded 1,000 CDs with free software (OpenCD/Knoppix) which we gave out. We called the operation "Free Software Flood" because it was raining like hell that day and because all the participants were "flooded" with free open software.

—Free/Libre Software Macedonia

...for a sharing society

MS Office has become the standard software package for office use. But try OpenOffice.org:

✋ Download Open Office from www.openoffice.org. Read the license conditions.

✋ Copy it onto as many CDs as possible.

✋ Distribute these to people who could use them—free, of course.

SEPTEMBER 3

SOFTWARE *freedom*

Ubuntu Linux is a complete desktop Linux operating system, freely available with community and professional support. The Ubuntu Manifesto states that software should be available free of charge, that software tools should be usable by people in their local language and despite any disabilities, and that people should have the freedom to customize and alter their software in whatever way they see fit.

***Ubuntu* is an ancient African word meaning "humanity to others."** The Ubuntu Linux distribution brings "the spirit of humanity to the software world." ♛ Ubuntu is funded by Mark Shuttleworth, a young South African entrepreneur who achieved fame as a space tourist, paying around $20 million to travel on a Russian Soyuz TM-34. ♛ Also from South Africa is www.translate.org.za, which aims to localize free and open source software by providing translations in the 11 official South African languages. Translation from English is a key task for bridging the digital divide.

Find out more about Ubuntu from shipit.ubuntu.com and get one, five, or ten CDs free of charge to install and share.

Find out more about Mark Shuttleworth at www.africaninspace.com.

Resources

The Open CD Project has free software to download. www.theopencd.org

International Open Source Network is an initiative of the United Nations Development Program (UNDP) to bridge the "digital divide" between rich and poor nations. It has a downloadable user manual for the Linux operating system, www.iosn.net.

NGO in a Box is a collection of advice, links, and software for small NGOs: www.tacticaltech.org/ngoinabox/contents.

Free Software Magazine, which is free! www.freesoftwaremagazine.com

Best free antivirus software, best free adware/spyware/scumware remover, best free browser, best free spam filter, best free software suite, and a whole lot more. Aloke Mullick is a practising surgeon who reviews free software. He circulates an e-newsletter with advice on what works best. Get on his mailing list: acmullick@yahoo.com.

...save a ton of money

While you're enthused by the idea of free and open source software, why not

♛ Change your PC operating system to Linux.

♛ Use Open Office for your day-to-day computer work.

♛ Download and use lots of other free software.

Be free. Be open. Save money. Take a stand for sharing on the Internet.

wearing RIBBONS

Ribbons are used as symbols by different causes for promoting awareness. One of the best-known ribbon campaigns is the red ribbon used to promote HIV/AIDS awareness. Here are some of the other ribbon colors being used, and a weblink to get more information about the cause:

Gold: childhood cancer (www.cancerindex.org/ccw/index.htm)
Gray: asthma/allergies (www.aafa.org);
diabetes (diabetes.diabetesjournals.org);
mental illness (www.miepvideos.org);
brain tumor (www.cancercenter.com/brain-tumors.htm)
Green: clean environment (www.greenpeace.org);
organ/tissue donation (www.organdonor.gov);
missing children (www.missingkids.org); leukemia (www.leukemia.org/hm_lls)
Lace: osteoporosis (www.nof.org)
Light blue: prostate cancer (www.prostatecancerfoundation.org)
Orange: hunger (www.hungerday.org); Lupus (www.lupus.org)
Peach: uterine cancer (www.4woman.gov/faq/cuterine.htm)
Pink: breast cancer (www.nationalbreastcancer.org)
Red: HIV/AIDS (www.unaids.org)
White: Alzheimer's disease (www.alz.org); free speech (www.aclu.org)

For a list of lots more colors and causes, check out
kiwijewels.com/awareness_colors_and_meanings.htm.

How to make a ribbon

1. Cut a 3-inch length of narrow ribbon.
2. Lay the ribbon out horizontally on a table with the shorter edge on top.
3. Hold down the ribbon's midpoint with one finger. Move the left end of the ribbon so that it points downward at a slight inward angle.
4. Fold the right end in the same way, so the ribbon crosses itself about half an inch below the fold.
5. Where the ribbon crosses itself, glue the top ribbon to the bottom ribbon. As an alternative, you can sew the ribbon at the crossover point using a thread of the same color.
6. Pin a safety pin to the back at the crossover point; use this to attach the ribbon to your clothes.

...show you care

⚑ **Build awareness of different causes** in your own school, office, or community by organizing a Ribbon Week.

⚑ **Make a different-colored ribbon** each day of the week, and encourage people to pin them on their dress, shirt, or jacket lapel.

⚑ **Make a poster or leaflet for each "cause of the day."** Hand these out with the ribbons.

SEPTEMBER 5

SOCCER BALLS *fairly traded*

Soccer ball production has a reputation for using child labor. This fact was brought to public attention in the late 1990s. The response of most big companies involved in the trade was to ensure that they could provide a "no child labor" guarantee. As a result production was concentrated in large factory units and many women lost what had been a good home-based earning opportunity.

The challenge for fair trade was to develop a way of producing soccer balls in the villages while ensuring that children are not involved in the production process, and that workers receive a fair wage and are covered by health insurance. The $2 "fair-trade premium" provides for this and also supports a microcredit fund for the families of stitchers to help widen their opportunities for generating income.

How a soccer ball is made: The inner structure of a soccer ball is made from layers of fabric, which are glued (with latex) onto the outer skin of stitched panels. A design can be screen printed onto the panels. A latex bladder is glued onto one of the panels. A professional ball has an air mattress, which helps reduce the time a ball needs to regain its shape after being kicked.

Play Fair Trade Fair: yfocus.ncf.ca/fairtrade

Alive and kicking

Although AIDS is one of the biggest killers in Africa, nine-year-old Alan Majisu has no idea what it is. Living in Karangware, a sprawling Nairobi slum, Alan loves soccer but misses out because his school lacks balls and equipment. Instead, he plays on the streets with a ball made from plastic bags.

Alive & Kicking was set up by Jim Cogan to revive local production of leather soccer balls in Africa. The leather panels are supplied by Bata and stitched by trained young Kenyans. The footballs carry an AIDS message and are sold at a small markup to schools and community projects.

Contact:
director@aliveandkicking.org.uk

...buy three and have fun

Buy three soccer balls:

- **Use one** to play soccer with your family and friends.
- **Kick one** into a playground (as an unattributable act of generosity).
- **Donate one** to a youth soccer project in an African slum, where the sport has a real role to play in engaging young people. Send it to the National Youth Organisation (Bidii Foundation), PO Box 28838, 00200 Nairobi, Kenya.

campaign for VOTES AT 16

Women worldwide have fought for the same voting rights as men.
Women were granted equal voting rights in 1920 in the US. ♪ In the UK,
suffragette Emily Davison gave up her life for the cause; she stepped in front of
the king's horse in the 1913 Derby and was trampled to death.

Young people are now campaigning to get the voting age lowered to 16.
The arguments against this are the same as those used by earlier generations to
deny women and the working classes the vote, that they are too innocent of the
world and that others know what's best for them. Those arguments are as wrong
now as they were then.

National Youth Rights Association: www.youthrights.org

Ten reasons for young people to have the vote:

Young people suffer a double standard of having
responsibilities but not rights.

Young people pay taxes, live under the law.

Politicians will represent their interests if youth
can vote.

Young people have a unique perspective.

Lowering the voting age will increase voter turnout.

If we let stupid adults vote, why not let smart
youth vote?

Young people will vote well.

There are no wrong votes.

Lowering the voting age will benefit the lives
of youth.

www.youthrights.org/vote10.html

...give young people a say

♪ **Sign a petition, and get all your friends to sign too.**

♪ **Download the poster from Youth Rights.** Stick them up in schools,
colleges, youth centers...wherever young people will see them. Stick them
everywhere.

♪ **Lower the voting age.**

The most important right in this country is the right to vote. Without it, youth are
marginalized, victimized, and ignored. Lawmakers cut education while protecting
senior benefits. Lawmakers take away the right to drive from teens but not from
the elderly. Why? Seniors vote. Youth can't.

Join the movement: Youth are taxed like adults and put to death like adults. They
should have the right to vote like adults....Join us....Together we can do this.

www.youthrights.org/flyers/votinage.pdf

SEPTEMBER 7

SUBTITLES *read and hear*

Nonliteracy in India has risen as India's population has grown. Despite a rise in literacy rates from 1961 (28%) to 1997 (62%), the population growth has meant that the number of nonliterate people grew from 249 million to 294 million over the same period. ♟ And many of those who have learned to read will relapse into illiteracy if there are no written words in their lives.

Same-language subtitling allows people to read words as they are spoken onscreen. The idea was hit upon by Brij Kothari, an Indian academic at a center for education innovation in India. Brij realized that same-language subtitling of Bollywood film songs on television could be a cheap and effective way of helping people improve their reading ability.

If the subtitles are there, people will see and read them automatically. If they can't read a particular word, they will hear it being read out to them while they are trying to read it, and this will act as a prompt. ♟ Over 200 million Indian TV viewers have had access to same-language subtitled programming. The technique has been evaluated and has shown to improve reading ability. The idea won a Best Social Invention award.

Find out more about same-language subtitling: www.planetread.org

BookBox

Brij Kothari has now extended the principle of same-language subtitling to videobooks, which he is distributing on the Internet. His new project—BookBox—aims to produce a book for every child in every language. Text, sound, and illustrations are synchronized to create an entertaining reading experience that allows the child to see the words as they are read.

BookBox plans to become a web-based jukebox of illustrated children's books for children under ten, published in many of the world's languages. The project was launched in 2004, with three titles: *Santa's Christmas* and *The Little Pianist* in English, French, and Spanish; and *Turtle's Flute* also in Hindi and Chinese. This is just a start. The eventual aim is to publish one book a week.

BookBox books are ad-free and violence-free, and care is taken to respect cultural diversity in story content. The books can be previewed on the website for free and cost $1.95 to download.

...to develop literacy

♟ **Read a BookBox book with a child.** Go to www.bookbox.com.

the power of COMICS

Comics are a powerful medium. Words and pictures combine to tell a story or raise an issue. Comics can be serious or funny. They can stimulate, provoke, and urge people to action.

You don't have to be a professional artist to draw a comic strip. World Comics Finland and World Comics India have been running comic workshops with some of the world's poorest people to help them communicate effectively using comics, within their local community or to the wider world. ♟ The idea is spreading, and World Comic projects have been active in India, Tanzania, Mozambique, Lebanon, and also in some European countries.

World Comics Finland: www.worldcomics.fi
World Comics India: www.worldcomicsindia.com

Tips for producing a good comic:

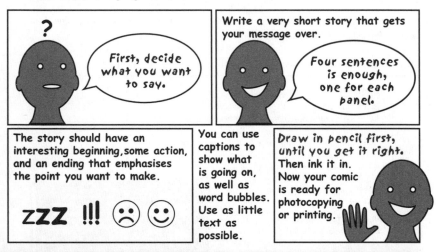

? First, decide what you want to say.

Write a very short story that gets your message over. Four sentences is enough, one for each panel.

The story should have an interesting beginning, some action, and an ending that emphasises the point you want to make.

zzz !!! ☹ ☺

You can use captions to show what is going on, as well as word bubbles. Use as little text as possible.

Draw in pencil first, until you get it right. Then ink it in. Now your comic is ready for photocopying or printing.

...tell stories in pictures

Take an issue you feel strongly about. Produce a wall-poster comic about that issue.

♟ **A wall-poster comic is a good format to use.** Stick your poster up on a wall in a prominent place. A simple format is two sheets of typing paper taped together. This provides space for a big headline and four panels, which should be enough to get your message across.

♟ **The how-to section on the World Comics Finland website** gives some basic advice on how to set about producing a wall-poster comic.

♟ **Being able to draw well is not the most important thing.** You need a good story with interesting and engaging characters with which the readers can identify easily.

♟ **Just try, and surprise yourself with the results!** When you have finished, pin your comic somewhere people can see and read it.

STOP SEXUAL *harassment*

Sexual harassment is "offensive behavior of a sexual nature." It includes sexual innuendo, such as lewd comments about appearance or sex life; unwelcome physical contact, such as someone deliberately brushing up against you or trying to fondle you; an unpleasant work environment created by the display of sexually explicit pictures, the circulation of lewd e-mails, or the downloading of Internet porn.

In two high-profile cases of "Sexism in the City," women won out-of-court settlements for alleged sexual harassment. In March 2001, Isabelle Terrillon, a 35-year-old trader working for Nomura Securities in London, alleged that a company executive told her to wear short tight skirts, another asked her to strip and give him a massage, and male colleagues passed around pornographic e-mails that she found degrading. ⊗ In July 2004, Elizabeth Weston, a 29-year-old lawyer working with Merrill Lynch, alleged that a senior employee had made lewd remarks, joked about her sex life, and caused red wine to be spilled down her front.

Sexual harassment and what to do about it, from the Equal Opportunities Commission: www.eeoc.gov/facts/fs-sex.html

Stereotyping: The word *stereotype* was originally a printing term, meaning a duplicate impression. The word developed into a metaphor for an identical idea used in different situations. *Cliché* has a similar meaning and also comes from printing; it expressed the sound of molten metal being poured to form the type to be used for printing. Today a stereotype is a simplified image of an individual or a group that is perceived to share certain characteristics. It is often used to portray negative qualities—of women, homosexual people, ethnic and racial groups, old people, young people...

Get the Don't Stereotype Me! sticker from "Bitches, Bimbos and Ballbreakers: The Guerrilla Girls Illustrated Guide to Female Stereotypes." Download it from www.guerrillagirls.com.

...for a better workplace

Challenge sexual harassment!

⊗ **When you encounter sexual harassment** or just sexist behavior at the workplace, challenge the person concerned.

⊗ **Download a postcard from the I Spy Sexism website.** Send it to the wrongdoer. Let him know that you are watching and that you will continue to watch, and that you will take firm action unless his behavior changes.

combat TERRORISM

On September 11, 2001, 19 hijackers hijacked four airliners. Two were crashed into the Twin Towers in New York, one into the Pentagon, and the fourth crashed into a Pennsylvania field following passenger resistance. Deaths totaled 2,986 including passengers and the 19 hijackers. The day had a significant impact on the US and how its citizens feel. It was the starting point for the invasions of Afghanistan and Iraq and for the "War on Terror."

Human rights can easily be violated in the name of national security. Violations include

Government interference with the judicial process.

Use of torture and cruel, inhuman, or degrading treatment or punishment.

Secret detention or denying detainees prompt access to lawyers, family members, and medical personnel.

Failure to produce charges or evidence against detainees, and failure to bring a case promptly before a court.

Denying detainees the right to challenge the lawfulness of their detention.

Not providing a fair trial through an independent and impartial tribunal or court.

Allowing evidence obtained by torture to be part of the prosecution case.

Failing to safeguard freedoms of expression, religion, conscience, belief, association, and assembly, and the peaceful pursuit of the right to self-determination and to privacy. Any restrictions should be "necessary and proportionate."

Not providing effective remedy and reparation to any person adversely affected by counterterrorism measures.

Expelling persons suspected or convicted of acts of terrorism to a state where there is a risk that they will be subjected to a serious violation of human rights.

Amnesty International: www.amnesty.org
International Commission of Jurists: icj.org

Download an ICJ Alerts Form from
http://icj.org/article.php3?id_article=69&id_rubrique=36&lang=en.

Declaration on Upholding Human Rights in Combating Terrorism

In adopting measures aimed at suppressing acts of terrorism, states must adhere strictly to the rule of law, including the core principles of criminal and international law and the specific standards and obligations of international human rights law, refugee law and, where applicable, humanitarian law. These principles, standards and obligations define the boundaries of permissible and legitimate state action against terrorism. The odious nature of terrorist acts cannot serve as a basis or pretext for states to disregard their international obligations, in particular in the protection of fundamental human rights.

—International Commission of Jurists, August 2004

...but uphold human rights

Be vigilant to see human rights upheld. There seems to be a resigned acceptance that a significant loss of our human rights is necessary following 9-11 and subsequent acts of terrorism. But this need not be the case. The War on Terror should be conducted while we uphold people's fundamental human rights.

Report any significant or disproportionate violation of human rights to Amnesty International and to the International Commission of Jurists.

TURN ON *and tune in*

There are many excellent radio and TV programs on international development, health, the environment, human rights, gender, and other global issues. Programs can be informative and inspiring.

Here are some good sources of information on what's happening in the world. And what people are doing to change things:

New Internationalist reports on the issues of world poverty and inequality. The site focuses attention on the unjust relationships between the powerful and powerless worldwide. It debates and campaigns for the radical changes necessary to meet the basic needs of all people. It brings to life the people, ideas, and action in the fight for global justice: www.newint.org.

Resurgence reports on environment and ecology, holistic science, creative living, spiritual well-being, and sustainable agriculture, with articles written by theorists, visionaries, activists, scientists and artists: resurgence.gn.apc.org.

Utne Reader reprints the best articles from over 2,000 alternative media sources. It contains "Provocative writing from diverse perspectives.... Insightful analysis of art and media....Down-to-earth news and resources you can use....In-depth coverage of compelling people and issues that affect your life....The best of the alternative media." Some of the magazine is available on the web, some you need to subscribe to: www.utne.com.

WorkingForChange, an online daily journal of progressive news and opinion published by Working Assets. Take action with ActForChange, which is part of the website: www.workingforchange.com.

Third World Network, a research and information service based in Malaysia providing a southern nations' perspective on global issues. It publishes a daily SUNS bulletin as well as the fortnightly *Third World Economics* and the monthly *Third World Resurgence*. It also distributes books published in the Third World: www.twnside.org.sg.

Radio Ga Ga
It's not just TV, websites, and newspapers that report on world events. Radio is also a great way to find out about current affairs. Listen to programs on OneWorld Radio: radio.oneworld.net. Or seek out pirate radio stations for a unique take on the world.

...get the latest news

Tune in to find out about what's happening in the world.

- **Listen to BBC World documentaries on your computer.** Go to www.bbc.co.uk and click on "Listen to shows you've missed" and then "World Service." If you don't have Realplayer, then you will be given instructions on loading a free version.

- **See the latest news in words and pictures at 10x10.** This website displays the top 100 words and pictures in the world every hour based on what's happening in the news. www.tenbyten.org

12 SEPTEMBER

wood-burning STOVES

More-efficient wood-burning stoves can change lives dramatically. The Escorts Foundation works with the people of the Changa Manga forest area in Punjab, Pakistan. They noticed that families spent many hours illegally pillaging the forest for the firewood they needed for cooking. This was damaging the forest; out of 760 trees grown per acre, 600 were being stripped for firewood. 🌐 The cooking process also meant that the women were spending hours every day near a smoky stove (known as a *chulla*), and this was causing serious respiratory and eye problems.

A new type of stove that used less wood and was less smoky had not caught on, partly because of the high cost of paying a local blacksmith to make the stove's steel chimney. 🌐 The Escorts Foundation first modified the design by introducing a simple mud chimney, and then adapted the design of the stove itself so that it could be made out of locally available raw materials (measured in units of cans and bottles) and using a cooking-oil drum as a mold.

This stove could be built by anyone anywhere. The materials needed were mud, straw, and clay. The challenge was to demonstrate to village women that the stove would actually work, and that it would save them time. The stove uses up to 75% less firewood, and it can use smaller branches and twigs. 🌐 Escorts then trained women to become "chulla mechanics." The women would go back to their villages and help other women make stoves. 🌐 One stove takes a day to make and costs virtually nothing. So far, 12,000 stoves have been installed, with an average 70% adoption rate in most of the villages.

The Escorts Foundation won a 2004 Ashden Award for projects bringing renewable energy to local communities in the developing world: www.ashdenawards.org

An evaluation has shown the following benefits from adopting more-efficient wood-burning stoves:
Children attend school more regularly.
Children are cleaner.
There is a 70% saving in time collecting firewood and a 50% reduction in the use of firewood, thereby reducing carbon dioxide emissions.

...life-changing solutions

Support the Escorts Foundation in this work.

It costs just $4 to build a stove (including all the training and support). Raise a small sum and make a huge impact on people's lives.

SEPTEMBER 13

POLLUTANT *persistence*

Persistent Organic Pollutants, or POPs, are among the most dangerous chemicals ever created. They include many pesticides, industrial chemicals, and chemical by-products. ♣ POPs have become an urgent global environmental health problem. POPs break down very slowly in soil, air, water, and living organisms. They persist in the environment for a long time. They get into the food chain, and then into the tissues of living creatures, including humans. POPs damage reproduction, the body's development and immune system, and create nerve disorders, cancers, and hormone disruption.

Every living organism on earth now carries measurable levels of POPs in its tissues. POPs have spread throughout the environment to threaten human health and damage land and water ecosystems all over the world. ♣ POPs travel long distances in air and water currents. They do not disperse in high-altitude, low-temperature regions of the globe. Peoples and ecosystems of the Arctic and Antarctic are at high risk. In 2001, a treaty banning the use of POPs was signed by 91 countries. It comes into effect when 50 countries have ratified it.

It's VOCs as well as POPs. Beauty comes at a price. Fragrances are chemicals that vaporize easily: that's why we can smell them. They are added to products to give them a scent or to mask other ingredients. ♣ The volatile organic chemicals (VOCs) emitted by fragrance and cleaning products contribute to poor indoor air quality and are associated with headaches, allergic reactions, and other side effects.

From fleas to weeds, factsheets for pesticide-free solutions:
www.pesticide.org/factsheets.html

Pesticide Advisor, alternatives at home, in the garden, and on humans and pets:
www.panna.org/resources/advisor.dv.html

Pesticide Action Network: www.pan-international.org
Fragranced Products Information Network: www.fpinva.org
Health Care without Harm: www.noharm.org

Chemicals in agriculture are not always essential to high productivity.

In Bangladesh 2,000 farmers were trained to grow rice without insecticides and with reduced amounts of nitrogen fertilizer. The yield was not affected, and the farmers saved money.

This innovation is being replicated across the country. Around 12 million farmers could benefit from higher incomes and improved living standards, while creating environmental benefits for everyone.

—www.irri.org

...threatens life on earth

♣ **Understand what POPs are and the danger they pose.** Know what you are buying and using.

♣ **Then take steps to reduce (better still, eliminate) your use of POPs.**

♣ **Don't use toxic insecticides,** for example. Careful sanitation, door and window screens kept in good repair, fly swatters, flypapers, and fly traps will all help reduce the fly population.

promote BREAST MILK

A mother has a right to independent information and freedom from pressure from companies. If she chooses to bottle-feed she should be aware of the risks and costs.

—International Baby Food Action Network

Breastfeeding is the best start in life: it is free and safe, and it protects against infection. Breastfeeding reduces the risk of illness in all countries. Breastfed babies need no other food or drink for about the first six months of life. They also have reduced risk of diabetes, pneumonia, ear infections, and some cancers. It is extremely rare for a woman to be physically unable to breastfeed.

In the developing world, formula milk is expensive. It is often mixed with unclean water, which can cause diarrhea, and it may be overdiluted to make it last longer, thus leading to malnutrition. Where water is unsafe, UNICEF says, babies are 25 times more likely to die if they are bottle-fed, and that reversing the decline in breastfeeding could save the lives of 1.5 million infants every year.

Nestlé says that it is socially responsible in distributing and promoting formula milk. They state that "breastfeeding is best for babies. Chemist Henri Nestlé stated this in his Treatise on Nutrition soon after founding our company in 1867, and it is still true today. We are committed to ensuring that the best interests of mothers and babies are served by our employees around the world." Nestlé is the world's largest baby food company. It sells formula milk in both the developed and the developing world.

International Baby Food Action Network: www.ibfan.org

For Nestlé's point of view: www.babymilk.nestle.com

Nestlé SA: www.nestle.com

Breastfeeding advocates say that Nestlé

Provides information to mothers that promotes artificial feeding and discourages breastfeeding.

Donates free samples and supplies to health facilities to encourage artificial feeding.

Gives inducements to health workers for promoting its products.

Does not provide clear enough warnings on labels of the benefits of breastfeeding and dangers of artificial feeding.

...save infant lives

Make up your own mind about who's right and who's wrong. If you think that Nestlé needs to do more, boycott Nestlé and bring pressure to bear:

- **Stop buying Nescafé coffee and other Nestlé products.** Tell your friends and workmates to do the same.
- **Write to tell Nestlé that you support the boycott.**
- **Collect petition signatures** to present to Nestlé at its AGM.
- **Encourage support** from community groups, unions, churches, and other organizations.
- **Hold a day of action** in your community and get publicity for it.

SEPTEMBER 15

GREENSCORE *yourself*

We can all live a greener, more environmentally sustainable life. But this will mean changing what we buy and how we live.

Some things will require a bit of effort. For example, reducing the number of car journeys we make or not buying cheap air tickets to get away on weekend breaks.

Some will require money: loft insulation, seals for windows and doors, double glazing. Some will be a bit less comfortable until we get used to them: turning down the heating and switching off the lights and TV remote. Some will be a bit more expensive, such as buying organic food and drink. But on the other hand, we will save money in the long run on things such as long-life electric bulbs.

GreenScore and Eco-Teams are projects of Global Action Plan: www.globalactionplan.org.

To take a test to measure your greenness, go to www.context.org/ICLIB/IC22/TestPPhtm.

The Green Guide: www.thegreenguide.com

Green Living: www.greenlivingnow.com

Flintham Crusaders

Seven young people from the English village of Flintham, aged between 12 and 17, formed a youth Eco-Team. They cajoled their parents into cutting down household waste, composting, and saving energy and water. Their efforts saved their families an average of about $36 per week and reduced the amount of waste going to the landfill by half.

Tom, the youngest member of the team, was fired up by his experience. After completing the program, he decided to expand his hobby of keeping ducks and chickens to provide eggs to sell to villagers. He produces over 200 eggs a week, which he delivers by Rollerblade to "increase the danger level"!

...reduce your impact

Take the GreenScore test to see how green you are.

♞ **The questionnaire covers around 80 practical things** you can do to become more energy efficient, reduce the impact of your travel, save water, shop sensibly, and reduce, reuse, and recycle your trash. How did you score?

♞ **Now try to improve on it!** Get together with half a dozen or so of your neighbors and set up an Eco-Team. Then over the next four months, together try to reduce your environmental impact from energy and water use, household waste, transportation, and shopping.

♞ **From time to time, take another GreenScore test** to measure your improvements. Improving your Eco-Team score will help create a cleaner, more sustainable future for everyone.

speak up SPEAK OUT

Speak up for what you believe in. If you have something important to say, if you disagree with what someone else is saying, or if you agree and want to add some points, then it is important for you to have your say.

Here are some opportunities for you to get your voice heard:

At conferences and public meetings you attend. Don't just sit there thinking about what you might say. Stand up and say something. Mention who you are (and any organization you represent). Then say what you need to say clearly and succinctly. And bring along lots of literature to hand out afterward.

Call into a phone-in program with your point of view. They will ask you what you would like to speak about before they let you on the air. So make sure that it's something sensible.

Send your views by phone or e-mail to viewers' and listeners' feedback programs on TV and radio.

Write a letter to the editor of your local newspaper.

Write to your representative. They often refer to their mail but in actual fact get very little correspondence except through orchestrated campaigns.

Your view may not be heard or be published this time. But no matter, try again. And keep trying. See yourself as an expert with something important to say on an important issue. And one day, perhaps, people will be trailing after you to get your point of view.

Tips for public speaking
Breathing: give yourself enough air to get the words out.
Eye contact: you're communicating with them personally.
Straighten up: speak tall.
Talk with your hands: gestures reinforce what you're saying.
Volume: don't eat your words.
Emphatic pauses: to make a point.
Slow down: make each syllable count.
Tonal variation: for emphasis and impact.
or **B-E-S-T V-E-S-T** for short. Give it your best shot!

...get your voice heard

👫 **Make a list of ten things** you could do to get your voice heard. Then try to do them all.

👫 **Make a diary of what you have done,** with the dates and details of each approach. If you get no response, then telephone to ask why.
It pays to be assertive.

👫 **Get something published or broadcast** at least once during the month, if you can.

SEPTEMBER 17

STORY *telling*

The imagination is a place all by itself. A separate country. You've heard of the French Nation and the British Nation. Well, this is the Imagi Nation. It's a wonderful place.

—George Seaton

Storytelling is as old as humanity. Thirty thousand years ago, hairy, grunting cave dwellers threw down their tools to sit by the fire and share tales about the day's hunt. A millennium ago, entire fiefdoms and kingdoms gathered together to hear their storytellers perform.

Through stories, we are introduced to the rise and fall of empires, the world's great and passionate loves. We taste what it would be like to live in another time in the past or in the future or in another body. Entire cultures and histories have been passed down through the ages through oral tradition. ⚫ Public libraries, schools, playgroups, day-care centers, women's shelters, afterschool clubs, and youth centers would all jump at the chance to have you come in and do some storytelling.

information about storytelling, conferences, tips, and networks:
www.storynet.org
stories and information about storytelling: www.storyteller.net
spooky stories from the American South: www.themoonlitroad.com
stories for all ages from all over the world: www.dancingponyproductions.com

It was a dark and stormy night...

...the rain fell in torrents, except at occasional intervals, when it was checked by a violent gust of wind which swept up the streets (for it is in London that our scene lies), rattling along the housetops, and fiercely agitating the scanty flame of the lamps that struggled against the darkness...

—from *Paul Clifford* by
Edward George Bulwer Lytton (1830)

"It was a dark and stormy night..." is the most quoted opening sentence of a story. The annual Bulwer Lytton Fiction Contest awards a prize for the worst opening sentence of an imaginary novel. Why not have a go? You might even win! www.bulwer-lytton.com

...become the local oracle

🌷 **Call your local library,** and arrange a time when you can come in and enthrall a group of kids with a nail-biting adventure or a heart-wrenching romance. Show them a wider world. Tell them stories about people who will inspire them to great things.

🌷 **Through your storytelling, you will become a feature of your local community.** You will feed people's imagination and you will brighten up their lives. And why not persuade your local talk radio to give you a weekly slot?

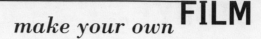

make your own FILM

Television, radio, movies, newspapers, magazines, blogs, websites, billboards, flyers...they all feed us continuously with images and words. We get stories of death, destruction, killing, bombings, natural disasters, and environmental damage. These negative images tell only half the story and help perpetuate feelings of fear and powerlessness.

With advances in video technology and new communication networks, ordinary people can now create and distribute their own films, addressing the issues that concern them, highlighting positive images of cooperation and social action. Refugees from a conflict country, youth from immigrant families, members of urban gangs can all have their say.

It is not enough just to say, "Right, I'm going to make a movie." A lot of work will be involved, so it's important to decide why you want to make it and who your audience will be before you get started.

Pick an issue that you want people to understand better—maybe something in your community that needs to change. Perhaps it is a controversial issue that affects everyone—such as sex, violence, or drugs. This will be the subject of your movie. Here's what to do next:

Step 1: Get some friends to work with you. Borrow a video camera.

Step 2: Write your script, Decide what you want your message to be. Think about the images as well as the words. Decide whom you want to interview.

Step 3: Shoot your movie. Then edit it.

Step 4: Get people to come and see your movie. Start with a "debut night" at your own home. Invite everyone you know to come and see the film. Find forums where you can show it to the public. Approach community centers, libraries, schools, film festivals, and TV stations. There are public access stations or public access slots on offer from mainstream broadcasters. Take advantage of these, and get your film on TV!

Scenarios USA: www.scenariosusa.com

How to get your film made by a Hollywood director!

Picture yourself a scriptwriter, a filmmaker, a visionary, the next Steven Spielberg? Picture getting your first big break in Hollywood? Then here's a way of getting your first film made by a major Hollywood director.

If you are age 12 to 22, write a short story about a difficult subject that young people have to face, such as AIDS/HIV, violence, or drugs. Send your story to Scenarios USA. Do this right now.

If your short story is selected, you will be paired with a big-time Hollywood director, and the two of you will turn your story into a short film.

Scenarios USA films are shown and distributed at film festivals and schools. They have been shown on Showtime, MTV, Oxygen, NBC, and ABC.

Scenarios USA is dedicated to giving young people a creative forum to explore and express who they are and how they see the world, with the goal of helping them make healthy decisions about their lives.

...and make a statement

To find out about festivals around the world where you can submit your film, go to www.britfilms.com/festivals.

SEPTEMBER 19

TRAVEL *to other countries*

Do you have any idea how many countries there are? Boundaries shift when wars, treaties, or totalitarians muddy things up, but there are currently around 190 countries in the world.

How many have you seen? Not many, very likely. So get moving! There's an entire world to explore, with cultures and styles of living that are very different from your own. Seeing the world may inspire you. It could even change your life.

Some ideas to inspire you:

Witnessing war and peace: Why not find out about countries that have experienced war and conflict? Don't just rely on what you see on TV. Check it out at firsthand. But check the security situation first. You can travel independently, but you could also join a peace tour.

From Fiji to Cyprus and back again: The School for International Training allows you to engage with regional experts, work with local organizations, and understand local and regional issues.

Palestine: The Palestine Summer Encounter, organized by the Holy Land Trust, aims to create a dialogue between overseas visitors and Palestinians. In two months, you learn Arabic, volunteer with a Palestinian nonprofit organization, and visit important sites in the region.

Colombia, Cuba, Mexico, Nicaragua: In a Witness for Peace delegation you will gain an insight into issues of peace, economic justice, and sustainable development, and have the chance to meet those fighting for a better world.

Bosnia: Builders for Peace is a summer program that includes hands-on restoration of historic sites damaged during the war that followed the breakup of Yugoslavia, plus teaching conversational English at a free summer school for high-school students.

Witness for Peace: www.witnessforpeace.org
Palestine Summer Encounter: www.http://travel.holylandandtrust.org
School for International Training: www.sit.edu/studyabroad/index.html

Get the money together to pay for your trip.

Put a big jar on a table just inside your front door. Stick a label on the jar that reads "BRAZIL" in big letters, or whatever country you'd like to go to. Every time you enter or leave your apartment, BRAZIL will be staring you in the face, reminding you of your plans.

Ask everyone who comes to your home (and that includes you) to put their change in the jar. It doesn't matter whether it's a dollar or a penny. It all adds up. As soon as you have enough money, pack your passport and go see the world.

...to broaden your mind

Be a net-jetter!
During your trip, write a travelogue and take photographs recording your daily experiences and encounters. E-mail this to everyone you know, or put it on a website or a blog you have created for your trip.

campaign for PEACE

All over the world people campaign for peace. In 2001 the United Nations General Assembly declared September 21 as the International Day of Peace (Resolution 55/282). It is intended as

a day of global ceasefire and nonviolence devoted to commemorating and strengthening the ideals of peace both within and among all nations and peoples... the observance and celebration of which alleviates tensions and causes of conflict ...an invitation to all nations and people to honor a cessation of hostilities for the duration of the Day...and an invitation to all Member States, organizations, and individuals to commemorate in an appropriate manner this International Day of Peace.

The US government spends twenty-five times as much on the military as it does on overseas aid; the UK spends over eight times as much; France six times as much; Germany and Japan five times as much.

International Day of Peace website: www.un.org/events/peaceday

Marching for peace and justice

In 1930, Gandhi, with 78 followers, led a Salt March to protest the injustices of the British Empire. The march became a turning point in India's struggle for independence. They walked 241 miles in 24 days from the Gandhi ashram in Ahmedabad to the seaside village of Dandi, where they proceeded to make salt from seawater (which was illegal at that time, as the British rulers imposed a hefty tax on salt).

The Salt March was reenacted in March and April 2005 in order to reawaken the people of the world to stand up for peace and nonviolence. Find out more from www.saltmarch.org.in

...seven simple actions

Here are seven things you can do for World Peace Day:

- ❧ **Organize your own event** to celebrate World Peace Day—a fast, or a disco with peace movement music: "All we are saying is give peace a chance."
- ❧ **Give $10 and get nine of your friends to do the same.** Then together use the $100 to support a peace initiative.
- ❧ **What's your big idea for world peace?** If a world leader could do something, what should he or she do? Write a letter to the leader with your idea, and send a copy to your local newspaper.
- ❧ **Be inspired by Gandhi:** "Be the change you wish to see in the world." If there is one small thing you could do for world peace, what would it be? Go and do it today.
- ❧ **Measure happiness in smiles per hour.** Today on World Peace Day, smile at people, people you meet, people in the street.
- ❧ **Choose an issue or a region of conflict,** and then find out as much as you can about what is happening there. Try to hear both sides. Keep up-to-date with breaking news.
- ❧ **Find a pen pal from the other side** and share your thoughts and ideas.

PEDESTRIAN *rights*

We're all pedestrians and many of us also drive cars. As drivers we demand congestion-free roads and the right to drive as we wish; when we are not in our cars, we hate the traffic noise, the polluted air, the dangerous driving, our streets jam-packed with traffic and parked cars, traffic signs everywhere. And when traffic is banned, we suddenly realize how much nicer our streets could be.

The car culture is not going to suddenly disappear. But we can fight to make it less dominant in our lives and landscapes.

Carbusters is an organization that campaigns against traffic. Members stage events and protests to cut down the use of cars. Carbusters organizes pedestrian-crossing actions to contest the fact that cars in practice always seem to get the right of way, even when they are outnumbered by pedestrians. Protesters dress in solid black or white outfits, march into the middle of the road and lie down, creating a human zebra crossing.

The World Carfree Network is a clearing house for information from around the world. Their annual World Carfree Day in September has over 1,500 cities in 40 countries participating: www.worldcarfree.net

Carbusters provides tools for taking on car culture: www.carbusters.org
Carfree.com, a website linked to the book *Carfree Cities:* carfree.com

Carbusters Campaigns

Get hold of an old car, park it in the center of town, and invite people to destroy it. While they are doing so, tell them about the destructiveness of the car.

Offer a free roadside counseling service for all car addicts. Give them the opportunity to undertake the "Eight-step Program to a Carfree Life" on the Carbusters website.

Hand out fake parking tickets, designed to look like the real thing, "fining" drivers for hogging public space or contributing to climate change.

Sticker a car parked on the pavement or in a pedestrian zone with footprint-shaped stickers and leave a note saying,

Warning, You have parked illegally
in a pedestrian area.
Next time your car
will be walked over.

...people before cars

♟ **Pay a parking meter** for parking time and use it as a venue for a party.

♟ **Make it a huge party,** using a whole row of parking meters in the busiest area of town at the busiest time of day.

♟ **Have lots of banners and placards** so that everyone knows exactly what you are doing.

have a healthy HEART

World Heart Day is observed at the end of September. It is held in more than 90 countries around the world and receives a great deal of positive publicity. The aim is to increase awareness of heart disease and encourage people to adopt healthier lifestyles. The World Heart Day slogan is "A Heart for Life."

Heart disease has become the number one killer, not just in Europe and North America, but across the developing world, especially among the middle classes in urban areas. Cardiovascular disease accounts for one in three deaths each year, adding up to 17 million people. ☺ Changes in diet, involving the consumption of more preprepared and fast foods, which contain too much fat, sugar, and salt, are one of the reasons for the growth. Smoking and lack of exercise are also important factors.

The main risk factors for heart disease include high cholesterol, which clogs the arteries, high blood pressure, smoking, lack of exercise, unhealthy diet, being overweight or obese, drinking too much alcohol, stress, and genetic factors.

World Heart Federation www.worldheart.org
World Heart Day www.worldheartday.com

Some ideas for incorporating exercise into your daily routine:

Get off the bus or train a few stops earlier and walk the rest of the way.

Go for a walk during the workday break or at lunchtime.

Take the stairs instead of the elevator.

Go and speak to someone instead of phoning or e-mailing them.

Stand while on the phone.

Schedule exercise time into your day.

Why not do salsa or go line dancing, or get together with a group of your friends to jog, play softball, or swim together on a regular basis?

...be fit for life

First start with yourself. Try not to die young. Small changes to your lifestyle can bring big rewards.

☺ **Check the shape you're in** by going to www.worldheartday.com/heartforlife/Obesity.asp.

☺ **If you smoke, stop.** It is also important to have a smoke-free environment at work and at home, so make others around you aware of the dangers of passive smoking.

☺ **A balanced diet and regular exercise are both important.** Even 30 minutes of moderate exercise several times a week will help.

FOOD *for thought*

While the human population grows, there is a crisis at sea. Nature's limits have been breached by too many fishing vessels catching too many fish, often in extremely wasteful and destructive ways.  Overfishing what is considered a "free resource" is leading to a catastrophic decline in fish stocks. Species that were once found in abundance have or will soon become endangered.

If nothing is done, the oceans will turn into fish deserts. The human communities around the world that depend on fishing will be forced to find alternative livelihoods. There will also be disastrous consequences for marine life.

In his book *The End of the Line,* Charles Clover suggests these actions: The fishing industry fishes less, especially the giant trawlers that scoop up everything. Consumers eat less fish, or eat fish that have been less wastefully caught. And we should all know more about how fish are caught and reject fish caught unsustainably.

For information on what not to eat: www.fishonline.org/advice/avoid

Don't eat

Atlantic cod	Skates and rays
Atlantic salmon	Snapper
Chilean seabass	Sturgeon
Dogfish	Swordfish
European hake	Tuna
European seabass	Tropical prawns
Grouper	
Haddock	
Ling	
Marlin	
Monkfish	
North Atlantic	
halibut	
Orange roughy	
Shark	

Do eat and enjoy

Bream	Mackerel
Brill	Megrim
Brown crab	Mussels
Catfish	Oysters
Clams	Pollack
Cockles	Poulting
Coley	Red mullet
Dab	Scallops
Dover sole	Turbot
Flounder	Witch
Gurnard	
Herring	
Langoustine	
Lemon sole	
Lobster	

...eat the right fish

Favor fish caught by the least wasteful fishing methods.

 **The Marine Conservation Society lists 20 fish not to eat,** giving reasons and suggesting possible alternatives, as well as 25 fish that you can eat with a clear conscience (see above). Follow these recommendations and you will know that you are not contributing (at least for the moment) to the destruction of a particular fish stock.

 **Campaign for the government to give fishermen tradeable rights to fish,** accompanied by new responsibilities for marine conservation, and to create in the oceans nature reserves where fishing is banned.

 **Think before you eat.** Eat fish with a clear conscience and make sure that you don't eat any of the fish from the "Don't eat" list.

 **Read** *Cod* by Mark Kurlansky, for the story of how a once abundant fish has come to be greatly depleted.

24 SEPTEMBER

Tell people how important they have been to you.

I decided that I was going to find one person a year and write them a letter and tell them how they had changed my life. I wrote to my 3rd grade teacher and said what I remembered most from what she had taught me. Then I forgot all about it. But I was visiting my parents on vacation and we went shopping. I heard my name being called. My teacher ran up to me to say that when she and her husband read my letter, it made them both cry and that it was such a nice thing to write.

Give other people a chance to do good.
A minister in Indianapolis preached about kindness. Then she held up 50 envelopes. An anonymous donor had filled each with a $50 bill. Anyone could take one, no strings attached. All the donor asked was that the money be used for good. "We can make this world a better place," the preacher told her congregation. Those who picked up the envelopes spent weeks pondering how best to spend the money and make a difference. The donor had trusted them to use the money wisely. They took that trust and passed it on.

Be unexpectedly kind.

One time when I was at a bookstore, I noticed that the shop assistant was the only person working. She was trying hard to be really pleasant even though she was overwhelmed with waiting customers. I crossed the road and bought a potted plant, walked back to the bookstore, handed the plant to the shop assistant, and said, "I hope your day gets better." She smiled and said, "It just did. Thank you so much."

You can visit the makesomeonesday.org website and write about what you have done as an inspiration for others. www.makesomeonesday.org

Some other ways to make someone's day:

Praise people and mean it: "I saw what you did, and it was really great!" "You're really important to me," "You're looking great"...

Smile at people as you pass them in the street, when you are sitting opposite them in a subway, or when you're stuck in a traffic jam.

Lend a hand when someone needs it. Help an old person across the street, or someone with a stroller trying to navigate some steps, or someone with heavy shopping. Do it without their having to ask.

And there are lots and lots of other ways to make someone's day!

...make people feel good

👫 Today, do something that will make someone's day.

👫 And if you've enjoyed doing it, then do it again tomorrow, and the next day, and every day!

SEPTEMBER 25

RETHINK *school lunch*

Children are not eating well enough. And many children today have little understanding of how food is produced, how it gets to our plates, and how our health and well-being are connected to what we eat. A school lunch should be seen as being more than just a meal.

Thinking outside the lunch box: Rethinking School Lunch is a program developed by the Center for Ecoliteracy to show that school lunches are more than just providing a plateful of food. ☺ Students visit local farms to understand the local farm economy and to see local small-scale food production. They can compare this with the global market for foods colonized by international brands. ☺ Students can work with kitchen staff to plan healthy meals. They also develop the messages that will persuade their peers to eat more healthfully.

The most important meal of the day. Children concentrate less well if they arrive hungry at school in the morning or if they've just had a bar of chocolate or a bag of chips. A quarter of children are turning up at school each morning without having had a proper breakfast.

Rethinking School Lunch: www.ecoliteracy.org
Feed Me Better: www.feedmebetter.com
Parents Jury: www.parentsjury.org

Feed Me Better

Jamie Oliver, nicknamed "The Naked Chef," is a young British celebrity chef with his own TV cooking show and string of best-selling books. In 2004, he started a campaign to improve school lunches by showing that something could be done. Working in an area of South London in a TV series broadcast on Channel 4, Jamie developed new menus, worked with school catering staff to prepare more nutritious food within the budget, and persuaded the children to abandon junk food and start eating better. Side effects were better concentration, better behavior, and better health. When the series ended, Jamie had persuaded the UK government to invest in feeding children better.

...more than just a meal

Download the "Road Map" to a rethought school lunch from www .ecoliteracy.org/rethinking/rsl-guide.html and send a copy to the principal of your local school.

freedom from HUNGER

Every day by 10 a.m., 12,083 children will have died from hunger. Here are more facts:

☺ There are two basic types of malnutrition. The first is protein-energy malnutrition; the second is vitamin and mineral deficiency.

☺ Poverty is the principal cause of hunger. There are an estimated 1.2 billion poor people in developing countries who live on $1 a day or less. An estimated 780 million are suffering from chronic hunger.

☺ Children are most susceptible because of their higher nutrition needs, and they are more vulnerable to infection. One in four chlidren is malnourished, 153 million are underweight, and 182 million are stunted.

☺ Pregnant women and breastfeeding mothers are also at high risk, because they are eating for themselves and their baby. Malnutrition during pregnancy will also affect the health of the child.

☺ The world actually produces enough food to feed everyone. Agricultural production provides 17% more calories per person now than it did 30 years ago, despite the 70% population increase. The principal problem is that many people in the world do not have sufficient land to grow their own food or sufficient income to purchase the food they need.

☺ Conflict is a major cause of hunger—as these hunger hot spots (source: World Food Program's "Hunger Map") show:

Haiti	North Korea	Bangladesh
Darfur (West Sudan)	Colombia	Nicaragua
Afghanistan	Democratic Republic of Congo	Peru

☺ The target set at the 1996 World Food Summit was to halve the number of undernourished people in 2015 from the number in 1990–92. The latest data show that numbers are *increasing* by 15 million people a year.

30 Hour Famine: www.30hourfamine.org
Hunger Notes, an online publication of the World Hunger Education Service: www.worldhunger.org
UN World Food Program: www.wfp.org

...the right to eat enough to live

Organize a 30-hour famine for hunger.

World Vision designates three National Famine Days each year, but you can hold yours anytime. Here's how to do it:

Get together a group of people who agree to go 30 hours without food (to experience what hunger is actually like); during this time everyone engages in some sort of community volunteering (you can choose what to do). Everyone asks as many of their friends and family as possible to sponsor them (each agreeing to give so much for each hour of the fast), and you can also donate the money you have saved by not eating. All the money you raise then goes to support your designated project.

SEPTEMBER 27

AIR *pollution*

Every time we breathe in, dangerous air pollutants enter our bodies. These can cause short-term effects, such as eye and throat irritation. More alarming, however, are the long-term effects such as cancer and damage to the body's immune, neurological, reproductive, and respiratory systems.

Air pollution is not just a city problem. Many air pollutants are dispersed hundreds of miles away from their source, and so can affect distant ecosystems. Some pollutants remain toxic in the environment for a very long time and will continue to affect ponds, streams, fields, and forests for many, many years. Most air pollution is the result of energy consumption: the burning of fossil fuels to produce electricity or to power transportation.

Pollutants in the air include
Sulphur dioxide and nitrogen oxides, produced from the burning of fuel, which cause acid rain.
Carbon monoxide, which is toxic, produced in vehicle emissions.
Particulate matter, such as smoke and vehicle exhausts. Legislation for cleaner air and substantial decreases in the amount of coal being burned have reduced this problem in America and Europe.
Lead, which is produced from a chemical added to gasoline to make engines run more smoothly (tetraethyl lead); lead-free gas has become the norm.
Other chemicals and increasing amounts of additives in gasoline mean that many other pollutants are being released into the atmosphere.

The Department of Homeland Security's Ready America website has simple advice for making your own face mask: www.ready.gov/america/clean_air.html
Find out more from the Clean Air Council: www.cleanair.org

How one man brought clean air to Delhi

In 1986, environmental lawyer M. C. Mehta asked India's Supreme Court to protect fundamental constitutional rights by directing government ministries and departments to implement the 1981 Air Act in Delhi. In 1986 in response, the court pressed Delhi's administration to explain what it was doing to reduce air pollution. In 2002, all public service vehicles (buses, taxis, and auto-rickshaws) had to convert to compressed natural gas. The impact on air quality was marked and immediate. www.cseindia.org

...every breath you take

Wear a face mask whenever you go out into the street.

♣ **This will protect you from pollution.** It will also make a public statement that the air is not clean enough for people to breathe safely. This will get others thinking.

♣ **Most cycle shops sell face masks** because cyclists are at more risk from vehicle pollution. They are in the street, with exhaust fumes all around them, at red traffic lights stationary vehicles pump exhaust fumes into their faces, and physical exertion means that their air intake is increased.

28 SEPTEMBER

responsible BUSINESS

All big corporations have a corporate social responsibility policy. It sets out how they wish to relate to their external stakeholders: the communities where they operate, the customers they serve, and the wider society.

These are statements made by some leading oil companies:

BP: "We support the fundamental rights of people around the world: we run our business in accordance with the principles set out in the Universal Declaration of Human Rights."

ChevronTexaco: "Our approach to corporate responsibility is to conduct business in a socially responsible and ethical manner; support universal human rights; protect the environment; benefit the communities where we work; learn from and respect cultures in which we work."

ConocoPhillips: "[Our] longstanding commitment to the communities in which [we] operate reflects our belief that no individual or corporation can be a good citizen without becoming involved; by exercising imagination, donating time and skills and providing financial support."

ExxonMobil: "We condemn human rights violations in any form. We seek to be responsible corporate citizens, and recognize that we have both the opportunity and responsibility to improve the quality of life wherever we do business."

Shell: "Contributing to sustainable development is not only the right thing to do, but it makes good business sense. It helps us to maintain our license to operate, manage risk better, lower costs through improving energy efficiency, and enables us to grow."

Download the Hands-on Corporate Research Guide from CorpWatch:
www.corpwatch.org

Corporate Social Responsibility Newswire for information and contacts:
www.csrwire.com

What makes a company socially responsible? Should it
Support community organizations in the local communities and the countries where it operates by donating cash and encouraging employee volunteering?
Pay fair wages and provide good working conditions to all its employees?

Trade fairly with its suppliers?
Make products according to accepted standards of safety and durability?
Have an environmental policy based on the principles of sustainability?
Deal with the pollution it produces?
Provide leadership on social and environmental issues?

...judge corporate policy

- **Find a company that interests you.** Go to its website and examine its corporate social responsibility policy. Read its annual report to see how it pursues this side of its business. Find out from other sources some of the issues and controversies around the company and its operations.

- **Make up your own mind** as to whether the company seems to be pursuing its role as a "good corporate citizen" in a satisfactory way. What can you do to make it more socially responsible?

SEPTEMBER 29

DIARRHEA *prevention*

Most people will be affected by diarrhea at some time in their life. But for many, especially babies and children, it can be deadly. ☺ Diarrhea leads to dehydration, the main cause of death in infants. Children are more likely than adults to die, because they become dehydrated more quickly. ☺ A drug that will stop the diarrhea safely within a few hours does not exist. Yet the deaths of more than a million children a year could be prevented by a method that is cheap, safe, and so simple it can be learned and used by anybody.

The treatment is oral rehydration therapy, which is effective in most situations. Oral rehydration does not stop diarrhea, but it does prevent the body from drying up by replacing the water and salts that help it retain water. This gives the body time and strength to do battle with whatever is causing the diarrhea. ☺ ORT consists of salt and glucose. It is extremely cheap, costing as little as ten cents per dose (or you can make your own from these commonly available household ingredients). It *does* need to be added to clean water, however, which can prove problematic in areas where none is available. ☺ No other single medical discovery of the 20th century has the potential to prevent so many deaths at so little cost. It currently saves the lives of around 1 million children a year.

The Rehydration Project: www.rehydrate.org
Find out how many people have had diarrhea so far today and how many people have died. Go to www.rehydrate.org/diarrhoea/index.html.

It is in the developing world that the impact of diarrhea is most severe:
1.8 million people die every year from a diarrhea-related disease (which includes cholera).
90% are children under five.
88% of diarrhea-related disease is caused by an unsafe water supply, inadequate sanitation, and poor hygiene.
Washing one's hands (better personal hygiene) and an improved drinking-water supply would do a great deal to improve the situation.

...with a little sugar and salt

Teach yourself how to rehydrate a child suffering from diarrhea:

☺ **Wash your hands** with soap and water.
☺ **Prepare a solution in a clean pot** by mixing one teaspoon of salt and eight teaspoons of sugar with one liter of clean drinking water (boil and then cool the water). Stir until the contents dissolve.
☺ **Wash your hands and the child's hands** with soap and water before giving the solution to the child.
☺ **Give the child as much of the solution as it needs,** in small amounts.
☺ **Give the child alternately other fluids,** such as milk and juice.
☺ **Continue to give solids** if the child is older than four months.
☺ **If the child still needs rehydration after 24 hours,** make up a fresh solution.
☺ **If the child vomits,** wait ten minutes and give more solution. Usually the vomiting will stop by itself.
☺ **If the diarrhea increases or the vomiting persists,** take the child to a health clinic.

be a PHILANTHROPIST

Money is sitting in your bank account right now, waiting for you to spend it. It may be collecting interest but only very slowly. It is contributing to the profits of the bank and doing nothing for you. You could be spending it to change the world.

If you could do one thing to make a positive impact on the world, what would it be? Think minuscule, think mammoth, think traditional, and think outrageous. If you have a vision, your money could help make that vision come true.

You could leave your money to charity in your will. But why wait? You could do something by yourself. Or you could join with others.

The Funding Network: www.thefundingnetwork.org.uk

The Funding Network is a group of people in the UK who meet regularly to give their money away. There are 100 or so active members of the network, and most give at least $1,800 a year.

Members of the network also suggest projects to support. This could be a disco run by and for people with learning disabilities, or an international Roma group lobbying for human rights, or a project that is making the Sahara green. Funding days are held every three or four months, when members get together. Half a dozen selected projects are each given ten minutes to present their case and answer questions. Most come away with at least $9,000 given by those present.

The Funding Network is a chance for like-minded people to get together, enjoy themselves, hear about some really interesting ways of changing the world, and give away their money.

...give away your money

You could join the Funding Network, or you could set up your own network of like-minded philanthropists.

Think of one thing that will make a real difference. It could address a problem, an issue, or a cause which you care about passionately. This is a chance to put your money where your mouth is.

Set up your funding network. Find nine friends who would like to join you in giving money away. Agree how much you each will give. It could be a lot or a little. It could be the same amount for everyone, or everyone could give a percentage of their income. You decide. Then look around for really interesting projects to support. Remember that your money will make much more of a difference if you support a small initiative or give directly to a project, rather than making a donation to a large charity.

OCTOBER 1

SEEING *is believing*

Witness.org is an amazing organization created by musician Peter Gabriel. It seeks to strengthen grassroots advocacy by making videos and video technology available to human rights defenders, so that they can mobilize public concern and move the issue to the center of political debate.

Video is a powerful tool. When there is footage of the human rights abuse taking place, it becomes impossible to deny what happened. And if you can get video footage, you may also be able to get media attention. TV is always hungry for good news stories with accompanying images.

Witness provides video cameras and training to activists and activist organizations so that they can capture on tape human rights abuses as they are actually taking place.

In 1995 Gillian Caldwell, then age 28, was in Russia investigating an organized crime ring that was peddling Siberian tiger pelts and women. Witness gave her a video camera to record trafficking of women into prostitution, and her footage led to the passing of the Trafficking Victims Protection Act in the US.

www.witness.org

Witness videos have been used:

- As evidence in legal proceedings.
- To complement official reports of human rights abuses.
- To contradict official versions of human rights performance as reported by offending governments and their allies.
- To stimulate grassroots education and awareness.
- To corroborate allegations of human rights violations.
- As a resource for news broadcasts and to produce documentaries.
- As a deterrent to further abuse.

...capturing human rights abuse

The Witness website is a great resource for information on human rights abuse occurring all over the world. Check out the Witness archives and find footage with interviews with victims, interviews with human rights abusers, police brutality, sweatshops, child labor, nuclear testing sites, sex workers, working conditions in diamond mines, and many, many examples of human rights violations all over the world. You can watch video clips, go to linked websites, and follow their suggestions for action.

- **Watch *Video for Change*** and *Tips & Techniques* (both 25 minutes long and on the Training section of the Witness website), and download the accompanying training manuals to find out more about using video for human rights advocacy.
- **Organize an evening** in front of the TV with a group of your friends, and watch a Witness video ordered from their website.

stay in an # EARTHSHIP

Earthships are solar-powered homes or work spaces. They're built from something that's causing a massive waste problem: used tires. They work with the planet's natural systems, using the sun's energy and rain to provide heat, power, and water. Earth-filled car tires also provide excellent insulation.

Earthship living is autonomous living: very cheap and very cheerful. Living in an earthship means that you do not need to make use of power stations emitting greenhouse gases, or rely on public water or waste services. ♣ Tires filled with compacted earth are strong and require a low level of building skills. Earthships create a use for a waste material that is a real and growing environmental problem. At least 240 million tires are scrapped each year in the US and 150 million in the European Union.

It is estimated that more than 2 billion scrap tires are stockpiled in illegal or abandoned piles throughout the US. Apart from being an eyesore, these cause serious health and environmental damage when they catch fire, and the fires are difficult and sometimes impossible to put out. ♣ Disposal options: retread the tires so they can be reused; extract the rubber for use as a raw material; use tires to generate energy in power stations, cement kilns, etc.; store for later reuse; dispose of in a landfill...and use them to build earthships. ♣ As many as 120,000 earthships could be built in the US each year from used tires. Building and living in an earthship makes a significant contribution to reducing greenhouse emissions. Cement manufacture causes 10% of greenhouse gas emissions worldwide. And in the developed world, other building materials create a further 10% of emissions. Energy used in the home for heating, lighting, cooking, and cooling contributes 30% of total emissions.

Earthship Biotecture: www.earthship.com
All you need to know about used tires: www.entire-engineering.de

Make use of used tires
John Dobozy, an Australian inventor, has developed a process to extract the greatest amount of value from a used tire, turning it into a number of useful and saleable products, leaving practically no waste, and with the potential to generate around $3 of income per tire. Find out more from www.abc.net.au/catalyst/stories/ s1185584.htm.

...for sustainability

Find out about earthships.

♣ **Have a holiday in an earthship.** Earthships were pioneered by Earthship Biotecture, which is based in Taos, New Mexico. They have earthships available for holiday rentals at around $50 per person per night for a party of four. Experience recycled zero-emissions living.

♣ **Buy the T-shirt.** If you're really committed, purchase a how-to book, plans, or even a fully built earthship.

WALK *to school*

When I was about 10 years old, I used to walk to school but was supposed to catch the bus home in the afternoon. My mother never knew that I used to spend the bus fare at the sweet shop. The walking journey home was always more pleasurable knowing that I'd got four fruit salad chews and a couple of sherbet flying saucers for the price of a bus fare.

The school run accounts for a sizable chunk of morning rush-hour traffic. It causes congestion, pollution, and danger outside most schools. If more children were to walk to school, then communities would experience the environmental and health benefits associated with having fewer vehicles on the road.

Children can walk to school on their own if they're old enough. Or they can be accompanied by their parents. Or you can organize a "walking crocodile," where parents and children meet up at some agreed point, and then walk to school together. The same can be done for bicycling to school.

There are also crocodiles in the jungle. In Gudalur, in the South India Nilgiris hills, children from tribal settlements in the forests walk together with a community worker one or two miles to school each day along forest trails. As a result, more children (and especially more girls) go to school.

International Walk to School Month: www.iwalktoschool.org
The USA Walk and Bike to School campaign: www.walktoschool.org
How to develop safe routes for kids to get to school: www.saferoutesinfo.org

10 reasons to use shoe rubber not tire rubber:

Strollers are easier to park than cars.

You save money.

You cut down on pollution.

You see more of your neighborhood.

You meet and make friends on the way.

You can chat with your children about this and that.

You can put road-safety theory into practice.

You're making life easier for those who need to use the road.

It can be fun.

It keeps you and your children fit.

...for healthy kids

Take part in Walk to School Month.

Three million children, parents, and community leaders from 29 countries around the world do something for International Walk to School Month.

Make sure all your friends and family know about it and participate. Go with them. Dress in fancy dress. Make a large placard with a catchy slogan. Play a big trombone...You'll be highlighting a major source of pollution and congestion.

International Walk to School Week is the first week of October **4 OCTOBER**

humane BORDERS

> *The news out of the Arizona desert could not have been more horrifying. Twelve people, migrants mostly from Veracruz, Mexico, had crossed the craggy desert into what they thought would be a promised land of new jobs and opportunity. But instead of the hoped-for new life in the United States, they met a terrible death in the desert, lost and abandoned by the "coyotes" who were supposed to guide them and finally succumbing to thirst and 115-degree temperatures.*
>
> —reported in Salt of the Earth,
> an online resource for social justice, June 2001

Every year millions of people attempt to cross the border between the United States and Mexico. They are all looking for a better life. There are hundreds of border crossing deaths every year, and these are just the bodies that are found.

Many are caught by the border patrol and sent back to Mexico. In one year alone, over 1.6 million people were apprehended attempting to cross the border illegally, and this was just the southwestern section. But many do get through and join the army of illegal migrants now settled in the US.

There are currently 11,000 border patrol agents working along the 2,000-mile US-Mexico border who are there to try to put a halt to this flow of humans. By contrast, there are approximately 1,000 agents working along the 4,000-mile US-Canada border.

No matter how much military presence is stationed along the southern crossing, Mexicans will continue to cross the border with the hope of a better life.

www.humaneborders.org

Humane Borders was founded in 2000 by the Rev. Robin Hoover to provide humanitarian relief to border crossers. It has set up and maintains water tanks along the border. Dehydration is a major cause of death. It distributes health kits at migrant shelters. Their work will have saved thousands of lives.

...saving lives of migrants

You can help save lives.

If you live anywhere near the border, you can volunteer your time. Wherever you live, you can put together health kits and send them to Humane Borders, which will distribute them to migrants.

Each kit should contain a hand towel, a wash cloth, a comb, a metal nail file or clippers, a bath-size bar of soap, a toothbrush, a tube of toothpaste, and 6 adhesive bandages.

Place all the items in a one-gallon-size zip-lock bag and ship them to Humane Borders, 740 East Speedway Boulevard, Tucson, AZ 85719.

BILLBOARD *liberation*

A can of spray paint, a blithe spirit, and a balmy night are all you really need.

—The Billboard Liberation Front

When was the last time you read a billboard with a positive message? Corporate giants have enough cash to bombard you with any message they want. Everywhere you look there are billboards sending out complex coded messages, trying to make you feel somehow lacking if you don't buy this or that product. No one spends thousands to put up a billboard that just says "Perform an act of kindness today."

It's time to fight back and turn billboards into a tool for good. As most of us don't have the spare cash to put up our own advertising, groups like the Billboard Liberation Front "adjust" someone else's message. But you must understand that liberating a billboard is completely illegal; you will get arrested if you are caught.

The opening to the Billboard Liberation Front's manifesto reads

In the beginning was the Ad. The Ad was brought to the consumer by the Advertiser. Desire, self-worth, self-image, ambition, hope; all find their genesis in the Ad. Through the Ad and the intent of the Advertiser we form our ideas and learn the myths that make us into what we are as a people. It is now clear that the Ad holds the most esteemed position in our cosmology.

Billboard Liberation Front: www.billboardliberation.com
Adbusters, a global movement fighting consumerism: www.adbusters.org

From the Billboard Liberation Front website obligatory disclaimer

This website is intended for entertainment purposes only. No one involved in the production and hosting of this website encourages any action which would violate state, federal, local or international statutes and treaties. We may be stupid, but we're not dumb.

...for positive messages

Dream about liberating a billboard! Think about what you would write. The Billboard Liberation Front offers these tips:

- **Consider just altering it** by adding a symbol, a word, or a thought bubble.
- **Plan escape routes.** Check the site out day and night for activity. How will you reach the billboard safely? Do you need a ladder?
- **Go up on the billboard prior to your "alteration";** make sure you feel safe.
- **Have a ground team to assist you** and to alert you to danger.

humanity for HARMONY

Daniel Pearl was a journalist working for the *Wall Street Journal*. In January 2002 he was in Pakistan, investigating the links between fundamentalism and terrorism. He was captured and beheaded. The video of his beheading was circulated by his murderers and shocked the world. His widow, Mariane, told her story in her book, *A Mighty Heart*.

Mariane has now set up the Daniel Pearl Foundation in memory of her late husband. In the spirit of Danny's love of music and commitment to dialogue, she has created Daniel Pearl Music Days, which are held during the first ten days of October each year (October 10 was Danny's birthday).

Concerts for peace are organized around the world. The number of events has been doubling each year. Tens of thousands have already joined this global community, celebrating the ideals for which Daniel Pearl stood: cross-cultural understanding, mutual respect, and tolerance. Small bands of amateur musicians to international music stars, drum ensembles to big symphony orchestras have all participated. Over 400 concerts were held in 39 countries in 2004.

Daniel Pearl Foundation: www.danielpearl.org

For participation guidelines in Daniel Pearl Music Day, please go to www.music-days.org.

Just Vision: www.justvision.org/profile

The Just Vision website presents the stories of Israeli and Palestinian civilians who are working for peace. By the end of 2005, there were 180 such stories, representing only a fraction of the courageous Israelis and Palestinians whose peace-related efforts receive too little media attention. There are four main criteria for being included. People must be engaged in work that involves people on both sides of the Green Line; they must be living permanently in Israel or Palestine; they must be pursuing nonviolent approaches to peace building; and they must be civilians, not elected officials.

Just Visionaries include people like Inas Radwan, from Jenin, who organizes summer camps in the US for young Israelis, Palestinians, and Americans; and Gershon Baskin, from Jerusalem, founder of IPCRI, an Israeli–Palestinian think tank.

...play music for peace

Stand up to hatred and intolerance in the world; play music for peace!

❧ **Promote the spirit of peace.** Have some fun. Give fun to others. Organize your own gig for Daniel Pearl Music Day, or persuade your favorite venue to dedicate a performance.

❧ **Participation is open to anyone** who wishes to promote tolerance, understanding, and global harmony. You are not expected to raise funds.

TV *helps*

Get a "dot tv" Internet address, and you will be supporting a threatened nation. All Internet and web addresses end in a suffix—.com, .org, .biz, .gov, .coop, .net, .info—which shows the nature of the organization that is registering (a commercial company, a government body, etc.). 🎋 Suffixes such as .uk, .fr, .pk, and .in show where the Internet address is registered (UK, France, Pakistan, India, etc.). Each country has a different suffix, apart from the US, which was the heartland for the developing World Wide Web.

Tuvalu, which is a group of islands in the South Pacific, has .tv as its suffix. This is a real asset for the country, as the two letters *TV* are recognized all over the world as having media glamour. But Tuvalu is so small that it does not even have its own TV station. When you get a .tv web or e-mail address, you will also be contributing to the economy of one of the smallest and strangest countries on the planet, as the .tv suffix has been leased to the VeriSign corporation under a profit-share agreement with the government of Tuvalu.

So get a .tv Internet address, and help the Tuvaluan economy. But also think about global warming and what you could do to bring the plight of the Tuvaluans to the attention of a gas-guzzling, complacent world.

Sign up for .tv at www.tv.
Find out more about Tuvalu by going to www.tuvaluislands.com.

Tuvalu

There are 11,500 Tuvaluans living on nine islands and atolls in the South Pacific with a total area of 10 square miles. The place is remote and really small. The islands are no more than 16 feet above sea level. Global warming and the melting of the polar ice caps means that the sea is rising. The islands are in danger of disappearing; they get flooded not from waves, but through water bubbling up from the ground, and the flooding is becoming more frequent. Tuvalu is likely to disappear off the face of the earth; it is likely to be the first nation to fall victim to global warming.

...support a threatened nation

Get a .tv Internet address. It's simple...and it's cool.

If your e-mail or website address is yourname.tv or yourorganization.tv, it will look different from most and get you noticed.

To register, go to www.tv. It'll cost you $50 for one year or as little as $300 for ten years.

Natural Disaster Reduction Day
is the second Wednesday of October **8 OCTOBER**

send a LETTER

We've stopped writing letters. We now send e-mails instead. But finding an e-mail in your inbox is not the same as getting a letter through the postal service. A letter has a personal touch; and it can be a real pleasure to get a letter that is not a bill or a piece of junk mail. So what can we do to encourage letter writing? ✊ Letter Writing Day is held in Japan in July each year. The Japanese postal service issues a commemorative 80-yen stamp to mark the day. July has traditionally been known as Letter Month in Japan, possibly because July 7 is Star Festival, when people write letters of wishes to their God. Letter Writing Day builds on this tradition.

International Letter Writing Week is held each year in October. This is the date when the Universal Postal Union was founded in order to facilitate international mail. The week encourages worldwide cultural exchange and friendship as a contribution to world peace. ✊ The union organizes a letter-writing competition for young people to mark the week. Each year, there is a different theme for the competition. The national postal services promote the competition and choose a national winner. UNESCO then chooses three overall winners. The competition is open to young people under 16. Letters must be between 500 and 1,000 words in length.

Past themes have included "How to build a better future" (2003), "My views on human rights" (1998), "A letter to the person I admire most" (1997), "How young people can help the children of a country at war" (1993). Themes are not always serious. In 2005, contestants had to write a letter to their favorite fairytale character.

Universal Postal Union: www.upu.int

Japan Letter Writing Day:
www.post.japanpost.jp/english/kitte_hagaki/stamp/tokusyu/2002/0723_letter

Amnesty's advice on letter-writing for activists:
www.amnesty.org/campaign/letter-guide.html

International Letter Writing Week Winner

Anuar Yasin, a 13-year-old Ethiopian, won first prize in 2004 for his letter describing how young people can contribute to reducing poverty in the world. He stressed that young people can play a pivotal role in this, and set out a number of actions that all young people could take to combat poverty around them.

...make someone's day

Write two letters. And send them by snail mail.

✊ **Letter 1:** To all your friends, just to say hello or to urge them to do more to change the world. Go on, make their day!

✊ **Letter 2:** To the president of the United States or to the secretary-general of the United Nations, urging them to do more to create a fairer world.

BULLY *awareness*

Question: What do Ms Dynamite, Tom Cruise, and David Beckham have in common?

Answer: All of them were bullied at school.

Bullying can happen at school, at the workplace, and within families. It's particularly horrid when the bullying is homophobic or racist. If you are being bullied, tell someone. Speaking up can be hard, so it may be easier to write a note explaining how you feel. ◀ Bullying won't stop unless you do something. Keep a diary of what's happening; record the incidents and also your feelings, so that you have a record if you need it. If you know someone who is being bullied, then it's important to do something to stop it. Antibullying websites give information on what to look out for.

The Wikipedia encyclopedia gives these as some examples of bullying:
Spreading (negative) gossip and rumors
Constant criticism for unspecified allegations
Taking the victims' possessions or exerting control over their work
Making victims do what they do not want to do with a threat of violence or disciplinary action if they refuse
Actually following through with a threat to ensure victims will comply with all future orders

Stop Bullying Now: www.stopbullyingnow.hrsa.gov
You Big Bully: www.youbigbully.com

Stamp out cyberbullying

Cyberbullying is sending or posting harmful or cruel text or images using the Internet or other digital communication devices. Cyberbullies
Send cruel, vicious, and sometimes threatening messages.
Create websites that ridicule others.
Break into e-mail accounts and send vicious or embarrassing material.
Engage someone in instant messaging, trick the person into revealing sensitive personal information, and then forward it to others.
Take embarrassing pictures of people using a digital phone camera and then send these pictures to others.
The Center for Safe and Responsible Internet Use provides advice and guidance on online cruelty: responsiblenetizen.org.
The Center's cyberbullying website is at cyberbully.org.

...bullies ruin people's lives

Do an antibullying survey.

◀ **Download some suggested questions from Bullying Online,** and include an open-ended question for respondents to tell you about how the bullying is affecting or has affected their life.

◀ **Survey school students, or adults,** asking them about their experience of being bullied at school. Make the response anonymous. You may well be surprised at the extent of bullying and the impact it has had on people's lives.

the gift of SIGHT

There are an estimated 45 million people in the world who are blind. The majority of these are poor people in the developing world. This year nearly 2 million people will lose their sight. If no action is taken, there will be 75 million blind people by 2020. ☺ More than two-thirds of blindness is treatable and preventable; 30 million people could see, if we could address the problem.

Restoration of sight is one of the most cost-effective interventions in health care. It costs surprisingly little to make a blind person see, and it brings enormous benefits to those who are enabled to see again.

The term 20/20 vision means perfect sight. Vision 2020: the Right to Sight aims to eliminate needless blindness by the year 2020. This initiative has been jointly launched by the World Health Organization and the International Agency for the Prevention of Blindness, working with more than 20 international NGOs involved in eye care and the prevention and management of blindness.

Vision 2020: www.v2020.org
SightSavers International: www.sightsavers.org.uk
Project Orbis: www.orbis.org

Main causes of blindness

Corneal blindness: caused by malnutrition.
Cataract: a clouding of the lens; 100 million people could benefit from a simple operation.
Glaucoma: caused by increased pressure in the eye through malfunction of the drainage system.
Trachoma: an eye infection caused by poor hygiene and environmental factors and transmitted by flies. Children can be treated with antibiotics, adults with a simple operation.
River blindness: endemic in sub-Saharan Africa and parts of South America, can be treated with drugs.
Childhood blindness: usually caused by Vitamin A deficiency. There are 1.5 million blind children worldwide.
Retinal detachment: caused by ageing or accidents.
Refractive error and low vision: usually correctable with glasses.

...give it to someone in need

It costs so little to help someone see again. There are lots of organizations that run eye camps, which involve setting up a "production line" for treatment and operations. They all want your money to help them do more work. Project Orbis (a US agency) and SightSavers (an international agency) both are actively looking for support. For example:

$25 buys enough antibiotics to treat 50 children with eye infections that could permanently damage their eyesight
$50 covers the cost of a month's training fo a local eye specialist who will go on to treat thousands of children
$100 helps train a doctor to treat premature babies at risk of long-term sight loss

Books document the ideas of a culture and a generation. For example, Jews settled in Calcutta (now known as Kolkata) at the end of the 18th century and developed a vibrant community with its own culture, cooking, and lifestyle that was significantly different from that of Jews in other parts of the world.

Today only a handful of Jews remain in Kolkata, and they are very elderly. Tomorrow their presence will be forgotten, their synagogues abandoned, their graveyards fallen into disrepair. All that will remain will be the memoirs, the genealogies, and the cookbooks published by this community. And if these are lost, so will all memory of the Jews of Calcutta.

Collecting and preserving books is a way of preserving a heritage. Whether it is the Jews of Calcutta, the antics of the hippies of the 1960s, or the early history of the Beatles.

National Yiddish Book Center: www.yiddishbookcenter.org

How one man saved 1.5 million books and an entire culture from extinction

In 1980, Aaron Lansky was a 23-year-old graduate student. He was alarmed by the fact that all over North America thousands of Yiddish books that had survived Hitler and Stalin were now being thrown away. The older generation was passing on, and their children and grandchildren were unable to read Yiddish. The books seemed to be of no value to anybody.

Yet this was an entire literature from a vibrant Jewish civilization from central Europe that existed until the pogroms and the Holocaust led to mass emigration and genocide. If this literature was destroyed, so would be our knowledge of the civilization that created it.

Lansky realized something had to be done before it was too late. So he took a two-year leave of absence from graduate school, rented an unheated factory loft, and issued a public appeal for unwanted and discarded Yiddish books. Lansky has now recovered 1.5 million books and established the National Yiddish Book Center, which translates books and supplies Yiddish books to libraries around the world. His efforts have been hailed as the "the greatest cultural rescue effort in Jewish history." Read Lanksy's story in his book, *Outwitting History*.

...for future generations

Think of some small part of today's civilization that particularly fascinates you.

- **Start photographing it,** keeping cuttings of newspaper articles about it, and buying all the books you can find on the subject.

- **Begin to build up a library.** Some time in the future this could become a valuable archive, preserving for future generations knowledge of this special interest of yours.

from iPod to E-WASTE

Digital equipment causes toxic waste. Lurking underneath Apple's beautifully designed digital music players and computers are poisonous chemicals like lead, mercury, and cadmium that can cause birth defects and disabilities. Every computer manufacturer, every mobile telecom provider, every digital download system is developing ever-newer products, and making the older models obsolete. These are then discarded. E-waste is becoming a major issue.

About 40% of the heavy metals in landfills comes from electronic equipment discards. If the toxins seep out, the impact could be horrendous. Just 1/70th of a teaspoon of mercury is sufficient to contaminate a 17-acre lake, making the fish unfit to eat. Silicon Valley Toxics Coalition estimates that up to 600 million desktop and laptop computers in the US alone will soon be obsolete. All these obsolete computers would create a pile 1 mile high covering 5 acres. This would be the same as a 22-story pile covering the entire area of Los Angeles. E-waste is growing almost three times faster than municipal waste.

Less than 10% of discarded computers are currently recycled. Most of the rest are either stored in basements, garages, offices, and cupboards or, in ignorance of the hazards, tossed out with the trash.

The Computer Take-Back campaign: www.computertakeback.com
Silicon Valley Toxics Coalition, calling to account the global electronics industry: www.svtc.org

Send a letter to Steve Jobs, CEO of Apple Computer.

On the principle that the polluter should pay, computer companies should be reducing their use of toxic materials and taking back their products for recycling. Steve Jobs has already agreed to take back iPods. This letter could encourage him to do more. Send this letter from the Computer Take-Back website:

Recycling iPods at Apple stores is a great thing; but why not go all the way and accept all obsolete Apple products at your retail outlets?

If you can do it with iPods, you can do it with all your products! Old computers like the Apple II, IIe, and the Mac Classic contain toxics like lead, mercury, and cadmium, and end up in landfills or incinerators, polluting our land, air, and water.

By offering free recycling for all Apple products, including to those who don't happen to live near an Apple store, you can be the real innovator and green leader I thought you would be.

...minimize toxic waste

🌳 **Continue to use your computer if it is still usable.** You almost certainly don't need the extra specifications that suppliers are offering.

🌳 **Donate your old computer** to a charity at home or abroad if you want to trade up.

🌳 **Find out how to dispose of your computer safely,** if you can't find anyone to donate it to (or if it's just too old or broken down).

OCTOBER 13

GRAND *challenges*

Most medical research is directed toward diseases of the rich. Similar efforts made toward healing the poor could save millions of lives. In 2003, the Bill & Melinda Gates Foundation challenged researchers to come up with solutions for some of the world's major health problems.

Fourteen "Grand Challenges" were selected from more than 1,000 suggestions to address these goals:

> **Create childhood vaccines** that don't need refrigeration, needles, or multiple doses.
> **Use the immune system** to guide the development of new vaccines for malaria, TB, and HIV.
> **Find ways** of preventing insects from transmitting diseases such as malaria.
> **Grow** more nutritious staple crops to combat malnutrition.
> **Discover** ways to prevent drug resistance.
> **Develop methods** of treating latent and chronic infections such as TB.
> **More accurately diagnose** and track disease in poor countries, where sophisticated laboratories or reliable record keeping systems are not available.

In 2005, the foundation gave $436 million for 43 projects.

Grand Challenges: www.grandchallengesgh.org
Bill & Melinda Gates Foundation: www.gatesfoundation.org

Crops play a part in malnutrition:
Many people's diet consists largely of a single staple food, but in many cases the food does not meet their nutritional requirements.

Cassava: This starchy root crop is a staple for more than 250 million Africans; it provides less than 30% of the protein needed for a healthy diet and can be toxic if not prepared properly.

Rice: Rice is the primary source of food for more than half the world's population, but it is deficient in many essential micronutrients.

Sorghum: More than 300 million people in arid regions of Africa rely on sorghum, but it is low on essential nutrients and difficult to digest.

...for health solutions

Define your challenge. It may be to solve a problem or to come up with good ideas.

🏆 **Get some money together.** See what you can afford to contribute; badger your friends; write to rich people, big companies, the newspapers, telling them about your dream of solving a major social problem and ask them to contribute something. Set yourself a challenging target, and see if you can reach it!

🏆 **Set up a judging panel** (of illustrious people) to decide the winner.

🏆 **Issue your own grand challenge.** Use websites, blogs, and newsgroups to spread the word. If the challenge is interesting and there's a cash prize, then lots of people might reply.

world-changing WOMEN

Did you know that women

Produce 60–80% of basic foodstuffs in sub-Saharan Africa and the Caribbean?

Undertake over 50% of the labor involved in intensive rice cultivation in Asia?

Perform 30% of the agricultural work in industrialized countries?

Head 60% of households in some regions of Africa?

Meet 90% of household water and fuel needs in Africa?

Process 100% of basic household foodstuffs in Africa?

Contribute an estimated $15-trillion worth of unpaid work in the home and the community?

But

Women have not achieved equality with men in any country.

866 million women live below the poverty line, two-thirds of all poor people.

20 million women are refugees, 75% of the world total.

660 million women are illiterate, two-thirds of illiterate adults.

86 million girls are not in school, two-thirds of all absentees.

Women earn about three-quarters of the pay of men for the same work, outside the agricultural sector.

Only 24 women were elected heads of state or government in the 20th century.

Only 7 of the 185 highest-ranking diplomats to the UN are women.

Women's Creativity in Rural Life: www.woman.ch/women/1-laureates.asp

Women who make a difference:

Amina Bio Yau Bio Nigan from Gomparu, Benin, created her own microenterprise: transforming local fruits, vegetables, spices, and roots into syrups, jams, and cosmetics, and selling quality products at an affordable price.

She uses traditional methods and organic ingredients.

Bio Nigan products are now well known and even sold in neighboring countries (Burkina Faso, Niger, and Togo).

Betty Makoni from Harare, Zimbabwe, teaches English. Most of her girl students have been victims of sexual abuse, so she created a club where they can exchange accounts of their experiences and encourage each other to sue the guilty. The club concept has spread over the whole country, with 166 (involving more than 3,000 girls) being formed. Betty grouped them into the Girl Child Network.

In 2001, Betty built a "safe village" in Rusape as an information dissemination center and a shelter for abused girls.

...a force for development

⊗ **Take part in Women's Rural Development Day.** Reflect on and learn from the extraordinary contributions that women are making.

⊗ **Read about the winners of the Prize** for Women's Creativity in Rural Life, and what they have achieved. Select some favorite stories. Tell other people about their achievements.

FEED *the world*

The good news: progress is being made in the war on hunger. The number of hungry people in the world dropped from 959 million in 1970 to 791 million in 1997.

The bad news: between 1995 and 2005, the number of hungry people has increased by almost 4 million each year. In 2002, there were 852 million underfed people worldwide (one in seven of the world's population): 815 million in developing countries; 28 million in transition countries; and 9 million in industrialized countries.

Hunger is the main risk to health worldwide. Its impact is greater than AIDS, malaria, and tuberculosis combined. ⊕ The hunger hot spots in the world are Haiti, West Sudan (Darfur), Afghanistan, North Korea, Colombia, Democratic Republic of Congo, Bangladesh, Nicaragua. ⊕ The main reason for hunger is poverty; war and natural disaster account for just 8% of the problem. ⊕ Causes of hunger include overpopulation and land degradation; population movements (refugees); shortage of water and drought; floods and tropical storms; locust infestation; severe heat or cold; natural disasters, such as earthquakes; man-made emergencies, such as the consequences of conflict.

The World Food Program is the food aid arm of the United Nations. It provides food aid to save lives of refugees in emergencies, improve the nutrition of vulnerable people including children in school, and help build infrastructure through food-for-work programs.

Food Force: www.food-force.com
FightHunger: www.fighthunger.org
Facts about hunger: www.bread.org/learn/hunger-basics

What is hunger?

Hunger: a signal that the body is running short of food.

Undernourishment: food intake does not provide enough calories to meet the body's minimum needs. This results in chronic hunger.

Malnutrition: food intake is insufficient to support natural bodily functions such as growth, pregnancy, lactation, and resistance to and recovery from disease.

Wasting: substantial weight loss usually associated with starvation or disease.

Stunting: shortness for age, which indicates chronic malnutrition.

Underweight: a low weight compared with a well-nourished, healthy person of the same age.

...and fight global hunger

- ⊕ **Download the World Food Program's video game,** *Food Force.* Play and enjoy it. Distribute copies. You will learn about the problems of hunger and the difficulties of delivering food aid. There are six missions to complete.

- ⊕ **Go to the FightHunger site.** Click and trigger a 19-cent donation, which is the cost of feeding one child for one day.

rock and WRAP IT UP

In December 1990, Syd Mandelbaum met rock music promoter Ron Delsener, who mentioned that at concert venues there was always leftover food that was just thrown away.

In June 1991, Syd arranged that food be picked up at a concert and given to a local soup kitchen. This was how *Rock and Wrap It Up!* began.

Concert venues, stadiums, arenas, theaters all had surplus food after catered events, as the caterer contractually could not run out. Syd thought that a clause might be put in the contract stipulating that leftover food be given to soup kitchens, shelters, and food banks. But if this was to happen, a network of distribution points would need to be created. The answer to this problem was provided by Second Harvest, which had food bank contacts in 180 cities.

In July 1994, *Rock and Wrap It Up!* went nationwide. The Rolling Stones were playing in 34 U.S. cities. The caterers were given a contact point for each city. In New York, the Claddagh Inn soup kitchen collected over 1,000 pounds of cooked and uncooked food—enough to feed 700 people.

By the end of 2005, *Rock and Wrap It Up!* had provided over 40 million meals, and it had a database of 41,000 places where food can be delivered. Some 5,000 volunteers were helping make all this happen.

Rock and Wrap It Up!: www.rockandwrapitup.org
If you have food or clothes to donate, call toll-free: 1-877-691-FOOD

Some Other *Rock and Wrap It Up!* Initiatives

☺ ***Rock and Wrap It Up!*** school program and ***College Wrap!*** teach students to recover food from school and college cafeterias and deliver it to places of need. Students are also encouraged to organize four major collections a year of clothing, baby items, toiletries, and book bags.

☺ ***Wrap Their Memory in Charity!*** both clothing following a death in the family or leftover food at a house of mourning can be donated. *Rock and Wrap It Up!* will suggest places to take it.

...distribute your leftover food

☺ **If you are organizing a conference, event, or party** where meals are being provided, get a *Rock and Wrap It Up!* clause put into the catering contract. If you are doing the catering yourself, find a distribution point and deliver the food yourself.

☺ **If your college or office has a cafeteria,** talk to the catering manager distributing each day's leftover food to feed the hungry.

☺ **Make friends with the manager of the local gourmet restaurant** and suggest that as an act of philanthropy they cook a meal for a homeless shelter one day a week. The publicity they get will repay their effort in spades.

WATER *monitoring*

Millennium Development Goal 7 pledges to ensure environmental sustainability. One of its targets by 2015 is to halve the proportion of people who lack access to clean water and proper sanitation. Water monitoring, to provide data on the state of the world's water resources, is essential if progress toward achieving this goal is to be measured. ♣ A water-monitoring kit costs $13 plus shipping. It includes everything you need to test the four key indicators, plus a step-by-step guide to using the kit. Each kit includes one set of hardware (collection jar, pH test-tube, dissolved oxygen vial, thermometer), and enough pH and dissolved oxygen tablets to perform 50 tests. ♣ The kit is suitable for all ages and experience levels. A large group will require more than one kit.

World Water Monitoring Day, held annually, was created

> **To promote** the importance of water monitoring.
>
> **To connect** people with efforts to protect and preserve their local watersheds, and get them involved.
>
> **To develop** information about the health of each watershed as it changes over time.

On October 18, people all over the world go out and test four key indicators of water quality:

> Temperature
> Acidity (pH)
> Dissolved oxygen
> Turbidity (how clear the water is, the amount of suspended particles)

They assess the health of their local rivers, lakes, estuaries, and other bodies of water. Everyone is invited to participate.

Water on the Web, all you need to know: www.waterontheweb.org
World Water Monitoring Day: www.worldwatermonitoringday.org
Young Water Action Team: www.ywat.org

The Young Water Action Team

YWAT is a global network of young water professionals, activists, and students, ages 18 to 30. Their mission is to increase awareness, participation, and commitment of young people to water-related issues. There are members in more than 40 countries. If you are in the right age range, interested in helping tackle the world's challenges regarding water, sanitation, and hygiene, and would like to be part of an international network, join YWAT.

...increasing awareness

Participate in this global water-monitoring initiative. Not just this year but next year too.

♣ **Order a water-monitoring kit.**

♣ **Go out and measure the water quality** of all the lakes, rivers, streams, and estuaries near you.

go on a PILGRIMAGE

We went into the depth of the bush in Highgate Cemetery. When the highest tombstone came into view, we saw the familiar statue: an amiable old man, wise scholar, fearless fighter and giant who predicted and created a new world. On the tombstone was inscribed: "Proletarians of the World, Unite!"

—Xue Baosheng

Karl Marx, founder of communism and author of *Das Kapital*, is buried in Highgate Cemetery in North London. Pilgrims from all over the world come to visit his grave.

The idea of pilgrimage is found within almost every religion. The In the Steps of the Magi tour organized by the Holy Land Trust aims to develop a better understanding between people from different regions and to give firsthand opportunities to explore the culture and people of the Middle East. The journey begins near Jerash in Jordan and ends in Bethlehem. Pilgrims visit Petra, Jericho, St. George's Desert Monastery, Jerusalem, Hebron, Nazareth, Ramallah, and Bethlehem. Travel is by a variety of methods, including car, camel, and a lot of walking—which gives the opportunity to observe and interact with local people and communities.

In the Steps of the Magi: http://travel.holylandtrust.org

Make a virtual pilgrimage without leaving your house. Choose to visit one of these heroes:
Nelson Mandela on Robben Island: www.freedom.co.za
Gandhi's virtual ashram: www.nuvs.com/ashram
Karl Marx in Highgate: www.redrocks.net/travel/london/image23.html

---

Shantum Seth is an adviser to the United Nations Development Program on volunteering and livelihoods. He is also actively involved in Ahimsa Trust, which is working on peace and development. Shantum is a Buddhist. He explains,

In the Footsteps of the Buddha provides an opportunity to explore areas that few tourists visit and to understand some of the structures and subtleties of Indian life. We go for country walks and visit villages that have changed little since the Buddha's time 2,500 years ago. We visit schools, stop at mango groves for picnics, take a boat ride along the Ganges, and even shop for silk! We go at a slower pace than tourists usually do, which allows us to be mindful, have discussions and time for ourselves. At each of the sacred sites I tell stories of the Buddha's life and teachings.

travel.vsnl.com/footstepsofbuddha/shantum.htm

...develop your understanding

What sort of pilgrimage would you like to make?

Would you like to go to

Woodstock, New York, the venue of the concert that defined a counterculture?

Rochdale, England, to see where the cooperative movement started?

Selma, Alabama, to see where Martin Luther King once stood?

Hiroshima, Japan, to see the epicenter of the first atomic bomb?

The choice is yours.

OCTOBER 19

ROOM *to read*

World change starts with educated children

—John Wood, Room to Read

School is unaffordable in many parts of the world. Many poor people survive on less than a dollar a day. Even if there is a school nearby, some children may be two hours' walk away, and there may not be a teacher in attendance. Or the child may be required to look after the family or work in the fields. The cost of books, school uniforms, and sometimes school fees can also make school beyond the reach of many families. 🔖 As a result, over 100 million school-age children in the developing world are not enrolled in primary school.

The situation is worst for girls. The girl child is last in the pecking order when it comes to allocating family resources. She may be required to look after the younger children in the family, do the housework, and fetch water, and in some societies will get married while still very young.

More than two-thirds of women in some countries never attain literacy. Room to Read is creating educational opportunities in Asia by building schools and libraries. Room to Read gets villages to raise part of the overall expenditure (through donated land, labor, materials, and cash). This community involvement has enabled Room to Read to grow quickly. In its first four years, Room to Read

Helped over 510,000 children.
Built 110 schools and 1,475 libraries.
Published 33 children's books in local languages.
Donated 300,000 new books.
Established 48 computer and language labs.
Funded 975 long-term scholarships.

Room to Read: www.roomtoread.org

The story of two eight-year-olds

Eight-year-old Karpali in Tennessee organized a read-a-thon, which raised over $6,000 for Room to Read to build a school in Nepal.

Eight-year-old Renu lives in Phutung Village in Nepal. She wants to become a doctor—a big ambition for a daughter of subsistence farmers. When her parents could no longer afford school fees, Room to Read provided a scholarship. Now Renu's goal of becoming a doctor is back on track.

...an opportunity to learn

Help Room to Read provide communities with schools and literacy.

🔖 **Go to the website.** See a slide show about their work.

🔖 **Adopt a project.** Raise money to help a community build a school or library. It's an achievable target. And you'll be proud of having done something really worthwhile.

🔖 **Become a virtual volunteer,** doing anything from website development to speaking at local schools.

20 OCTOBER

build MOUNT EVEREST

When most people think of Nepal, they think of trekking and Mount Everest. They don't picture thousands of young people who are ignored and ostracized from society. Nepal is a land of extremes, a land where there is tremendous natural beauty alongside grinding poverty. The south of the country is just above sea level and in the north you will find the highest mountain in the world. If you cannot visit Everest for yourself, then why not build your very own Mount Everest to help the young people of Nepal have a better future?

The Esther Benjamins Trust was started by Philip Holmes in memory of his first wife. It is a small organization working with Nepali children who have been trafficked across the border into India to work as performers in traveling circuses.

Esther Benjamins Trust: www.ebtrust.org.uk

Rescuing child slaves in circuses

Circus children in India are denied the most basic rights, suffering regular physical and often sexual abuse. They are kept in extremely poor conditions and given little food and rest. They have no schooling and minimal (if any) remuneration. They can work 18 hours per day, rehearsing and performing difficult and often dangerous acts. They are effectively kept as prisoners. Many lose contact with their family.

The Esther Benjamins Trust Circus Children Project began with an undercover survey in 2002, which revealed more than 200 children working in 29 Indian circuses. Most were

Nepali, 82% were girls, some as young as five. All the children desperately wanted to go home but were bound to the circuses by illegal contracts of up to ten years' duration.

The project aims to get child performers in Indian circuses made illegal by 2007. It retrieves children from the circuses by engaging with circus owners and through direct action. The Esther Benjamins Trust provides education, work skills, and emotional and psychological support for the rescued children.

...free Nepali children

Create a mountain for the Esther Benjamins Trust.

- **Build as high a mountain as you can** with household items (newspaper, egg boxes, empty cans, etc.). Use whatever items you like, stuck together with glue, tape, or pins.

- **Ask friends and family to sponsor you,** paying you an agreed amount per item in your mountain.

- **Turn the idea into a competition** at work, at school, or as a party game. Give a time limit. Offer prizes for the highest mountain and the mountain made from the most items.

- **Send the trust photos of your mountains,** together with the money you raise. Young people in Nepal will thank you for your efforts.

OCTOBER 21

GO MAD *in October*

Make a Difference Day started in 1992 with a simple idea: "Put your own cares on hold for one day to do something for someone else or for your local community." It is America's largest single day of volunteering, with 3 million people doing their bit. It is being copied in other countries. Soon it will become a worldwide event. ♦♦ Make a Difference Day is always the fourth Saturday in October. But if you can't make that day, just do something that week or that weekend. ♦♦ Here are some inspiring examples of what people have done for Make a Difference Day:

In Hurricane, Utah, Tonya Jocelyn collected food, clothing, and blankets for the Navajo Nation, America's largest Indian reservation, where Jocelyn's mother came from. Jocelyn had distributed flyers, but things really started to happen when she contacted nearby hotels. Soon her yard filled with donations. She crammed a U-Haul trailer with 80 boxes of clothing, dozens of shoes, 100 hotel blankets, 300 toothbrushes, 4 cases of fresh peaches, and 10 boxes of nonperishable food and baby formula, then drove 370 miles to Window Rock, Arizona, to drop it all off.

In Warren, Ohio, 1,000 residents were mobilized to do something by the local newspaper, the *Tribune Chronicle,* which ran weekly articles for two months. Among them, they worked on 78 projects. They donated 150 pints of blood; collected 3,500 used tires; collected 162 bags of fallen leaves; picked 100 bags of apples; recycled 32 bags of clothes, toys, and books; fixed homes; cleaned parks; and much more.

Make a Difference Day: www.usaweekend.com/diffday

In Denver, Colorado, teen girls gave a former welfare mother of six a much-needed day off. Denver has a teen birthrate two to three times the national rate. The Girls of Promise Club helps its members avoid the pitfalls of teen pregnancy and poverty. Fifteen club members decided to help Oshanette Neal, a struggling single mother with six young children. Oshanette had been trying to stay off welfare with a $7-an-hour day-care job. The girls raised $5 each by doing chores or sending letters to neighbors asking for support. On Make a Difference Day, eight girls prepared a spaghetti dinner with salad and dessert, and seven others took the kids to a matinee of *Finding Nemo.* A little difference really can make a big difference.

...on Make a Difference Day

♦♦ **Why not do something this year for *Make a Difference Day*?** Register as an official participant. Or just do something independently.

♦♦ **Do something big that involves lots of people.** Or do something quite small by yourself or with a friend—such as picking up the litter in your street, planting a few flowers around the base of a tree, or helping old people across a busy road.

♦♦ **You can make a difference.** And *Make a Difference Day* is the day to do it.

sleep ON THE STREET

There is no single reason why children run away from home. They may be suffering sexual or physical abuse, violence, bullying, depression, loneliness, feelings of failure or low self-worth. A breakdown in communication with parents could be a deciding factor. ● According to ChildLine, the free helpline for children in distress, "Many of the children and young people who call us about running away or being homeless have argued with their families; most desperately want to reestablish good communication, and get on again with their parents and siblings." Others may have been released from child-care institutions with nobody they can turn to.

It is estimated that more than a million children run away from home every year. Most go on the streets because there is nowhere else to go. Street life then lures them into crime, drugs, and prostitution.

Most of us will never have to experience homelessness. If we could understand better what homelessness is like, then we might be able to deal with the problem more effectively. ● With this in mind, MuslimYouth.Net devised a homelessness experience project for young people to directly experience homelessness (under controlled conditions) and to report on it.

The MuslimYouth.Net online magazine for young Muslims: www.muslimyouth.net

Experiencing two days of street life

In March 2005 a group of six young people took part in the 2 Dayz of Street Life project. Each participant was given £3 ($5.75) spending money, which had to last them two days (the duration of the event). There were strict rules. The following were not allowed:

Additional funds or credit/debit cards

Mobile phones or other electronic equipment

A change of clothes or personal hygiene products (such as toothbrush or soap)

Sleeping bags, blankets, and other bedding materials

They could only make contact with family and friends through a payphone (paid out of their spending money), and all food had to be purchased from their allocated spending money.

The group was asked to keep in contact with a Project Manager during the two days. Participants were photographed and videoed discreetly. They had to submit a detailed diary, which was published on the MuslimYouth.Net website.

...end homelessness

Organize your own homeless experience.

● Sleep out with limited funds for as long as you dare.

● Get a friend to photograph you.

● Write up a record of your experience.

You must think about your personal safety before you embark on this.

SCORE *a Millennium Goal*

The world community came together in 2000 to agree on a plan to solve world poverty. They would work together to achieve eight goals by the year 2015. They set themselves eighteen targets, so that they could measure their success.

The Eight Millennium Goals are:

1. **Extreme poverty and hunger must be halved.** Halve the number of people living on less than $1 a day, and the number who suffer from hunger from the 1990 level.
2. **Universal primary education must be achieved.** All boys and girls must have proper schooling at primary level.
3. **Promote gender equality and empower women.** Eliminate gender disparities at all levels of education by 2015.
4. **Child mortality must be reduced by two-thirds.** Reduce the under-five mortality rate by two-thirds from the 1990 level.
5. **Maternal mortality ratio must be reduced by three-quarters.** Reduce the maternal mortality rate by three-quarters (from the 1990 level).
6. **The spread of HIV/AIDS and malaria must be halted.** Halt and begin to reverse the incidence of HIV/AIDS, malaria, and other major diseases.
7. **Environmental sustainability must be ensured.** Reverse the loss of environmental resources. Halve the proportion of people who lack access to clean water and proper sanitation. Improve the lives of at least 100 million slum dwellers.
8. **A global partnership for development must be developed.** Rich and poor countries must work together. All rich countries should increase their development aid to 0.7% as a minimum. There must be equitable rules of trade. Heavily indebted poor countries should be helped.

Millennium Development Goals: www.developmentgoals.org
The Millennium Campaign: www.millenniumcampaign.org
Global Call to Action against Poverty: www.whiteband.org

Only with your voice...The Millennium Campaign

The Millennium Campaign has been set up to ensure the eight goals are met. As part of the program a number of celebrities have dedicated their support for the cause. Actors like Angelina Jolie and Richard Gere, and singers like Shakira, have publicly joined the Only with Your Voice campaign and spoken out on these issues.

...solve world poverty

◉ **Score a soccer goal for the future of the world.**
Organize a "penalty shoot-out." Invite your friends along. Get them to pay a small entry fee for each kick. Hand out explanatory literature.

◉ **How to play:**
Players shoot at eight hoops hung from the crossbar with string, one for each millennium goal.
When the ball goes through a hoop, play stops for a discussion of the relevant goal.

war on the ARMS TRADE

> *I watched a Hawk attack a village in the mountains. It used its machine guns and dropped incendiary bombs....They have a terrible sound when they are coming in to bomb, like a voice wailing....They fly in low.... and attack civilians, because the people hiding in the mountains are civilians. Four of my cousins were killed in Hawk attacks near Los Palos.*
> —Jose Gusmao, refugee from East Timor

In the recent past, Indonesia waged a brutal war in East Timor, involving bombings, arbitrary arrests, torture, kidnapping, sexual abuse, and extrajudicial killings. 🕊 After 1994, over half of Indonesia's weapons came from abroad. These included the Hawk jets described by Jose Gusmao, and tanks used in attacks on peaceful demonstrators in 1998, which killed students and protestors. 🕊 These are just a couple of examples of the worldwide impact of the arms trade: fueling wars, snuffing out lives, and consuming vast sums of money.

Money spent on arms is money *not* being spent on development by poor countries. In 2004, wealthy countries sold arms worth $22 billion to developing countries. 🕊 Half of this amount would enable developing countries in Africa, Asia, the Middle East, and Latin America to put every child in primary school. 🕊 The deadly trade continues because of massive government support to the arms industry, providing large financial subsidies, promoting arms sales abroad, and watering down export controls.

The Campaign against Arms Trade suggests three ways of reducing the arms trade:
Genuine export controls, putting human rights, development, and an end to conflict before arms company profits
Ending government subsidies to the arms industry
Converting arms production to civilian industries

Control Arms: www.controlarms.org

The major exporters of arms are all wealthy countries.
In 2004 the value of the arms being exported was
USA $18.6 billion
Russia $4.6 billion
France $4.4 billion
UK $1.9 billion

...to make peace in the world

🕊 **Stopping the supply of arms in conflict zones** and to dubious regimes should be a part of the ethical dimension to any country's foreign policy. Write to your representatives asking that they press the government to end arms export subsidies.

🕊 **The next time newspapers report a massive arms deal,** write to the editor of your newspaper pointing out the potential suffering to the inhabitants of the recipient country.

🕊 **Get involved in campaigning** for an end to the deadly trade in weapons. Join a local CAAT group in your area.

OCTOBER 25 *Disarmament Week is the last week of October*

WORDS *for the future*

New words and phrases are added to our vocabulary every day. As society evolves, as new technologies are developed, as new ideas become current, so new words and phrases are created and existing words and phrases come to acquire new meanings. For example:

> **Spam,** once a brand of canned meat, is now used to describe junk e-mail.
> **Bootylicious,** an amalgamation of *beautiful* or rather *bootiful* and *delicious.*
> **Nuke** and **Mutual Assured Destruction (MAD),** part of Cold War speak.
> **Text messaging** and **ringtone** are part of our mobile phone society.

The *Future Dictionary of America* lists words compiled in 2004. Intended to be read as though it was produced 30 years in the future, and to reflect the social and political issues of our times, the dictionary comes with *The Future Soundtrack of America,* a musical expression of current policies. Nearly 200 contributors, mostly famous writers, have invented words. For example:

> **Wolfowish:** Hoping for that which is highly unlikely. Believing that the residents of Sadr City would greet the approaching Humvees with rose petals and chocolates was, in hindsight, probably indulging in a bit of wolfowishing.
> **Errorgance:** A feeling of smug superiority over those who do not share one's own erroneous or misguided convictions.

Wiktionary: en.wiktionary.org
McSweeney, the publishers of *Future Dictionary*: www.mcsweeneys.net

Theofandtoainthatiswas....
WordCount is an interactive presentation of the 86,800 most frequently used English words, ranked and scaled in order of commonness and displayed side by side as one very long sentence. www.wordcount.org

...add one to the Wiktionary

🖋 **Invent a new word or phrase for a new idea or a recent innovation.** That's the easy bit. Now try to get it in the Wiktionary. Wiktionary is a free online dictionary of words in every language with definitions of words and information on their origins and pronunciation. It is a companion to the Wikipedia free encyclopedia.

🖋 **To get into the Wiktionary,** a word needs to satisfy at least one of the following criteria:

> The word is in widespread use.
>
> The word has been used in a well-known work.
>
> Common usage of the word has been confirmed in a reputable work.
>
> The word has been used in at least three independently recorded instances over a period of at least one year in publicly available written texts or in audiovisual productions.

🖋 **Once your new word qualifies,** write the Wiktionary entry for it.

change your NAME

You might want to change your first name or family name for any number of reasons. This could be because you

> **Are getting married** or are making a commitment to live with a partner.
> **Are getting divorced.**
> **Want to reclaim an old family name** that has gone out of use.
> **Are fed up with the silly name** your parents gave you.
> **Want to be noticed.**

These are some of the more usual reasons. You might also want to change your name to bring attention to a cause or an issue, but you need to feel really strongly about the issue to do this.

Names can be changed in two ways. You can pick a new name and consistently use it. This is called "common usage," and is used for stage names and aliases. But you will still have to use your original name to sign official documents. 👫 Or you can get a court order changing your name.

Type "change your name" into Google, and you'll find a lot of online name-change services which will do the necessary.

The Soyouwanna website will tell you more:
www.soyouwanna.com/site/syws/changename/changename.html

Lesley Presley

Name-Change Limitations

You cannot change your name with fraudulent intent, for example to try to avoid bankruptcy or impersonate someone else.
Your new name should not be blasphemous, offensive, or vulgar.
You should use only letters, hyphens, and apostrophes.
Use of your new name should not result in a breach of a trademark. (If you are a singer, giving yourself the name Mick Jagger to promote your music would not be allowed.)

...to promote a cause

👫 **Is there a cause you feel absolutely passionate about?**
Do you want to draw attention to this cause by giving yourself a new name?
Do you want to be seen as being intimately identified with that cause?
Are you prepared to give up your existing name (although you can always use the same process to change your name back to what it was originally)?
Do you have the courage to have a really unusual name that people will notice, comment on, and even have a good laugh about?

👫 **If the answer to all these four questions is yes, then start making plans for your new name.**
What's it going to be? You can be sensible or outrageous. For example:
Edward Goldsmith, an environmentalist, could become Edward Going Green.
Emily Pankhurst could become Emily Votesforwomen.
John Potter, a cycle activist, could become Free Wheeler.
Hans Blix, a UN arms inspector, could become Guantánamo Sucks.

OCTOBER 27

DIRTY *hands*

In the western world, we all have access to soap and water. In 1848, Ignaz Semmelweis discovered that simple hand washing could prevent passage of infection from one person to another. ● Despite the discovery, over 150 years ago, of the most simple form of disease prevention, global poverty is such that many people in the world still do not have access to the two basic requirements: soap and clean water.

As a result of not being able to wash their hands, children may suffer several bouts of diarrhea each year—a dangerous and dehydrating condition. A major way of avoiding diarrhea and other infections is washing your hands properly when they are dirty.

Cole Brothers has recipes and step-by-step guidance on how to make soap: www.colebrothers.com/soap

Steven Baumrucker's website has lots of information and contacts on soap making: www.hospice.xtn.net/soap

How to make soap

Soap forms when fats are converted into fatty acids through a process known as saponification. This occurs in the presence of water and a strong base. Lye, the base used in soap making, is sodium hydroxide, an extremely powerful chemical. So take care when using it; it's best to wear rubber gloves.

There are hundreds of soap recipes to choose from. Here are the ingredients for one:

    coconut oil
    palm oil
    lard
    lye
    water
    coconut essential oil or trace of fragrance oil

—www.colebrothers.com/soap

...getting clean

Help the world to become a cleaner place.

● Make some soap. This is an easy and a fun process. It will be a new skill for you.

● Give some to your friends.

● Send some, via a suitable aid organization, to a country where many people can't afford soap, for distribution to the community.

living on LESS

The average person requires 2,500 calories a day to survive. In the developed world, and also among the rich in the developing world, people are consuming 40% more than this norm. ● Obesity is fast becoming a problem of epidemic proportions, while 600 million people in the developing world, mainly the rural poor, are seriously malnourished.

Plenty and waste are taken for granted in the rich world, while hunger and need exist in the poor world. The inequalities are growing wider. Could you live on less? ● Doing this will make you more sensitive to what many of your fellow human beings are experiencing, simply as a result of where they happened to have been born.

Human Development Reports: hdr.undp.org/statistics/data
Living on Less, reflections of a blogger: livingonless.journalspace.com

Living on less than a $1 a day
2004 selected countries

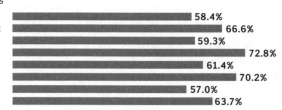

Burundi	58.4%
Central African Republic	66.6%
Gambia	59.3%
Mali	72.8%
Niger	61.4%
Nigeria	70.2%
Sierra Leone	57.0%
Zambia	63.7%

...could you do it?

Live on less. Try some of these exercises in marginal living:

● **Go without having your trash collected for a month.** Go through the bin to analyze what you have been throwing away.

● **Confine your water consumption to 2½ gallons a day,** equivalent to one flush of the toilet.

● **Live without electricity** for a day or a week.

● **Do without motorized transport.** Walk or cycle if you need to travel.

● **Spend as little as you can for three months.** Make a diary of everything you spend, with your comments on each spending decision.

● **Buy only basic food,** no convenience foods, and with as little packaging as possible.

● **Entertain yourself for a week:** no TV, no radio, no CDs, no video games.

Examine the things you did to make do. What were the things you most missed? How much reduction in consumption could you bear without feeling excessively inconvenienced? What can you do about global inequality?

OCTOBER 29

AIDS *living with it*

Shawn Decker has a story to tell about living with HIV/AIDS:

I'm a positoid. In the early 1980s I was infected with HIV through the use of tainted blood products. At the age of 11, after being diagnosed HIV positive, I was expelled from the sixth grade because local school officials thought I was a danger to other students. That was in 1987, a time when certain communities believed that HIV/AIDS was something that could not happen to them.

Eventually I was readmitted to high school and graduated as homecoming king. In part, I think this gesture was my classmates' way of showing that they not only liked me, but they supported me as well. Even though I wasn't speaking openly about HIV at the time, they respected me for being "goofy, wisecracking, HIV positive Shawn." ☺ Later, when I came out of my AIDS closet, I used that humor as my main tool in educating others about life with HIV. Nearly twenty years later, I'm healthy, happy, and in love.

One way that I try to raise awareness about HIV/AIDS issues is through public speaking. My partner, Gwenn, shares my passion for HIV education, and we travel the US through CAMPUSPEAK, talking to college students about our relationship: I'm HIV positive and she is not. ☺ Much of the conversation has to do with our sex life, and by "opening our bedroom door," so to speak, we give people a chance to learn that those living with HIV are normal beings with normal emotions.

My advice to young people is to be open and honest about the topic of sex. Know that you cannot tell that someone is HIV positive by looking at them, and in many instances people who are HIV positive themselves do not even know; so how could they tell you?

Shawn's websites:
www.aboyagirlavirus.com
www.mypetvirus.com

Love, Shawn Decker and Gwenn Barringer

Aboyagirlavirus.com is an engaging, honest look at two people in love. Shawn has HIV and Gwenn doesn't. They answer all the questions you can think of, and then some.

Gwenn has her own site, and she makes one excellent point; if she can stay HIV negative, then anyone should be able to.

...keep informed, keep safe

☺ **Go to Shawn's website** to see what it's like to live with HIV/AIDS.

☺ **Wear a red ribbon** to show your support for people with AIDS.

☺ **Never put yourself at risk of contracting HIV.**

some more GREAT IDEAS

In compiling this book, we invited people to submit ideas for ways of changing the world. Here is a selection of the ideas we received but did not have space to give them their own page:

Campaign to get empty housing back in use. Do a survey. Think about who might need it. Homeless people? Asylum seekers and refugees? Students? Visitors and tourists? It's doing no good remaining empty.

Organize a carnival to kick racism out of the community. Celebrate the diversity of all the different peoples who live in your neighborhood.

Do a litter walk with some friends. Pick a mile of road or beach, and pick up all the litter you find. Wear heavy-duty gardening gloves. Take great care with sharp objects (including discarded syringes). Start a Stop Litter campaign.

Make a banner to promote an issue horizontally or vertically, and hang it up.

Befriend an elderly person. Have tea with them, do their shopping, tend their garden. Share experiences from the past and the present. Collect their stories of life long ago.

Hold a swap-shop party. Everyone brings ten things to swap for something they like better. Everyone leaves with ten new things.

Get people in your office to stop printing out e-mails. This change could save up to 40% of office paper use.

Make recycled paper. It's fun and it makes great gifts. All you need are scraps and a blender.

Organize a communitywide "I have a dream" contest to find the best ideas in your community for addressing some of its key problems and opportunities.

Organize a Talk-to-your-Neighbors day in your neighborhood. Or just invite your neighbors in for a cup of coffee.

Create a catalog that features locally made items, to stimulate the local economy.

Set up a coffee shop in your neighborhood that is cheap, fair-trade, and healthy. Fill it with posters, publications, and music on how to change the world. This could be the best franchise idea since Starbucks!

Use pavement chalk as a protest tool—or just to brighten up the street. Create a floor mural. Unlike paint, chalk will wash away with the next rain.

Petition Sara Lee to reduce cake packaging. Do a survey of food packaging. Start a campaign to get manufacturers to reduce the amount they use.

Send your great ideas to us: www.365act.com

...do something with a pumpkin

- 🖤 **After Halloween, pumpkins go to waste.** But there are many things you could do wth them. Why not arrange a pumpkin soupfest? Or a competition for the best pumpkin jam? Or even a prize for turning one into Cinderella's coach?

- 🖤 **Take one of these ideas and make it happen.** Or think of a better idea and send it to us.

AFGHANISTAN *women*

We work hard for women's rights in Afghanistan. We need the solidarity and support of all people around the world.

—RAWA

The perception of Afghanistan as a country where women are most oppressed was reinforced under the rule of the Taliban (which ended in 2001), when women were only allowed out in public dressed in a burka, and many suffered substantial abuse to their human rights.

RAWA, the Revolutionary Association of the Women of Afghanistan, was founded in 1977 by Meena, then aged 21, for Afghan women to fight for human rights and social justice. Meena was assassinated ten years later in Pakistan by Afghan KGB agents, in connivance with fundamentalist warlord Gulbuddin Hekmatyar.

RAWA runs education, health, and income-generation projects alongside its political campaigning. RAWA needs all the support it can get. Since the overthrow of the Soviet-backed regime in 1992, the focus of RAWA's struggle has been against fundamentalism and its ultra–male chauvinistic and antiwoman outlook.

RAWA: www.rawa.org

In France, FemAid works closely with RAWA: www.femaid.org

What FemAid supporters worldwide are doing:

US: A large number of kites were donated and distributed to two RAWA orphanages. Kite flying had been banned by the Taliban. A jazz musician gave a concert for his fortieth birthday and sent the proceeds.

UK: A charity soccer match was organized, and supporters of both teams raised money. Stella McCartney sold signed and numbered T-shirts for a RAWA orphanage.

France: Schools in the Bordeaux area collected school supplies to send to Afghan refugees in Pakistan.

Canada: Funds were raised for medical aid for a Quetta hospital (in Pakistan near the Afghan border) and for training midwives.

...act in solidarity

- **Read** *Meena, Heroine of Afghanistan* by Melody Ermachild Chavis.
- **Buy some music** to support RAWA. There is a choice of two CDs:
  Azadi, a benefit compilation for RAWA; 100% of proceeds go to RAWA: www.museumfire.com/azadi.htm.
  Dropping Food on Their Heads Is not Enough; 50% of proceeds go to RAWA: www.gcrecords.com/benefit.html.

1 NOVEMBER

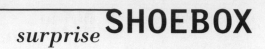
Christmas is still weeks away. But you may already be finding the commercialization distasteful, and you will almost certainly be wracking your brains as to what to buy your family and friends. Why not give yourself a treat, and enjoy putting together a box full of small items for someone you can be sure will appreciate them? ● There are several schemes that distribute donated gifts, packaged in shoeboxes, to people in countries where children are living in such poverty that a toothbrush, a packet of crayons, or a skipping rope will be a treasured gift.

But why wait until Christmas? This really simple idea was found on the www.honduras.com website:

> When you pack your luggage, please include a shoebox full of school supplies such as pens, pencils, chalk, paper, crayons, etc. Also take an extra $20 along. When you arrive in Honduras, keep an eye out for a small, poor school. Walk up to it, and give your box to a teacher or to the director. Then as you continue your vacation, keep an eye out for an obviously poor person (preferably a woman). Walk up to her and give her the $20. The reason for giving to a woman is that it is usually a woman who has to feed and clothe the children; so your money will more than likely go where it is desperately needed.

> You will be surprised at how good this will make you feel. And believe me, you will have done a great service to Honduras, even though it may seem to be a very small amount. Have a great trip! Have a great vacation! And have a great life! Thanks.

—*Gringo Jak*

Samaritan's Purse is a Christian organization that runs a shoebox scheme in North America, Northern Europe, and Australia: www.samaritanspurse.org

The Rotary Club distributes shoeboxes year round: www.rotary1280.org/shoebox

How to pack a box

If it's a gift box, indicate whether it's for a boy or a girl and the approximate age.

About 14 items fill a box. For a school, pens and pencils, marker pens, solar-powered pocket calculators, geometry instruments, scissors are all useful. Toy suggestions include doll, ball, toy car, cards, marbles, skipping rope, yo-yo, dominoes.

Other popular items are toothbrush, toothpaste, soap, comb, sunglasses, caps, socks, T-shirts, hair clips, watches, small books.

Don't include used items, knives, battery-powered or electrical equipment, perishable items, medicines, breakable items, flammable or caustic materials, or religious items.

Tie your box with string so that it can be opened easily in case of enquiries at customs. Take it with you when you travel abroad. Or deliver it to a charity running a gift-box program.

...a gift that really helps

Remember to keep the shoebox next time you buy a pair of shoes.

● **Wrap the box** with some bright wrapping paper. Wrap the lid separately.

● **Collect things** to fill up your shoebox: assorted supplies for a school, or gifts for a child in an orphanage.

● **Get a group of friends** to join you in filling a shoebox.

NOVEMBER 2

NONVIOLENT *movies*

Every day we are bombarded with images of violence and death. Video games, music lyrics, television shows, commercials, radio, and movies entertain us, but they also spew out images of aggression, violence, and killing. ✻ *Rambo*, *The Terminator*, *James Bond*, *Spider-Man*, *Indiana Jones* are all about men who win out by blowing up buildings, shooting opponents, pushing the enemy off a cliff.

Some movies you could watch:

***Gandhi* (1982):** This film swept the 1983 Oscars, winning eight awards, including Best Picture, Best Actor (Ben Kingsley), Best Screenplay, and Best Director for Richard Attenborough. It is the awe-inspiring story of how a diminutive lawyer stood up to the British Empire and became an international symbol of nonviolence and understanding.

***Martin Luther King, Jr.: The Man and the Dream* (2004):** This is a film about one of the most loved, respected, and influential leaders in American history. In this look at the life and work of Martin Luther King, writer and director Tom Friedman explores how Dr. King's ideas evolved in the face of the rapidly changing climate of the Civil Rights Movement.

***Free at Last: Civil Rights Heroes* (2004):** Watch the incredible stories of Emmett Till, Medgar Evers, the Birmingham Four, Viola Liuzzo, and more. Their deaths contributed to the forward momentum of the civil rights struggle.

An online magazine for movie buffs: www.movies.go.com

Or for a different thought-provoking movie marathon:

***Amandla! A Revolution in Four-Part Harmony* (2003):** The struggle to eradicate apartheid in South Africa and the vital role music played in this challenge.

***Apocalypse Now* (1974):** Possibly Francis Ford Coppola's greatest work, based on Joseph Conrad's *Heart of Darkness*.

***Hotel Rwanda* (2004):** Amid the genocidal butchering, one ordinary man musters the courage to shelter more than 1,000 people in the hotel he manages.

***The Killing Fields* (1984):** All hell is breaking loose in Cambodia; Khmer Rouge's genocide has begun. The true story of *New York Times* journalist Sydney Shanberg, who stayed on after the American evacuation.

***Schindler's List* (1993):** Steven Spielberg's Holocaust epic shows factory owner Oskar Schindler exploiting cheap Jewish labor. In the midst of WWII, he became an unlikely humanitarian, losing his fortune while saving 1,100 Jews from Auschwitz.

...for a peaceful night in

Challenge the culture of violence.

✻ **Invite your friends** to join you in a Nonviolent Movie Marathon.

✻ Get some popcorn, fluff up the couch, and enjoy several movies that do not contain explosives, car chases, guns, bombs, or punches.

✻ **Explain to your guests** the idea of your movie marathon, which is to think about the impact of violent images on society.

✻ **Challenge your guests** to come up with ideas for addressing this issue.

3 NOVEMBER

theater of PROTEST

A simple play reading can become a theatrical act of protest.
In Aristophanes' ancient Greek play *Lysistrata*, a group of women organize a sex strike to try to stop the endless warfare that their menfolk are pursuing. On March 3, 2003, the Lysistrata Project organized 1,029 readings of Aristophanes' play in 59 countries around the world to protest against the war in Iraq. ✊ A secret reading in northern Iraq was organized by members of the International Press Corps, who had to keep quiet about it or risk losing their jobs. A reading in Patras, Greece, was held by Greeks and Kurdish refugees in an abandoned factory serving as a Kurdish refugee camp. There were secret readings in China. ✊ The readings raised $125,000 for peace and humanitarian aid in the Middle East and elsewhere.

How they did it: The organizers wrote a letter that said, "Are you frustrated by the buildup to war? Do you feel like there isn't anything you can do? Well, here's something you CAN do..." They e-mailed this letter to everyone they knew, who in turn forwarded it to everyone *they* knew. The next day the organizers started hearing back from people all over the world. Within two weeks, they had been interviewed on national radio, readings were scheduled in over 70 cities, a documentary team started filming, and a couple organized an Internet auction to raise money.

> The Lysistrata Project: www.lysistrataproject.com
>
> Kathryn Blume's account of how it was all organized:
> http://kathrynblume.com/AcAc.htm
>
> "Put the Act Back into Action," a Friends of the Earth how-to guide to using street theater: community.foe.co.uk/resource/how_tos

Ten steps for a successful local play reading:

1. Clarify your aims: Why are you doing it? What do you want to achieve? Be realistic, but also be ambitious.

2. Get a location: in a living room, at a community center, on the steps of city hall, anywhere!

3. Pick a time.

4. Pick a charity to benefit.

5. Get the script: online or from a library or a bookshop.

6. Cast the roles: friends, celebrities, whoever's willing.

7. Get help! Send an e-mail asking for volunteers. Give everyone who offers something to do.

8. Make the project visible: get as much publicity as you can.

9. Put up a website.

10. Be green: Show that you also care about the environment. Use recycled paper for programs and flyers.

...be an accidental activist

Stage a public reading of a political play.

✊ **Try a play by Richard Norton-Taylor**. The words are entirely those spoken by participants at an important public inquiry. *The Colour of Justice*: racism and the police response; *Bloody Sunday*: civil rights in Northern Ireland; *Justifying War*: the legitimacy of the invasion of Iraq.

✊ **Or read** *The Accidental Death of an Anarchist* by Dario Fo; *Execution of Justice* by Emily Mann; *Fires in the Mirror* by Anna Deveare Smith; *The Syringa Tree* by Pamela Gien; *Jody's Body* by Aviva Jane Carlin.

NOVEMBER 4

LAND MINE *adoption*

Each year, 26,000 people are killed or mutilated by land mines, 8,000 of them children. The lives of 71 people each day are being damaged or destroyed. ❧ They didn't lay the mines, but they suffer the consequences. And their lives are at risk with every step they take.

There are between 60 to 100 million land mines in the ground worldwide. It costs between $3 and $30 to purchase an antipersonnel land mine. It can cost as much as $1,000 to remove it. Land mines destroy livestock and prevent the cultivation of arable land. They are an ever-present menace to those who live in affected areas.

Rebuilding war-torn communities and economies is difficult in any circumstances. But in many communities, recovery, reconciliation, and long-term development are all but impossible because of land mines. ❧ The Ottawa Convention on the Prohibition of the Use, Stockpiling, Production and Transfer of Anti Personnel Mines, and on their Destruction, has now been signed by 136 nations—but not by China, Russia, and the US, three of the world's most powerful nations.

International Campaign to Ban Landmines: www.icbl.org

The Night of 1,000 Dinners

Coordinated by Adopt a Minefield, this event takes place on or around the first Thursday of November each year, although people can hold dinners whenever it is convenient for them.

Thousands of people around the world host dinners in their homes, at work, or in community venues to raise funds to clear land mines and help land mine survivors.

Dinners have been hosted on the sand dunes of the Sahara, in embassies, in studio apartments, and in all sorts of weird and wonderful places.

...help mine casualties

Host an Adopt a Minefield dinner. This is a chance for you to make a difference while cooking and eating a meal with your favorite people.

❧ **Find out this year's date** from the Adopt a Minefield website, put it in your diary, invite your friends, and download some of the recipes that have been donated for the occasion.

❧ **Raise lots of money.** It costs about $2.25 to clear a square yard of minefield, and about $100 to help an amputee child walk again.

Adopt a Minefield passes 100% of the funds received from the general public to projects clearing land mines and helping land mine survivors. Adopt a Minefield tells every donor where their money is allocated and, when the project has been completed, what impact their money has made.

plant a PEACE POLE

Peace is a daily, a weekly, a monthly process, gradually changing opinions, slowly eroding old barriers, quietly building new structures.

—John F. Kennedy

Peace Poles are a memorial to peace. Wherever a peace pole has been planted, it is an indication that that specific place on earth has been designated a place of peace. ❧ A peace pole ceremony can serve as a memorial to a tragedy that has taken place. The major of New York City, Michael Bloomberg, planted a 9/11 Memorial Peace Pole. ❧ A peace pole can also be a symbol of a community making a commitment to achieving peace. It can serve as the symbol of a new beginning between two previously warring factions.

Over 200,000 peace poles have been planted in over 180 countries. There are peace poles at:

> The Pyramids of El Giza, Egypt
> The magnetic north pole in Canada
> Sarajevo
> The Allenby Bridge between Israel and Jordan
> Baghdad
> Robben Island, South Africa
> New York
> Gorky Park, Russia
> The Confucius burial site, Taiwan

The Peace Pole Project, a project of the World Peace and Prayer Society: www.worldpeace.org/peacepoles.html

Peace Pole Makers (USA): www.peacepoles.com

Peace poles are usually 8 feet tall. They can be made out of a sustainable material; for example, in North America they are often constructed out of western red cedar cut from renewable forests. They can also be constructed of metal or plastic.

They are planted in the ground or placed on stands if they are indoors. Desktop models, 20 inches high, are also available.

Every "official" peace pole has the words "May Peace Prevail On Earth" written on one side; and often that phrase is written on the other sides in different languages.

...reserve a space for peace

Plant a peace pole in your community.

❧ **Pick a spot** such as a public space or park, or even someone's backyard. The more people who pass by and see it, the better. You can make your peace pole. But make sure it is solid and durable in sun and rain.

❧ **Or if you prefer, buy a ready-made peace pole.** The Peace Pole Project publishes a list of suppliers in countries all over the world. Outdoor poles cost between $200 and $1,350. A miniature travel version costs $12.

❧ **Organize a dedication ceremony.**

NOVEMBER 6 *International Day for Preventing the Exploitation of the Environment in War and Armed Conflict*

CELLPHONE
recycling

You know how it is, you're now with the latest model. And your old mobile phone, the one you used to love and take everywhere with you, is left at home, unwanted and abandoned. It doesn't have to be like this. Your old mobile can have a new life, full of meaning and purpose... but with someone else...

—Oxfam, Bring Bring

Millions of cellphones are obsolete, broken, or otherwise unused. And more are discarded every year. Most are put into the household waste. They end up in landfill sites, where the toxic material contained in the battery and LCD display leak out. Your old phone really does need to be disposed of safely. The best thing to do is recycle it.

The developing world is taking a technological leap into the mobile phone age. A really interesting village phone program is run in Bangladesh by Grameen Telecom, in partnership with the Grameen Bank. Rural women are given mobile handsets, which they pay for with a small Grameen Bank loan, and they are taught to use them. They then sell phone services to villagers, and this provides affordable telephone access to the village and contact with the outside world. It also provides the women with a livelihood.

Donate Your Phone: www.collectivegood.com/donate1.asp

Grameen Telecom: www.grameenphone.com

Turn your old mobile into a sunflower

Researchers at the University of Warwick in England have developed a mobile-phone case that you can plant and transform into the flower of your choice.

The case is made from an easily biodegradable plastic. When it is placed in a compost heap, a seed, embedded behind a small window in the case, germinates. The prototypes have used dwarf sunflower seeds. Watch a film about this:

www.research-tv.com/stories/technology/mobilephones

...new owners, new uses

When you get a new cellphone, make sure that your old one is recycled.

If it is in good enough condition to be reused, it can be tested, refurbished, rebranded, and sent to a developing country for reuse.

If it is not, metals can be extracted for reuse from handsets, batteries, and chargers. The handsets are incinerated to generate heat. The plastics from chargers are recycled into such things as traffic cones and buckets.

*world*KINDNESS

No act of kindness however small is ever wasted.

—Aesop

Glen Bornais from Ottawa, Canada, writes,

Despite my preoccupation with the big problems of the day (perhaps because I've studied political economy at a critically spirited institution) and despite my natural tendency towards the dramatic, I've recently come under the power of one truly simple idea: we could improve our lives, our communities, our families, our friendships, our world simply by engaging in a random and unsolicited act of kindness every day.

This approach to life will not likely resolve or reverse the unequal distribution of wealth, nor the damage we do to our planet, nor third-world debt, nor suffering and hunger of the deepest kind, but acts of kindness such as unsolicited compliments, smiles, simple charity, community trash pickup can help us regain faith in each and every person, and sometimes even in ourselves.

The World Kindness Movement was set up in 1997 to promote kindness. There are now branches in a dozen countries. Their work is "in acknowledgment of the fundamental importance of simple human kindness as a basic condition of a satisfying and meaningful life." ♦♦ The second week in November has been designated World Kindness Week, and one day in that week is World Kindness Day.

Inspiring quotations on kindness: www.kindness.com.au/quotations.htm

Calendars and bookmarks with ideas for acts of kindness from Random Acts of Kindness Foundation: www.actsofkindness.org/inspiration/graphics.asp

Or send an e-card: www.actsofkindness.org/inspiration/ecards.asp

Join the Coinspiracy

The Coinspiracy is an initiative of the KindActs Network Association of British Columbia in Canada to engage young people in creating positive global change.

The campaign uses a kindness coin called a UNI, which is short for the "universal" nature of kindness. To participate, the "Coinholder" commits three kind acts: one for him or herself, one for the environment, and one for someone else. The coin is passed on to the recipient of the kind act, who in turn commits the three kind acts and passes it on.

The first Coinspiracy campaign was piloted in 2002. Over 100,000 humanitarian acts were performed, and an estimated $30,000 was raised in donations. Clothing, books, medical supplies, and food were donated to orphanages, families in need, and inner-city schools.

On World Kindness Day in 2003, 77 schools and youth groups in Australia, Bermuda, Canada, India, Italy, Nepal, New Zealand, Nigeria, Scotland, Singapore, South Africa, and the US, participated in the Coinspiracy.

...make people happy

♦♦ **Perform an act of kindness** right now to the person you next see. Think of this act as a start for leading a kinder life.

♦♦ **Join the Coinspiracy campaign** and experience for yourself the multiplier effect of kindness and its endless possibilities. Find out more about the Coinspiracy: www.investinakinderworld.com.

SEND BOOKS *to prison*

Treat people as if they were what they ought to be, and you help them to become what they are capable of being.

—Goethe

The US has a huge prison population—possibly the largest that has ever existed on earth. Over 2 million people are incarcerated. Many of these men and women try to use their time in prison to make a new start for themselves. They educate themselves to get a high school diploma or a college degree. But they need textbooks...badly.

Getting an education will make a huge difference to their life. It will open doors for jobs that would otherwise remain closed. It will give them a sense of pride and purpose. It will show that hard work can lead to tangible results.

This is where you come in. Prison libraries are drastically short of books. They especially need textbooks—those battered books that you are so glad to get rid of at the end of your studies. Instead of leaving them forgotten and gathering dust on a shelf, or having a massive bonfire, send them to your local prison.

www.books2prisoners.org

Some prisons have rules about what they will or will not take. Some don't want paperbacks or won't take books about certain subjects. Sometimes there are particular needs—a prisoner doing an engineering degree, for example. Find out as much as you can about their rules and needs before you get going.

Most prisons would love to take more than just your textbooks. See what other books you could send as well.

...help someone make a new start

Send your books to prison. This is how to do it:

Step 1: **Make contact.**
Telephone your local prison or ask at your local police station. Tell them you want to send your books to prison. Ask them for details of the nearest prison and the name of the person to contact. Or go online and look up prisons in your area. Some prisons even have information on book donations. When you eventually do make contact, ask if there are any types of books they would be particularly interested in having.

Step 2: **Collect the books.**
After you have found out what they need, go through your bookshelf to see what you can provide. Start collecting books from all your friends. And if there are some particular types of books that you have not been able to get, try writing a letter to your local newspaper asking for someone to donate those books.

Step 3: **Deliver the books.**
Put all the books in a box. Wrap it up nicely in giftwrap. And deliver it in person. See if your local newspaper will send a photographer to record this momentous event. If not, find a friend to do it for you.

Step 4: **Sit back and relax.**
Enjoy the knowledge that your little gesture is helping people change their lives.

prevent GENOCIDE

After WWII the international community pledged never again would genocide occur. Yet it has. And it is occurring again and again. Genocide is defined as the systematic and planned extermination of an entire national, racial, political, or ethnic group. It has eight stages:

1. **Classification.** Dividing people into "us" and "them."
2. **Symbolization.** Giving names or symbols to the group.
3. **Dehumanization.** One group denies the humanity of the other group. People are equated with animals, vermin, insects, or diseases.
4. **Organization.** Genocide is always organized, usually by the state, though sometimes informally, or by terrorist groups. Special militias are armed and trained. Plans are made for mass killing.
5. **Polarization.** Extremists drive the groups apart. Laws are passed denying rights or forbidding social interaction.
6. **Preparation.** Victims are identified and separated. Death lists are drawn up. People are often segregated into ghettoes, forced into concentration camps, or confined to a famine-struck region and starved.
7. **Extermination.** The killing begins and quickly escalates.
8. **Denial.** This follows the genocide. The perpetrators dig up the mass graves, burn the bodies, try to cover up the evidence, and intimidate the witnesses. They deny that they committed any crimes and often blame what happened on the victims.

Genocide Watch: www.genocidewatch.org
The Genocide Watch pledge: www.genocidewatch.org/Pledge.htm
Prevent Genocide: www.preventgenocide.org

Websites for more information:

The Nazi Holocaust	www.nizkor.org
Armenians in Turkey	www.armenian-genocide.org
Rwanda	www.hrw.org/reports/1999/rwanda/
China	www.gendercide.org/case_infanticide.html
Sudan	www.genocidewatch.org
Cambodia	www.yale.edu/cgp
Iraq	www.gendercide.org/case_anfal.html

...pledge "never again"

Sign Genocide Watch's pledge:

I pledge to do my part to end genocide: the intentional destruction, in whole or in part, of a national, ethnic, racial, or religious group.

I commit myself never to be a passive bystander to genocide anywhere.

I will assist the victims of genocide and will help them escape from their killers. I will support the victims with humanitarian relief.

I will not stop my protests against a genocide until that genocide is stopped.

PEACE *for a moment*

After catastrophic events—either natural or human-induced—there is now a well-established tradition of people gathering together, or just pausing in their daily routine, and spending some moments in silent contemplation.

November 11 is Armistice Day or Remembrance Day. At the eleventh hour on the eleventh day of the eleventh month, two minutes' silence is observed to remember all those who died in WWI, and in subsequent wars. 🕊 In the UK, as well as the red poppies distributed by the British Legion, there are white poppies distributed by the Peace Pledge Union to symbolize the belief that there are better ways to resolve conflicts than killing strangers.

On August 6, 1945, the first atomic bomb ever used in warfare was dropped on Hiroshima; on August 9, the second was dropped on Nagasaki. On August 9, 2005, Pax Christi Ireland observed One Minute for Peace at 10:02 GMT.

Global Minute for Peace Day takes place on December 22, the winter solstice—traditionally a time for rejoicing, as the days start getting longer, bringing a new hope into people's lives. On the first Global Day, the voice of President Kennedy speaking at the United Nations was broadcast. He said, "Together we can save our planet." GMPD is an initiative of John McConnell, who also promotes International Earth Day on the spring equinox.

Just a Minute of Peace (JAMOP) is a Canadian initiative, linked to an international concert for peace. People are urged to spend a minute in silence on July 7, 2007, at 23:59 GMT.

See what conflicts took place in the world during the 20th century by exploring the Conflict Map: nobelprize.org/peace/educational/conflictmap

Just a Minute of Peace: www.jamop.com

Total deaths in the 20th century from war and oppression:

Genocide and tyranny:	83 million	
Military deaths in war:	42 million	
Civilian deaths in war:	19 million	
Manmade famine:	44 million	

—Matthew White's *Historical Atlas of the 20th Century*: users.erols.com/mwhite28/20centry.htm

...time to commit

🕊 **Sign up to JAMOP** and make a symbolic gesture to advocate peaceful solutions to international conflict, to advance human rights, and to promote responsible economic and social development in the world. And join together with others on July 7, 2007.

🕊 **One minute of silence provides a time for reflection,** a time for you to think about what part you can play to end war. Take a minute now to think about this and commit yourself to taking one simple action for peace. Sit down; stand up; write a letter; lobby your elected representative; do something.

compile a DIRECTORY

Right under your nose, there's a whole heap of things going on, most of which you probably don't even know about. There may be

A sailing club that meets to sail model boats on a nearby lake.
A kite-flying group showing off their latest creations.
People learning salsa, yoga, karate, tai chi, or flower arranging.
Poker or bridge clubs.
Reading circles, amateur dramatic societies, and groups that play music.
One o'clock clubs for young mothers to meet and share their experiences.
Dances for senior citizens.
The local soccer or baseball team that's about to make it big in the local league.
Self-help groups such as Alcoholics Anonymous, Weight Watchers.
Local chapters of Greenpeace or Amnesty International planning a campaign to change the world.
Church groups, school groups, youth groups
... and much more.

Groups are a good indicator of how well the community is functioning. The more the better. If people knew about what was happening when and where, or if organizers had a place to advertise what they were doing, then many more people might join in. It would become easier to find what to do and easier to

Nicholas Albery, a social inventor, created two initiatives to foster participatory activity. He needed to take regular exercise, owing to a medical condition, so he created a Saturday Walkers Club. Based on the *Time Out Book of Country Walks,* it consists of walks ranging from vigorous to relaxed to creative (with a 30-minute break for silent reflection or creative activity). Walkers meet at a time and place specified on the website to take part. Walks are free; everyone is welcome.

Nicholas also created DoBe, as an electronic community bulletin board for local communities to post news of participatory events being organized in the area. You can use the software to create your own bulletin board.

...of community activities

Create a Neighborhood Yellow Pages for your local community or town.

🏠 **Make a list** of all the activities and services taking place in your neighborhood. Provide enough information on each for people to know if it is something they might be interested in.
🏠 **Provide contact details** for people to find out more.
🏠 **Publish your list**. Set up a website, which will cost little or nothing.
🏠 **Produce a printed directory,** and try to recoup your money from sales of a hard copy or from advertising.

FOOD *not bombs*

It is a scandal that there is hunger in the midst of plenty. Hungry people include single-parent families, low-wage employees, the unemployed, the elderly, and those unable to work through illness or disability. Before you eat the meal in front of you, your food has gone through a chain of farmers, distributors, manufacturers, wholesalers, and retailers. At every point in the chain, perfectly good food is discarded. The US wastes 22 million tons of food a year (about 175 lbs. per person). Just one-tenth of this would end hunger in America.

Food Not Bombs started in 1980 with two ideas: bombs, militarism, and war are a bad thing, and no person should go hungry in today's world. Food Not Bombs provides free vegetarian food to hungry people. They recover food that would otherwise be thrown out, fresh produce near the end of its shelf life, and turn this into hot vegetarian meals, served in city parks to anyone who wants it. Food Not Bombs also campaigns against war and poverty throughout the world.

Food Not Bombs groups have been started in nearly 50 countries. Join or start a group in your city: www.foodnotbombs.net

Food for Life: The International Society for Krishna Consciousness runs free vegetarian food programs in about 16 countries: www.ffl.org

Many homeless projects organize soup runs going out in the evenings to provide free meals to people on the streets. This is what McKenna's Wagon does in DC. Working 365 days a year, they provide 558,000 meals and snacks to 1,200 homeless families and 500 day-care toddlers and to 85 seniors on weekends, plus groceries once a month to 200 families and holiday meals 3 times a year to 6,500 homeless people at Martha's Table. Five vans distribute 3,000 sandwiches, 65 gallons of soup, and 65 gallons of hot beverages. Food is donated by groceries, cafeterias, bakeries, and others. A lot of food for a lot of hunger. www.marthastable.org/wagon.html

...feed the hungry

- **Collect food for** distribution to the hungry. You'll need a vehicle and a small group of committed volunteers.

- **Approach supermarkets,** grocers and greengrocers, markets, restaurants, and ask them to donate food to you on a regular basis. Take literature to explain what you are doing.

- **Deliver the food** you collect to shelters, day centers, and soup kitchens. Find out what they need and arrange a regular delivery schedule.

- **Prepare meals** to serve on the street. This is hard work but also fun. Pick central locations, as they will make the problem of homelessness more visible.

- **You've just started a Food Not Bombs group.** The *Food Not Bombs Handbook* on their website will tell you all you need to know.

become an ENTREPRENEUR

Social entrepreneurs do for society's problems what entrepreneurs do for business: they provide practical solutions by combining innovation, resourcefulness, and opportunity. They innovate by finding a new product or service to meet a need, or by developing a new approach to an existing problem. They get started immediately, confident that they will find a way of succeeding.

The Ashoka Foundation supports social entrepreneurs around the world by providing them with three-year grants to develop and implement their ideas. ✋ Veronica Khosa was a nurse in South Africa. Around her she could see sick people getting sicker, elderly people unable to get to a doctor, and hospitals with empty beds that would not admit patients with HIV. So Veronica started Tateni Home Care Nursing Services, pioneering the concept of home care in her country. Starting with practically nothing, her team took to the streets providing care to people in their homes. ✋ A few years later, the government adopted her ideas, and home-care services are now spreading beyond South Africa.

Mohammed Mamdani set up the Muslim Youth Helpline when he was 17, so that young Muslims in the UK had somewhere to turn with their problems. Rupert Hawley is trying to build affordable housing out of straw bales and eventually set up a museum of alternative building. Social entrepreneurs are unstoppable people with great ideas—people who get things done.

These organizations support social entrepreneurs. Visit their websites to see the sorts of people and projects they are supporting:
Ashoka Foundation: www.ashoka.org and www.changemakers.net
Skoll Foundation: www.skollfoundation.org
Schwab Foundation: www.schwabfound.org
Social Capitalist Awards: www.fastcompany.com/social

Join these networks to meet other change makers:
Pioneers of Change: www.pioneersofchange.net
International Young Professionals Foundation: www.iypf.org

Ashoka success story

Rodrigo Baggio wanted to help poor people make use of information technology to improve their communities and their own lives. In 1995, he set up a technology school in a Rio de Janeiro slum. This worked so well that his organization, Committee for Democracy in Information Technology, has since established more than 900 schools in Latin America, and in South Africa and Japan.

The students learn how to use computers and discuss issues facing their communities. They then devise a project that involves the use of computers—such as publishing a community newspaper or launching a small business or organizing a civic group—which they then work to make happen. Over ten years, more than 600,000 people graduated from CDI schools.

...lead social change

Get on with it! If you see a problem, and if you have an idea for how it could be dealt with, do something. Don't make excuses for doing nothing; don't wait for someone else to do something. Do it yourself...and do it now!

IN-YOUR-FACE *politics*

The Biotic Baking Brigade is a movement that actually moves: a network of political pranksters who literally practice in-your-face politics. They target assorted greedheads, hitting them right in the smacker...with pies! But it is worthy work. The BBB's pies are the Boston Tea Party of our modern day, sending a serious message softly to the corporate oligarchy.

—Jim Hightower

It's an assault on public officials. It's an assault on government. It should not be condoned.

—Michael Yaki, San Francisco Supervisor

Humor is an important weapon in the armory of an activist. What do Bill Gates, Milton Freidman, Sylvester Stallone, Canadian premier Jean Chretien, Swedish king Carl Gustaf, Ronald McDonald, Timothy Leary, Eldridge Cleaver, World Trade Organization Director Renato Ruggiero, and Andy Warhol have in common? They've all been "pied" by the Biotic Baking Brigade and its sympathizers around the world. 👫 The brigade consists of activists involved in ecology, social justice, animal rights, and feminism, with a sense of humor and an "in your face" courage.

Slapstick and politics can mix. The fine art of landing a freshly baked cream cake in the face of a reactionary, pompous, but otherwise deserving person has a long and venerable tradition. 👫 As a way of highlighting a particular cause, gaining often spectacular media attention, or merely bringing a lofty demeanor down a crust or two, there is nothing quite as good as a pie.

Biotic Baking Brigade: www.bioticbakingbrigade.org

Watch *The Pie's the Limit,* a delicious documentary featuring a cornucopia of political pie throwings in San Francisco and beyond, plus behind the scenes interviews with real underground pie tossers. Watch with delight as half a dozen demagogues are served up their just deserts! View it or download it at www.whisperedmedia.org/piepage.html.

Pie Any Means Necessary: buy the book

This anthology cooks up an intoxicating mélange of history, analysis, tactics, and recipes for the most edible of the political direct action techniques. Tips from experienced pie-ers on the best way to slip into a shareholders meeting unobserved, ammunition in hand, blend deliciously with tried and tested recipes for delectable vegan pastries (perfect for launching, or dining upon). Generously sprinkled with some of the punchiest, wittiest communiqués explaining just why those responsible for environmental destruction might be in line for their just desserts.

...how to pie for publicity

Step 1: Get hold of a copy of *Pie Any Means Necessary: The Biotic Baking Brigade Cookbook*. Find it in bookstores, cafés, bunkers, caves, and police station lockups everywhere. Or order it straight from the publisher, AK Press: www.akpress.org.

Step 2: Choose a recipe from this or another cookbook, and bake your pie. Sloppy is good!

Step 3: Choose your target, and go for it.

people MIXING

You are probably missing out. There are interesting people everywhere, but most of us tend to stick with the groups of people we're used to. Most of us remember the way cliques or gangs formed at school, and most adults still experience them to a degree. Every group has its own territory and its own rules. Almost everyone remains locked into their small group.

The reality is that people can't really be slotted into types. One of the human race's most spectacular attributes is its phenomenal diversity. You might share the political opinions of your bank manager, or a favorite food with your boss at work. You really don't know until you ask. There may be lots of really interesting people out there whom you never get to talk to.

Some people are dedicated to mixing up their social groups. On November 16, 2004, more than 4 million students at nearly 8,000 schools across the US participated in the third annual Mix It Up at Lunch Day. They stepped out of their comfort zones to meet someone new.

So try mixing it up. Organize a day where everyone gets to meet new people. It's a great way to break down social, economic, racial, gender, ability, disability, and even age barriers. You could allocate tables according to birth month, or the first letter of last names. Break down the barriers, and you might find people have more to talk about than they realize.

Tolerance.org: www.tolerance.org/teens/lunch.jsp

Where else you can mix it up?

In bars and restaurants, make a point of sitting next to strangers and chatting with them.

At parties, go and talk to all the interesting-looking people you don't know.

Using a telephone directory, invite everyone in town with the surname Rice or Bush or whatever to meet for a drink one evening after work.

Mix It Up encourages people to cross lines and meet new faces. You want to make a difference, so start by meeting someone new.

...meet someone new

Organize a Mix It Up event:

A Mix It Up at Lunch Day.

A Mix It Up at Work for employees at your office, college, or wherever you can.

Tolerance.org has instructions on how to set up a Mix It Up Lunch. It includes e-cards to send to everyone and posters to download.

NOVEMBER 16 *International Day for Tolerance*

COOPERATION *is the key*

Anyone can make a difference and feed hungry people. Eric Samuel gave up a full-time job as a banker to fight food poverty and health inequality as a volunteer in the London borough of Newham, one of the poorest parts of the city. ✋ He started off by going to the wholesale market once a week early in the morning and getting fresh fruit and vegetables. He then sold these at a 10% markup. Eric has now created a whole network of food projects in the area through the Newham Food Access Partnership.

Eric's food programs have spread. His food access programs include food co-ops (with 14,000 customers), breakfast clubs (serving 40,000 meals a year), free fruit for primary school children, fruit snack shops, lunch clubs, and fruit delivery services. ✋ While Eric has been encouraging food access, he has also been developing a sustainable social enterprise, which aims to alleviate food poverty, create local jobs, and enable the community to play an active role in improving its health.

All this started with one man in a borrowed van getting up early to go to market!

Cooperatives are businesses based on collective ownership. Instead of having an a partnership of directors, the executive decisions are handled by a team.

Cooperatives can be an extremely difficult business model to start up, but once up and running often prove a superior decision-making body than other companies. A cooperative aims to trade fairly with its customers. Profit is rarely a primary aim.

You could set up an informal cooperative buying group for you and your friends or neighbors. You'll get fresher fruits and vegetables a whole lot cheaper, because you will be buying from the market at wholesale prices.

...to decent living

✋ **Get a group of people together** who would like to join the co-op, and make a list of the things that everybody seems to want.

✋ **Go and buy from the wholesale market** (or you could buy direct from a local farmer). Everyone gets what they ordered, and everyone contributes their share of the cost.

✋ **Next month another person from the group will go and do the buying.** Everyone will take their turn doing this. Everyone has to do something for the group. Everyone will benefit.

To start with, just buy a few boxes of the things that are in season. As the scheme develops, you can decide to expand the range of the things you buy. Shopping will never be the same again!

pay it FORWARD

Pay It Forward, a Hollywood movie inspired by a book by Catherine Ryan Hyde, has now become a movement.

In the movie, which starred Kevin Spacey and Helen Hunt, twelve-year-old Trevor is living in Las Vegas, alongside hookers, homeless people, and addicts in a wasteland of rundown motels and shanty houses. The teacher challenges Trevor's class to come up with ideas to make the world a better place. Trevor's idea is a "pay it forward" pyramid scheme, which will start a chain reaction of good deeds and random acts of kindness throughout the community.

The essence of the "pay it forward" idea is altruism. Do something for someone else without any expectation of gain or reward... and the act may change your whole perspective on life. And those who receive can in turn find a way of paying back what they have received by paying it forward—spreading the ethos of voluntarism.

The Pay It Forward Movement website has lots of examples of inspiring projects and people who are paying it forward. Join them, and share your experience on the website.

www.payitforwardmovement.org

The Extreme Kindness Tour

The Extreme Kindness Tour was a three-month marathon to connect the world through kindness. In 2002, four friends set off in one motor home to commit random acts of kindness in as many Canadian communities as they could manage. They knocked on people's doors offering to cook dinner, dragged office workers out for a game of hockey during the coffee break, and entertained kids at the children's hospital. This was "Kindness 24/7." They were the "Kindness Crew." www.extremekindness.com

...save the world with kindness

Commit an act of kindness. Do something for someone else today. Not necessarily someone you know, but perhaps a complete stranger whom most likely you'll never see again. Or it could be something for your partner to let him or her know you don't take your relationship for granted.

Pay it forward. It's a movement; it could become a way of life. It could take only 30 seconds, but the effect could last a lifetime!

There are hundreds of things you could do. Here are some to start you thinking:

👫 Shovel someone's driveway.

👫 Buy a homeless person lunch.

👫 Whenever you pass a playground or area where kids play, drop some coins. Do you remember how excited you were when you found coins?

👫 If you know people who are having a hard time financially, put a $5, $10, or $20 bill in an envelope, and mail it to them anonymously. They'll talk about it for weeks, remember it forever, and wonder who sent it.

👫 Offer to babysit so parents can have some time to themselves.

👫 Start up a conversation with a stranger. You might find that you have a lot in common.

STOP *child pornography*

The Internet can be a dangerous place for children. 🐾 A research group at the University of Cork collected more than 50,000 child pornography pictures via the Internet over a two-year period. There were about 2,000 children involved in these pictures. On average, two children, not previously seen, were added each week. 🐾 Perhaps up to 70–80% of these pictures are as much as 30 years old. For the children forced to participate, this violation continues as long as the pictures circulate. It is like a rape that never ends.

Complaints about child pornography are on the increase. Between 1997 and 1998, Save the Children Sweden received three tip-offs. The following year the number rose to more than 700. New sources of Internet child pornography include Russia, Romania, the Baltic states, and the Czech Republic. Live webcasting of sexual acts involving children is now being reported. All indications are that Internet use will increase, and that the problem of child pornography will grow with it.

Pedophile organizations and networks are becoming more daring and cunning in using the Internet. They use it not only to display images of children but also to make contact with children through chat rooms. 🐾 Police appear to lack the resources to deal adequately with the problem—despite the fact that the distribution of pornography in any form is illegal virtually everywhere.

Radda Barnen's Child Pornography Hotline: www.rb.se/hotline/ehome.htm

In Sweden 53 pedophiles created a net community whereby members could post photographs and film clips in categorized archives. There was also a message site and a chat room, where members could discuss pictures and fantasies and exchange images. The members used only nicknames and anonymous e-mail addresses.

A technical oversight by the group allowed an intruder to listen in to members' exchanges. This person tipped off the Child Pornography Hotline, and the police were able to investigate, gather evidence, and take action.

The pictures and film clips on view in the room were hard-core child rapes involving children as young as four years old and even a three-month-old baby.

The pedophiles included an unemployed twenty-seven-year-old, a university faculty head, and a female farmworker.

...police the net

Support the campaign. Save the Children Sweden (*Radda Barnen* in Swedish) is campaigning to end the use of the Internet as a marketplace for child pornography.

🐾 **Join them in their fight against child pornography on the Internet.** They need our help.

🐾 **Report any instances of child pornography** on the Internet you come across.

rights for CHILDREN

Of the world's population, 2.2 billion are people under 18. Almost all of these are protected by the Convention on the Rights of the Child, apart from the 80 million children who live in Somalia and the US, neither of which has signed the convention.

The convention was launched on November 20, 1989, with these basic ideas:

Every child has the right to have his or her basic needs fulfilled.

Every child has the right to protection from abuse and exploitation.

Every child has the right to express his or her opinion and be respected.

Some important children's rights:

The right to have a name and be registered as a citizen in your home country. *Of 132 million born each year, 53 million children are never registered. There is no written proof that they exist.*

The right to a home, food, clothing, education, health care, and security. *Around 600 million children live on less than $1 a day, 900 million on less than $2. Three-quarters of the world's children are very poor.*

The right to be protected from economic exploitation and against work that damages health or prevents the child from going to school. Children under 12 years may not work at all. *Over 100 million children under 12 do work: 90% of these are involved in harmful work; 9 million are enslaved; 1.2 million are sold each year as merchandise.*

The right to go to school. Elementary school should be free of charge to all. *Over 113 million children never begin school, 60% of these being girls. Around 150 million children leave school before the fifth grade.*

The World Children's Prize: www.childrensworld.org
Information on the Convention on the Rights of the Child: www.unicef.org/crc

The World Children's Prize for the Rights of the Child (WCPRC)

The WCPRC invites all schools and children to be part of the world's largest annual forum and educational program about the rights of the child, democracy, and global friendship.

The WCPRC has one unusual feature. Only children can vote to choose the laureates. In 2005, 2.3 million votes were cast from 7,821 schools and young people's groups in 73 countries.

Past laureates have included

Maggy Barankitse (Burundi), for child welfare work.
Barefoot College and Children's Parliament (Rajasthan, India), where the prime minister is just 12 years old.
James Aguer Alic (Sudan), for fighting to free slave children.
Nelson Mandela (South Africa) and **Graça Machel** (Mozambique).

Hear their inspiring stories on the WCPRC website.

...defend them

Enlist your local school or young people's group as a Global Friend of WCPRC. They will then receive the prize magazine (which, as well as the prize website, is published in nine languages) and can vote from January to April for the person or group who has done the most for children's rights.

TV-FREE *zone*

Bhutan is a Buddhist sanctuary, a refuge from the world and its ills. In the 1930s all that was known of Bhutan in the western world was what could be gleaned from James Hilton's novel, *Lost Horizon*. He called Bhutan "Shangri-La." ✊ The king of Bhutan decided that, as a spiritual society, Bhutan recognized happiness as the most important thing, and in 1998, he defined Bhutan's key aim as "Gross National Happiness."

Bhutan was the last country in the world to introduce TV. It arrived in 2002, with 46 cable channels. This has thrown Bhutan headlong into the global culture of the 21st century. Everyone underestimated the impact that TV would have on local life and culture. One-third of Bhutan's girls now want to look more American (whiter skin, blond hair). A similar proportion of girls also aspire to a new approach to relationships (boyfriends not husbands, and sex before marriage).

An editorial in a Bhutanese newspaper warns, "We are seeing for the first time broken families, school dropouts and other negative youth crimes. We are beginning to see crime associated with drug users all over the world, shoplifting, burglary and violence." Swapping Gross National Happiness for the joys of *Big Brother*, *Baywatch*, and *I'm a Celebrity, Get Me Out of Here*, may not be such a good thing after all.

The TV-Turnoff Network encourages children and adults to watch less television in order to create healthier lives and communities. www.tvturnoff.org

White Dot is an international campaign against TV. Read their survival guide "Get a Life" for what to do after you've turned your TV off. www.whitedot.org

TV-B-Gone: www.tvbgone.com

Technology to the rescue

TV-B-Gone is a universal remote control device that hangs on your key chain. It enables you to "turn off virtually any television" at home or in a public place from a distance of about 45 feet. Point, press, keep pointing for just over a minute. It's that easy. Launched in October 2004, the TV-B-Gone device was sold out in just two days, and the suppliers have been battling to keep up with demand ever since.

It must have been a useful tool in late April 2005, when TV-Turnoff Week was celebrated in countries as far apart as the US and Australia, the UK and Brazil.

...turn off the box

Spend less time watching TV. American children spend more time each year in front of the television (1,023 hours) than in school (900 hours). A recent survey showed that children spend an average of three hours a day in front of TV. Adults are also "glued to the box."

✊ **Turn off your TV.** Reduce your viewing by 50% for starters. Later, consider reducing the number of TVs in your home to just one.

✊ **Think about what you could do with all this extra free time...**talk, exercise, change the world?

say THANK YOU

Giving thanks is traditionally associated with autumn. Throughout history and all over the world, people have celebrated the harvest each autumn with some sort of thanksgiving ceremony. ❧ Demeter, the ancient Greek goddess of grain, was thanked at the festival of Thesmosphoria. On the first day of autumn, married women built leafy shelters. The second day was a fast day, and the third was a feast with offerings to Demeter. ❧ The Romans had Cerelia on October 4, when the fruits of the harvest were offered up to Ceres. Cerelia was celebrated with music, parades, games, and a feast.

The Chinese harvest festival is Chung Ch'ui, held at full moon in the eighth month. This is the moon's birthday, celebrated with special moon cakes, stamped with a picture of a rabbit (the Chinese see a rabbit, not a man, in the moon). ❧ The harvest festival of the Jews is called Sukkoth, the feast of tabernacles. They build small huts out of branches and foliage, which are decorated with the fruits of the harvest. ❧ Thanksgiving commemorates the first year in the New World of the founding Pilgrims, and a harvest that was plentiful. This is a day of family get-togethers and turkey dinners.

Find out about Tim Berners-Lee: www.w3.org/People/Berners-Lee

Health-care achievements in the 20th century to be thankful for:

Antibiotics, vaccines, and anesthetics, which have transformed medicine.

Insulin, which saves the lives of diabetics.

Antiretroviral drugs, which mean that those with HIV don't need to die of AIDS.

The understanding of malaria, which means that it can be treated.

The Human Genome project, which has the potential to eliminate hereditary disease.

...count your blessings

Thanksgiving is a great day to say "Thank you." In every area of human endeavor, you will find things that have made life much better. Today's the day to reflect on all that's good in the world.

👫 **Say thank you to all your funders and supporters.** To be good at fund raising, you need to build good relationships with those who give you their money or time. This means thanking them nicely. Keep in touch; tell them what you have been able to achieve with their help; share your successes. Today, tell them how much you value their support.

👫 **And say a special thank-you to Tim Berners-Lee.** Tim devised the World Wide Web, one of the great ideas of the 20th century, which has profoundly changed all our lives.

STICK,_{'em up}

A bath and a washing machine both use 20 gallons of water, a power shower uses 18, a dishwasher 9, flushing a toilet $2\frac{1}{2}$. A garden hose will use 115 gallons an hour. This water is delivered to your door. It's high-quality stuff too, clean enough to drink. It's usually available on demand. And although you may be charged for the amount you use, it's almost free. This is amazing when you consider that people in other parts of the world may need to walk several miles each day to get a few gallons from the local water source.

Turning off the tap should be a reflex action. But people often forget to do it. They leave the water running when they are brushing their teeth, when they are staring at themselves in the mirror, when they are combing their hair...or even after they have left the bathroom. This is a waste of a precious commodity— especially in long hot summers or in areas where demand is threatening to exceed supply. The same is true for turning off the lights when you leave a room. It's so basic, but your laziness or forgetfulness will translate into higher electricity bills, more pollution, and more greenhouse gases contributing to global warming.

Sticker slogans

To put next to taps:

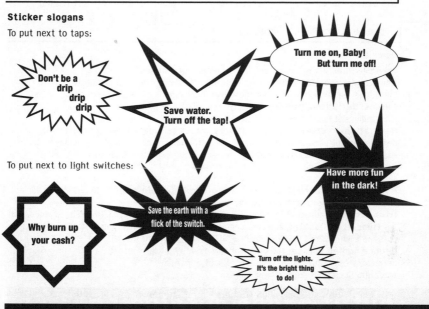

To put next to light switches:

...and turn them off

Make some stickers. Buy a pack of large blank labels. Cut them into interesting shapes. Think up some provocative slogans and use marker pens (non-water-soluble will be best for obvious reasons) to write and illustrate your slogans.

Put them next to taps and light switches as a reminder to everyone (including yourself).

Put your stickers up at home, at work, and in public places.

information is POWER

The Open Directory describes itself as "the Republic of the Web." The project is the largest, most comprehensive human-edited directory of the Internet. It is constructed and maintained by a global community of volunteer editors.

The World Wide Web continues to grow at staggering rates. In fact, growth is such that automated search engines are increasingly unable to turn up useful results to search queries. So, instead of fighting the explosive growth of the Internet, the Open Directory provides a means for the Internet to organize itself.
  ♪ Volunteer editors each organize a small section, culling out the bad and the useless, and keeping only the best content.

So far the Open Directory has cataloged over 4 million websites: 590,000 categories in 76 languages, using 66,849 editors. Just as the *Oxford English Dictionary* became the definitive book on words through the efforts of volunteers, the Open Directory aims to become the definitive catalog of the web.
  ♪ The Open Directory has been founded in the spirit of the open source movement. It is free. There is no cost for submitting a site to the directory, and use of the directory's data is free, subject to terms of the Copyleft license.

Open Directory Project: dmoz.org

Damn it!
The Open Directory has eight entries in English for "Curses":
Breaking curses from our lives; biblical curses, how they affect the lives of Christians, and how to be free of them. www.bible.com/answers/acurses.html
Curses: Definition, history, modern usage.
www.themystica.com/mystica/articles/c/curses.html
Generational curses, sins of the fathers; curses carrying down a family line, with descriptions of various types of curses: hometown.aol.com/godswaitn/genealgy/index.htm
Global psychics, the truth about curses; fraudulent scenarios by unethical practitioners claiming to remove curses for cash: www.globalpsychics.com/lp/Tips/curses.htm
Gypsy curses incorporated; free random curses or individually tailored curses for a fee: members.tripod.com/~Curses_Inc
Irish curses, traditional Irish curses: www.ncf.carleton.ca/~bj333/HomePage.curses.html
An tinneall Mallachtai, the curse engine; choose from English phrases to generate a curse in Irish: hermes.lincolnu.edu/~focal/scripts/mallacht.htm
Understanding curses; the effect of curses in a biblical context: hermes.lincolnu.edu/~focal/scripts/mallacht.htm. Also dmoz.org/Society/Folklore/Magic/Curses/

...but it needs cataloging

  ♪ **Join the Open Directory Project.** Apply to become an editor using the form on the website. Editors select, evaluate, describe, and organize the websites to be included in the directory. Indicate a category that corresponds with your interests.
  ♪ **All you need is an interest in the subject area**, plus a computer, and a genuine interest in building a global directory that is objective in its outlook and free from commercial interests.

NOVEMBER 24

DEFEND *yourself*

There are all sorts of situations where we may be in physical danger of attack—whether it is a mugging, a sexual assault, or simply a random act of violence, and whether we are in Houston or Harare, Moscow or Manila.

Girls are particularly vulnerable to assault. In the US:
Women and girls represent 86% of all victims of sexual violence.
Children 6–17 years old account for 53% of all victims of sexual assaults.
A young woman is at greatest risk of sexual assault at age 14.
40% of all young people have witnessed violence.

These startling facts should shock us all into finding ways to create safer lives for ourselves, our families, and our communities. We need to understand the threats and the best course of action in a violent situation. We need to think about acquiring basic self-defense skills, which will help to conquer fear and boost our confidence.

Girls' Leap, a community program to help girls understand and deal with violence: www.girlsleap.org
AWARE: arming women against rape and endangerment: www.aware.org

Question 1: You are walking to your car in a deserted parking area after working late one evening, and you hear someone behind you quickly approaching. You realize that they can reach you before you can get to your car. What would you do?

a Don't look back, walk faster, try to get into your car before they reach you.
b Put your hand on whatever defensive tool you are carrying, turn your head so you can see who is approaching.
c Stop and turn around, pull out a weapon if you are carrying one.

Question 2: You are on a long drive and stop at a fast-food restaurant late at night. When you return to your car in the deserted parking lot, you encounter a man with a knife in his hand who orders you to go with him. What would you do?

a Scream.
b Cooperate with him and look for an opportunity to escape.
c Try to talk him out of it.
d Refuse to go with him and resist in the strongest way possible.
e Pretend to faint.

Find the answers at: www.aware.org/quizzes/quizindex.shtml

...learn martial arts

❌ **Answer the questions above.** Think carefully about what's the best course of action. One day you might find yourself in a similar situation.

❌ **Download and photocopy the four "Fighting Back" posters** on self-defense for women and girls published by *the F word*, an online magazine on feminist issues: www.thefword.org.uk/static/fightingback/page1

stop SPENDING

About 20% of the world consumes over 80% of the world's natural resources. This is in part because we buy so much stuff we don't need. World Buy Nothing Day is when "you can turn the economy off and talk about it." ⚽ Buy Nothing Day gives you a breather to think about whether you need to buy the things you feel you need. It will focus your mind on the environmental and ethical consequences of consumption: whom you buy from and whether they are socially responsible businesses.

Buy Nothing Day is held near the end of November each year. There is only one rule: don't spend a single penny all day for the whole day. It all started with No Shop Day in 1994, organized by Ted Dave, a Canadian advertising executive, as a collective protest against the unrelenting calls to overconsume.

These are some of the things that people do to support Buy Nothing Day:
    Ask friends to bring stuff to swap.
    Create a shopping-free zone, hanging out with friends in a public space.

World Buy Nothing Day: www.ecoplan.org/ibnd/ib_index.htm
Buy Nothing Christmas: www.buynothingchristmas.org
Adbusters: www.adbusters.org/metas/eco/bnd

And some more things to do instead of buying:

    Turn your cellphone off and chill out.

    Go to the top of a tall building and look at the view.

    Paint your fridge or washing machine a bright color.

    Collect wild food: windfall apples, blackberries, mushrooms.

    Have a bath in candlelight.

    Learn to count up to ten in ten languages.

    Grow your own beansprouts.

    Go out in the evening and look for bats.

    Take up jogging.

    Take your toaster apart and try to fix it.

...buy nothing for a day

⚽ **Buy nothing on Buy Nothing Day.** Throw a Buy Nothing Day Party. Spend the whole of the day with friends instead of spending hard-earned cash.

⚽ **Read Judith Levine's account of her year without spending,** *Not Buying It.*

DEFEND *your right*

Our liberty depends on the freedom of the press, and that cannot be limited without being lost.

—Thomas Jefferson

The Thomas Jefferson Center exists for one purpose: to defend freedom of expression. They have no political agenda and no backdoor aims. They exist so that we can all have the freedom to say what we want.

Every April 13, on Thomas Jefferson's birthday, the center releases the Muzzle awards. These awards direct attention to individuals or organizations that have committed particularly heinous affronts to the freedom of expression.

Read about the recipients of the Jefferson Muzzle awards. Learn how organizations such as CBS, the US Secret Service, and the US Department of Defense have impeded your freedom of expression.

It is not just activists who suffer under the tyranny of censorship. It could be anybody and everybody: the 14-year-old boy who is forbidden to wear an antiestablishment T-shirt to school, and is forced to change his clothes... the family that turns on their TV each night, not realizing that the news they watch has been censored, sometimes very crudely, sometimes in a much more sophisticated way... the cartoonist who has a political cartoon published and finds a Secret Service agent at his front door that evening... anyone in the US who falls under the jurisdiction of the US Patriot Act.

Anyone who wants to write, publish, or say what he or she thinks could be facing the danger of censorship. Anyone who wants to read the truth may be reading "the truth that they want you to know."

www.tjcenter.org/muzzles.html

Muzzling in the Big Apple

Staten Island resident Terence Hunter heard that a local community center was going to be closed. He wrote a letter of protest to an elected official. The letter was highly critical of the official, claiming that the closing of the center in an area with a significant African-American population showed the official was a "bigot" and a "Jim Crow" politician "who would approve things like this." Attached were photographs of lynchings of African-American men copied from a book.

Two days later, five police officers took Hunter to the precinct house, where he was questioned about the letter. After several hours' interrogation, he was charged with aggravated harassment, arrested, handcuffed, fingerprinted, and had his shoelaces and the drawstring from his sweatpants removed. He was then placed in a cell with another prisoner who forced him to stand against the cell wall. After standing for some time, he collapsed, and an ambulance had to be called.

Next morning, shackled to other prisoners, he was driven to the Staten Island Criminal Court. The district attorney's office reviewed the case and decided not to prosecute. Hunter was released but had to walk back to the precinct to retrieve his apartment keys, holding his pants up the entire distance.

A subsequent internal police investigation concluded that the arrest had been a mistake. The First Amendment permits citizens to criticize their elected representatives without fear of government sanction. In this incident the authorities completely disregarded this fundamental right.

...to speak your mind

If you know of an act of censorship that is serious enough to merit a Jefferson Muzzle award, send your nomination in to the Thomas Jefferson Center.

freedom of EXPRESSION

Writers have a critical role to play in countries where freedom of expression is denied. They can write about what's happening and get their writings smuggled out and published in the free world. But if they remain true to their convictions and write the truth, they lay themselves open to imprisonment.

Alexander Solzhenitsyn, Nobel Prize–winning author of *One Day in the Life of Ivan Denisovich* and *The Gulag Archipelago*, was the first to bring to the world's attention the scale and barbarism of the gulag system in the Soviet Union. He had been imprisoned and exiled in his country for many years and was eventually allowed to seek refuge in the US.

Václav Havel, a prominent Czech playwright, spoke out against Soviet oppression. The publication of his plays was banned, and he spent five years in prison because he had cofounded Charter 77 and was a member of the Committee for the Defense of the Unjustly Prosecuted. In 1989 he was elected his country's first post-Communist president.

Writers need to speak out. It is important to show solidarity with those who do, and who are imprisoned for doing so. PEN is an international campaign against the persecution and imprisonment of writers anywhere in the world. PEN has 130 branches in over 100 countries.

PEN American Center: www.pen.org
International PEN: www.internationalpen.org.uk

Raul Rivero Castañeda, poet and journalist, founded the independent news agency Cuba Press in 1995. Together with nine others he called on Castro to free prisoners of conscience and reform the socialist regime. In April 2003 he was charged with "crimes against the state" and given a 20-year sentence, following a one-day trial for which he was given insufficient time to put together a proper defense. He was released in November 2004, after being transferred from prison to a military hospital.

Naushad Waheed, cyberdissident and a prominent artist in the Maldives, has been an outspoken critic of his government for many years. His most recent arrest took place in 2001. He was then held in detention for about five months before being transferred to house arrest. In October 2002, he was tried without access to a lawyer or the opportunity to defend himself, and was sentenced to 15 years imprisonment. In an account smuggled out of jail, Waheed describes the horrific scenes of torture inflicted on himself and others.

...support writers' rights

Join the campaign.

- **PEN organizes a Writers in Prison campaign.** Each month one writer is featured. Find out as much as you can about that writer by searching on the web. Go to www.amazon.com, and see if any of that writer's books are available. If so, order copies. Read as an act of solidarity.

- **Join PEN's Rapid Response Network** to campaign against the oppression of writers.

NOVEMBER 28

PALESTINIAN *olive oil*

Olive oil is the backbone of the Palestinian agricultural economy. Since the 2000 Intifada, farmers have encountered enormous difficulties in picking their olives. Some cannot reach their fields without a special permit, as they are cut off by the so-called "separation wall" (the barrier the Israelis are building between Israel and Palestine). In other villages, the olive groves are near Jewish settlements, and access is hazardous or impossible.

The Israeli Occupation is devastating the lives of many Palestinians, who depend on olives for a living. Ironically, the olive branch is a symbol of peace in a region where olive picking is wracked by conflict. ✹ As part of the Olive Picking Coalition, 255 peace activists from the Gush Shalom peace movement (in Hebrew, this means "the Peace Bloc") took part in the olive picking at Yassouf and Jama'een villages in Palestine. The villagers feared harassment by the settlers of neighboring Tapuakh and that dogs would be set on them.

Gush Shalom staged a peaceful protest. Together, the families who own the groves and the peace activists shook the trees and climbed to the highest branches, while talking in a mixture of Hebrew, Arabic, and English. The olives were collected on nylon sheets, put into sacks, and taken away by tractor.

Gush Shalom: www.gush-shalom.org/english/index.html

Holy Land Olive Oil sells Palestinian extra-virgin olive oil in the US and Canada: www.palestineoliveoil.org

Gush Shalom members want to see:

An end to the Israeli occupation.

An acceptance of the right of the Palestinian people to establish an independent state in all of the territory occupied by Israel since 1967 (with possible minor exchanges of territories agreed between the parties).

Jerusalem as the capital of both states, united physically for municipal governance.

A recognition of the right of Palestinian refugees to return, allowing each refugee to choose freely between compensation and repatriation, with a fixed annual quota for those able to return to Israel.

The security of both peoples, ensured by mutual agreement and guarantees.

An overall peace between Israel and all Arab countries, and the creation of a regional union.

...buy it in solidarity

✹ **Buy olive oil from Palestine**. Holy Land Olive Oil imports oil from five Palestinian cooperatives; some is organic. Help the olive growers earn an income. Find out more about the olive oil industry and Palestinian politics.

✹ **Go olive picking in Palestine** next October with Gush Shalom.

support LOCAL ARTISANS

Robib in rural Cambodia is six small villages, with a total population of 4,000. The annual average income per person is around $40. The villagers harvest rice once a year, and this barely feeds their families. There is no surplus to sell. In bad years or when there is a flood, there is not even enough food to go around.
⚜ Robib has a health center but there is a shortage of medicine. Seriously ill patients have no access to expert medical care, so little chance of survival. Like most of rural Cambodia, Robib's population is vulnerable to malaria, TB, and some tropical diseases. AIDS, which is growing uncontrollably in the larger urban centers, has not yet hit Robib because of its isolation.

Bernard Krisher, a 69-year-old former journalist, has brought IT to Robib. A satellite link was provided free by the Thai company Shin Satellite. The dish provides a continuous 64,000-bits-per-second connection to a small group of computers in the village, which are run for part of each day using solar power.
⚜ In addition to providing computer education and Internet access to the school (attended by 400 students), the project has brought telemedicine to the village, using doctors in Boston.

Krisher is showing how the Internet can really help a single village. His American Assistance for Cambodia program has also constructed 200 rural schools, using matching funds from the World Bank. ⚜ Villagers have been trained in traditional weaving skills, which vanished during the Pol Pot years. Silk scarves and table runners are now produced. The hotel in Tokyo where Krisher lives processes credit-card purchases made from the village website.

American Assistance for Cambodia: www.cambodiaschools.com
Robib Village Website: www.villageleap.com
Arts and crafts from Ghana: www.eShopAfrica.com
Arts and crafts from Novica, which is run in association with National Geographic: www.novica.com

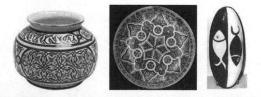

...via the web

Next time you want to give someone a present,
⚜ Buy a silk scarf from Robib.
⚜ Or buy a product from another website linking producers with consumers.

AIDS *is preventable*

AIDS is a global challenge. It is having a huge impact on the world's most vulnerable and poorest people. The HIV virus infects 13,500 people every day, swelling the total number infected with HIV to 37.2 million adults and 2.2 million children at the end of 2004. ● Of these people, 95% live in the developing world. ● In 2004, 3.1 million people died of AIDS, which means that, on average, somebody died every 10 seconds; 25 million people have died since AIDS was first diagnosed in 1981, 6 million of whom were children. More than 15 million children have been orphaned by AIDS.

There is hope for the future. The political will exists. The resources are there. Medicines that inhibit new infections now allow many to survive with the disease, and they are becoming more affordable through pressure on the drug companies and the wider availability of generic drugs. ● The UN has set up UNAIDS to encourage global action, and the Global Fund to mobilize funds. The Apathy Is Lethal campaign promotes awareness and encourages action. You can

Educate yourself to better understand the disease, and what you can do to minimize the risk to yourself.

Educate others as to what actions they can take on a personal level.

Volunteer with an AIDS organization—providing anything from office help to buddying. Raise funds for the global effort.

Apathy Is Lethal: www.apathyislethal.org
United Nations Program on HIV/AIDS: www.unaids.org
AVERT has a useful website: www.avert.org

Major challenges

Women account for 57% of the people living with HIV in sub-Saharan Africa, largely as a result of gender inequality, sexual violence, and ignorance.

Young people (aged 15 to 24) account for nearly half of all new HIV infection worldwide.

Prevention programs currently reach only 1 in 5 people at risk of infection.

Only 1 in 10 pregnant women in poorer countries is offered services for preventing mother-to-child HIV transmission.

Antiretroviral treatment is available for only 7% of the people who need it in developing countries: a total of 400,000 people at the end of 2003.

...apathy is lethal

Erase the tax on condoms. The high price of condoms acts as a disincentive to consistent use, particularly for at-risk groups and young people. Condoms can be obtained free of charge from your health-care provider.

have another CHOCOLATE

When people eat chocolate, they are eating my flesh.

—Drissa, a child slave in Côte d'Ivoire

Child slaves may have made your chocolate. According to the television program, *Slavery*, made for the BBC by Kate Blewett and Brian Woods of True Vision, thousands of children in Central and West Africa are being stolen from their parents, shipped to the Ivory Coast, and sold as slaves to cocoa farmers. These children earn no money for their work and are barely fed. They are beaten if they try to escape, and most will never see their families again. Nearly 50% of the world's cocoa supply is grown in the Ivory Coast.

Steven Millman saw the television program and was so appalled he had to act:

Suddenly I could taste every bit of chocolate I'd ever eaten in my life, a taste so sour at the thought that child slaves had produced it that I thought I would vomit. Since then I've done some research to see where chocolate might safely be purchased, and I decided to make that information available to the world.

This information takes two forms. First, I've written over 200 letters to many of the world's great chocolate manufacturers to find out who is making sure that their chocolate has no slavery involved and I am posting their responses. Second, I have compiled a links page with relevant information about news sources and organizations.

Steven Millman's website: www.radicalthought.org
True Vision website: www.truevisiontv.com/

How to avoid slave chocolate

This is the letter that Steven sent to over 200 chocolate manufacturers:

Hi! There has been a ton of information in the news over the last few months about the child slavery used in the harvesting of cocoa in the Ivory Coast. I love your chocolates, but I can't bear the thought of eating chocolate made by child slaves. Do you guys do anything to ensure that no child slavery is used in the production of your cocoa?

Thanks, Steven

All replies and the names of companies that didn't reply are posted on Steven's website.

...but be sure it's slave-free

Go to Steven's website: www.radicalthought.org.

- **Click on the Companies Page** to find out whose chocolate is made with child slavery. Don't eat it. One easy way of being sure of purchasing slave-free chocolate is to buy chocolate made organically. There are no organic farms in the areas where slavery is used. Any chocolate bearing a "Fair trade" or "Max Havelaar" logo will also be free of slavery.

- **If you are inspired by what Steven did,** then do something similar about an issue close to your heart.

DISABILITY *access*

It is part of a modern, humane society that people with physical disabilities should have proper access to the offices they might work in, the public buildings they might need to visit, the events they might wish to attend, and the streets and public transportation they might wish to use. ⊗ The Graphic Artists Guild Foundation in New York designed 12 symbols that can be used to promote and publicize accessibility of spaces and activities for people with a range of disabilities. These include

An event or location accessible to people who are blind or have low vision.

Accessible to people with limited mobility, including wheelchair users: step-free access, disabled toilets, and low public phones.

AD)))) Audio description at performances for people who are blind or have low vision.

Availability of a text telephone.

Amplified listening systems, such as loop systems to amplify sound via hearing aids.

Large Print Large print books, pamphlets, guides, and programs for the visually impaired.

Availability of telephones for the hard of hearing.

OC Open Captioning, where captions are available all the time.

Braille Availability of printed material in Braille.

Symbols can be downloaded from www.gag.org/resources/das.php.

...it's a basic right

⊗ **Download these symbols** and print them onto sticker paper.

⊗ **Design a second version** with a diagonal red bar superimposed on the symbol contained within a red circle to indicate that these facilities are **NOT** available, but should be made available in order to provide disability access.

⊗ **Use your stickers to praise good practice** and publicize a lack of proper access.

More than 250 million children are working illegally in the world today. Some work because they have to earn money to survive, others because they are forced to: their parents may have sold them into bonded labor, for example.

The hand-knotted carpet industry is a major user of child labor. It is estimated that at least 500,000 children in South Asia are involved in producing hand-knotted carpets, which are then sold all over the world. Many are working more than twelve hours a day for an absolute pittance and are being denied both an education and a childhood.

The Rugmark Foundation has been working to end child labor in the South Asian carpet industry by persuading loom owners and factories to end the practice, by developing consumer labeling for carpets made without child labor, and by encouraging carpet exporters and importers to trade only in carpets that are free of child labor. The Rugmark label offers an assurance that a carpet is not produced by children.

www.rugmark.org

Laws against child labor

The International Labour Organisation adopted a Minimum Age Convention in 1973, which binds ratifying countries to pursue a national policy for the abolition of child labor and to work toward a minimum age for employment of fifteen years old. In 1999, the ILO adopted a Worst Forms of Child Labour Convention, which calls for immediate and effective measures to prohibit and eliminate the worst forms of child labor. "Child" applies to all persons under the age of eighteen. "The worst forms of child labor" refers to child slavery, forced labor, trafficking, debt bondage, serfdom, prostitution, pornography, and forms of work that harm the health, safety, or morals of children. India has not yet ratified either convention.

At the age of six, Laxmi Shresta was rescued from a Nepali carpet factory by a Rugmark inspector who found her balling wool on the factory floor. Rugmark now pays for her education. She is studying English, Nepali, math, and science. She loves drawing and, aged ten, dreams of being an artist. You will be helping children like Laxmi fulfill their dreams if you purchase a Rugmark carpet.

...help stamp out child labor

Send this letter to your local carpet store. If you don't get a reply, telephone. If the response is unsatisfactory, think what else you might do.

Dear Store Manager:

I am concerned about the widespread use of children in the carpet-making industry, which is completely illegal under international law. I want to do what I can to end this practice.

Could you please tell me if all the carpets on sale at your store are child-labor free? One way of determining this is if they carry the Rugmark label, which guarantees that no child labor has been used in making the carpet.

Child labor in carpet manufacture will only be ended if consumers like me and retailers such as you insist on buying only carpets that are guaranteed to be child-labor free. I hope you will play your part in trying to end child labor.

Yours sincerely,

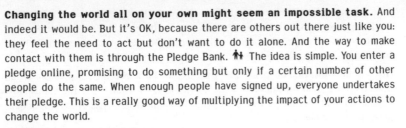

Changing the world all on your own might seem an impossible task. And indeed it would be. But it's OK, because there are others out there just like you: they feel the need to act but don't want to do it alone. And the way to make contact with them is through the Pledge Bank. ♦♦ The idea is simple. You enter a pledge online, promising to do something but only if a certain number of other people do the same. When enough people have signed up, everyone undertakes their pledge. This is a really good way of multiplying the impact of your actions to change the world.

Tips for successful pledges:

> **Keep your ambitions modest.** Why ask for fifty people when five would be enough? Every extra person makes your pledge harder to meet.
>
> **Think about how your pledge reads.** Will an outsider understand it? Read it to someone else. If that person doesn't understand it, you'll need to rewrite it.
>
> **Make your pledge imaginative,** worthwhile, fun, and reasonably easy to complete.
>
> **Don't imagine that your pledge will sell itself.** Tell the world. E-mail your friends, print leaflets, and stick them through your neighbors' doors. Get some publicity in the local newspaper.

Pledge Bank: www.pledgebank.com

Some examples of successful pledges:

Jeff edited 100 pages for Project Gutenberg (www.pgdp.net) once 50 other people had agreed to do the same.

Andy installed low-energy long-life bulbs throughout his house once 20 other people had agreed to do the same.

Matthew bought only fair-trade tea, coffee, and chocolate bars during July 2005 once 20 other people had agreed.

Ellie did all her shopping locally and not in a supermarket chain in July 2005, along with 20 other people.

Find out why these things are the secret of a successful pledge

Tom wrote to his congressperson asking for wireless internet access to be provided at his local library, and 200 other people pledged to write to their representatives with the same request.

Other pledge requests include displaying posters on "How TB kills 1,500 Africans a day" in your car, planting 10 trees to offset your carbon dioxide emissions, giving 1% of your gross annual salary to charity, refusing to register for an ID card but pledging $20 to a legal defense fund, switching to green electricity, and cleaning up a river bank.

...but only if others do too

♦♦ **Pledge to do something to change the world.** Put your pledge on Pledge Bank. Persuade family, friends, colleagues, and complete strangers to sign up. Achieve your target by the cutoff date.

♦♦ I will...*(enter your pledge)*, but only if...*(enter number)* of other people will do the same. The other people must sign up before *(enter date by which the pledging has to be completed)*.

an edible PLAYGROUND

An edible playground or schoolyard is a wildlife garden with an edible foods theme. In a school, the pupils will help build it and maintain it. In the community, a youth organization will do this. Members will learn from their experience and enjoy the garden.

The young people can plan the garden, which might include habitat areas (such as a wildflower meadow or a pond with boggy margins), and the planting of a range of edible species (such as fruit and nut trees, wild fruiting hedges, vegetables, and herbs).

An edible playground can not only find a new use for a bit of vacant land or bring life to an asphalted area, but will also introduce nutritional and environmental issues to younger people and encourage a greater appreciation of trees and plants (and their importance to wildlife).

Community Services Unlimited, a project initiated by the Southern California Black Panthers: www.globalpanther.com/csu.shtml
Edible schoolyard: www.edibleschoolyard.org

A researcher asked a group of elementary schoolchildren what they like to eat for breakfast. "Pepperoni pizza" was a popular answer. "Okay, so what is pepperoni? Where does it come from?" Blank stares. "It falls from trees?" or "It's like a carrot?" were some of the suggestions.

In a 10-by-15-block area where these children live, there are 50 fast food restaurants and 39 liquor stores/mini-markets, but only 8 restaurants and 4 supermarkets. In addition, supermarkets in low-income, minority areas usually only carry half the types of fruits and vegetables that stores in higher-income areas carry.

Community Services Unlimited, Inc., has been building edible playgrounds in Los Angeles to teach children about health (especially obesity) and diet, and to bring a taste of nature into their lives.

The gardens use companion planting: squash plants grow next to corn, which shades the soil, and beans release nitrogen, which is essential for the corn. These three crops sustained indigenous populations in America for thousands of years. Apple trees attract hummingbirds that pollinate the garden, while the leaves of tall Chinese paulownia trees shade the crops and oxygenate the air. The garden is actually five degrees cooler than its surroundings—evidence that green space mitigates inner-city heat.

These techniques are now spreading out into the community. Private lawns and public spaces, which require a lot of watering, are being transformed into thriving sources of healthy produce. "We're educating people in nutrition, from those who use the farms, to those who buy produce in the market. And we're reconnecting them with their food."

...so good you'll want to eat it

Find a piece of vacant land. Get together a group of friends with some experience of gardening and growing vegetables. Plan an edible playground for the vacant land. Draw a picture of what it might look like. This could be a starting point for turning the land into an edible playground. Or you could just start planting fruit trees and vegetables on a part of the land; look after them and watch them grow.

DECEMBER 6

LIGHT UP *your message*

Do you want to change the world while you sleep? You can be curled up in your warm bed, dreaming of desert islands and exotic fruit cocktails complete with miniature umbrellas—and still be sending out a message to passersby. 🏠 We all have our own ideas about how to improve the state of the world. Why not write up a message in lights and hang it up outside your house or apartment?

Be as political, as fun, as serious, or as silly as you want. You are only limited by your ideas, your spelling, the space you have available, and how many lights you can afford. Change your message whenever you feel like it...or when you think up an even better slogan. 🏠 This is a great way of spreading a message in an innovative way. Don't be surprised when people all over your neighborhood pick up on your idea. Here are some ideas for messages to light up the world:

P-E-A-C-E	if you're antiwar, or just as a seasonal message
V-O-T-E	at election time
W-A-L-K--T-O--W-O-R-K	to reduce greenhouse gas emissions
S-M-I-L-E	because tomorrow will be a nice day
S-A-V-E--W-A-T-E-R	in a drought
S-M-O-K-I-N-G--K-I-L-L-S	a dear friend has just died of lung cancer
F-A-I-R--T-R-A-D-E	to support fair trade, of course
U-S-E--A--C-O-N-D-O-M	do your bit to combat HIV/AIDS

There are lots of novelty lights on sale. Try matching your lights to your message: yellow ducks for a watery theme, red chilli peppers for a particularly spicy slogan, and pink elephants to give people a laugh. Rope lights are especially easy to write with and come in a range of colors.

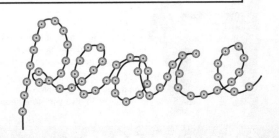

...while you sleep

🏠 **Get one or several strings of lights.**

🏠 **Spell out a message for nighttime drivers and midnight amblers to see.**

🏠 **Hang it up in your front garden**, a window, or a balcony facing the street.

7 DECEMBER

effective FUND RAISING

Fund-raisers donate their time to raise money and change the world. There are many causes worth donating to, and a number of routes to raise the cash.

1 Prepare a short talk, perhaps with a PowerPoint presentation. Contact local groups (such as the Chamber of Commerce) or the local school. Ask if they would like a speaker. Then invite the audience to support you or to raise money for you.

2 Ask your friends, family, and colleagues at work. You only need 50 people to give you $2 a week for a year, and you will have raised over $5,000. This is little more than the price of a cup of coffee. Prepare a leaflet explaining your project. Ask everyone you can think of—in person, by telephone, by e-mail, or by letter.

3 Organize a fund-raising event—party, a disco, a quiz evening, a picnic, or an outing. There are lots of ways of raising money!

4 Organize an Auction of Promises. Get people to promise to do something for you, such as babysit once a month, mow your lawn every week through the summer, or serenade a loved one's apartment. Then auction these promises at a fund-raising event.

5 Run in a marathon or cycle from one end of your state to the other. Do something that seems very difficult, and then ask people to sponsor you.

6 Make a wish list of all the things that you need, which people or companies can donate or lend to you. Think about who might have these things, and then ask them for help.

How to be a Fundraising Champion is a simple, practical, lively workbook for improving your fund-raising skills. Download it from www.millenniumcampaign.org.

Effective fund raising

To change the world you need a great idea, lots of time and energy, tenacity, and friends to help you. You will almost certainly also need money to pay the costs of your project.

First draw up a budget. Write down all the things you need. Estimate how much each will cost. Once you know how much you need, you can start raising funds.

Remember to say thank you to all your supporters. Report back on progress. If your project is going well, then people might be happy to give you more support next time you ask.

...how to do it

Raise some money today.

👫 **Set yourself a target.** This could be $10 or $50 or $500.

👫 **Think of who might be interested in giving.** Then find a way of asking them.

👫 **Make people so excited by your project** that they want to help you.

DECEMBER 8

PRESERVE *material culture*

To understand the present, it is important to know about the past. We can learn about it through documents and what is written in books (personal memoirs as well as great histories) but also through the buildings, landscape, and historic artifacts that survive.

How will future generations view the present period if nothing remains? How will they get a balanced view of our age if the great events of our time are remembered but the experience of ordinary people living ordinary lives is forgotten? ♣ Each of us has a responsibility to value the objects of our contemporary culture, to help ensure their preservation, and to use them to tell our story. ♣ One way of doing this is by making a time capsule. About 10,000 people around the world have already done so.

International Time Capsule Society (Oglethorpe University, Georgia): www.oglethorpe.edu (then type name of society into website search engine)

The Smithsonian Center for Materials Research and Education tells you how to make your own time capsule with a contact list of suppliers: www.si.edu/scmre/takingcare/timecaps.htm

Ideas for what to put in a time capsule: www.appliedhistory.com/suggest.html

The rescue game

Gather a group of friends and ask everybody to imagine that they have been given a ten-minute warning that their house is in imminent danger of being flooded.

Invite everyone to make a list of the ten things they would rescue and a brief explanation of why they would save each item and what it means to them.

Compare lists. Look for similarities; look for differences; examine each other's choices, rationales, and histories. The aim is to give you all a better understanding of the meaning of the objects in your world and how they define you.

...make a time capsule

Make a time capsule.

♣ **It needs to be airtight and watertight.** Or you can buy one made in lead (around $500) or plastic (around $100).

♣ **Include in it some of the things** that you think best represent life on earth as it is now—photographs, recordings, CDs and DVDs, articles from newspapers and magazines, predictions about the future, clothing, equipment, objects, seeds, identity documents, whatever.

♣ **Produce a guidebook for your collection.** Try to explain to someone who might be opening it in 100 or 500 years' time what the objects are, how they work, their significance, and why you selected them.

♣ **Bury the capsule,** but not too deep, in the hope that someone sometime in the distant future will unearth it and discover the secrets of the early 21st century.

9 DECEMBER

stand up and **BE COUNTED**

Human rights provide a foundation for building a just and peaceful world. Every human being on the planet has the right to dignity, respect, and freedom—whatever their race, color, sex, sexual orientation, language, religion, political or other opinion, national or social origin, wealth, or other status. ⚡ On December 10, 1948, the General Assembly of the United Nations adopted and proclaimed the Universal Declaration of Human Rights. This has been translated into over 300 languages and dialects—from Abkhaz to Zulu. It is the holder of the Guinness World Record for the document that has been most translated. ⚡ Unfortunately, unlike the US Constitution or the European Convention on Human Rights, the Declaration has no legal force.

The Declaration contains 30 articles. Among these are

Article 1: All human beings are born free and equal in dignity and rights.

Article 3: Everyone has the right to life, liberty, and security of person.

Article 4: Slavery and the slave trade shall be prohibited in all their forms.

Article 5: No one shall be subjected to torture or to cruel, inhuman, or degrading treatment or punishment.

Article 18: Everyone has the right to freedom of thought, conscience, and religion.

Article 19: Everyone has the right to freedom of opinion and expression.

Article 20: Everyone has the right to freedom of peaceful assembly and association.

World Human Rights Day is a time to reflect on how lucky we are to have our rights enshrined in a UN Declaration, and to pledge to do something for the many people across the world who are denied these rights.

Information on the UN and human rights: www.un.org/rights
Read the Declaration in almost any language: www.unhchr.ch/udhr

 **Ngawang Gyaltsen** is a senior monk from Drepung monastery near Lhasa. He was imprisoned for a year in 1987, rearrested in 1989 and sentenced to 17 years in prison, plus 5 years' deprivation of political rights. He had been singled out as the leader of a group of monks accused of producing literature critical of the Chinese government and "passing information to the enemy." The group's first publication was a Tibetan translation of the Universal Declaration of Human Rights.

...celebrate your human rights

⚡ **Put human rights on a T-shirt.** Get together with a group of friends and each choose a basic right from the Declaration. Get a local T-shirt screening shop to design colorful shirts with your chosen slogans. Assemble in a public space, stand in a line, and proudly advertise your selection of human rights to promote World Human Rights Day.

⚡ **Make a series of Tibetan prayer flags,** each one focusing on a different human right. Visit the website of an Amnesty International group in Pasadena, California, whose idea this is: www.its.caltech.edu/~aigp22/flags/home.shtml

SHARE *your books*

bookcrossing n. the practice of leaving a book in a public place to be picked up and read by others, who then do likewise.

—added to the ***Concise Oxford English Dictionary*** in August 2004

You probably have lots of books on your shelves, gathering dust. Why not share them with others? Select one that you really like. Nobody is reading it at the moment. Register it on the BookCrossing website, and start its journey into the unknown.

BookCrossing is a book-lovers' community. It's a global book club that crosses time and space. It's a reading group that knows no geographical boundaries. It has 300,000 members, sharing 1.5 million books, all over the world. And it's completely free. ♟ A BookCrossing member leaves a book around for someone else to pick up and read, and registers this book on the BookCrossing website. The person who finds the book reads it and then passes it on to another reader. The book continues from one reader to another, until it gets lost or someone breaks the chain by not passing it on. ♟ Each reader can comment on the book, putting their comments on the BookCrossing website. The person who originally supplied the book can keep track of its journey.

BookCrossing: www.bookcrossing.com

The Three Rs of BookCrossing

R1: Read a good book—a book that you would recommend to others.

R2: Register the book with BookCrossing. First you log in your details. This takes a couple of minutes. You will be given a BookCrossing identification number and the URL of the BookCrossing website. Label your book with these references, and put in a note asking the reader to pass it on after they've finished reading it. You can buy printed labels from the BookCrossing website.

R3: Release the book for someone else to read. There are three ways of doing this. You can give it to a friend. You can leave it somewhere for someone to pick up—on a park bench, in a coffee shop, etc. Or you can release it "into the wild," which means that people have to search for it. The BookCrossing website enables you to say you have left it or give clues to help people find it.

Then wait and see what happens.

...help create a public library

♟ **Sign up** as a member of BookCrossing.
♟ **If you happen to find** a BookCrossing book left by someone else, read it, enjoy it, and pass it on.
♟ **Encourage all your friends to join.** The more BookCrossing grows, the better it will get!

buy a GOOD GIFT

There are all sorts of occasions when you may need to buy a present: someone's birthday, Christmas, Mother's Day, Valentine's Day, to celebrate a wedding, as an in memoriam gift for someone who has just died, because you've been promoted, or just because you feel like giving someone something.

How often do you find that you can't think what to give? How often have you given (or been given) something that the recipient doesn't need and doesn't like, which is then quietly hidden away and forgotten, or taken to a thrift shop, or given to someone else as a present (which they won't like either)?

So here's a really great alternative: *buy a good gift.* Choose a gift from the *Good Gifts Catalogue* and your Good Gift is actually delivered by a charity to a person or a family or a community in need. What you are paying for enables something very specific to happen. 👫 The recipient gets a card with details of the project and a badge to tell them that they are "gifted." They can take pleasure in their gift, which is doing something positive, and they do not need to worry about how to get rid of yet another unwanted and unneeded present. You feel good, and your gift will make a difference to someone's life.

The Good Gifts Catalogue: www.goodgifts.org

A selection of Good Gift ideas:

Life Cycle: Give a bike for a midwife in places like Cambodia and Ethiopia. This will enable her to get around more quickly when she's needed. — $70

Swords into plowshares: Help a village blacksmith turn a Kalashnikov or a tank into farm implements in war-torn Sierra Leone. — $50 and up

Adopt a vegetable, and save it from extinction. — $25

Pedal power in Kigali: Give a young Rwandan a bicycle with a passenger seat, and he'll earn an income by giving people rides around the city. — $100

A nomadic camel for a nomadic family, to provide transport, milk, and good company as it wanders between Ethiopia and Somalia. — $250

Ducks for peace: Cows, goats, bees are all given to families to generate more income. The latest good idea is ducks—four plus starter feed. — $30

There are gifts for all occasions, and for all sorts of people. You can even give your worst enemy a brain cell—for medical research! The gifts are fun to give and fun to receive.

...make three people happy!

👫 **Buy a Good Gift** for someone's Christmas present.

👫 **Once you've done it,** do it again for someone else. Giving will never be the same with a Good Gift.

👫 **If you're getting married,** put Good Gifts on your wedding list. Everything you're given is sure to be wanted.

DECEMBER 12

HUNGER *banquet*

Our planet produces enough food to feed every woman, man, and child—and with some left over. The problem is that the food does not reach everybody who needs it. And we're not talking here only about those who go hungry as a result of drought or conflict, but about people who are just too poor to buy enough food to keep them alive and healthy. ● Children are particularly at risk. Malnutrition stunts their physical and mental development and makes them more prone to disease.

Millennium Development Goal no. 1 is to halve the number of people suffering poverty and hunger by 2015. But if hunger is not really about an overall shortage of food but about its unequal distribution, we should be able to do much better than that. We should be able to abolish malnutrition altogether.

Oxfam America's Hunger Banquet website gives you a chance to learn about hunger from the point of view of those who experience it every day:
www.hungerbanquet.org
www.oxfamamerica.org

Gloria Narua is surviving on the edge, and it wouldn't take much for her life to fall apart. She lives in Mozambique, where she grows crops on a small plot of land called a *mashamba*. It's not much, but most years she can produce enough maize, groundnuts, eggplant, carrots, and kale to feed three children. She even owns a few chickens.

Unfortunately, she doesn't earn enough to send her children to school. Her oldest, Eduardo, is nine years old and desperate to learn how to read and write. She'd do anything to educate him but simply can't afford it. Besides, this year, she'll need his help in the field. It's October—time to bring in the maize. Last year, her husband gathered the harvest with her, but he died in the spring. People say it could have been AIDS, but she can't be sure.

She misses her husband—now more than ever. For as she looks forward to the harvest, she's worried. The rains were not good this year. This could make for a tough year to come...

...experience life's lottery

Organize a Hunger Banquet. Each person attending is randomly assigned a role.
● **Of the guests, 15% are in the high-income group;** they sit at a table and enjoy a three-course meal.
● **Another 25% of the people are in the middle-income group;** they sit on chairs and eat rice and beans (delicious and nutritious).
● **The remaining 60% are the world's poor;** they sit on the floor and get only rice and water. They will be suffering the fate of the billions of poor people throughout the world who are undernourished and go to bed hungry each night.

You can use a hunger banquet to raise money to fight global poverty. But make sure the rich pay more!

13 DECEMBER

go on a SEX STRIKE

Sometimes there is nothing to do but to show you mean business. If you want to bring about change, or at least persuade your partner to see your point of view, you may just have to hit them where it hurts.

Sex strike in Sudan: Samira Ahmed, a university professor, launched a sex strike in 2002 to try to end nineteen years of civil war. She called it *alhair*, Arabic for "women sexually abandoning their men." The action (or rather the inaction) began with twenty women from the Lou and Jekany tribes, who were most involved in the fighting.

Stripping against strip mining: Birsel Lemke campaigned against a proposal to develop highly poisonous cyanide-based gold mining in sites across Turkey. Inhabitants of one village near the site of a proposed mine ran naked, bearing signs with the slogan, "Before Eurogold strips us, we'll strip." The women refused to have sex with their husbands until the men had expelled the gold mining company.

Sex strikes have been used around the world:

> **In Colombia:** to protest against the violent drug wars.
> **In Poland:** to fight for legal abortion
> **In Amsterdam:** by sex workers to protest against harassment.

Birsel Lemke's Right Livelihood Award: www.rightlivelihood.org/recip/lemke.htm

The Global Women's Strike held on March 8 each year to highlight how much of the world's work is done by women, and how much difference it makes when their contribution is withdrawn: www.globalwomenstrike.net

---

No Water, No Sex

In 2001, a group of women in the village of Sirt in Turkey banned their husbands from their bedrooms in an effort to get a water main to supply their village. The 27-year old water system had broken down, and the women were having to collect water from a

fountain and carry it home over long distances.

The strategy had an immediate effect. The men petitioned the authorities to repair the water system and offered their labor free. The local authority provided pipes to bring a nearby water source to the village. The women continued their protest until water actually started gushing out of the taps. Islam requires people to bathe after sex, so there was a connection between the method of protest and what was being fought for.

...to get things done

If there's an issue you care passionately about, write to the partners of those who are causing the problem urging them to go on a sex strike. Get as much publicity as you can for your campaign.

If there is something your own partner is doing that is causing harm to others or to the planet, why not start your own sex strike to persuade him or her to desist.

DECEMBER 14

MEET *Reverend Billy*

Shopping? We're spoiled for choice. We have enough, and we buy too much. When we feel down, we just go out for a bit of "retail therapy." When we get home, and the buzz wears off, we start worrying about where we're going to put all the stuff we've bought. ⚽ How about trying something really therapeutic: *stop shopping*.

Reverend Billy is the Archpriest of the Stop Shopping movement. His particular targets are Starbucks and Wal-Mart. Visit his website for fun and ideas.

Reverend Billy and the Church of Stop Shopping: www.revbilly.com

THE CHURCH OF STOP SHOPPING — REVEREND BILLY

Buying nothing at Wal-Mart

Twenty of us walked into Wal-Mart—the largest retail company in the world. We each took a shopping cart and walked silently and slowly in an unbroken line up and down, down and over, pushing our empty carts through endless canyons of products. Sometimes the line got split up, by a real shopper, or a curious child, or a near convert; but the line always reformed, rejoined, moving randomly, inexorably toward what? Toward the sex of our church picnic, toward the mouth frothing, eye rolling, religious fervor of sheer not-shopping...

The cop finally approached us—and we were tentative with our entreaties. "The Church Officer, the Church, the Church of Stop Shopping." He came to understand that we had simply and lawfully worshipped in a Wal-Mart. Maybe we were Odd. Maybe we put the Odd in our God! But he understood we were just celebrating buylessness...

We heard him murmur something to himself. Then a pause, silence, he looked across the street to the big box no man's land and said, "Well, our founding fathers did say that every healthy democracy needs a little revolution once in a while." Revolution? Who said anything about a revolution? Let's just Stop Shopping! Amen.

Bill Talen
Ecologistonline, November 1, 2003

...and stop shopping

Where $Bucks Prison Laborers Get Their Buzz...

Two lead actors walk in together and start the action at the shelves near the cash register, which should be central, like a stage. Support actors walk in with them to distribute literature when the play is climaxing.

Ex-prisoner: Oh gosh, look at this place.

Friend: It's just a Starbucks.

Ex- prisoner: Well it beats the penitentiary cafeteria, I'll tell you.

Friend: Yeah, it's a beautiful coffee shop, everything is real...arty.

Ex-prisoner: That's the thing about prison. They don't let graphic designers in there.

Friend: Well, prison is supposed to be depressing.

Ex-prisoner: Just look at those packages over there, everything looks so...wait a minute.

Friend: What?

To find out what happens, download the full script from www.revbilly.com.

Then go and perform this (or one of the four other Reverend Billy playlets) at your local Starbucks.

🏠 *support* HOSPITAL CLOWNS

> *The hospital clowns have become shooting stars in my life. I can count on them when I need some cheering up. Thank you for your smiles, your jokes, your fun. No words could ever describe what you have done for me!*
> —Brooke

Humor relaxes people, reduces pain and stress, makes people laugh and feel good, and generally promotes a positive outlook. All in all it's a good medicine. And it doesn't have the side effects of some more potent drugs. 🏠 This is where hospital clowns come in. Imagine being in a hospital, away from the comfort of your home, and feeling sad, anxious, frightened, lonely, or in pain. Hospital clowns treat children in the hospital with a dose of fun and laughter. 🏠 The hospital clowns program was developed by the Humour Foundation in Australia, where 40 hospital clowns entertain about 60,000 patients a year. A similar program was set up by the Theodora Foundation all over Europe. In the UK, the Theodora Children's Trust recruits and trains special clowns to work in selected hospitals in England and Wales.

The Hospital Clown website: www.hospitalclown.com

Hospital clowns receive considerable training in the very special skills needed to divert children's attention during painful procedures, help calm them in an emergency, or just brighten up their day. They learn how to develop their mastery of magic, storytelling, acting, mime, balloon sculpture, and juggling, and adapt these skills to each child's needs in widely differing situations. When working on the wards, they have to behave with sensitivity, only approaching children when it is clear that they will be welcome, judging how best to involve the children and their care givers, and bring them some relief from the distress and pain they may be feeling. As one grateful parent remembers:

> *It was an extremely stressful time, but as if by magic the hospital clowns would always arrive on the ward at the right time and brighten everyone's day. The children would perk up, parents would have their minds taken off the awful and often harrowing situations they were finding themselves in, and even the staff would smile!*

...bring happiness to a hospital

- 🏠 **If you think you have what it takes to become a hospital clown,** join a volunteer group in your area. Or you could make a donation.
- 🏠 **If you know a child who is ill** and could do with some cheering up, download the *Clown Doctors Activity Book* from www.humourfoundation.com.au
- 🏠 **Bring a little happiness** into an old people's home or a day center for homeless people, and organize a Christmas entertainment for them.

DECEMBER 16

STREET CHILDREN *speak out*

Children are living on the streets for many reasons. They have run away from physical or sexual abuse at home. Their families are too poor to feed an extra mouth. They are physically disabled and unwanted. They are attracted by the idea of "the bright lights." ▲ In the developing world, they are "street children." In the rich world, they are "runaways." The causes may be slightly different, but the result is the same: vulnerable children living on the street, having to fend for themselves just to survive.

Once on the streets, they need to earn money just to eat. Some beg. Some sell—anything from sweets to magazines. Some do shoe-shining. Many are ragpickers—recycling cloth, plastic, glass, metals, often in dangerous conditions. And some work is traditionally done by gangs of street children, such as erecting wedding tents in India. ▲ It is hard to comprehend what life for children on the streets must be like. When we encounter street children, we see them as a nuisance. But they are human beings who are being denied access to some fundamental human rights we take for granted.

Consortium for Street Children: www.streetchildren.org.uk

Street children have their own ideas about the world and its problems:

> *With unity amongst ourselves, we can do anything!* —Mannar

> *We should work to protect all children and uphold their rights. We should see that the police who make the lives of street children so miserable are punished.* —Suresh

> *Education is the most important thing to bring about change. With education comes respect. And with respect we can build our lives.* —Papu

> *Employment is the big issue. Every young adult should have the opportunity to earn a living.* —Anuj

After a brainstorm on how to change the world, a group of children in Delhi aged from 9 to 17 came up with the idea of organizing a National Street Children's Day, when they would do things for other people for free, which would challenge the stereotype that street children are parasites who are up to no good.

...listen to what they say

- ▲ **Remember** George Bernard Shaw's wise words: "The worst sin towards our fellow creatures is not to hate them, but to be indifferent to them; that is the essence of inhumanity."

- ▲ **Understand:** Read *Trash* by Gita Wolf, a storybook that shows the life of a group of ragpickers in South India, compiled from a workshop when the children told the stories of their lives.

- ▲ **See:** Contact the Consortium for Street Children to find out about street children's organizations in countries you plan to visit. When you get there, visit a night shelter and meet some of the children. Take some of your old toys (such as Legos) or school materials to leave with them.

- ▲ **Do:** Next time you are accosted by street children, buy them an ice cream!

17 DECEMBER

make friends with AFRICA

The state of Africa is a scar on the conscience of the world. But if the world as a community focused on it, we could heal it. And if we don't, it will become deeper and angrier.

—Tony Blair, British prime minister, 2001

People are the real wealth of nations. The United Nations Development Program (UNDP) defines "human development" as much more than the rise or fall of national incomes. It is about creating an environment in which people can develop their full potential and lead productive, creative lives in accordance with their needs, interests, and choices. Economic growth is only one means, although an important one, of enlarging those choices.

The Human Development Index is a rating compiled by the UNDP. It tries to reflect the wider view of human development by taking into account the following factors: life expectancy, adult literacy rate, education enrollment, and gross domestic product per capita. The bottom 20 nations in 2002 were

East Timor	0.436	Malawi	0.388	Mozambique	0.354
Rwanda	0.431	Angola	0.381	Guinea-Bissau	0.350
Guinea	0.425	Chad	0.379	Burundi	0.339
Benin	0.421	Dem. Rep. Congo	0.365	Mali	0.326
Tanzania	0.407	Central African		Burkina Faso	0.302
Côte d'Ivoire	0.399	Republic	0.361	Niger	0.292
Zambia	0.389	Ethiopia	0.359	Sierra Leone	0.273

All but East Timor are in Africa, and most of the other sub-Saharan African countries are not far behind.

Substantial numbers of Africans now live and work in Europe and North America. Some are passionate about doing something for Africa and have started their own organizations to raise money and support development programs.

News from all over Africa can be gleaned from www.allafrica.com.

UNDP human development website: hdr.undp.org.

Stand up for Elsie

Elsie Nemlin, who is from the Ivory Coast, founded Stand Up for Africa in 2003 with three main objectives:
To raise funds for the disadvantaged in Africa and facilitate their self-sufficiency
To provide volunteers from the African diaspora to share skills for African development
To lobby for justice and fairness
SUFA's first program addresses the child slave trade in West Africa.
www.standupforafrica.org.uk

...help it to a better future

Volunteer to help one of the small African diaspora development initiatives in whatever way you can. You will be working with a group of highly motivated people and make some exciting new friends.

EAT*in darkness*

See what it's like in the dark. Here, we're on an equal footing with other people. And for once we can hold a hand out to others.

—a visually impaired waiter in a pitch-black restaurant

The idea of eating in total darkness may seem strange if you are sighted but of course is perfectly normal to an unsighted person. In 1999, a blind clergyman, Jorge Spielmann, had the idea of opening a restaurant in Zurich staffed by blind waiters. It is called Die Blinde Kuh (The Blind Cow), and the waiters wear bells on their feet so you can hear them approaching. Diners are met at the entrance and led in procession to their tables. The toilets are lit, but diners have to be guided there by a waiter. ✖ The venture has a serious purpose—to give blind people work, and at the same time to teach sighted people what it is like to live in a blind world. ✖ Before opening his restaurant, Spielmann sometimes used to blindfold guests at his home to encourage them to pay more attention to the food and the conversations going on around them. "I just want people to experience the world on our terms."

Dans Le Noir? (In the Dark?), which has branches in Paris and London, is run on much the same lines. The venture was established by the Paul Guinot Association, which helps France's blind and visually handicapped. "We hope the restaurant will serve as a bridge between people who can see and people who can't." ✖ The idea is certainly of interest to experimental psychologists, who are eager to find out how lack of vision affects our experience of taste. And, if an account of a one-night experiment along these lines in New York is anything to go by, the darkness can make for a very intimate dining experience.

Die Blinde Kuh: www.blindekuh.ch
Dans le Noir?: www.danslenoir.com
Unsicht Bar: www.unsicht-bar-berlin.de

Adapting a building to make it totally blacked out is an expensive and time-consuming process. It also runs into difficulties with health and safety regulations. The Unsicht Bar (Invisible Bar) in Berlin gets round the problem by requiring diners to wear masks over their eyes. The restaurant was started by an organization of blind and visually impaired people, and most of the staff are blind.

...a blinding experience

- ✖ **Is a blind restaurant a good idea?** Could the idea catch on? Might blind restaurants spring up in other cities? What do you think?
- ✖ **If you go to any of the cities** featured above, make a point of going to dine at a blind restaurant, and find out for yourself.
- ✖ **Back home,** contact an organization for blind and visually impaired people active in your town or city, and suggest that you work together to organize a blind evening (with masks) at a local restaurant.

become an ENCYCLOPEDIST

Thanks to the Internet, you can play a part in creating the world's most ambitious information project. Wikipedia is an Internet encyclopedia (*wiki* means "quick" in Hawaiian) created entirely by volunteers, who contribute new articles and update and revise existing ones. Contributions have to comply with Wikipedia's "neutral point of view" policy, so that there is no bias in what is published. ✋ Articles can be edited by anyone (except by banned users, and there are a few protected pages). The entries in the encyclopedia develop, as amendments and additions are made, and flaws are quickly repaired. Everything is copyright-free.

Wikipedia is the world's largest and fastest-growing encyclopedia. It was started in 2001, and in its first year over 20,000 entries were created. By September 2004, over 1 million articles had been completed (350,000 of which are in English). ✋ There are articles under active development in over 100 languages. Nearly 2,500 new articles are added to Wikipedia each day, along with ten times that number of updates to existing articles. Wikipedia is one of the ten most popular Internet reference sites.

There are a number of related projects supported by the Wikimedia Foundation, including *Wiktionary* (a dictionary and thesaurus), *Wikiquote* (a compendium of famous quotations), *Wikibooks* (a collection of manuals and textbooks), and *Wikisource* (a repository of public domain documents). All of these projects are being developed using similar principles to Wikipedia. ✋ The Wikimedia Foundation is funded by appeals on its websites, which have raised $150,000 for this work. Compare this with the cost of creating a new edition of the *Encyclopaedia Britannica*.

en.wikipedia.org
www.wikimediafoundation.org

Translators wanted
In France, between 1751 and 1772, a remarkable book was published that attempted to put all human knowledge between two covers. This was the *Encyclopédie*. Compiled largely under the direction of Denis Diderot, it comprised 28 volumes, 71,818 articles, and 2,885 illustrations. A second edition, in 66 volumes, was published from 1782 to 1832.

You can help translate the *Encyclopédie* into English: www.hti.umich.edu/d/did/call.html

...contribute to Wikipedia

✋ **Write an article** for Wikipedia on some obscure subject that you are an expert on. Start by finding out whether the subject already has an entry and what related subjects have entries.

✋ **Open your article** with a concise paragraph defining the topic and mentioning the most important points. The reader should be able to get a good overview by reading only this first paragraph. Then write the rest of the article. Guidance for contributors is published on the Wikipedia website.

✋ **Or take a subject that you are really interested in** and know something about, find the article in Wikipedia, and then edit it, adding all the bits that are missing.

DECEMBER 20

BRIGHTEN *up your community*

It's the middle of winter. The days are short. Some people in northern states suffer from seasonal affective disorder (also known as SAD), which is the most common winter depression. It is caused by a biochemical imbalance in the hypothalamus (the gland responsible for regulating body temperature and food intake) caused by the shortening of daylight hours and the lack of sunlight in winter. The symptoms include a general lassitude and depression.

Many of us find the winter months bring us down, even if we are not as badly affected as sufferers of SAD. Our surroundings never look as good under gray skies as they do in the summer sunshine. But maybe this is the time to take a fresh look at the community we live in—when it is at its worst. 🏠 What can be done to improve it? Remove the graffiti? Paint a mural? Hang up banners in the streets? Encourage window boxes? Plant trees? Tidy up the road signs, pedestrian barriers, and other street features? Banish cars? Build outdoor seating areas? Encourage live music? Provide more sunlight? Whatever it is, if you want it done by the end of the summer, you had better get started now.

Resources for redesigning your community:
The Community Planning Website: www.communityplanning.net
Christopher Alexander's famed *Pattern Language*: www.patternlanguage.com

From SAD to happy

On one side of a valley is the Austrian village of Rattenberg, with a population of 455. This sits in the shadow of a high mountain, which deprives the village of sunlight for four months of each year. On the other side of the valley is Kramsach, which basks in the winter sun.

An array of computer-guided solar reflectors known as "Heliostats," each computer programmed to adjust direction according to the sun's position, bounces the sun's rays from above Kramsach to a rocky outcrop close

to Rattenberg, where a second bank of mirrors directs the light to the village.

There is not enough reflected sunlight to brighten the whole village. But selected streets, building façades, and public spaces are lit up, and the villagers now feel much less sad during the long winter.

...with a ray of sunshine

Spend an afternoon walking around your neighborhood. Make a note of all the things you don't like and all the things you would like to have but which are not there. Then categorize your suggested improvements:

🏠 **Things that can be done easily** and with very little or no money.

🏠 **Two or three things** that are really important and that would bring maximum community gain.

🏠 **Everything else.** Talk to your neighbors and try to get a consensus for your community improvement plan. Talk to your local representative to see what your town board could do. Talk to your neighborhood association to see how they might help. Try to get at least one thing on your list done within the next three months.

don't buy COCAINE

For once the politicians and the police are actually right: cocaine is bad news. But not just for the reasons you might be thinking. You've probably heard all about how coke rots your nose, causes heart attacks, is highly addictive, and fuels cartels and corruption.

But there's another reason not to buy cocaine that people don't talk about. It is that cocaine isn't fair-trade. Far from it. Although many farmers initially turn to growing drugs because low commodity prices mean that they can't make a decent living from more traditional crops, less than 1% of the profits from cocaine go back to the producer.

Every time you purchase an ounce of cocaine, the people who cultivate coca leaves are being ripped off. They are breaking their backs and employing child labor just so you can get high for a few hours. It must be a bit of a downer knowing that kids have had to work themselves to the bone just so that you could indulge yourself.

The Drug Policy Alliance website explores the drug war and is a good source of information on every drug under the sun: www.lindesmith.org

Educate yourself on what people have been eating, inhaling, and injecting for centuries. HuumeBoikotti is a Finnish website with lots of interesting information on the drug trade: www.huumeboikotti.org/english.htm

Drug facts to share with your friends:

Opium was being cultivated from 6,000 BC.

In the 19th century, the opium business was one of the most profitable businesses of the British Empire.

When Coca-Cola was first produced, the "health tonic" contained small amounts of cocaine in the recipe.

According to rough estimates, there is more money in circulation annually in the drug trade than in the refinement of oil, and almost as much as in arms trafficking.

...it's not fair-trade!

Support fair trade.

☺ **Stop using cocaine.** If you haven't yet started, more power to you!

☺ **Tell your friends to stop.** Spread the word.

☺ **Eat fair-trade chocolate,** unzip a fair-trade banana, have a fair-trade cup of tea instead. It's better for you...and better for the world.

DECEMBER 22

COMPUTING *power*

Two heads (or in this case tens of thousands) are better than one. Some problems are so complicated that it is difficult to find enough computer power to solve them. To get over this, a mechanism has been developed for harnessing together the unused computing capacity of PCs all over the world so that they can work together.

One very complicated problem is predicting climate change. The climateprediction.net project has over 95,000 computers in 150 countries. They work together to investigate how sensitive the different climate change models are to small changes in the underlying assumptions that have been used to create them, and also to changes in climatic conditions.

www.climateprediction.net

Climateprediction.net

This is the world's largest climate modeling experiment. It will provide decision makers with a much better scientific basis for creating policies to address global warming.

Each simulation divides the globe into thousands of sectors and estimates the future temperature, based on certain assumptions such as cloud coverage, the rate of heat movement, and rainfall rates.

The first results of climateprediction.net suggest that average temperatures could rise by as much as 20°F by the middle of the 21st century unless deep cuts are made to greenhouse gas emissions. This is double the warming predicted by the Intergovernmental Panel on Climate

...help predict the future

Link your computer to the 95,000 others around the world that are already working on the climateprediction.net project.

To run a simulation will take between 10 and 22 days, depending on your computer power. If you switch your computer off and then back on again, the simulation will continue from where it was left off until it has been completed.

What to do

🌳 **Decide to join in.** It's not a huge decision to make. You are not using your computer up to its full capacity. If you want to use your employers' computer, get their permission.

🌳 **Check whether your computer meets the minimum requirements.** If it's less than five years old, it probably will. The operating system can be Windows, Mac, or Linux.

🌳 **Go to climateprediction.net,** which should answer any questions you might have.

🌳 **Register** and accept the license agreement.

🌳 **Run the program;** the results will be sent back automatically to climateprediction.net.

23 DECEMBER

Christmas Eve is make-or-break time for children fortunate enough to be expecting gifts. Has anyone paid attention to their wish list? Will Santa Claus bring them that much-desired gift?

What is on your wish list? Maybe you don't care too much what you receive by way of a Christmas gift but would dearly love to see a more caring society, a more peaceful world, or a healthier environment. Well, these certainly aren't going to be brought by Santa Claus—or by any single individual. They are problems that you are going to have to help sort out yourself.

Letters to Santa is a website that was inspired by New York's Operation Santa Claus. You can download Christmas carols (words and sheet music), classic Christmas stories, safety tips, and even track Santa's progress on Christmas Eve. www.operationlettertosanta.com

Operation Santa Claus

At the New York Post Office in the 1920s, postal clerks started opening some of the letters to Santa and, touched by some of the requests, dug into their own pockets to pay for presents. This has now become Operation Santa Claus, and the idea has been copied by other post offices in the US.

The idea is simple. Postal staff volunteer to sort through the mail (around 200,000 letters to Santa are received each year) and select those that appear to be from needy inner-city children. Members of the public come to the post office, read through some of the mail, and take away letters they would like to reply to with a gift.

...write a letter to yourself

Write a letter to yourself, which you will open and read in 10 or 25 years' time.

🏃 **Write about the issue** that you want to do something about. What impact do you think you will be able to make? How would you like things to be in the future? And what do you think things will *actually* be like then?

🏃 **You could add some personal thoughts**—your current state of mind, how you spend your time, if you are in love with anyone, how you see your life evolving, your ambitions for the future...

🏃 **Hide the letter,** or if you think you will lose it or be too tempted to open it before the time is up, give it to someone else to keep for you.

It will be fascinating to read your letter in the future. You will be able to compare how things are now with the world as it will be then, and your current aspirations and emotional state with those of the person you will have become.

BAND AID

November 25, 1984: There was widespread famine in Ethiopia. Images were being shown on TV of people literally starving to death. Bob Geldof, a rock singer with Boomtown Rats, felt he had to do something. So, with Midge Ure, he wrote a Christmas song, called up his famous singer friends to help record the song, and produced "Do They Know It's Christmas?" All the proceeds were given to the Band Aid Trust for African famine relief.

January 28, 1985: Inspired by what Geldof had done, 45 musicians got together in New York to record "We Are the World," written by Michael Jackson and Lionel Richie. The group called itself USA for Africa—United Support of Artists. This was also a number one hit.

July 13, 1985: Geldof organized Live Aid: a rock concert held simultaneously on both sides of the Atlantic (in London at Wembley Stadium and in Philadelphia at the JFK Stadium) and broadcast around the world. (Geldof estimated that nearly 85% of the world's TVs were tuned into it.) The concert raised nearly $100 million.

Geldof raised millions for Africa. But he also invented two big fund-raising ideas: the pop single recorded and produced entirely free, and the megaconcert broadcast globally. He alerted a whole generation of young people to the idea that the world needed fixing. And he went on to help set up the Commission for Africa and organize ten Live8 concerts on July 2, 2005, to get the G8 rich nations committed to eliminating poverty in Africa.

Live Aid: www.liveaiddvd.net
The 20th anniversary version of "Do They Know It's Christmas?": www.bandaid20.com
Live8: www.live8live.com
The unofficial Live Aid site: www.live-aid.info
All about Band Aid: en.wikipedia.org/wiki/Band_Aid
All about USA for Africa: en.wikipedia.org/wiki/USA_for_Africa

Band Aid Charitable Trust

New recordings of "Do They Know It's Christmas?" were made in 1989 and 2004. The Band Aid Charitable Trust continues to receive income from sales and royalties, which it donates as aid for Africa.

In 2003, it supported food security, fresh water, eye-care and health-care projects in West and East Africa. The 2004 recording helped victims of famine in Darfur, Sudan.

...do they know it's Christmas?

Buy the various Band Aid, Live Aid, and USA for Africa CDs.

Almost everyone has some assets, and everyone is going to die sometime. Your life expectancy might be high, but the unexpected can happen—today, tomorrow, whenever.

It is important to make a will, because it allows you to

Choose how to dispose of your assets. If you die without a will, there are rules that dictate how your assets are distributed. This may not be in the way you would wish.

Inherit from an unmarried partner. Unmarried couples (same sex or not) cannot inherit from each other without a will.

Make arrangements for your children. Couples with children under 18 may want to consider arrangements for their children if either or both die.

Minimize tax payments. It may be possible to save inheritance tax.

It is your most recent will that determines what happens. So if your circumstances change, for example if you separate from your partner or you hit the jackpot in the lottery, then you should make a new will.

Why not include a charitable bequest in your will? This could be a simple charitable gift, or you might establish a fund for a specific purpose, which will continue to operate for many years (for example, a fund to provide books, uniforms, and school fees to a child in the developing world). Or you might fund the planting of a grove of trees as a memorial.

Take the Make-a-Will quiz at moneycentral.msn.com/retire/home.asp.

Living Wills

A living will sets out how you would like to be treated as you near death, when you are no longer able to make decisions for yourself. It covers such things as the degree of medical intervention, pain management, feeding that should be administered, and where you would like to die. This can take the burden of decision away from your family.

A living will is an expression of wishes rather than a legally enforceable instruction. Buy *The Natural Death Handbook*, or download an older version from www.globalideasbank.org/natdeath/ndh0.html

...give something to charity

Write your will today. Type "make a will" into Google, and you will find many do-it-yourself guides and online will-writing services.

Include a charitable bequest in your will. Think about how much you would like to give and what you would like to support. Remember that a small bequest to a large charity will be almost unnoticed, but the same money could support really interesting work by a smaller organization.

Remember that the charity will get nothing until you die, and that the gift will cost you absolutely nothing and may save tax when you die. So be generous!

DECEMBER 26

STUFF *do we need it?*

Michael Landy, a British artist, cataloged and destroyed all 7,226 of his possessions in a 2001 art installation called *Break Down*, held in a vacant C&A clothes store on Oxford Street in central London. ⚽ Landy stood on a platform overseeing a production line staffed by ten assistants. Every single one of his possessions was first cataloged and then destroyed—his passport, his keys and his credit cards, right down to a last dirty sock. The objects were shredded or ground up and then put into plastic trays and sacks for disposal.

The things Landy valued most he had left until last. One of the last objects to be destroyed was his father's sheepskin coat. Over 45,000 people came to see what was happening, and the final day attracted a crowd of 8,000.

> *When I finished I felt an incredible sense of freedom, the possibility that I could do anything. But that freedom is eroded by the everyday concerns of life. Life was much simpler when I was up on my platform.*

The event got a huge amount of publicity. Sermons were preached on the morality of consumerism. Landy was attacked for wanton destruction. Some saw it as an attack on capitalism. And others saw it as an act of madness and offered counseling. Landy described the event as an "examination of consumerism." ⚽ Since then, he has been drawing street flowers. These are flowers that live in the cracks in paving stones in the street. They don't need many nutrients. They can survive in harsh conditions.

Find out more about Michael Landy at
www.tate.org.uk/magazine/issue3/michaellandy.htm

We live in a consumerist society. We are urged to purchase much more than we need. And when fashion changes, we just buy something else—whether or not the thing we have is still functioning. Maybe, like Michael Landy, you could experience a sense of freedom by ridding yourself of possessions—maybe not all of them, just those you no longer need.

...or are we better without?

⚽ **Make a catalog of everything you own.** Think about each item on your list: about how and why you came to acquire it, whether you still use it (or indeed ever used it), whether you still need it (or think you need it), and whether you really do want to keep it.

⚽ **Set aside everything that you don't need or want.** Then either take these to a charity shop or sell them on eBay. Or if they are completely worn out or of no use to anybody, throw them away (in a recycling bin, of course).

⚽ **Keep your list. In five years' time,** repeat the exercise and see if you have continued your consumerist ways, buying more than you need.

auction it on EBAY

If you no longer need it, someone else might really want it. And they may be prepared to pay good money for it. So why not auction it on eBay? You will find a new user, liberate some space in your home, and raise money to help you change the world—all in one go!

The site eBay was created in 1995 by Pierre Omidyar as an online marketplace for buying and selling. He wanted to create an efficient Internet trading space for individuals and small businesses. ♀♂ He pioneered an auction format with a simple, easy-to-understand mechanism that lets buyers and sellers decide the true value of items, build relationships with others, and become part of the eBay community. Pierre and cofounder Jeff Skoll are now major philanthropists.

About 114 million registered users, trading in more than 50,000 different categories in 29 different countries, now use eBay. At any time there will be more than 25 million items for sale; 3.5 million new items are added each day. ♀♂ If you are not already hooked on eBay, there are simple instructions on the website on how to buy and sell. You can also buy a guidebook to help you through the process.

eBay charity page: givingworks.ebay.com

Download a factsheet on buying and selling on eBay: www.harriman-house.com/ebay/factsheet.htm based on *The eBay Book* by David Belbin.

Information about the charitable foundations funded by Omidyar: www.omidyar.net and Skoll: www.skollfoundation.org

The Great Chicago Fire Sale

This was the first charitable eBay auction, organized by a municipality to raise money for the arts. Items donated for the sale included a 1960s Playboy bunny costume, a dinner party prepared by Art Smith, personal chef to Oprah Winfrey, the opportunity to dye the Chicago River Green, and much more.

...create hope from junk

♀♂ **Go through your possessions,** identify all the things you no longer need and which you think someone else might want to buy from you. Then start selling. See how much you can raise!

♀♂ **Go to the eBay Charity Page,** where nonprofit organizations can publicize their auctions. Selling fees still have to be paid, but you will get some free additional publicity.

♀♂ **Approach celebrities,** and see if they will give you things to sell. They may sign something, provide some bit of memorabilia, or get you tickets to an upcoming film premiere. Dave Rowntree, drummer with Blur, offered to auction two hours of his time for a drumming lesson and a glass of champagne.

THINGS *to do*

In this world, nothing is certain but death and taxes.

—Benjamin Franklin

The rest of your life is up to you. But remember that you have only a limited amount of time before you go.

So start making a list of all the things you want to do before you die. Then start doing them. Right away. You never know how much longer you have left.

A list of 100 simple things to do: brass612.tripod.com/cgi-bin/things.html

Grow a Brain is a website all about things to do before you die, with lots of links: growabrain.typepad.com/growabrain/things_to_do_before_you_die/

Some things you simply must do:

Scour the night sky for comets, with the chance of following Halley or Donati and having a comet named after you.

Extract your own DNA. Spit gargled saltwater into diluted dishwashing liquid and slowly dribble ice-cold gin down the side of the glass. The spindly white clumps that form in the mixture are, basically, you.

Measure the speed of light by melting chocolate in a microwave oven. You measure the distance between globs. Various calculations produce the answer. You can still eat the chocolate afterward.

Write your name in atoms at IBM's Almaden research laboratory, San Jose, California. While you're saving up to go there, simply go and see an atom by visiting a university lab with equipment to trap and cool atoms. Barium is best.

Help nail a murderer. Register ahead with Tennessee's body farm and donate your corpse. It will be left out in the open to decompose before a trainee forensic scientist gets to work on it. An estimated 100 murderers have been convicted as a result of this training.

Become a diamond. LifeGem of Chicago, Illinois, will take a few grains of your cremated remains, subject them to high pressure and temperature. You emerge from the process 18 weeks later as a sparkling one-carat diamond.

From *100 Things to Do Before You Die*, ideas from scientists put together by Valerie Jamieson and Liz Else, Profile Books.

...before you die

Think about all the good you might do before you die.

♟ **Make a list of things you would like to do** to address some of the world's big problems. Your list can be as long or as short as you like. The problems are those you believe important. The actions are what you want to do to address them.

♟ **Put the list where you can see it.** Make sure you do at least one thing on the list each month, and try to do everything before you die.

The World Social Forum is a huge annual event, attended by people from NGOs, community groups, and civil society movements from all over the world who are "opposed to neo-liberalism and world domination by capital." ⚽ The WSF is an open meeting place for reflection and creative thinking, for democratic debate of ideas and issues, for free exchange of experiences, and for networking and linking up with other people and groups in order to plan effective action for a better world.

The first WSF was held in January 1998 to coincide with the annual World Economic Forum in Davos, when 192 organizations from 54 countries launched a "Declaration against the Globalizers of Misery." The next year, in 1999, a Davos Forum aimed to show that the economic issues addressed by the World Economic Forum only served a small group of interests, and that other mechanisms were needed for addressing issues of social justice and world development. This led to the first World Social Forum held in Porto Alegre, Brazil, in January 2001. Some 20,000 participants came together around the slogan "Another World Is Possible."

The number of people attending has continued to grow. Over 55,000 people from 131 countries came to the second WSF in 2002, and 100,000 attended in 2003. ⚽ In 2004, the WSF was held in India, attracting around 250,000 participants. There are also regional and thematic WSFs, which explore specific issues and issues of regional significance.

World Social Forum: www.forumsocialmundial.org.br

There are a number of regional forums linked to the World Social Forum. In 2005, these included forums for Europe, the Mediterranean, the Pan-Amazonian American, and the Caribbean regions. Details of future forums are posted on the WSF website.

What it's like at the forum
The program includes lectures, presentations, workshops, film and video, cultural events, marches and demonstrations, the issuing of declarations, and much else. If you go, you will learn about the world and its problems, what people's movements are doing to address these, new ideas for development, and new skills for making change. You will meet old friends and make new friends, and you should come away believing that another world *is* possible.

...another world is possible

Change your plans for January. Take a trip to the next World Social Forum. It will open your eyes to what people are doing to create a better world. It could inspire you. And you should have a great time.

NEW YEAR'S EVE

Never doubt that a small group of thoughtful committed citizens can change the world. Indeed it is the only thing that ever has!

—Margaret Mead, anthropologist

New Year's Eve is a time to look back and to reflect on all that has happened in the past year. What have you been able to achieve in your efforts to change the world? What has been your most successful action? What was most fun? What had most impact? What have you learned? What new friends have you made? How have you changed?

But it is also a time to look forward—to make a commitment to continue your efforts next year and into the future.

Through your actions, you can do your bit to change the world. You can also inspire others to action. Congratulations on what you have done so far. Keep up the good work. And best wishes for an enjoyable and successful New Year of making a difference!

Bethesda Arts Centre: www.bethesdafoundation.org

Nieu Bethesda is a poverty-stricken township in semiarid desert of South Africa attached to the town of Bethesda. It has become a popular tourist attraction because of The Owl House, a tiny museum devoted to the work of the eccentric sculptor Helen Martins, who lived and worked

there. The township also has underground pools from which the local people draw water with windmills.

The New Year of 2005 was welcomed in by a choir and a procession of lantern bearers, who walked through the streets and alleyways of Nieu Bethesda. Before the event, workshops were held to involve as many local people as possible in lantern making. Long withies (willow sticks) were bound together to form a three-dimensional framework, which was covered with tissue paper and decorated with patterns. Some of the lanterns were geometric and others were in the shape of wild animals and birds.

When night fell, candles were placed inside the lanterns and the procession started off. The local police and volunteers were there to ensure safety. It was a great night, which will be long remembered.

...light up the future

🙌 **Say good-bye to the old year and welcome in the new** with an outdoor celebration, even if it's only in your street or garden. Use some kind of illumination—homemade lanterns, torches, tea lights—anything you can lay your hands on at short notice to symbolize your hopes for a bright future.

🙌 **And next year,** think about involving your whole community in a lantern parade.

Turn your ideas into actions:
24 tips for social inventors

Here is some advice for making a success of your project:

Idea generation

1. Define the problem as clearly as you can; then think how you can solve it. Brainstorm to overcome worthy but dull ideas.

2. Look for synergy, for win-win-win situations that solve lots of problems all at the same time.

3. Gather other people's ideas and find a way of rewarding them for their contribution.

4. Be prepared to be flexible. Lots of ideas develop in ways you can't foresee at the outset.

5. Be patient. Take a long view. Some ideas might take ten years or more for the results to develop.

6. Use humor. It can tilt the scales when confronting bureaucracy and can be much more effective than simply arguing with people.

Structural

7. Involve your friends: together people can move mountains.

8. When you start out, think about linking with an NGO that is able to receive grants on your behalf.

9. Delegate as much as possible to other people (for particular initiatives, to run a committee, etc.). But make sure everyone who promises to help actually delivers.

10. Invite celebrities, business leaders, politicians, and other important people to become patrons and to attend events.

11. Celebrate successes as you go.

Financial

12. Make a budget for your project. Keep your overheads low and try to get as much as possible for free.

13. Ask friends and colleagues to support you by giving you regular (small) donations.

14. Find the funds you need. Persevere. There will be someone out there who is interested in supporting what you are doing.

15. Think about charging for things that you might otherwise provide for free.

16. Keep your accounts simple, and keep them up-to-date.

Outreach and publicity

17. Create a great website, and use it to disseminate information. Make it interesting and interactive.

18. Polish up your DTP (desktop publishing) and design skills, and make your leaflets and posters look really nice. But remember that simple = effective.

19. Get access to a good photocopier that does double-sided leaflets reliably. Some offices may help you by providing this facility as an "in kind" donation.

20. Get to know journalists, especially those who are most likely to be interested. Try to get publicity at every opportunity.

21. Maintain an e-mail press list. Send out regular press releases telling people what you're doing.

Keeping going

22. Keep a diary charting how your project is progressing.

23. Ask for advice when you need it. There are lots of people with the experience and skills you need.

24. Keep up the momentum. Don't give up. Deal with the problems that come up from time to time.

Adapted from advice given by Nicholas Albery, social inventor, to students at the School for Social Entrepreneurs, London. To help you plan your project, download "How to be a Community Champion" from www.millenniumcampaign.org.

ACKNOWLEDGMENTS

The idea for this book had been in the back of my mind for some time, but it was only after discussing it with Vicki Saunders, a Canadian social entrepreneur, and her telling me to get on and do it, that I felt able to get started. Christen Eddy got the original website going to solicit ideas, arranged brainstorm evenings, and got a team of young volunteers involved. Particular thanks should go to Victoria Stanski for agreeing to contribute to, and edit, the Peace section, and to all the contributors who submitted material for the book.

Thanks to the team at Myriad Editions: Jannet King for such excellent project management; Candida Lacey and Bob Benewick for making it happen; Corinne Pearlman and Isabelle Lewis for the design and graphics; and Martine McDonagh, Sadie Mayne, Catherine Quinn, and Helen Kingstone for additional editing. Thanks also to Colin Kennedy and Roger Harmar for additional design and graphics.

For the use of other photographs and illustrations, the publisher and author would like to thank the following:

January: 1: James Parr; 7: World Food Program/Robert Maas; 13: Derek Chung/Tactile Pictures; 14: GLINN Media Corporation, Gay/Lesbian International News Network; 27: Erik Millstone; February: 5: WaterAid; 13: Jason Stitt; 15: Neve Shalom; 20: Robert Benewick; March: 9: Daniel Tan; 20: UNICEF India/Ami Vitale; 22: WHO/P Pirot; 23: WHO; 25: David Lawson/WWF-UK; April: 3: Simon Edwin; 5: Laurie Knight; 7: Rotary International; 14: Phototag; 15: Dania Lolah; 16: Linda Bucklin; 20: World Bank/Francis Dobbs; 25: Sean Locke; May: 5: World Bank/Tran Thi Hoa; 23: World Bank/Ami Vitale; 24: USDA/Bill Tarpenning; 26: Marc Gold; 31: Woodrow Phoenix ©Comic Company; June: 2: Friends of Nature Burial Ground; 3: worldnakedbikeride.org; 7: Nancy Durrell McKenna; 17: Excellent Development Ltd.; 24: Colin Kennedy; July: 8: Anna Mockford ©BareWitness.org; 16: US State Department; 17: Augusta Riddy; 18: Lee Dowse; 19: Kenneth C. Zirkel; 24: Jonathan Ling; 27: Peter Morenus; 28: Daniel Fletcher; August: 1: Judi Ashlock; 3: Zed Nelson; 4: Björn Kindler; 6: Greg Nicholas; 9: Anupam Mishra; 10: Rene Mansi; 13: Dane Wirtzfeld; 17: ©Vo Cong Thong/Street Vision/PhotoVoice; 21: Rafal Zdeb; 25: Kamila Kingstone; 26: Stefan Klein; 29: Woodrow Phoenix ©Comic Company; September: 7, 22, 23, & 24: Colin Kennedy; October: 14: Graham Higgins ©Comic Company; 16: WFP/Tom Haskell; 18: FAO/J Holmes; 20: Room to Read; 21: Esther Benjamins Trust; 30: Jen Fariello; November: 27: World Bank; December: 9: Tina Rencelj; 10: Paiwei Wei; 11: Daniela Andreea Spyropoulos; 13: World Bank/Eric Miller; 14: World Bank; 16: Theodora Children's Trust; 17: World Bank/Curt Carnemark.

Every effort was made to obtain necessary permissions for use of copyright material, both illustrative and quoted. If there have been any omissions, we apologize and will be pleased to make appropriate acknowledgment in any future edition.

Index

Holy Land Trust, 267, 296
Homeless
    children, *see* Street children
    clothing for, 170
    food for, 321
    helping, 98
    refugees, 201
    soccer teams for, 94
    street papers sold by, 20
Honduras, 7
Honore, Carl, 115
Hoover, Herbert, 121
Hoover, Robin, 282
Hospitals, clowns in, 354
Housing
    designing, 89
    green, 31
    in slums, 114
    solar-powered, 280
H2G2, 224
Huang Qi, 127
Human capital, 147
Human Development Index, 11, 356
Humane Borders, 282
Human rights, 9, 208
    of children, 92
    combating terrorism and, 258
    videos of abuses of, 279
Human Rights Watch (HRW), 9, 166, 231
Human waste, disposal of, 77, 91, 114,
    229
    see also Sanitation, lack of
Human Writes, 75
Hume, John, 153
Humour Foundation, 354
Hungary, privacy violations in, 209
Hunger, 10, 158, 245, 274, 306
    combating, 293, 321, 351
Hunger-Free World, 164
Hunter, Terence, 335
Hussar, Bruno, 49
Hyde, Catherine Ryan, 326

Ideas, 308
    party for generating, 63
    websites for, 14, 80
iEarn, 228
Illich, Ivan, 50
Illness, *see* Diseases
Immigrants, 175
    illegal, 282
Incinerators, 248
Independence Day, 189
India, 28
    air pollution in, 275
    bio-piracy in, 152

British rule in, 54
casteism in, 212
children in, 246, 298, 355
Coca-Cola in, 119, 128
comics workshops in, 256
computers in, 37, 40
cooperatives in, 186
disasters in, 193, 206
forests of, 118
Jews in, 289
nonliteracy in, 255
polio in, 101
population growth in, 216
religious conflict in, 13
solar energy in, 200
tea growing in, 225
women in, 42
Indonesia
    arms sales to, 302
    endangered species in, 146
    human rights abuses in, 9
Indymedia, 24
Injustice, fighting, 19
Insects
    diseases carried by, 34, 198, 230
    natural repellents, 105
Institute for Transportation &
    Development Policy, 178
Intellectual property, 117
International Agency for the Prevention
    of Blindness, 288
International Baby Food Action Network,
    262
International Bicycle Fund, 178
International Campaign to Ban Land
    Mines, 153
International Coastal Cleanup, 163
International Commission of Jurists, 258
International Decade for Action, 185
International Labor Organization (ILO),
    342
International Monetary Fund, 11
International Network of Street
    Newspapers, 20, 94
International Storytelling Center, 138
International Women's Day, 71
Internet, 113
    activism on, 16
    addresses, 285
    blogging, 59
    books on, 137, 138
    bullying on, 287
    buying and selling books on, 74
    carpooling on, 125
    child pornography on, 327
    citizens of, 140

Thank you for changing the world
www.365act.com

ABOUT THE AUTHOR

Michael Norton is a social entrepreneur who actively sets out to change the world. In 1964 he set up the UK's first language teaching program for non-English-speaking immigrants that was run entirely by volunteers. In 1975 he founded the Directory of Social Change to provide grants information and advice and training on fund raising, management, and communication to nonprofits (the UK equivalent of the Foundation Center and the Grantsmanship Center combined). Since 1995 he has been designing and promoting new initiatives to promote volunteerism, including Changemakers (which encourages young people to go out and change the world), and YouthBank (which enables young people to make grants in their community). He is currently working on a young person's cooperative bank. In India, he has developed literacy and village library programs, and he is working on village reading circles, where semiliterate women come together to read books with the potential to improve their lives.